A Sense of Place

Great Travel Writers Talk

About Their Craft, Lives,

and Inspiration

A Sense of Place

Great Travel Writers Talk
About Their Craft, Lives,
and Inspiration

with MICHAEL SHAPIRO

Travelers' Tales
San Francisco

Travelers' Tales and Travelers' Tales Guides are trademarks of
Travelers' Tales, Inc., 330 Townsend Street, Suite 208, San Francisco,
California 94107. www.travelerstales.com

Art Direction: Michele Wetherbee and Stefan Gutermuth
Interior Design: Melanie Haage
Cover Photographs: © Bullety-Lomeo/The Image Bank.
Page Layout: Melanie Haage, using the fonts Minion,
Koch Antiqua, and Belucian

Distributed by: Publishers Group West,
1700 Fourth Street, Berkeley, California 94710

Library of Congress Cataloging-in-Publication Data
Shapiro, Michael, 1962–
A sense of place : great travel writers talk about their craft, lives,
and inspiration / by Michael Shapiro.-- 1st ed.
p. cm.
ISBN 1-932361-08-1 (pbk.)
1. Travel writers--Interviews. 2. Travel writers--Biography. 3. Travelers'
writings. 4. Shapiro, Michael, 1962---Travel. I. Title.
G154.49.S52 2004
910/4'092'2--dc22
2004011873

First Printing
Printed in the United States of America
10 9 8 7 6 5 4 3 2 1

For my father, Larry Shapiro, who exhorted me onward even as his own world was turning in.

TABLE OF CONTENTS

INTRODUCTION

IT WAS ON AMERICAN AIRLINES FLIGHT 44 THAT I FIRST PITCHED THE idea for this book to Travelers' Tales Executive Editor Larry Habegger. We were flying from San Francisco to New York, en route to a travel journalists' conference in Bermuda. Somewhere over Nebraska I knelt in the aisle next to his seat and shared my nascent thoughts for a book of interviews with travel writers. I felt like I was kneeling at the altar of publishing, seeking benediction for my project. When a flight attendant approached with a rolling cart and a nasty glare, I thanked Larry for his consideration and went back to my seat.

That was September 4th, 2001. A week later the Twin Towers crumbled and the Pentagon was shattered, sending shock waves through the American psyche and economy. Few industries were hit as hard as travel, and travel publishing was reeling for months.

Yet the idea stuck with me. Each year I spend the week between Christmas and New Year's on silent retreat at the Sonoma Mountain Zen Center. During my 2001 retreat I kept thinking about this project, and it began to take shape. Initially I considered interviewing each author about travel writing, but soon realized I wanted to discuss much more: their lives, their hopes, their aspirations, and their thoughts about the world. That last part—their thoughts about the world's politics and people—seemed especially relevant after the September 11th disaster. Who better to shed light on global issues than the people who have explored the planet so widely and so sensitively, and who have written about it so eloquently?

Another thought occurred to me during that retreat: In the coming year I would turn forty, and I wanted my life to take a new turn. For the past seven years I had written mostly about travel-tech issues, such as how to use the Internet for travel planning. I didn't want to abandon that completely, but I sought something more engaging to my soul and intellect. I sensed I was embarking on a pilgrimage, as well as a journey of tribute to the writers who have inspired me to explore the world in new ways.

I wanted to learn from the masters. And the best way would be to interview them where they lived. After roaming the planet they had settled—or not quite settled in some cases—in places far from their native homes (Pico Iyer) or on their native soil (Jan Morris). I was curious about what influenced their choices of place and whether being rooted somewhere helped them understand the world.

This would require extensive travel and some expense, but rather than hope that the project would pay off in financial terms, I chose to view it as a personal graduate school. I would learn from the interviews and from the travel. By simply being in the presence of so many prominent authors, I'd soak up knowledge and wisdom by osmosis.

The following spring I submitted a proposal. Travelers' Tales Publisher James O'Reilly saw potential but wanted "proof of concept." That's when the fun—and the hard work—began. I interviewed Simon Winchester in Great Barrington, Massachusetts, and Jeff Greenwald in Oakland, California, and wrote introductions to each conversation. The editors liked what they saw and sent me a contract.

In the spring of 2003, I began setting up interviews. That April I met Bill Bryson—Bill Bryson!—in Hanover, New Hampshire. He was as kind and congenial as you'd imagine from reading his books. I returned home on a high, enthralled by the prospect of one-on-one conversations with Pico Iyer, Jan Morris, Tim Cahill, and so many more of my literary heroes.

The exultation didn't last. When I returned from that trip my father complained of pain in his abdomen. At the Passover Seder he couldn't sit at the table through dinner and excused himself to lie on the couch. Tests showed nothing wrong, but when my father's pain became unbearable a week later, he checked into a San Francisco hospital. A CT scan showed he had cancer of the pancreas, one of the fastest-growing and most lethal types of cancer.

The weeks he spent in the hospital were a living hell that Dante and Kafka might have concocted. But we rarely left him alone—my mother, brother, wife, and I worked out a schedule that enabled one of us to be with him almost around the clock. Throughout his life, my father had been diligent about work and didn't want his illness to forestall my project, encouraging me to keep my interview appointments. To prepare for them, I spent many nights in a sleeping bag on the floor of his hospital room, reading Frances Mayes and Pico Iyer by the light of my headlamp. After twenty-six days in the hospital, my father was released and vowed never to return.

Soon I was on the road again, driving down to the Santa Barbara hills to meet Pico. I spoke to my father daily as I continued south to Arizona to interview Tom Miller, and each time he sounded stronger. The night I got back from that trip, we went out to his favorite restaurant, Gary Danko, in San Francisco, celebrating his recovery with a triumphant parade of delicacies and wines.

But his pain had already returned. On Friday, June 13th, we learned the cancer had spread. I canceled an upcoming trip to Britain, where I'd planned to interview Jan Morris and others, and spent much of the summer hanging out with my father, talking in the backyard and watching Giants' games on TV. Chemotherapy had contained the cancer for the moment, and my father insisted I get back to work. I told him I would dedicate the book to him and he said, "Then I better stay alive long enough to see it in print."

It was against this backdrop that I interviewed Tim Cahill in October and Isabel Allende in November. With each of them I discussed death and dying, and, probably without realizing it, they helped me cope with my father's loosening hold on life. The day after Thanksgiving I left for Europe to interview Frances Mayes, Redmond O'Hanlon, and Jan Morris. I told my father I could cancel the trip, but he insisted I go. He planned to stick around for a while and said that if I was dedicating the book to him then it should be the best book possible.

I called daily from Europe and each time my father's voice sounded strong, belying his deteriorating condition. Even after a discouraging doctor's appointment my father kept his spirits up—at least during our phone conversations, and encouraged me to continue on. But I sensed his condition was worsening, and I canceled my appointment with Morris. I flew back to San Francisco the day after I interviewed O'Hanlon.

During the flight I reflected on how fortunate I'd been to interview so many of the world's leading authors. (I hesitate to call them travel writers because many don't see themselves that way and because their work typically ranges well beyond travel.) How fortunate to jet around the world, to have plenty to eat, to buy any book I wanted.

I got home just in time. My father was conscious but in terrible pain. He said he knew what was happening to him and that it was O.K. He listened with interest as I told him all about my trip, and later we watched a basketball game on TV. The next day, a hospice nurse arrived with a morphine pump. That evening, while holding his wife's hand and flanked by his two sons and daughter-in-law, my father departed for his final destination. I'm certain he was upgraded to first class.

Spurred on by my father's courage and determination, I continued with the interviews. In the three months before my deadline, which had been generously extended, I met Arthur Frommer in New York, Rick Steves and Jonathan Raban in Seattle, Jan Morris and Eric Newby in the U.K., and Peter Matthiessen at the far end of Long Island. It was a stirring conclusion to a project that has enriched my life in ways that are just starting to become fully apparent.

—Michael Shapiro
Sonoma County, California
April 2004

Working-Class Hero

Tim Cahill
LIVINGSTON, MONTANA

NIGHT IS ENVELOPING THE COLOMBIAN JUNGLE CAMP; YOUR traveling companion is insulting one of Colombia's most ruthless guerrilla leaders, and said guerrilla is dropping less-than-subtle hints that you may soon be kidnapped. Leave it to Tim Cahill to defuse the situation with an off-the-cuff remark about his companion's fondness for drink.

After more than a quarter-century of travel to the world's most challenging places, Cahill has developed a knack for doing the right thing at the right time. Cahill doesn't court danger, but when he encounters it, which is often, he responds shrewdly and emerges to recollect his adventures in tranquility. Whether scaling a cliff or descending into a cave, he's the kind of guy you'd want by your side when it all hits the fan.

Cahill grew up in a small Wisconsin town. When he was ten, he joined a swim team so he could travel around the state. He put himself through the University of Wisconsin on a swimming scholarship and soon he found himself in UW's law school. But when it dawned on him that most law students become lawyers and go on to careers in law, he dropped out and headed for San Francisco.

A *San Francisco Examiner* story led to a job at *Rolling Stone*. Later he became a founding editor of *Outside* magazine, where he invented the world's greatest job: traveling to some of the planet's most remote places and writing about them. He's swum with great white sharks, plunged into caves with lethal levels of CO_2, pursued Caspian tigers, and taken a dip in the ice-encrusted waters of the North Pole. But unlike many adventure writers of yore, Cahill's stories don't come from his gonads. He writes from the heart and hopes his tales make you laugh and make you cry.

Cahill, an imposing presence, stands six-foot-one and has filled out a bit since his collegiate swimming days. *The New York Times* has called him "a working-class Paul Theroux," and when he's wearing a tattered t-shirt and sipping a beer, he looks like he just got off the day shift. But looks can be deceiving. Though Cahill can joke about dog farts on one page, on the next you'll find lines by William Blake. He's a serious student of the craft of writing, and his stories are seamlessly structured.

Among Cahill's collections are *Pass the Butterworms, Pecked to Death by Ducks,* and *A Wolverine is Eating My Leg.* He called his first book *Jaguars Ripped My Flesh* to rile colleagues who felt adventure travel writing was traditionally "subliterate." Cahill's 1991 book, *Road Fever,* recounts a caffeine-fueled road trip from Tierra del Fuego to Alaska's Prudhoe Bay that set a speed record recognized by the *Guinness Book of World Records*.

"Let me know when you're getting in and I'll pick you up at the airport," Cahill told me when we set a date for the interview. The Bozeman airport is thirty-five miles from his home, so I declined and rented a car. But when he said I could spend the night on his couch—"I doubt you got a big advance for this book, so you may as well save your motel money"—I accepted. I drove under Montana's big sky to Livingston, where Cahill lives in a modest, century-old house in town, with his wife Linnea, two dogs, and two cats.

We corralled Grace the springer spaniel and Mac the 105-pound giant schnauzer and asked them that rhetorical question: Wanna go for a walk? It was a sunny, Indian summer afternoon. We circled a broad valley framed by the Crazy Mountains to the north and the snow-streaked Absarokas to the south. The dogs took off ahead of us and when a herd of antelope sprung past us, Gracie leapt after them. But even a speedy dog is no match for America's fastest land animal.

Tim and I talked about the death of his mother five weeks before— he and his siblings had to decide when to pull the plug. I asked Tim how his neighbors felt about wolf reintroduction. "Polarized," he said. He told me how he learned to hunt antelope by shadowing other hunters. Later he pointed to a nearby peak and said one day he wants to walk out his front door, swim across the river, scale the peak and be home in time for dinner.

Back at his house, in the company of a fearsome Dogon figure from Mali and a wild-eyed mask from Bali, we conducted the interview. Mac's deafening barks punctuated Tim's remarks and he often derailed his train of thought to shout "*Plotz!*" to Mac, figuring the dog would respond better to commands in its native German.

For dinner we went to The Pizza Garden, a homey restaurant owned by Tim's close friend, Jim Liska. Ten people crowded around a table for eight—many were Tim's friends—and they squeezed us in. One guy was a documentary filmmaker, another had been a photo-journalist for *TIME*. The woman across from me had helped ghost-write Hillary Clinton's book. Our waitress, Courtney, was the young woman whose heartrending story of life-threatening spinal surgery is recounted in Cahill's tale "Trusty and Grace" (in the 2002 collection, *Hold the Enlightenment*).

Halfway through dinner, an effervescent woman named Margie blew in and pulled up a chair next to mine. She told me she'd recent-ly starred in the touring production of *The Vagina Monologues*. Turned out it was her birthday so we all sang for her. On the way home I asked Tim who she was and he said, "Oh, Margie. That's Margot Kidder." Well, my wine-addled mind thought, I might never emerge from a phone booth with a big red S on my chest, but at least I've sung happy birthday to Lois Lane.

The next day Tim asked if I'd like to see his cabin in the woods and help him pull his plastic water pipes out of the creek. As yellow aspen leaves rustled in the breeze, we drove on dusty roads past the small house where he lived when he first moved to Montana in the late '70s. "See that long driveway—it wasn't plowed in winter so I had to post-hole it up that road with bags of groceries and the dog." Nearby ranches belong to Tom McGuane, Robert Redford, and Tom Brokaw. "See that place up there on the hill—you'll never guess who used to own it: Whoopi Goldberg," he said. "But she sold it after a year."

Cahill's cabin is nestled in heavily forested woods just north of Yellowstone. PVC pipes stretched to the nearby creek, bringing water to the cabin. In anticipation of winter we yanked the pipes out from the creek bed. Tim marveled that this was the first time he'd ever managed to pull the pipes without getting his feet wet. I was soaked up to my knees. Just as he asked if I'd like to take a hike, the phone in his cabin rang. It was Linnea—they needed to leave for a dinner date in an hour.

The drive to the cabin had taken an hour and fifteen minutes. "It'd be great if we could get back in time for me to take a shower," Tim said. "Would you mind driving?" I hadn't really bargained for this: piloting a bulky Chevy pickup at hair-raising speeds across Montana's back roads with a passenger who'd set an overland speed record. "Don't worry," he said, "I'll let you know when there's a curve or a bump coming up." My sodden foot put the pedal to the metal. We flew over ditches, kicked up clouds of dust, sped past a herd of befuddled buffalo. We made it in about forty-five minutes, as fast, Tim said, as he'd ever driven it himself.

≈≈≈

What are you working on now?

A very short book called *Lost in My Own Backyard,* which is about walking in Yellowstone. I was asked to write about my favorite place to walk so I said, "Could it be Yellowstone Park?" And they (the publisher) said it certainly could be. Good lord, what a job! They're going to pay me to walk in Yellowstone Park—I love it.

Not everything you've done is travel. You started by writing for Rolling Stone.

Let me start a little bit further back, and I'll tell you a story. I wanted to be a writer from the time I was a teenager and I think a lot of my adolescent fantasies of travel were tied up with being a writer. Big-time writers in those days were Ernest Hemingway and guys who went to Africa. However in the little town that I grew up in there was nobody who was a writer, and since I really did love to read, I thought writers were some kind of gods. Now you and I know many writers (laughs) and we know this is not the case. Some of the most poetic and wonderful writers are somewhat less than gods in their personal lives.

But at the time I thought if I said I wanted to be a writer, it would be a kind of vanity. It would be like saying I want to be a god. So I never told anybody until I went to the University of Wisconsin. I went to law school and did pretty well in my first semester. A professor, one of those scary law school professors, a *Paper Chase* kind of guy, called me into his office and said, "This is one of the five best briefs I've ever read from a first-year student."

I recall walking out of that office and feeling very depressed and thinking, Why was I depressed? What I realized was that if this kept up the way it was going, I was going to be a lawyer, and I'd never actually tried to be a writer. So I went to San Francisco—this shows how backwards I was; the capital of the American literary world is New York—and enrolled in San Francisco State in a creative writing program. I wrote a mercifully unpublished novel…

What year was that?

1968 or 1969—I'm vague on years. The Summer of Love—I got there in the fall (laughs). I was there certainly in time for Altamont. In those days in San Francisco, prices were cheap enough that young people who had big dreams, artistic dreams, could actually live in the city, and there were a lot of us. I had this friend who was an oil painter and a lithographer, and he did birds. He wanted me to write something about birds so that the popular media would carry one of his lithographs.

The only problem with that is that I have ornithological dyslexia. I can't tell one bird from another. I have gotten better at it. What I did know were the turkey vultures on Mount Tamalpais. I used to just lie down in the meadow, and the vultures would begin to circle trying to figure out if you were dead or not. So I said I'll write about the vultures.

So Jim—the artist's name was Jim Gorman—said "I can do vultures" and he did some. I wrote the article and submitted it with some of Jim's lithos to the magazine of the *San Francisco Examiner* and they accepted it. Now here's the interesting thing: I'd never had a journalism course. I knew nothing whatsoever about journalism—I was going to write the great American novel.

But it was just the beginning of New Journalism. I didn't know I was a new journalist. I was just a guy who had never been taught the proper pyramid lead, the structure of a journalistic piece. I knew the structure of a dynamic scene; I knew the structure of novels. I knew how to carpenter scenes together. At that time it turned out to be a very good idea for me to do things like that. The editor liked my story on vultures and asked what else I'd like to do something on.

I'd been told: Write about what you know. So I did one on beer, and then I did one on this guy who had won the 100-meter breast stroke in the Olympics. As it turned out, I had been a swimmer at the University of Wisconsin and I knew what swimming was like. I knew that in the big race you can remember every second of that fifty-eight seconds—you can remember precisely what you were thinking—and how much more so an Olympian than someone like me who was just a pretty fair Big 10 swimmer.

So I went and I asked him, "What were you thinking? You're standing on the block and the gun goes off, what do you think now?" And I followed him all the way through—I did about 2,000 words on what he thought from start to finish. It was all an internal monologue, which is a novelist's technique. And that made my work in the *San Francisco Examiner* stick out, because I just didn't know how to do journalism properly. I would use the techniques of fiction, like internal monologue.

It's always good to be in the Sunday papers because everybody reads them, even the people of *Rolling Stone*. I had friends who had friends and somebody said, "Why don't you come down and ask about a job?" So I did. And they said, "Yeah, we need an editorial drudge." That was my title. *Rolling Stone* was so amazing in those days because you could travel very quickly from editorial drudge to associate editor. I think almost all things are more stratified these days. Two months later I was writing about rock-and-roll stars that nobody else wanted to write about, like Donovan. So that's how I got started, long story.

Was writing about travel a conscious decision for you, or did you just find yourself propelled by your curiosity and start going places and writing about them?

I've thought about that a lot. I can remember when I was a kid in Wisconsin in a little town called Waukesha. I told my dad, this guy got to go to Florida and that guy went to New York, I never get to go anywhere. I was ten at the time, and my dad said if you join the YMCA swimming team, they go all over the state. So I said O.K. I made the team and I got to go to really exotic places like Beloit, Fond du Lac, Green Bay. I think I associated this reward of travel with hard, physical work.

What happened at *Rolling Stone* is they wanted to start an outdoor magazine and there were only two of us in the office who liked to go outdoors, Michael Rogers and myself, and we along with Harriet Fier started putting together the plans for *Outside* magazine. I said, "Let's have an adventure travel article in each issue." And they said, "Well, see Tim, you don't seem to get it; *Outside* will be a literate magazine for people who go outdoors." You have to think back to '76, there wasn't such a thing. It was either a magazine that told you how to paddle a canoe twelve times a year, very service-oriented, or there were those magazines called *Man's Adventure* or *Man's Testicle*, and they were all about our death race with the Jungle Leper Army, stuff that you can hardly credit as being entirely true.

I said, "Hell if I can write about lying out and watching vultures and make an interesting story, how much more interesting would it be if I went diving, for instance, and saw a shark." In the old men's magazines I'd have to pull out a pen knife and battle it to death. In what I saw, you could talk about what it felt like to see one, and talk about whether you were scared and the core of wonder that would be wrapped up in all that. If you did that well you would have an adventure article.

They said, "O.K. Tim, do it." And hence I sort of invented my own job, to travel to different places and often put myself in jeopardy, hard physical work being something that travel had been about for me since I was ten.

I'm curious about how you see your terrain. You talk about the interior landscape as well as the external landscape. What do you view as your beat?

If I have a beat, it is the remote places on earth. Remote places have changed a great deal since I began writing. Twenty, twenty-five years ago you could go to places such as Peru, and as a white man from the United States, you looked a good deal different than most people there. They would grab you by the arm and take you to one of their children who might have blond hair and blue eyes. And it was just such a novel thing. Now there are adventure travel tours that go through there all the time. People see gringos all year long.

The places that are now remote are the places that cannot be visited by adventure travel companies because the adventure travel companies can't get insurance. I'm talking about places that generally have some kind of civil insurrection going on. For me to get remote anymore, I'm being driven more and more to the lines of guns. I used to have to figure out ways to ford a river that was running high in the springtime. Now I have to figure out how to get past the soldiers with the guns.

The air was filled with a light snow that didn't precisely fall but seemed to drift aimlessly under a pearly, opalescent sky. Everything else under that crystal dome was flat, an endless prairie of sea ice, white with the newly fallen snow, and I could see the curve of the earth in the far distance in any direction I cared to look. That direction was south.

I was, for the moment, facing due south. Behind me, the direction was due south. It was due south to my right, due south to my left, and if I wanted to quarter off on my left side, I'd be facing south by south-south.

—TIM CAHILL,
Pass the Butterworms

One thing that strikes me about your writing is its youthful sense of wonder and exuberance. How do you keep that alive—does travel help you cultivate that?

I talk about my travel as being sort of an adolescent dream that I never let anybody know about. The word adolescent is used often as a pejorative, but when I was fifteen, sixteen, seventeen, I was the most idealistic I ever was in my life; the most doors were open to me. Adolescence has some good qualities and I try to cultivate those qualities. The benefit of travel writing is you can always keep that gate to wonder open—it's a great big huge world. Say you'd been to every single place I'd been to in my life except that you were ten feet to my right. You would have lived a totally different trip.

Or if I followed the exact same line ten days behind, it would still be entirely different.

The world is inexhaustible so it leaves that gate to wonder open.

After researching and writing Buried Dreams *(about mass murderer John Wayne Gacy), did you travel to get away from the psychotic mind of the murderer?*

I lived in a sewer for three years when I was in that guy's mind. The subtitle was *Inside the Mind of a Serial Killer.* I tried to get inside there. And when I did I was not very happy; it was not very good psychologically for me. This guy had a certain type that he killed. After I got to know him pretty well I could look at somebody on the street and say, "Victim. Victim." Walking down the street looking at people and thinking: victim; that's not real healthy for you.

What's good about the travel I do, a certain rough travel, stuff that makes stories, is that usually there is something, some obstacle that has to be overcome. It may be that your tent and all your gear has been stolen and it's going to be ten below zero tonight. You better figure out something to do about it right now. When things like that happen, they require your entire attention. Coming off a bad serial-killer hang-over, things that required my immediate attention took my mind completely off the problems.

You say adventure is physical and emotional discomfort recollected in tranquility—that's in Hold the Enlightenment, *right?*

That's right—I can't recall which poet I stole that from. I think I said it was Wordsworth, but I think it's Emerson. But the two met, so they stole it from one another, you know, they thought alike. They said, "Poetry is strong emotion recollected in tranquility." And I said, "Adventure is physical or emotional discomfort recollected in tranquility." An adventure is never an adventure when it's happening. An adventure is only an adventure when you've had time to sit back and think about it.

Now, a book that I admire is the one that Tracy Johnston wrote called *Shooting the Boh*. This was supposed to be a simple river-running trip and everything went wrong. Suddenly she's clinging to life at the end of her fingernails, and she's also beginning to get the first hot flashes of menopause. What a wonderful book, and a book, by the way, that no man could have possibly written.

Hardly anything bonds you to someone stronger than an intense physical challenge met together. I don't have any problem with adventure travel tours. I worry a little bit about the Disneyfication. The idea is you can't get hurt because this is a tour—people have lost the idea that indeed they can.

I'll give you one quick story: we were in Namibia in southwest Africa. A guy broke his ankle very, very badly. We had to carry him in a homemade stretcher for quite some distance—it was 120 degrees at the bottom of the canyon. We had to get a satellite phone with a dying battery to get somebody to come down and get this guy out of there. The helicopter said they couldn't make it till the next morning so we spent the night there. It was like *Gilligan's Island*—it was supposed to be a day hike.

A three-hour tour?

(Laughs.) Yeah, a three-hour tour. And there we were with this guy with a broken leg and I was with Richard Bangs, the famous river runner and writer, the founder of Sobek. And this guy with a broken ankle asked Richard: "Is this the worst that's ever happened on one of your trips?" He said, "No, people have died." That's the nature of adventure travel. I think people should keep that in mind when they book their next adventure travel trip.

You've said you don't need to travel halfway around the world to enjoy the discovery of travel. But I find that unless I get away from familiar surroundings, I can't really see the world with fresh eyes. Do you feel that it's possible to write travel about your hometown? Can you feel that sense of discovery that you feel when you're in a new place for the first time?

I hope, with over twenty-five years of experience going to far away and remote places, that I have learned enough about how to write travel that I will be able to write travel right here at home. I have come to many conclusions during the past years—I'm approaching sixty years old—frankly I've lost a step or two. I used to be able to make this climb or make that climb. Now I will quite often say, "Boys go ahead. This one's beyond me—I'll meet you on the other side." As I begin moving away from the more remote places, I want to write about the area right here at home.

I'm a writer—I can live any place on earth that I choose to. I choose to live here. It distresses me to know that there are people that come here for two-week vacations at dude ranches and they know more about these mountains than I do because they've ridden all around them. I am hoping that I can see this land, this country, the place that I've lived for twenty-five years...I hope the same gate of wonder opens here, and I think it has.

Hell, the only national magazine award I ever won was for writing about Yellowstone. It wasn't for writing about chasing Caspian tigers along the border of Iraq and Iran or swimming under the ice in the North Pole, or walking around Antarctica. It was for Yellowstone; it was for my back yard. So maybe I do have the capacity to see it with fresh eyes. I think maybe the fact that I have traveled widely and I've seen a lot has helped me see what this is. I live here because—don't tell anybody—it's the best place on earth. There is no place better than this to live.

Why? Why did you choose it and why do you love it?

Remember when we took a walk this afternoon and I was rambling on about how the prairie meets the mountains here? Now you go over on the other side of the Continental divide, the western side, and you will have all trees, and you will be stuck in a forest, and in this forest you won't be able to see more than ten feet in any direction. There won't be a whole hell of a lot of wildlife. And if there is you won't see it. You might see signs but you won't see a lot of wildlife. It's claustrophobic over there.

Yeah, the mountains are pretty spectacular and the glaciers look great, and the big lakes are terrific, but for game, just for the natural concentration of animals, you're going to see it where the prairie meets the mountains, where the prairie meets the forest. That's why Yellowstone, which is largely a flatland surrounded by mountains, is America's version of the Serengeti. There are animals in there, herds in the thousands—that's what I like. I like the collision of prairie and forest. I like the ability to have a long view.

When we were standing up there and I was saying, my friend from Hawaii says that what you can see would encompass all of O'ahu. Think about what humans must have wanted back as the ice left this land maybe 10,000 years ago. You're going to want a place where there's lots of game, on the prairie there's lots of bison; there's lots of elk; you're going to want a place that's a little bit high to give you the military advantage. You want to be able to see for miles and miles in any direction—you do not want to be in the middle of a forest surrounded by trees. It might have been good for Robin Hood but it wasn't good for Crazy Horse.

You showed me that place where there was continuous human habitation for 9,000 years.

The Myers-Hindman site, found by two ladies probably in their sixties at the time. They would walk around and look for arrowheads and the like. Archaeologists started digging up there and found 9,000 years of continuous human habitation, which by the way is not nearly the oldest around here. What I like is continuous human habitation—just over that little hill they would be out of the wind, they'd have a view forever—you can see why people would live there continuously for 9,000 years.

I remember when I was working as a whitewater rafting guide on the Kern River, there were grinding holes in the rocks at our campsite. It was so cool to sit up there knowing that a few hundred years ago people were sitting on the same rocks, hanging out, talking, grinding acorns into flour...

Around here you can do the same thing: find a spot that commands a view so that you can't be snuck up upon but is really quite pleasant and out of the wind, and then start looking for arrowheads and they're all over.

I love it around here. I like the river, floating the river. I'd row the river. I used to hunt and fish a great deal more than I do now. I believed at one time that if I was going to be a meat-eater that there was a necessity to hunt and to fish. I don't do it much anymore—I'm busy. If I have a chance to hunt antelope and I have the time, I love to cook it—it's the best tasting meat.

Having lived here for twenty-five years, do you feel that this place gives you a foundation that helps you feel better about traveling for long periods?

Yeah, it certainly does. This is a small town, 7,000 people. You pretty much know who doesn't like you and who does. There are people I know here whose values are ones that I respect: honesty and integrity and loyalty to their friends, and it gives you a very, very solid base.

The weightlifters have an expression about how you should tense your body if you're trying to lift something over your head with one hand, and that is: "You can't shoot a cannon from a canoe." In other words, if you don't have a solid base, you're not going to be able to do that. This is my solid base, this little town.

When you go to a new place how do you make sense of it or understand it?

You have to let everything happen around you and try not to make whatever happens happen solely because you're there. Some things will happen solely because you're there because you're a stranger who is out of place. What's always struck me as strange is you read about these tragedies in which soldiers from some country, say England, crashed onto the shores of Hudson Bay and died—they froze to death, one after the other—in the midst of other people who have lived there for centuries. It would seem to me that those Englishmen might have thought, Wait a minute, this is the way you live here.

Or maybe: We should talk to these people and make friends with them.

Yeah, find out how they do things. In general the way they do things wherever you're going—they've had centuries to think about it—is probably better than the way you were taught. So watch them, listen to them, have them teach you. A side note: Just about everything you need is going to be available there. If you're driving yourself nuts in Denver trying to find a proper machete—listen, they're all over Honduras. Just walk into any marketplace and buy one for a tenth of what you would pay in Denver.

You've said preparation is scintillating when your life may depend upon it. What do you feel is most important when going to a place where there could be risk or challenge? What should one read—how should one approach it mentally?

I think knowing one's limits is real good. If someone said, "Tim, we have a space on the K2 climb for you," I'd have to say, "Guys, that's out of my league." I know what my limits are. I can do things that push my own envelope, but it's my own envelope, so I will have the exact same feeling when I get to the summit of my 20,000-foot mountain that elite climbers have when they get to the summit of Everest.

Aside from that, if you're going to a place where there are going to be guns, it really does help to know what everybody is mad about. Do a lot of reading. Find out who's who and what's what so that if you happen to be in the hands of somebody who may have reason not to like you, you would be able to say some things that person might agree with. Spontaneously perhaps say those things.

I think, to a large degree, preparation—I'm not talking about traveling; I'm talking about writing—is having a pretty good idea of what your quest is, what you're going to try to do and what you're going to try to find out. If you go to a country or continent that you don't know much about, you're going to be overwhelmed with things that you could write about and you want to be able to follow a story line. So have an idea of what your quest is.

What's in your tool kit? Obviously you take a pen and paper. What else? Camera, tape recorder?

I use reporter's notebooks—I usually use just one side and then when I'm thinking about it later at night I use the other side. I bring a large spiral notebook and if I have time I transfer the notes from the smaller notebook into the larger notebook. I build whole scenes and sometimes things go almost directly from the big notebook into print.

I may have a tape recorder, or two, because if things are going so fast that I don't have time to take notes, I can speak my notes into the tape recorder as I'm moving. I did that on a six-week walk across a forest in the Congo, and the woman who transcribed my work came out with 750 pages. I think taking notes in the notebook is such drudgery that I truly keep my mind on what I am trying to do and trying to say.

Clearly your work is journalism, so are you allowed any leeway with facts to put together a good story?

I am allowed no leeway whatsoever—the facts are the facts—what happened happened. Remarkable things have happened to me maybe because I have sought out remarkable events. Believe me, all journalists who are just starting out: if you fib, they will catch you. And since I have had the remarkable good luck of seeing some astounding things, I must be totally trustworthy as a narrator. Otherwise I am nothing—there is no leeway for me.

Even when exaggerating? What about the half-pound centipede in your story "Bug Scream"?

Yeah, it was no bigger than an ordinary Polish sausage. Frankly I may have exaggerated a little bit, but yeah the thing did fall on my chest and people did come over, and the pygmies did spend a great deal of the evening laughing at me—all that is true. I suppose I couldn't resist "only about as big as an ordinary Polish sausage." Was it that big? Hey, it could have been pretty close.

Structure. I think anyone who has read your work and is interested in writing knows that you take structure very seriously.

Yeah, I work on structure. I take voluminous notes—what I do when I'm about to begin writing a story is look for something a little different. On a three-week trip I'll fill two to three of those large notebooks. I read them over and I read them over until I have basically memorized what I have written.

David Quammen, my friend who lives over in Bozeman and is one of the great writers of our time, says it's like you hold this unformed thing up to the sun and you keep turning it and turning it until suddenly like a prism, a rainbow pours through it. And that's what you do with the raw material of a story: you keep reading it and thinking about it until it suddenly becomes a story. How and why does it become a story? It becomes a story because we are story-telling creatures—that's how we keep from going mad. 'Cause there's too much happening all around us—too many things to describe, too many things to think about.

There's 8 million stories in the naked city—how many can you encompass in your mind? Only a few. You have your own story. You look at your notes—your mind wants to put that into a story structure, one that has a beginning, a middle, and an end and is somehow satisfying or insightful and leaves you with a punch. That's the philosophical part, I suppose: we're storytellers. We are also entertainers. Unlike in school where you're paying a professor, nobody has an obligation to read what you've written. So you must make them want to read you. You do that by telling stories well.

Let's talk about time. Your stories jump from the past to the present and back—they rarely unfold chronologically. How do you work with that?

You're looking at your notes, raw material, and you're trying to figure out what makes the best story. If I was telling this as a story, wouldn't the listener want to know this part first. But I only learned that toward the end of my trip. So how am I going to manipulate the story so that all the information that the reader knows, the reader has to know to make a story convincing, is up front. You do that by fracturing the timeline, but you tell the reader that.

Readers are used to it; they've been to movies—they know what a flashback is. You use the techniques of suspense. I think Alfred Hitchcock said something like, if there's a bunch of guys in a meeting room and suddenly a bomb goes off, that's shock. But if these guys are in the room and you know there's a bomb and you know it's going to go off at twelve o'clock and the clock is ticking towards twelve, that's suspense. Sometimes you have to tell the reader ahead of time things that you didn't know to produce that suspense. I don't think that's cheating—that's storytelling.

You've said that you want to make the reader laugh and you want to make the reader cry. I also feel from reading your stuff that you want to teach the reader something. I always learn something, like why animals' eyes shine at night.

Why do different animals eyes shine differently in light at night? Why are some red—why are some green? Some say, well predators have the red eyes, and prey populations like deer have the green eyes, and I wondered whether that was true or not. But here's the thing: I find the answer is fascinating; it's a scientific principle of reflection that has to do with a coating on the back of the eyeball.

So if I said, Reader, I'm going to tell you about a coating on the back of the eyeball that reflects light back through the pupils and makes animals eyes shine...some people may read it and some may not. But if I put you into a dark forest and I have a light and I start shining it around and I'm looking at all these different colored eyes staring at me, then the reader may be ready for me to tell him what I

That's why the words "Let's go!" are intrinsically courageous. It's the decision to go that is, in itself, entirely intrepid. We know from the first step that travel is often a matter of confronting our fear of the unfamiliar and the unsettling—of the rooster's head in the soup, of the raggedy edge of unfocused dread, of that cliff face that draws us willy-nilly to its lip and forces us to peer into the void."

—Tim Cahill, "Exotic Places Made Me Do It," *Outside*

know about why animals' eyes shine differently. The reason I put that stuff in there is that I just found it fascinating. But I can't put in the purely scientific or historical stuff until I've aroused the reader's curiosity to the point where the reader might say, "I wonder why that is." And if I'm really good, that's when I come in and say, that's because...

In a lot of your work you deal with fear, whether going to places where men have guns or risking your life in physical adventures. I wonder what scares you most?

What scared me most in my early career was physical disability, if I lost a leg or something like that. I don't think this now, but as a very young man I thought it would be better to be dead than to be an invalid. Now I see the value of life—my mother just passed away. She had written me many times saying if it's a choice between me being an invalid and living with machines keeping me alive, please have the courage to pull the plug.

And we did what she wanted us to do. Dammit, you say, we could have had her around for a little bit more. So, yeah I could live very well without a leg.

What scares me today: the same thing that scares everybody else: heights. Who wants to fall to their death? And I'm scared of talking in front of an audience.

But in terms of your trips, you've suggested people with guns scare you more than a raging river, for example, because you can sort of gauge a river, but you can't really tell whether or not somebody is going to pull the trigger.

You've said it exactly the way I would say it. You cannot tell what a person with a gun is going to do. As the world turns, I'm afraid that gunmen get younger and younger. You're getting a fourteen-year-old with an AK-47 on you. I've had a chance to test my physical limits. I kind of know what my limits are. I can look at a river and say, no, not me—I'll walk around. I didn't do that early on.

One of the first stories I did was I learned to fly a hot-air balloon—one had never been flown over Pike's Peak in Colorado. We got all set to do it—I had two experienced pilots with me and we got ready to go. One of the experienced pilots said, "I don't like it." He didn't like the way the mountain looked. This is one of the guys who taught me how to fly a hot-air balloon, and he didn't like it. These days I would say, the guy who knows more than me doesn't want to do it, but I was too dumb call if off. We managed to get over, but...

I greatly admire Bill Bryson's book on the Appalachian Trail because he just said, "Oh hell, this is way too hard—I'm not going to do this." He wrote a wonderful book about it. I never never never never would have not done that entire trail. What am I trying to do—

I'm only trying to write good books, but somehow that Calvinist thing in my brain would have said: You said you're going to walk the trail and you're going to walk the trail. Bryson made it wonderfully hilarious, and it was a better book for it.

I agree. You and Bill have such different approaches. When I interviewed him he expressed great admiration for you and your sense of adventure and daring. He said, "I don't like that." His favorite trip is walking through England from inn to inn, with a lovely fire and a nice dinner when you get there. He can write beautifully about that.

Oh, he can. I didn't used to work out to try to keep in shape. I always figured I'd get in shape on the trip—let the trip get you in shape. Now, with age creeping up on me, I've got to work out. I gotta walk, I gotta lift weights. But you know what, if I do what I do properly, it isn't about the peril or the adventure. It's about the writing, it's about the laughing, the crying, and maybe a little bit of the teaching. As I segue into a maybe less adventuresome writer, I hope those things will become obvious, that I've been doing them all along.

I would like to walk from hut to hut. I would like to spend a great deal more time getting to know these mountains around here. They're 10,000-foot mountains, but hey, I was on search and rescue around here: you make a mistake up there.... We took more people who hadn't made it out of there than we ever rescued alive. You'd think that I would know the area having done search and rescue. I'm talking about really knowing the area, and I can see spending a great deal of time up here. How many stories on Yellowstone or the greater Yellowstone ecosystem can I write before somebody says, "Oh, he's the guy who always does this."

I'm curious about the scariest trip you've ever been on. I know you've traveled with Robert Young Pelton (author of The World's Most Dangerous Places*). Was that it or were there other times when you were even more imperiled?*

First off, Robert Pelton is an extremely good reporter. We were traveling in Colombia at the time—we interviewed the FARC, the revolutionary Marxist forces that were opposing the government, and

America was their deadly enemy. They'd killed a couple of American indigenous rights workers, by mistake they said, and kidnapped a great deal more. So that was real scary.

Another extremely scary one was when I went to the Maranon River down in Peru where my friend Paul Dix's twenty-six-year-old son was killed, shot by people on that river. Those people had to imagine that when we came down there to find out what happened that Paul was a father looking for revenge. And they'd killed before, in the night, so that was an extremely scary story.

Recently I was in northern Thailand going into caves that have lethal levels of CO_2. It's a lot of rappelling and stopping on a moment's notice and pulling out your CO_2 sensor because it can change in six feet from being O.K. to being deadly. And if it is, you gotta be able to change from your rappelling-down thing to your climbing-up thing— that's tough to do when you're worried about the gas belching up at you in total darkness. I hadn't done any serious hard-core caving for almost fifteen years, so I found that frightening as well.

The scariest one is not scary at all for anybody except me because I made a mistake. I was stupid.

The fall?

Uh-huh. I was in the Queen Charlotte Islands—we were kayaking. The thrust of my story was that the Queen Charlottes are the Galapagos of Canada. They have a lot of endemic species, species seen nowhere else, among them a kind of woodpecker, a kind of bear, but it's heavily forested. The kayaking was spectacular. There were killer whales all over, sea lions going nuts—it was not to be missed. But I thought my assignment was to at least look for some of these endemic species, and there were orchids out there—I thought for sure I could find those.

So I asked people, "Who wants to come on a walk with me?" But nobody wanted to come so I thought I would go alone. I told you I was on search and rescue—I knew that it was the dumbest thing that I'd ever done. This is a temperate zone rainforest and the trail went from our kayaking camp and disappeared. So I bushwhacked over the spine of the mountain while the rest of my friends were enjoying their kayaking. On the way back I was really screwed. I was probably three, four miles north of the campsite. That wouldn't be so bad, except imagine a big spine of mountains with rivers coming down. So I had probably a seven or eight drainages to get by, up and down, up and down.

On top of that I hadn't prepared myself for a really long walk. I was wearing Wellingtons, irrigation boots, these rubber boots that come up to your knees. As I was coming through one of these drainages, there was a cliff wall. And I said, "O.K. I can go quite a ways out and cross the stream there and come back down and keep going, or I could just climb this cliff." And the cliff, to me, was such an easy cliff that I kept my walking stick in my hand. I didn't even need both hands.

The problem is, the Queen Charlottes must be the world's capital of moss. There was moss a foot and a half thick on that wall and so I had to thrust my hand through the moss, find a handhold, and then kick with my foot until I found a foothold. We're only talking about climbing ten or fifteen feet here, and I was just about at the top, and there was a small tree there. I reached out with one arm to sweep and catch the tree and somehow missed it.

I was falling face first. I thought, This is really not good, but luckily it's all moss down there. I got my hands out in front of myself—it felt almost as if I was doing kind of a swan dive, as if my heels wanted to touch my head. You see this scar here—since it was all moss there, the only way I figure I got that was my walking stick.

I realized that I torqued my back extremely badly. I heard a cracking sound when I went down. Now here I was, alone in a temperate zone rainforest. It rains there all the time—I had my rain gear on, black pants, green shirt, Wellington boots—I looked just like the forest all around me. I was off trail—nobody was ever gonna find me. I realized that I should get up immediately—you know how when you fall you say to yourself, I wonder how bad it is, I'm just going to lie here...I didn't even think that.

I got up—I usually wear a bandanna around my neck when I'm walking. I took that off and tied it around my head to stop the bleeding. You know the way head wounds bleed; I was just covered in blood, and I started walking out of there. Well it's all downed timber, so you're going up and down, climbing over these things. I remember having this stupid conversation with myself, and it went like this: O.K., you always thought if it came down to it you could be a hero, so be a hero and walk out of here. Then the other part of me said, heroes don't do really stupid things. You can't be a hero because you're a moron (laughs).

So this conversation went on back and forth, and the question about whether or not I was ever going to get out of there was moot.

I got down to the beach—and you could walk for long periods on the beach and then you would come to a rocky point with waves crashing up against it. Now remember I said that I was a swimmer and I got through the University of Wisconsin swimming. I'm a strong swimmer. And I said, You know what, I can't go back up in those trees—if my back finally gives out I'll be stuck up there. I better stay down around this beach and it doesn't hurt to swim. But what about these boots, these irrigation boots are going to fill up with water. So I thought about these irrigation boots—I said, O.K. what am I going to do with these?

Tim, you know that if you lose your boots, you're not going to be able to walk anymore. If you keep them on they're going to weigh you down and you're going to have to get out beyond the breakers when you go around the point. And I thought, O.K., I'll wear the boots and swim around the breakers, and I did that and came back to the beach and walked to the next point. I think I swam about three times.

It's Canada—it's way up there near the border of Alaska so it was probably 10, 10:30 at night. It's going to get dark pretty soon. I figured my kayaking buddies are going to come looking along the beach. But I couldn't stop—I knew that if I stopped my back would seize up. So I went to a far point that stuck out and I got as much kindling as I could find. If it got dark I was going to light that fire—I figured that would be a signal fire.

How'd you start the fire? I've read the story in Hold the Enlightenment *and I've wondered that since.*

As it happened I didn't have to light the fire, but among the other stupid things that I did, I was a smoker, and I had a couple of Bic lighters. Believe it or not, you can dry those things out and light them up. Just blow on 'em.

So smoking almost saved your life?

(Laughs.) Yep. I still carry Bic lighters with me—it's part of the tool-kit. But that was as close as I've ever come, I think, to actually dying on a trip. I was MedEvac-ed out of there the next day and was immobile for about three days. And I thought I was O.K.—it took about a year and a half until it got to the point where I could not walk again. I literally could not walk more than six steps. I'd have to make a plan to brush my teeth because I couldn't stand. I eventually had a back operation—now I'm about 85 percent. I lift weights and do things like dead lifts and snatches that I think strengthen my back. But if you wanted me to move a couch for you, nah, I've got a bad back.

I'd like to ask about your encounters with dolphins and great white sharks. I think our culture has a lot of myths about dolphins being the good guys and sharks being bad.

Remember when you were a kid and you would say if a gorilla got into a fight with the lion, who would win? Well if a dolphin got into a fight with a great white shark, who would win? The dolphin. I saw an amazing thing when I was diving with great white sharks just off South Africa, this island where Southern fur seals gather. They have to get in the water every once in a while or they'll die from overheating. The fur seals go into the water all at once and—boop!—a great white will get one.

I was watching all this happen in a shark cage. Now you think a shark cage is something with big steel bars—it's more like chicken wire, a heavy grade of chicken wire but...I said to the guy putting me in there, can't they bite right through this? And he said, well it's more like bobbing for apples for them. It's a cylinder, just big enough for me and maybe one other person to be in there, and it's hanging on a rope so if the shark tries to bite it, it kind of moves away from them, the same way an apple moves away when you bob for apples. At least that's the way it was explained to me.

Nobody there had been eaten by a shark, and they'd been running this program for about five years. And the guys that I was with had all their arms and legs so I figured, maybe they know what they're doing. Never go shark diving with a guy that's only got one arm.

So there I am, and I see two guys who are swimming free among the great white sharks. They're not in a cage. And this one guy is shooting video of the great whites and the other guy is his safety diver. The safety diver swims just above—you gotta look 360 degrees—you usually have a shark club, a sharp pointed thing, which is really no more than a broom handle that you poke 'em with.

But this guy had something else: he had a plywood board, and this board was in the shape of a killer whale and the colors of a killer whale. This great white got a little close—it banged up against the cage that I was in. You could just see all these sickly ghost-colored muscles. And boom, he went towards the cage and the safety diver held up the board. The shark was twenty or thirty feet away and saw this thing, a great white shark that weighted maybe fifteen hundred pounds, and boom! I had never seen one move fast. When it saw this orca— boom!—it turned like a trout and disappeared.

There are a lot of people who are disillusioned about some of the things I found out when I wrote about dolphins, especially bottlenose. They can be bullies. They kind of knock their smaller cousins, the porpoises, around, just throw 'em around. Porpoises weigh what we weigh. The bottlenose dolphin can weigh one thousand pounds or more, and they'll just throw them around and kill them. They're not competing for the same food; they're just doing it for fun. It appears that some dolphins are involved in non-consensual sex like a gang-rape. To suppose that dolphins are smiling at us all the time is to misunderstand what they're doing. On the other hand, they do truly seem curious about us and they will approach us.

I quacked out the duck's furious rage. I quacked about loss and change; about the current that drives us ever forward, and entombs each moment as it passes, leaving only memories before we run out of air. I quacked so long and so fervently that I could feel moisture forming at the corners of my eyes.

—Tim Cahill,
Hold the Enlightenment

You learn all sorts of dolphin etiquette when you swim with them in the wild. One thing you learn immediately is that they attack and kill their enemies by banging them broadside. So you never get in a T-formation with these guys—they will see it as aggressive. You're always curving away from them.

So what you do is you start making your own circles and arabesques, and then they come with you. You're swimming right with them and you can look into their eye, and you feel that there is some sort of species-to-species communication.

One of my favorite stories of yours is "The Entranced Duck." One thing I really like about that story, beyond the humor, is the recognition of how much has changed without a lot of judgment. You don't say Bali is spoiled now with traffic and noise and cars. As someone who's been traveling for a quarter-century or more, what do you see as the most notable changes in the world and how do you view those?

In the world of travel, places that you go to see something different than you are likely to see every day in the United States are getting fewer and fewer. Western culture, and I include the Japanese in this, seems to be enfolding the earth. Remember that old 1950s horror movie called *The Blob*?

Of course—it's a classic!

Well, Western culture is like *The Blob*. It comes over the mountain…and people want your blue jeans. I had an argument with a photographer friend of mine once—we were covering stuff in the Marquesa islands. He wanted the Marquesans to take off their watches and dress in traditional things so he could take pictures. And I'm saying, "Wait a minute, this guy is wearing a bowling shirt that says Tahiti Lanes, and he's wearing a Seiko watch. I'm going to write about that and your pictures are going to be something different." We argued about it for quite some time. I think no matter what kind of romantic view we would like to have of the world, I think you have to tell it like it is and get those cultural cross-currents in there. And think about the people who are wearing a Seiko watch in the middle of Borneo.

Who don't know how to tell time…

They may not know how to tell time, but if you look there you'll see I have a Dogon mask. I have a bunch of stuff from Africa, I have bows and arrows from Indonesia. All these things in my house mark me as a great traveler, and the Seiko watch on the guy's wrist in the middle of Borneo marks him as a great traveler. I think you need to be able to see it from the other guy's point of view. So many people say, "He's got a watch on. I'm so disappointed; the fantasy is over."

As if these people exist for our fantasy.

As if they exist for our romantic fantasy—that's right. The question is, what do these people want? If you're a traveler like I am, you think, Maybe someday I'll run into a group of people who have not been contacted by the outside world. I came pretty close—I got to a group of people that had only seen the outside world just the year before.

But then I was talking to my photographer friend Chris Rainier who works with indigenous people in preserving their culture. We talked about what these people might want. Did they want the cure for common diseases? Did they want axes and fishhooks? Chris asked the question: Is this some kind of cultural imperialism that we're engaged in, wanting them to be real hunters and gatherers and not people that are aware of other cultures?

I like what you said, something like: Imagine if aliens came from another planet and had the cure for cancer and AIDS but they didn't want us to have it because we're very quaint the way we are.

They admire our quaint courage, and it would spoil us. That's one thing I just hate to hear people say, "Don't give that guy a tip, you'll spoil him." I think if aliens did have the cure for cancer and AIDS, I would do everything in my power to get the damn thing, and to hell with my quaint experience.

Who are your favorite authors and how have they influenced you?

In college I read Tom Wolfe's book of magazine stories and I was amazed. I read that book and said, "You can do that in nonfiction!" What Tom Wolfe had done was open up all doors. You could use all the techniques of fiction in writing nonfiction—that was amazing. I like Loren Eiseley because the man is not only a scientist but a poet. And David Quammen's *Monster of God* is brilliant.

Probably one of the greatest influences on me, or anybody that does what I do, is Edward Abbey. He could write about the outdoors, and preserving the outdoors, in a way that wasn't shrill or self-righteous, which so many conservation- and ecological-based things are. It's what makes our enemies hate us so—we are self-righteous. Edward Abbey could write about what was great about the outdoors without whining. He could make you laugh; he could make you cry, and he could make you think the big thoughts. If anybody wants proof of that, go to *Desert Solitaire* and read the piece called "Dead Man at Grand View Point." It's a brilliant piece—if you've ever heard him read it, he was a brilliant reader.

And I like many of the people you're speaking with. Bill Bryson has this blithe way about him that I absolutely admire. I like Pico Iyer; you would think he was writing a piece about the movie industry in Bombay, and it taught me more about India than several books I'd read. Why are these Indian movies the way they are, so full of this and so full of that? Pico was able to show us through the culture why the movies are the way they are. You could never look at those movies the same way, nor could you look at India the same way after reading that piece.

I am looking forward to a book by Lynne Cox—she's the long-distance, cold-water swimmer. She wrote a piece in *The New Yorker* not long ago. I kind of beat my head against the wall because I've been in contact with Lynne for a long time and we've talked about swimming. She is obviously a great athlete and she was looking for somebody who understood swimming and travel, and maybe I would write a book. I was probably not going to do that, so Lynne decided she would have to write the book herself. Unlike many other people who've tried, she has got a way with words. Her book (*Swimming to Antarctica*) may be spectacular.

If you had one last trip, where would you go?

That's the problem with travel writing. If you find a place that you like, say you like southern Italy, you can't go back a whole lot of times, otherwise you're the guy who always writes about southern Italy. I have a place that I like and that I've been back to many times, and that is Patagonia. It's the American West, except it's all just a little bit off. It's the bizarro version of the American West.

You'll be driving along in a landscape very much like what we were in today, golden grassy fields, fat cows, fast-looking horses, gravel roads. It will feel like the American West. Suddenly you'll see running along the side of the car, an ostrich-looking creature; it's a lesser rhea. Or you go down to Rio Gallegos where Butch Cassidy and the Sundance Kid robbed a bank in 1901. It was a daring, daylight bank robbery with six-guns and everything, and the bank is still there in a little square that could be a little Western town, except there's penguins there. It's all just a little bit different. It's my favorite place.

Is there a literary quote that defines your philosophy?

(Laughs.) Can I say the one that just popped into my head? I'm not sure I'd want it to define my life, but it always pops up and that is, let me get it just right, it's a William Blake quote, ah, I've got it: "The roads of excess lead to the palace of wisdom."

Yearning for the Sun

Frances Mayes
CORTONA, TUSCANY

A POET AND TEACHER, FRANCES MAYES AND HER SECOND HUSBAND Ed had rented vacation homes during the late 1980s in Tuscany and dreamed about buying a place of their own someday. In 1990, they stumbled upon an abandoned, centuries-old house in the Tuscan hill town of Cortona. The home was called Bramasole, meaning "yearning for the sun." When Mayes heard the translation, something clicked within, and she transformed those wistful dreams to action.

As Mayes fell in love with life in the Italian countryside, she kept an impressionistic journal recording Tuscany's sensual pleasures. A lover of food and entertaining, Mayes embraced Italy's fresh seasonal delicacies, welcoming new friends to her refurbished home. After writing a newspaper article about a nearby farmers' market, Mayes began thinking about writing a memoir.

Prior to the publication of the book that would change her life, Mayes had authored five volumes of poetry. A native of Fitzgerald,

Georgia, Mayes had crafted a comfortable career writing and teaching in San Francisco, the kind of life most people would settle into for decades. But after getting divorced from her first husband, Mayes wanted something big to move towards, and the restoration of Bramasole was nothing if not big.

Frances and Ed hired local contractors, scrubbed crusty floors, reinforced crumbling walls, and refinished wooden beams, working round the clock for weeks on end. The discoveries—about the house and about themselves—kept them going. One day a faded pastel fresco emerged while Frances was cleaning a kitchen wall, which now infuses the home with added grace and beauty.

In 1996, *Under the Tuscan Sun* appeared with an initial print run of 5,000 copies. Readers devoured its evocative descriptions of Bramasole, of luscious banquets, of the Italian verve for life. Three years later, Mayes followed with *Bella Tuscany*, which picked up where *Under the Tuscan Sun* left off and then followed Mayes through Venice, Sicily, and other Italian destinations. Her next book about Italy, *In Tuscany*, is a collaboration with her husband, Ed Mayes, and *National Geographic* photographer Bob Krist. She's also recently published a novel, *Swan*, that reaches back to her small-town Georgia roots.

I met Frances and Ed on a mild December day, just weeks after the film *Under the Tuscan Sun* premiered on thousands of screens around North America. To my utter surprise, Frances and Ed met me at the train station, about three miles from Cortona. Ed drove in an assertively Italian style while Frances noted the historical sites: "That's where Hannibal defeated the Romans in 217," she said, pointing to the valley nestled into the time-smoothed hills below.

In Cortona, Frances showed me the Teatro Signorelli, the historic theater featured in the movie. Though it took liberties with her story, Mayes said she loved Audrey Wells's adaptation of her book. Walking along the narrow streets, we stopped to chat with a florist, and then had a simple yet richly satisfying pasta lunch. To complete the meal, the osteria's owner brought us each a chilled glass of sea-green *alloro* (bay laurel liqueur), a gesture emblematic of the generosity Mayes so eloquently evokes in her books.

Under a sky the color of stone, we drove past a massive Etruscan wall, whose boulders date back to 800 B.C. Frances mentioned that

Under the Tuscan Sun was up to 134 weeks on *The New York Times* bestseller list. "It's not something either of us expected as poets," she said, with genuine modesty and disbelief. "We have workers today," Ed said as we pulled into Bramasole's driveway. "As usual," Frances replied.

Located a couple of miles from town, Bramasole is an imposing three-story stone house, approached by a stone path flanked by roses, sage, and rosemary. The land, a plot that would take two oxen two days to plow as stated in the property's ancient deed, is dotted with olive trees. Alongside the house is the Strada della Memoria, a thoroughfare lined by 600 cypress trees, each a tribute to a soldier who died in the first world war. Mayes had won a $10,000 award from Barilla, an Italian pasta company, and donated the money to Cortona to replace dying trees and to install plaques with the name of each soldier.

Frances gave me a tour of the house—I was especially moved by the shimmering pastels of the fresco—and we sat down to talk. Afterwards, ever the gracious southerner, Frances showed me the sturdy Polonia stone wall on the way out and stopped for a moment so we could quietly admire the arched shrine built into another wall nearby. Frances and Ed dropped me in town en route to another house they were restoring. At dusk I began descending the long hill from Cortona to the train station. As I walked past the nearly three-thousand-year-old stones and peered into the ancient cemetery shrouded by the hills below, a gibbous moon rose in the east. I took a last look back towards Bramasole, and just for a moment, through the misty shadows, I could have sworn I saw its original builders laying its foundation.

What first attracted you to Italy and what kept you coming back?

I studied Renaissance art and architecture in college, so I especially wanted to come to Italy to see the things that I had studied. But of course the minute I got here, I saw all the Italians in the piazza greeting each other and having coffee and enjoying life. I said to my husband then: "These people are having a lot more fun than we are—what's going on here?" What keeps us coming here forever is the people—that was the beginning. After that I always came to Italy anytime I could.

In 1985, Ed and I, with two other poets, by chance rented a farmhouse near Cortona. The very first day we were there, I saw a tumbledown farmhouse in the distance and I said, "I wonder how you can get one of these places and plant your basil and live here." I liked it immediately—I liked life in the country. So after that we rented houses around Tuscany for several years, and finally in 1990, which is a long time ago by now, we bought this place.

This house is called Bramasole, which means "yearning for the sun." Beyond the literal meaning, can you tell me what that symbolizes for you?

The house is named for the big Etruscan wall near the house which is part of the original city wall of Cortona, and it's called the Bramasole wall. But when I came here and got out of the car the first time, a real estate agent said, "*Bramare*, to yearn for and *sole*, sun, something that yearns for the sun." That just really hit, because metaphorically I was hoping for a connection with the light, something transformative, something big.

So the name of it immediately made me think, I would like to live in that house because that house is already very much at home in the landscape. It's been here; it's going to be here; anything with me is just going to be a passing through. The house itself is very important on this position, and if I can live in the house I think I can learn from the house how to live here in Italy.

And that has been the case actually—it's been the house that has led us here, that profound sense that there's the Etruscan wall, the Medici wall, this house, the valley down below where Hannibal defeated the Romans. It's these literal layers of history that you fold yourself into, and if you feel at home there, something radical has changed in your mind. It changes you.

I think for me, a Southern writer, I think I've always been very aware of a sense of place. You just have it with your grits in the South. But I came to understand it in a different way here. I came to understand really how much of a shaping force this place is and how what we loved about Tuscany was so much related to how the people have been shaped by living in such a beautiful place. In the South it's very different, so the two realizations kind of crystallized some things about place for me that never had quite clicked into place before.

You write in Under the Tuscan Sun *that you and Ed were not going to have children but that this house would be your child.*

I'd have to revise that statement. It's been more that we have been the children of the house because it has taken the lead and introduced us to the culture. This house was abandoned for so many years, and it's on this Strada della Memoria, this street out of Cortona where all the local people take their walks—they're passing here every day. So they always saw this big empty house on the hill and some people thought it was haunted. A lot of people used to climb up and take the wild lilies and daffodils and irises, the cherries. They had used the land as they were growing up, so they had a relationship to the place. They were particularly intrigued by the crazy Americans who had taken on the project. And they did think we were nuts because nobody in Cortona had ever bought this house. Now they say to me, I could have bought that house.

In the beginning it was working on the house, actually doing the work that gave us a place in the culture. I think working on the house probably saved us five years of getting to know people. Because we were working along with a lot of Italians here, they saw that we were actually on our knees cleaning the bricks, and on the ladders cleaning the beams. We weren't just standing there with our hands folded, giving directions, but we were in it. And I think that made them feel that they could invite us, and they began to very quickly bring us gifts: eggs, olive oil, bags of spinach, things from their own land. Then they began to invite us to their christenings and weddings—it was through the house that we were able to get to know people and to be recognized in town.

There is a wonderful kind of gift exchange among people who know each other here. Yesterday, Beppe brought us eggs, Giorgio brings a bag of wild boar, Giuseppina brings biscotti. We take people things from our garden—there's this kind of constant giving. You find things left on your doorstep, squashes and melons, you don't even know who left them.

I love the book, *The Gift*, by Lewis Hyde. He talks about the kind of psychology and economy of gift-giving in primitive societies. Well, this is far from primitive society; I think the Italians are anciently sophisticated, but there is this constant generosity: you go in town and somebody has paid for your coffee. It exists in one little way in the Bay Area, where sometimes the person in front of you pays on the Golden Gate Bridge. It's kind of like that (in Cortona), multiplied a million times.

Like fanning through a deck of cards, my mind flashes on the thousand chances, trivial to profound, that converged to re-create this place. Any arbitrary turning along the way and I would be elsewhere; I would be different. Where did the expression "a place in the sun" first come from? My rational thought processes cling always to the idea of free will, random event; my blood, however, streams easily along a current of fate. I'm here because I climbed out the window at night when I was four.

—FRANCES MAYES,
Under the Tuscan Sun

How nice. One of the most appealing aspects of Under the Tuscan Sun *for me was the leap of faith. And I think that's part of the reason people respond so strongly to the book. You went for it, you had this dream, you followed your bliss as you say. I just wonder what gave you the courage to make that leap, to say: I know it's crazy; I know the house is too expensive; I know it's going to be years of restoration, but what the hell, let's do it anyway. Where did that courage and sense of assurance come from?*

Just crazy, I guess (laughs). I'll take a risk—I've never been averse to taking a risk. I had never done anything like this, but I felt very much instinctively that it was the right thing to do. And a lot of people told me it wasn't, my sisters, my mother, everybody. My ex-husband said, "You're always like that." Everybody said no, and that made me think even more, this is the right thing to do.

Was it both you and Ed in equal parts wanting to go for it?

Yes, I think it was pretty equal. We were both ready to take a chance like that, and my daughter thought it was an excellent idea. She was in high school at the time and she thought, this is fantastic, go for it, as they used to say. So who knows why you act in these ways? It's sometimes good to surprise yourself.

The other surprise after that was writing a novel. I had always wanted to write a novel about the South, but I had put it off and put it off and particularly after coming here, I let Italy take over. I loved writing about Italy, so I just thought it was something that I was not going to do. And I had one of those things that kind of happen to you now and then: I think, I'm going to do that. As soon as I decided, I was able to do it. I think that is probably the secret to a lot of things: when you really decide, then you do it.

To act right away, and not say, someday I'm going to…

I'm a big believer in will, the kind of will to power and all that. I think you have to trust your will and that's the way things happen. People are always saying, luck, luck, luck. I think you make your own luck in a lot of ways. And if you are then lucky, it works. You can try to make your own luck and maybe nothing happens. I believe in kind of wrenching what you want out of whatever circumstance there is.

Restoration is a strong theme in your work, beyond the restoration of this house and the land, it's an internal restoration too. Could you say a little bit about how you restored yourself as you restored this house?

I think change is good; I think taking chances is good. Sometimes after you've had a career you think, Well, I already know how to do this, and what are the next twenty years going to be like? So I had that feeling to some extent. I loved teaching—I always totally enjoyed my job, but I thought, I want to do more than this. Also at a time when I was getting a divorce and reinventing my life, I wanted something really big out in front of me, something as big or bigger than what's behind me. Italy is that way; it's just endless. You could write about it forever—it's always new.

What have the most exciting discoveries been?

The way of life here, the gentleness and the great good manners people have, the hospitality, the generosity, those things have just been huge gifts. We love the people here, they're fun. They do their work, but they're not work-obsessed. They always have time to stop in, to go have a coffee. We had a coffee with the police chief this morning. It's more intimate here—it's partly that it's a very small town, but there's more to it than that. There's a sense of delight in living here. People love their town, they love their history. The Tuscans are nasty and fatalistic and cynical, too—they're not simple, happy go lucky, welcome everybody, that's it. They have a lot of levels, and they're very critical: they will tell you what they think of your garden or your clothes. They're very blunt in a way, but they're complex. There's this underlying basic generosity and sweetness that you can revel in here.

We like the life in the piazza, the constant interchanges that you have with all kinds of people, all kinds of classes, all kinds of educational levels. There's not as much stratification as we felt in our lives in America, where college teachers hang out with college teachers and writers with writers. You cross professions somewhat among your friends but basically everybody operates within the strata of their own educational or economic situation. And here it's not like that, it's everybody and you find yourself having dinner with all kinds of people—it's fun. It's interesting too because you get such a variety of perspectives and personalities and histories. The thing we have found the most liberating here is living among the Italians.

What have you learned about yourself by taking on this project and living here in Tuscany?

I've learned that I can work very hard physically. I've always worked hard mentally, but I've done so much hard work here, and Ed has, too. We've really pushed ourselves in many ways. I've learned to be more open with people—I'm basically a rather reserved person. Here I have felt the liberty to be much more open, just because other people are so open. So I feel like my personality has expanded here, and Ed feels the same way. He has so many friends here. And the men have a good time together: they walk down the street with their arms around each other, and they play cards, and they smoke cigars. They just have a big time together. It's so much fun to be here, and we have a lot more fun here than we've ever had in our lives.

We've also just felt the satisfaction of being able to contribute something to the town itself, being able to restore this place to its former life. It's now producing olives, producing grapes, big vegetable garden, herb garden. To bring it back to life has been very satisfying. And we like the restoration process so much that we got ourselves into this other restoration project which has been going on for two years. It's satisfying, too, but we're not doing the work up there. We just don't have time, although we do search for all the materials.

Where is that and how far from here is it?

It's just about fifteen miles out, but it feels very isolated. It's more in the mountains, in a chestnut forest. We discovered it by chance. We were picking blackberries with a neighbor and we saw it in the distance. I said, look there's where Little Red Riding Hood lives. So we scrambled over to it and we thought it was very sweet, a little stone cottage. We found out it was built in the 1200s by the followers of St. Francis of Assisi, so we thought it would really be fun to bring it back to life. We've done a historical restoration on it. That's why it's been so slow: we've done everything very, very carefully, working with a fantastic restorer who makes sure that everything is just right. It's been a process—we're ready for it to finish.

Will you write about that place as well?

I am writing a new book about the concept of home in Italy, and it will definitely be a part of it. It's called, *A Home in Tuscany*. I've been very interested in the concept of home because it relates so much to sense of place. I'm writing a travel book at the same time which is called, *A Home in the World*. In that book I'm exploring six or seven or eight different countries, and investigating what the concept of home means. And actually renting a house in each country and staying awhile, going to the markets, reading the papers and literature, listening to the music, and trying to see what it would be like to live there.

Do you write here more, or primarily in California?

It's odd, this used to be my escape place. I still write here a lot but now that I've quit my job in California I have more peace and quiet there than I do here. With the movie and all the things going on around my books, there's a whole lot going on here. Not to mention restoration of the mountain house. So it's kind of flip-flopped. I wrote the novel here, but I've been getting a lot more done in California recently.

I wonder if your books have helped Italians more greatly appreciate what it means to own a historic house in Tuscany. I know they appreciate their heritage and their history, but do you think that you as an outsider could look at this house with fresh eyes and say, this is a treasure. Whereas people who have lived here thirty years might say, it's just an old, abandoned house.

Definitely. That's been kind of fun. When I first wrote *Under the Tuscan Sun*, my friend, the writer Ann Cornelisen, said the Italians are not going to like it. And I thought, Maybe not, it's such an American perspective. But much to everybody's surprise, they did like it. It was a bestseller here. I've had hundreds of letters from Italians saying, I never appreciated my own country until I saw it through a foreigner's eyes. And I'm so ashamed that it took a foreigner to show me (laughs). It made them happy and proud.

And they also say things like, you could have gone anywhere and you came here. So that makes them think this must really be special. But I think a lot of Italians don't appreciate how great it is to live here. Of course if you live somewhere forever, you always have a lot of complaints about it.

Or you take it for granted.

Yes. They have an expression here: I found America. It means, Eureka, or I found something great. And they're always saying to me, you found America here.

But there's a certain irony in that because the Italians are such a proud people, especially here in Tuscany, and it took an American to make this place so appreciated.

When I wrote *Under the Tuscan Sun*, I changed some people's names for their privacy. I never thought anybody here would read it because I never thought it would be translated into Italian.

After the book became popular in Italy, people from town came up to me over and over and said, "*Senora*, why did you change my name?" They wanted to be known. And now it's really quite moving for me that often very old people in town come up to me and say, "I want to tell you something because you can write about it." That impulse to have your life mean something, to go beyond your own memory, is very surprising to me and I've heard a lot of wonderful stories. I've actually written some of the things that people have told me about: walking back from Russia after World War II, just stories. To be known as the town writer, even in such a small town is nice.

I'm curious about your hopes and expectations for sales for Under the Tuscan Sun. *Were you hoping to sell 20,000 books, or maybe 50,000?*

That would have been my biggest dream. I published it originally with Chronicle Books in San Francisco. I had written six books of poetry, and then here I started spontaneously writing prose. So I called an editor at Chronicle Books and they published it. It was an edition of 5,000. That was, I thought, a lot, because my poetry books had sold maybe a thousand. Then it started getting a lot of press and a lot of sales. It got a great review in *The New York Times* and all these things started happening. They called me up from Chronicle and said, this book is really selling—we think it's because of the cover. I thought, Oh, oh the cover. (Laughs.) But as I had, they expected it to be a small literary project so it was a big surprise. We didn't have any big expectations—of course you always dream that something will happen and in this case it did.

How many languages has it been translated into?

I think twenty.

And do you have a sense of total sales?

No, I have no idea—it's about 3 million in America. With the movie it's sold almost another million.

That's amazing. That's wonderful. It must have a really nice cover. Has your poetry sold more since the success of your books about Italy?

No, you would think there would be some blip, but maybe 100 more copies a year.

While reviewing your books to prepare for this interview, I kept thinking about a story my grandfather used to tell me about a traveler coming into a town. He asks the first man he sees, what are the people like in this town? The man replies, what were they like in the last town? The traveler says, they were miserable, horrible, terrible. So the man says, I think you'll find the people here are just like that. A second traveler asks the man, sir tell me what are the people like in this town? So the man replies, how did you find the people in the last town? Oh, they were wonderful, generous, kind. And the man says, I think you'll find the people here are just the same.

I think that's your perspective, too: you come to a place with an open heart and a generous spirit. You go into a restaurant and say, "What's the specialty of the house?" Not, "I demand this." I wonder if you have any advice for travelers as to how they can receive the best by bringing their best.

I think trying to leave America as far behind as possible and realizing that the world is still really various. To come here wanting what you get in America is really a sad way to travel. Try to open up to it; order the thing you don't know on the menu. Talk to people, get to know the place on its own terms. For me the fun of travel is what you can learn about another place. I like to really prepare for a trip and learn as much as I can about the place, just read exhaustively about it, and then when I get there not follow guidebooks. I experience it as much as I can on its own terms, not through the eyes of some guidebook writer.

Walk by a restaurant and sniff what's coming out the door. That sense of discovery is why I travel. I don't want anything pre-digested to guide me through a place. Remain open, I think, as much as you can. Of course, we always carry our prejudice with us to some extent, but I hate it when people come here and they want Coca-Cola all the time, they bring their candy bars. It's just so bad not to leave everything you can behind and see what's out there that you don't know.

When you first started writing about this place, you kept a journal for several years…

It was the kind of journal I'd always kept as a poet. It wasn't: I did this and I went here. It was lists of words, images, ideas, not narrative, but more just writerly things that I like to look at when I start writing. I can open the book and see lists of words and say, oh, I'd like to use that word. I describe colors of things and impressions. I also have a note-book that I keep in my bag all the time, but I've never been the kind of writer who keeps narrative journals.

Did you have any thought when you started keeping a journal that it might become a memoir of your time here?

I think I did pretty early on because I was asked by *The New York Times* to write an article on the market down in Camucia. It's still a fantastic market, every Thursday, and I loved writing that article. So as soon as I did that I started looking at my notebooks and thinking what thematically has come up for me here, and maybe I should do some other articles for magazines.

And then I just started writing. I had this rickety table with a primitive computer, just found myself writing more and more—it was a spontaneous change of form. And I think that, too, is one of those things about place. The place changed the rhythm in my brain, and I could no longer write in lines. I was writing in sentences.

I am about to buy a house in a foreign country. A house with the beautiful name of Bramasole. It is tall, square, and apricot-colored with faded green shutters, ancient tile roof, and an iron balcony on the second level, where ladies might have sat with their fans to watch some spectacle below. But below, overgrown briars, tangles of roses, and knee-high weeds run rampant. The balcony faces southeast, looking into a deep valley, then into the Tuscan Apennines. When it rains or when the light changes, the facade of the house turns gold, sienna, ocher; a previous scarlet paint job seeps through in rosy spots like a box of crayons left to melt in the sun.

—FRANCES MAYES,
Under the Tuscan Sun

That was a very big difference to me. I was suddenly into another form. So when I changed my life, I changed my form. Yeats said, "When I changed my syntax, I changed my life." It was the other way to me. When I changed the world, it changed the writing.

So how has poetry and being a poet shaped the way you approach other forms of literature, such as the memoir or the novel?

I always told my students that writing poetry is the best training for any kind of writing because you study imagery, you study the rhythm of phrases, you study the psychological impact of certain syntactical structures. All that translates quite easily to prose. And I've always read a lot of poetry. Ed, of course, is a poet, and we read poetry together, so I'd say the biggest shaping force for me as a writer is a background in poetry. I think it makes writing prose easier. You probably see your mistakes more clearly if you have training as a poet because you're used to winnowing down. The word-by-word selection you do as a poet can only benefit prose. After I write something in prose, I always go back through it word by word thinking, Is there a better word than this?

Ed often gives me suggestions that come straight from his psychological take on things as a poet, how to jump from one thing to the other without having to say, first I unlocked the door, and then I did this. But to have some kind of way over that, that still makes sense and creates more of a dynamic, he's very good at that.

You write, "Whether or not you leave somewhere with a sense of place is entirely a matter of smell and instinct."

If you let yourself experience a place physically, bodily, take it in, let it have its effect on you, then it will. If you're not open to that, it won't happen.

In Under the Tuscan Sun, *I think you say you're going to let this place have its way with you.*

Yeah, I was ready for it. I was ready for a kind of transformation. And now I'm ready for another one. Doing this new travel book and going to other countries has been fabulous. It's kind of an ambitious project, and it has become a more complicated project because three of the countries I planned to write about in depth were Turkey, Egypt, and Morocco. Going to the Muslim countries now is not good for Americans.

I don't know whether I'm going to be able to include those, but I loved going to Spain for a month and really studying the whole background of Andalusia. And we had two trips to Greece—it's part of that great sense of continuing education that you get as a traveler. You get to learn, you get to read, you get to go there, you get to read the poetry, you get to learn the history. I wrote about that a little bit in the introduction to *The Best American Travel Writing 2002*, that my sense of travel has a lot to do with reading. I'm not much interested in reading travel writing that has some kind of false adventure associated with it. I'm much more interested in what happens internally to someone when they go to a new culture and try to absorb what that culture means. So for me the traveling is much more ontological.

You say Southerners believe that place is fate, where you are is who you are. It's never casual, the choice of place is a choice of something you crave. You've chosen Italy; you didn't choose Georgia, and I wonder if the experience is different when you choose a place.

It's quite different—it's an act of freedom when you make your own choice of a place according to what you need, want, love, crave. Whereas if you don't choose, if you're born and bred in the briar

I heard Ramsey Clark, then Attorney General, speak when I was in college. All I remember him saying was something like, "When I die, I want to be so exhausted that you can throw me on the scrap heap." He wanted to be totally consumed by his life. I was impressed and adopted that as my philosophy, too.

—FRANCES MAYES, *Bella Tuscany*

patch, the place moves into you anyway, you don't have any choice. It becomes who you are. But I feel lucky that I've had both. I've never had that sense in California. I've lived there since 1973, and I've always liked living there. There were the greatest opportunities for women in California. I loved my job and have lots of friends there, but I could walk out of there tomorrow and never look back. I don't have that I-love-this-place feeling about it. I like it, but it's not in my metabolic pulse.

As somebody from the South, do you feel you've been more open to the Italian way of life, the slowness, the community, in a way perhaps a New Yorker might not be?

Well, Ed's from Minnesota, the coldest place in the universe, and he loves it, so I don't know. I do feel a lot of crossover here with life in the South. As we were talking about earlier, the hospitality, the fatalism that's common among Italians is very familiar to me. Southerners are hospitable, but they're also secretive and fatalistic. But there's no place like Italy because Italy has it all: the beauty of the landscape, the people, the art, fantastic cuisine and wine. Everything for me comes together here.

Sometimes people say to me, "Your books are popular because Italy is so trendy; next year it'll be Morocco." And I think: No it won't, because, they say Rome is the eternal city. Italy's just got that eternal aspect to it. It can't be duplicated. France has a lot but it doesn't have the Italian people.

That warmth and gregariousness of the people here…

… and the love.

I noticed when we walked just a couple of blocks through town you probably stopped four or five times to say hello to your friends or shopkeepers. I wonder if you like the balance of the community here and the anonymity you have in California.

I would prefer to have more community in California. I had it more when I was teaching because I had colleagues and we all lived in San Francisco. Now that I don't live in San Francisco anymore, and I don't teach anymore, I don't have it nearly as much as I used to. But it was never like here where you meet people from every age and walk of life.

What has living here in Italy helped you see about the United States, and what do you think Americans can learn from Italians?

You want me to write a second book? I like the perspective on America that we get here, and it's definitely turned my head around because I always thought America was the center of the universe. I was very much taught to believe that Americans were the luckiest people in the world and everyone envied us. And I find that is definitely not the case. It's just mind-expanding to read the European papers versus the American papers and to realize how much more of a global interest and outlook they have in Europe than we do in America. The news of the rest of the world in America is so shoddy, it's so small. It just keeps reinforcing that we-lucky-Americans sense that I've totally become disillusioned with. I don't find that to be true at all. I find life in Europe much richer on a day-to-day basis than life in America.

I think if you are lucky enough to spend some time in a foreign country it will change you. It will open your eyes to the kind of provincialism that we have. Of course every country has its own kind of provincialisms, I'm totally aware of that, but I think Americans are particularly parochial.

One question about food and dining here in Italy: what do you find so appealing about the food, the dining, the sharing, and all that you write about?

The food reflects the culture so much. Food always reflects culture, but here it's even more than in other places because there is still the sense of the long table, the table that's endlessly accommodating. The fact that someone shows up for dinner with two friends that you haven't invited used to shock me, but the assumption is, there's plenty, and it's fine to bring cousin so-and-so. At home if somebody brings the children and you haven't invited them, you think, Oh my Lord. But here it seems fine.

The philosophy of the long table reflects the kind of relationships Italians have with their family, friends and neighbors. The grandmother's at the table. There is not an exclusion of people—there's an inclusion. Yet the social life here is absolutely crippling. I get exhausted here from the social life—you're invited constantly. You could go out every single night of the week. The food is always fabulous, but sometimes I think, Please, I just want to stay home one night.

But they think that eating alone is sad. And they think it's unhealthy. When Ed's here by himself, he never, ever, gets to eat at home alone. Our neighbors, they love him, they say, "You come to our house, you're not eating alone." And that's just the way it is. Even in restaurants, like today, after we had that very simple meal, there's the little gift of the laurel liqueur that they make and give to their friends when they come in. It's always something more than just what you pay for. There's always the gift. The sense that, we're having polenta tonight, come on over. The sense that we're out walking and we find some wild asparagus, come to my house, let's make a frittata. You eat together, you eat, it's ancient and basic.

You dine. I imagine they don't have any policies here like Denny's had in the U.S., where if your meal doesn't come in ten minutes or less, it's free.

(Laughs.) Probably not. But Italy is changing. In the cities it's getting more and more the way it is in America, but in this area it's not. I should probably preface everything I say with, "In this area…" because Italy's big and there are many different kinds of cities and towns. The South is totally different from the North and it's such an amazingly varied country, probably anything I say could be contradicted somewhere.

Now it's early December and we're coming into winter. This is a time when far fewer travelers visit, but it seems to me a really nice time to be in Italy. Could you say a word about the low season and about the change of seasons here?

I love staying here in the winter because it is so quiet and the food is different every season of the year. If you're here in the winter, all the hunters are bringing in their woodcock and pheasant, and wild boar, and wild mushrooms, and chestnuts. A whole different thing appears on your plate in the winter than in the spring and summer and fall. Florence is much more wonderful in the winter when all the tourists clear out. It returns to itself. You see the Florentines in their woolens having hot chocolate and you just get more of the sense of Florence as a place where people actually live.

I like the change of seasons here. We do have changes of seasons in California, but they're subtle. Here they're very dramatic. The spring is just astonishing. The whole place is covered with wildflowers and the little wild asparagus are coming up, and the green almonds that you eat raw, all the little fava beans and wonderful little lettuces are coming up. So every season has its own culinary pleasures, and I like that very much.

The changes in the food are also the changes in the activities. You go looking for mushrooms with friends; you go into the woods and pick up chestnuts. In the early spring you start looking for the aspara-gus. In the summer, it's the little wild strawberries. In the late summer it's the blackberries. People do all these things together so the table again is not just the eating, it's the whole way that food becomes part of your life and part of the table. You are bringing things to the table that you've grown and found. It's a profound difference from going up to Whole Foods.

Now you're an honorary citizen of Cortona, right?

Yes, and also of Arezzo.

So it seems like people are very happy with the books, and the attention they've brought to the town, but are there any old, crusty, traditional peo-ple here who say, I wish you had never written that book and brought all the tourists here?

Not that I know of, but I'm sure there must be some people. I would think if someone disapproves of my having written this book it would probably be more people like me, people who came here for Cortona to remain a peaceful little place that no one knew about. And it's not like that anymore. So there are probably foreigners who've bought houses here who wish they had never heard of *Under the Tuscan Sun*. I probably wouldn't like it myself if somebody had done this.

But for the town the change has been really good. The town has awakened in a good way. You always think that change is bad, but it's a much more prosperous town. People can take vacations, and they can open shops. A lot of artists have told me, Now I can live here and make a living for my family—I was going to have to leave.

You edited The Best American Travel Writing 2002, *so I'd like to ask, what do you find makes the best travel writing? What strikes you? What makes you say, that's one for the book?*

That was a process of self-discovery. The travel writers I like are those who create some kind of particular world where the experience could only be had by that person. The writing is so precisely theirs that you get a sense of who that person is in that place. I like when I know the person is there, and they make the world of being there. And that's a power of writing—it's also a sense of their perception of the place, but re-creating it in words that are not just telling the story but are creating the story, making it come alive again. It takes a good writer to do that. So I'm always looking at the writing—I love Freya Stark; she's one of my favorite travel writers because she says things that surprise you so. She can go around something and come back underneath it in a way that just makes a lot of other writing seemed very pedestrian.

So is it the sensual aspect of the writing that appeals to you?

The imagery and the precision, the ability to re-create in words the experience, not to tell the experience, but to re-create it. I think that's just a mark of good writing. It's partly through the imagery, partly through the word choice, through narrowing to a very precise point what you have to say.

I'd like to close with that image near the end of Under the Tuscan Sun *of you as a four-year-old girl jumping out the window of your home and running. I wonder if all this, this house, this life, is ultimately fate or will, or some combination of the two?*

Probably a combination of both, but that little moment of climbing out the window is kind of the impulse: Go. And I always feel that, I feel very split always between the desire to stay, the desire for home, the desire for the nest, the desire to gather people around in the home, and that equal passion to shut the door and go, to leave it all behind and seek what's out there. So I think for me the writing partly comes from the tension between those two things. And it's odd because they both involve a sense of place, the place being the home, the domestic, and then the place being out there to be discovered.

A Long Way from Home

Jonathan Raban
<small>SEATTLE, WASHINGTON</small>

LIKE A MODERN-DAY DE TOCQUEVILLE, JONATHAN RABAN HAS traveled the length and breadth of the United States, observing Americans with the keen eye of a foreigner. His 1990 book, *Hunting Mister Heartbreak*, traverses the pathways of American immigration from late nineteenth-century Ellis Island to late twentieth-century Seattle. In the book, Raban fully inhabits each place he visits, even borrowing an old black labrador named Gypsy in Alabama to feel more at home among the locals. Jan Morris called *Hunting Mister Heartbreak* "the best book of travel ever written by an Englishman about the United States."

The son of a Church of England parson, Raban read *Huckleberry Finn* when he was seven. Thirty years later, he piloted a sixteen-foot motorboat down the Mississippi, making insightful and sometimes caustic observations along the way. Before setting sail he finds himself at a state fair in Minnesota: "These farming families from Minnesota and Wisconsin were the descendants of hungry immigrants from Germany and Scandanavia. Their descendants must have been lean and anxious men with the famines of Europe bitten into their faces. Generation by generation, their families had eaten themselves into Americans. Now they all had the same figure: same broad bottom, same Buddha belly, same neckless join between turkey-wattle chin and sperm-whale torso."

Though relieved to ditch his boat after his Mississippi journey, Raban found himself at sea again in the early 1980s, trolling for stories along the coast of Britain for his book, *Coasting*. His most recent work of travel literature, *Passage to Juneau*, navigates not just the coastal waters of western Canada, but the rocky shoals of his tumultuous marriage and father's death. Reading Raban's touching accounts of his father's journey into eternity just before our interview was especially heartrending for me because my father had died, also from cancer, just a month before.

Though Raban says he doesn't distinguish between fiction and non-fiction, he's the author of a couple of books created predominently from his imagination. His most recent work of fiction, *Waxwings*, is a tale of a Hungary-born British ex-pat in Seattle during the dot-com boom of the late 1990s. The themes of immigration and terrorism provide a sharp counterpoint to the phenomenal wealth and excess of the days before the bubble burst.

I first met Raban in the fall of 2003, during his tour to promote *Waxwings*. Projecting the resonant baritone of a Shakespearian actor, Raban captivated the audience with his literary insights and political discourses. The following February, I met him at his Seattle home on the north flank of Queen Anne Hill, not far from where the boat he took up to Alaska was tethered. The roads near his house were so narrow I felt like I'd stumbled onto London's back streets.

At dusk, I found Raban's home behind the "once-white picket fence" he described in his precise directions. Raban greeted me without his trademark baseball cap, which he wore in Berkeley and has described as "the only known cure for baldness." On one wall were two framed covers of *The New York Times Book Review*, one featuring Raban's award-winning *Bad Land*, about early twentieth-century settlers in Montana, and the other reviewing *Passage to Juneau*.

The room, which felt a bit like the inside of a ship's cabin, smelled strongly of cigar smoke, but it wasn't offensive. Raban asked me if I'd mind if he smoked and I said of course not. At first, I felt slightly intimidated by the six-foot-tall, professorial Raban, but that passed as the interview progressed and the bottle of wine emptied. Before I knew it, almost three hours had passed.

Jonathan and I repaired to Ponti Seafood Grill, along the nearby waterfront. Over wild salmon and a second bottle of wine, our conversation leapt from Orwell (Raban feels he's overrated) to CBS's decision not to air a MoveOn ad critical of President Bush. Shortly before eleven P.M., I bid Raban goodnight, pointed my car away from the water, and hoped somehow that I'd find my way home.

I've been asking writers whether the best travel writing comes from the insider's perspective or the outsider's perspective. What really struck me, especially when reading Hunting Mister Heartbreak, *was that you do both: you create a character like John Rayburn in Alabama, who is the insider, and then you as Jonathan Raban, the outsider, perceive him.*

It seems to me that outsiderdom is something that happens to you, not something that you deliberately construct. And my sense of my own displacement is the grit in the oyster that kind of nags at one. But I think that's a sort of a consequence of fate, really. It's the product of having grown up in a certain way, very much as an outsider, an outsider in terms of class—we're talking about England where class is important. It goes deep into two things, both a very peripatetic childhood, moving around from one place to another, so we were always outsiders in whatever place we landed. We started off in Norfolk and then before we got used to Norfolk we were hauled off to suburban Merseyside, which could not have been more different. Two years in suburban Merseyside, then two years in Sussex, then away to boarding school.

So I sort of spent this traveling childhood in which the family were always strangers and outsiders, trying to learn the ropes of the new place and never quite fitting in. And not fitting in another way, too, because of the class thing, which was interesting. My family was, in the nineteenth century and in the early twentieth century, sort of well-heeled, robust, dull English upper middle-class, with a foot in the East India Company, which it had had since the eighteenth century, and other feet in the army where somebody in every generation was an army officer, and in the church where somebody in every generation was a Church of England parson.

My father continued that because he, like my grandfather, took holy orders, became a student, which is another odd outsider thing to do. He became a theological student in his thirties and then became a priest relatively late. My father was an anomaly in all sorts of ways—he didn't have a university degree—he'd been through a teacher's training college. And without a degree, high office in the Church of England was closed to him. And he had this other career behind him as an army officer.

We were always in these funny social situations where we had a sort of lower middle-class or working-class income with these pretensions to upper-middle-class grandeur: family portraits on the walls, gilt-framed, the ancestors looking importantly down with their uniforms on from the eighteenth and early nineteenth century, boxes of my great uncle's medals—he was a general; the family coat of arms, the sort of relics of upper-middle-class grandeur. We were living on watery ground beef and instant mashed potatoes, eking out on a really tiny income. The proper way of being a Church of England priest is to have a private income, and then what the church pays you is just pocket money. But my family was actually living on the stipend from the church which was very little, about five hundred pounds a year in the 1950s, which didn't go far.

Once my father started having parishes, we were a strange kind of the island. We lived in the vicarage in rather a grand house, which took well to the ancestors. We had these pretensions, which made us natural invitees to the houses of the gentry, but we didn't have anything like their income. And equally we were far too snobbish to have to do with the people from—in England they are called Council Estates—here they'd be the projects. We were neither flesh nor fowl. We weren't upper-middle class; we weren't working class. We stuck out as oddities wherever we went. We were far too threadbare to be gentry and far too well spoken to be working class.

So this sense of oddity in place, this sense of the outsiderness, of not quite belonging where you are and therefore having to figure it out, I think that sense of always trying to know what you're doing here—that's the title of a Bruce Chatwin book: *What Am I Doing Here?*—I thought, Dammit, you've stolen the title that I should have used for one of my own books, because it seems to me that I've been asking that question ever since I can remember being of any age to ask questions. I was asking what I am I doing here when I was four years old in Norfolk and six years old in Merseyside and seven years old in Sussex, and so on, always with a sense that I didn't quite belong and, therefore, I had to work out my own relation to the landscape and the people and the place.

So probably the relationship between the overall narrator of *Hunting Mister Heartbreak* and the personae of Rainbird and Rayburn and the other characters, I think is related to that. But I don't think it's a calculated pose—I think it's more a fate.

But do you think, given the way you were brought up and your childhood, that perhaps you have a certain comfort in the role of the outsider?

I have a certain comfort in the role of the outsider not because of my childhood at all but because I found something to do that was consonant with my childhood, which was to be a writer. And I think that it's no bad thing for a writer to be aware of his social outsidernesss, to be both inside and outside at the same time, to be able to step back and look in, and to be conscious that you're not necessarily a part of this; you're a person on the edge of a party taking notes.

Your nonfiction work often has the feel of a novel. Do you find that perhaps truth lies somewhere between fact and fiction?

No, I don't believe in the distinction between the two. I really don't. I think that my so-called travel books, with the possible exception of *Arabia*, the first one...let's deal with the issue of the travel book, which is a genre in which I don't believe. I just don't believe that it exists. It isn't as though I think I do something more than write travel books—it's just that I don't believe in the travel book as a legitimate form. The travel book of the kind that I have written, and I think this is true of several other people, I'd say Redmond O'Hanlon certainly, Paul Theroux, Chatwin, I feel a certain commonness of interest with those people in a way that I don't with Jan Morris or with most of the traveling, see-the-world journalists. But with Chatwin, Theroux, O'Hanlon, I feel a sort of common identity. Our books all come out of the same essential impulse: the drift of the novel as the major prose narrative form as it began to move out from being about just imaginary characters. I mean the emergence particularly of the total-recall memoir.

With pages of dialogue...

Yes. The modern memoir seems to me to be a straight outgrowth of the novel. It requires the teller of the tale to both imagine and invent the past. Which doesn't mean to make it up. I can never tire too much of pointing out the origin of the word fiction. "Fiction" comes not from this imaginary Latin verb *fictia* meaning I make it up as I go along. It comes from the actual Latin verb *fictia* meaning, I give shape to.

When I was a kid, what memoir meant, and they were always in the plural, it wasn't a memoir, I would have found that a very odd term. What we all wrote were memoirs—they were largely done by retired generals and politicians. And it was usually a dry-as-dust recitation of the triumphs that made their career. It was certainly a million miles away from the memoir of seeming total recall, the entirely shaped life looked back on by somebody who was primarily a writer. They weren't describing their campaigns; they were simply shaping a life on a page and imagining that life as if it were the material of fiction.

And it seems to me that the modern travel book is an outgrowth of that. It's only really in the 1930s when novelists like Evelyn Waugh and Graham Greene turned to alternating fiction with accounts of their travels that you had this really ambiguous form emerging. I'm thinking particularly of Graham Greene's *Journey Without Maps*. It's interesting because Greene boasted afterwards that he'd come out of this journey on foot through Africa with no notebook—he hadn't taken a note on the journey. Months after he'd got back, he re-created the journey on the page, but re-created it out of his imagination and his memory.

Decades after *Journey Without Maps* was published, there was a cousin of Greene's who I actually met in Malta—there's this shadowy figure in *Journey Without Maps* of "my cousin." Sometime in the 1970s, forty years later, the cousin produced her own memoir of that trip and what the memoir did, of course, was contradict Greene's narrative at almost every point. She just remembered it entirely differently. And it's quite fun to put those two books together, not to disprove *Journey Without Maps* at all but simply to have this binocular account of the journey in which neither narrator agrees with the other as to anything at all, where they were, who they saw, what they met, the condition of Graham's illness, whatever. There is just no consonance between these two accounts.

And they revealed the privacy of the journey, the fact that you and I could make exactly the same journey side-by-side down a road and write our accounts afterwards, and the journey I had been on, even though we were joined at the hip, would be entirely different to the journey that you had been on.

Sure, it's the lens through which you perceive it.

So I think there is that inherent fictionality about the writing of these books which does come up partly from the tradition of the novel and comes straight out of the newer tradition of the total-recall memoir. And I see the kinds of books that I've written as variants of memoir. They're not travel books. They are books about journeys to some extent. And I think the thing about the journey is it's a very nice scale model of a life. But it's a life that has a beginning, a middle, and an end. And the person who makes the journey metaphorically survives his own death to write about a life posthumously.

So what you're saying is that you get to interpret your own life.

Yes, looking back on it from having passed into the afterlife of the post-journey. But I think that sense of a journey as being a life in miniature, and therefore the book about the journey being a posthumous memoir, makes much more sense than talking about the travel book, where you just get teliologically fucked up. How do you figure the difference between what I do and what Jan Morris does—they are utterly unlike each other. I do think that Redmond and Paul and Bruce and I, though, could probably agree to quite a large extent—Paul would pretend not to—Paul loves to pretend, and perhaps to some extent it's true, that everything he says in his travel books is true, but it's a pose.

I've read his work, and you read these pages and pages of dialogue and think, how could any human being remember, and then you realize he remembers the essence of it and works with that.

I think, though, there is an element of channeling. When I was sailing around Britain in 1982, I sailed up to Hull where I'd been at university, and I went to see Philip Larkin, the poet who had been the chief reason for me wanting to go to Hull University in the first place. I didn't feel then that Larkin would have any place in the book that I wanted to write. I just wanted to have dinner with him. We went out to dinner; I didn't take any notes. I went on sailing around Britain and then three years later Larkin died, and I went to his memorial service in Westminster Abbey.

I was in the middle of writing *Coasting* then, and I thought, Dammit, I'm going to put Larkin into this book. It was just one day's writing— usually I write very slowly and this came easily: the whole of the conversation we'd had that evening, though it was three years away, appeared to come back to me as I wrote. You sit there daydreaming and it seems to come back. I wouldn't vouch for its blow-by-blow, word-by-word accuracy, but I was very pleased when Larkin's biography came out. There was a reference to my description of Larkin in *Coasting* as "an uncannily truthful likeness." He caught my Larkin and believed it to be sort of photographic. Well, it wasn't photographic at all—it was remembered after three years without a single note, and yet there is Larkin going on as I had remembered him going on, in a Lebanese restaurant in Hull.

I think that sometimes total recall is not as suspicious as it may look. Writing in a state of almost trancelike memoriousness, you are able to recapture things that you ought, by all the sort of normal laws of memory physics, to have forgotten. But somehow just the very slowness of writing brings those words back. I do believe that very often memory is more accurate in certain ways than a tape recorder can be. What the tape recorder picks up is dreck, junk. It picks up the kinds of things that I'm saying now, but what it doesn't pick up are those salient details, a curl of the lip, a turn of phrase, a certain look that will itself recall the phrase… [Raban pauses to re-light his cigar.]

Momentarily slipping behind a veil of cigar smoke?

(Laughs.) Yeah, that kind of thing. Whereas memory is very accurate in that sort of way. When I'm writing a novel, I spend a lot of time day-dreaming my way back into a situation until I feel I've remembered it enough to write about it. Whereas coming back from a trip, I spend most of my time forgetting rather than remembering until I feel I can write about it, until I've got something very much like what I have inside my head when I'm writing fiction, in other words, a memory that is not overpolluted by irrelevant details. It does seem to me that a kind of forgetting has to take place first, because otherwise you're just landed up with the shapelessness of the journey instead of that imagined shape the journey begins to take on once you're far enough away from it for the irrelevancies to have leaped out of it, and you're left with various essential bits which you can then draw on when you write.

Sort of a settling of the details that might not play a part so you can get to the essence of that journey.

Until you can see it as something that has a plot, like a novel.

Do you ever sense that during a trip?

No, I don't. During a trip, I usually think I'm never going to write anything about this. I don't have a sense of an emerging book as I'm traveling, ever.

Really, even with Hunting Mister Heartbreak?

Actually, you're right about *Hunting Mister Heartbreak*. It was an experiment that only very partially came off. I wanted to try out an experiment, which was to know where the journey began: to get on a ship and follow the immigrant route from Europe to the United States. I knew that once I got to New York there would be a chapter set in New York. But then I wanted to see where the writing of that chapter would lead next—I had no idea. Only once I'd finished the chapter on New York did I make up my mind where the next chapter was to be. And after New York it had to be some rural place; it had to be in the South. I spent a little while with the atlas trying to figure out the likeliest possible destination and hit on Guntersville, Alabama, practically by sticking a pin there. So I wrote the Alabama chapter and then decided that I wanted to set a whole chapter aboard a plane. Then I would go to Seattle.

The idea was that one would be playing a game of Snakes and Ladders as one wrote. I wanted the book to find its own plot as I wrote. It was an untidy way of writing, not one that I would like to repeat. I don't think it was entirely successful either. My grand notion of it at the beginning was that this would be an organically developing book, that it would be more novel-like because of this. The problem with writing about a single journey is you're stuck with the journey. I wanted a journey that could develop along with the writing of the book.

There were the Street People and there were the Air People. Air People levitated like fakirs. Large portions of their day were spent waiting for, and traveling in, the elevators that were as fundamental to the middle-class culture of New York as gondolas had been to Venice in the Renaissance. It was the big distinction—to be able to press a button and take wing to your apartment. It didn't matter that you lived on the sixth, the sixteenth, or sixtieth floor; access to the elevator was proof that your life had the buoyancy that was needed to stay afloat in a city where the ground was seen as the realm of failure and menace.

—JONATHAN RABAN,
Hunting Mister Heartbreak

That gives it freshness and spontaneity. I was curious to see where you'd go next. You go from Alabama to Seattle to Florida. I never expected you to end up in the Florida Keys.

Well, after hard-working Seattle, being a boat bum in Florida seemed the natural next destination, and a way of dying. That book literally ends with the purchase of a coffin or the prospective purchase of a coffin.

That book has such brilliant descriptions. In New York you talk about the gulf between the Street People and the Air People—that was New York in the late 1980s, people heavily bound to the ground, unable to soar, and then people flying up these elevators to these lofty apartments.

On the wings of money.

I'm sure at some point this conversation is going to veer into politics because that's one hat you wear (writing for The Guardian*). But before we talk about politics, let's talk about the sea because the sea is a central element in so much of your work. It's like a crucible. Could you say—and I know this is broad—how the ocean has shaped you or your work?*

[Opens a bottle of wine.]

Don't let's talk about the ocean—let's talk about water. It's terribly hard, of course, to talk about something about which you've written, but, back to Norfolk, and back to being about four or five and feeling sort of odd about the world, my great pleasure, the place I always wanted to go to was just down the road. There was a small river with a ruined mill and a narrow bridge over the river. The river had some trout in it, and it was pretty clear water. You could actually look down into the water, which was running quite fast and there was this magical world of fish and waterweed and rock and things going on beneath the water. The water was constantly in motion, which I found absolutely transfixing—it was my sort of counterworld.

From as long as I was able to hold a bit of bamboo I went fishing, mostly fruitless fishing, just having some kind of contact with a worm hanging down into this counterworld, a feeling that it was mysterious and clear and vivid to me. I was certain of my place in relation to it. I was never self-conscious leaning over the bowl of that tree—I was completely lost in it and lost self-consciousness in the process. Otherwise I was incredibly self-conscious and awkward.

And something of that sort of clung. I fished for a long time—lakes, rivers, ponds, very occasionally the sea—though I didn't much like fishing in the sea. I really liked fly-fishing for trout when I was a good deal older. And somehow that translated into wanting to go down the Mississippi, which was the first watery book that I wrote and that came relatively late—I had written a bunch of books before I wrote *Old Glory*. The Mississippi, I did find completely transfixing; the whirlpools, the rips, the way of the current, the sense of being both outside society completely as long as you were afloat on that river, but also being very close to it. It seemed like a metaphor.

After finishing *Old Glory*, it's funny, towards the end of that trip it became kind of nightmarish. There was one stage where I left the boat loosely tied up in a pretty thievish town. I had deliberately tied up the boat and left it in an utterly conspicuous place in the vague hope that perhaps somebody would steal the damn thing and I wouldn't have to keep on going down the river. However I went back the following morning and sure enough the boat was there, and I continued on down. Then I got myself into the bayous of southern Louisiana and began to like the boat again because it was sort of made for those bayous. I finally got it back to New Orleans and gave it to a boatyard with an immense feeling of relief, thinking I never wanted in my life again to set eyes on a fucking boat, let alone be inside one. I'm through with that. It's a horrible way of being.

Did this have anything to do with approaching the Mississippi with an almost mythical, Huck Finn vision, or was that more a literary device that you used for the book?

No, it had to do with very practical things like the difference between the upper river and the lower river. After the Mississippi lock-and-dam system stops just about at St. Louis, the river becomes a whole different animal and really nasty, with long stretches between towns and villages, just miles and miles of cane break and strong current and chutes and sloughs. I began to get fixated by cottonmouths [snakes]. They're not exclusively aquatic but they swim—their bite is deadly.

Half the time I'd be looking down from my boat and I'd just see the cottonmouths. And the other half of the time the wind would be blowing from the south, blowing up against the current so it was raising three- and four-foot waves, and I had a boat that was really designed for fishing in a Minnesota lake. It was a completely open boat; it did have buoyancy built in, but it seemed shaped like a spoon, designed to just spoon up the river. The combination of huge wakes from towboats crossing these substantial waves produced by the wind—it was just nightmarish. I felt out of my depth.

I remember getting into the plane to fly from New Orleans to New York, thinking, Thank Christ that's over, never again. When I got back to London I had a sequence of very, very vivid dreams in which the river kept on coming at me in mushroom-like boils and whirlpools and rips and all of those things. And I thought they were dreams of relief, of having gotten away, until it came to me they were actually dreams of unhappy divorce. And the only way of stopping them coming was to get another boat.

So I went out that day and bought myself a boat about the size of the one I'd taken down the Mississippi, which I kept on the Thames for a year. And while I was writing *Old Glory*, weekends I was pottering up and down the Thames in a boat very much like the boat I had taken down the Mississippi. That boat led to the boat I had for *Coasting*, which was a very substantial, wooden-built sailing boat, which I took around Britain. And that boat led to the boat I got just down there, which is the one that I went up to Alaska in. So it became kind of an addiction, but an addiction as much as anything because I feared the sea, and I got to fear the Mississippi, in its lower reaches.

I understand that completely—I used to work as a river raft guide and I still fear moving water, but I love it. I love the waves, I love reading the water, the weird currents, and how a river at low water is entirely different from a river at high water.

Right. Well, we share an obsession in that case.

It seems you've been sailing now twenty or twenty-five years. I imagine the technology has changed considerably in terms of navigation systems—has that affected the way you travel on the water?

It's weakened the hold the water has for me. When I sailed round Britain in 1982, I did have radar, but I didn't have any kind of electronic navigation system. I didn't have GPS. When I sailed round Britain, I was basically navigating with a hand-bearing compass and a pair of binoculars, and making little cocked hats where the three lines intersected. And constantly studying the coast through binoculars, trying to figure out where I was, and taking bearings on everything that I could identify, obsessively. Every fifteen minutes I'd do another cocked hat on the chart.

Sure, because your safety and survival depended on it.

And consequently I have an absolutely total memory now for the British coastline. I could spool it through my head. Give me any starting point in Britain and I could see those headlands coming up because I spent so much time studying them, taking sights on them, navigating by them. Now there's a GPS on the boat—it looks like the TV remote; instead of lifting up the binoculars to study the coastline, I put on my reading glasses to look at the digital readout on the GPS. There is no need to look at the coast anymore.

I find this immensely depressing. It's lessened the interest of sailing for me quite a lot. That sense of being out in wild nature trying to figure out where you are and place yourself has just gone because this damned instrument tells you where you are, without your having to do anything. You become a sort of spectator to what's happening— you don't really study what you're passing by. Consequently, my memory for these coasts is not a patch on what it is for the coast of Britain because I've never had to look at it with the same seriousness.

And consequently it's taken from me what was, I don't know about the great pleasure, but certainly the great necessary interest in the business of managing a boat and sailing it round a coast. So much of that is gone: I find myself less and less interested in sailing. I do do a bit of it—I had a fine time taking my daughter—she was ten last summer— around the San Juan and Gulf islands. That was wonderful, but I don't feel as impelled, as I once used to, to take the boat off at every opportunity. Something very serious has gone out of sailing for me.

What you're saying about the navigation tools reminds me of Barry Lopez's essay "Flight," where older pilots still know how to navigate visually. For the younger pilots, it's all the screen. And those screens can save your life in a whiteout, but the downside of that is that you don't learn how to navigate by eye.

Well, think of the complete loss of knowledge that happened at the point at which the magnetic compass was introduced. People previously navigated their way across seas by things like swells, prevailing wind direction, all those arcane secrets of early navigation, primitive navigation. South Pacific islanders would sense by the shape and the direction of the sea where you were and where you're going. There was a sort of instinctual relationship between the seaman and the sea on which he traveled, because he just had to know every quirk of its surface to be able to figure out where he was.

And suddenly with the invention of the compass, he transferred his attention from the surface of the sea to this funny little needle in a box, and started watching the needle instead of watching the sea. A comparable shift has taken place with the change from compass navigation to electronic navigation, where you're dependent on these military satellites floating around in the sky.

I am afraid of the sea. I fear the brushfire crackle of the breaking wave as it topples into foam; the inward suck of the tidal whirlpool; the loom of a big ocean swell, sinister and dark, in windless calm; the rip, the eddy, the race; the sheer abyssal depth of the water, as one floats like a trustful beetle on the surface tension. Rationalism deserts me at sea. I've seen the scowl of enmity and contempt on the face of a wave that broke from the pack and swerved to strike at my boat. I have twice promised God that I would never again put out to sea, if only He would, just this once, let me reach harbor.

—JONATHAN RABAN, *Passage to Juneau*

It's another order of magnitude removed from direct experience. Redmond O'Hanlon talks about fear and says that if somebody sneaks up behind you in the jungle with a blowgun, that's extremely personal. That person is taking the time and trouble to kill you. When you're on the ocean, it's entirely impersonal and he finds that more frightening. The sea doesn't give a damn whether you live or die.

Though my experience of it is you believe that it does. There are certain conditions where the sea actively appears to have malignancy built into it. And its malignancy is focused on you. I remember once going around a tide race somewhere in Dorset. I was well clear of what I took to be the main body of the race, and then I saw this white wave of broken water moving fast but in a zigzag direction, as if it were trying to search out where it was going. And it was heading for me. I was absolutely convinced at that moment that the sea had a will, it really meant to get me. I've felt that sometimes, I've seen the curling lip of a wave with eyes for me.

I'd like to ask you about coming to America. When you came here fifteen years ago, did you come with the idea of settling here?

Yes, but that was to do with having an affair with somebody. At that stage I was very excited by the idea of coming to live in the United States. Increasingly it was the place that I wanted to write about. Every time I'd go to Heathrow Airport bound for New York, I'd feel a sort of lightness in my step: I'm going to America! And every time I'd catch a plane back to Heathrow, I'd think, Oh Christ, back to London.

So the prospect of actually living in this place, which I found hugely entertaining as an outsider, was uplifting. I wanted to do nothing more. I felt it was a terrific sort of break—I was forty-seven. It seemed like, as they say, a new life, and fun. But it was all on a kind of whim: I was having an affair and I was in a marriage which had grown intensely boring in London and it was an irresponsible escape. It wasn't a rational decision, but the kind of decision which writing makes so easy because you can do it anywhere. All you need is a pen and some paper and they have that kind of stuff in America, so why not do it there instead of here?

Hearing you speak about it, it sounds as though you're almost gleeful about writing about the United States. What interested you about this country?

Oh, it's all in the books. I was fascinated by the insane mobility of Americans, the way in which they were able to move around within their own country. People in England are rather bound by place. They're quite reluctant to move—unless they grow up in a real hellhole—they have a natural attachment to the place in which they're born.

I met some woman in a bar who'd just moved to Seattle from Denver. She'd gone to Denver, she told me, because she'd read about it in a magazine, and then read in some other magazine that Seattle was the hot place to be, so she packed up all her stuff and got on a plane to Seattle. I thought, Who are these people that they take their own enormous geography so lightly? Whimsically moving from one city to another, as if cities were kind of desserts on a dessert trolley and you just sample a little bit of chocolate decadence and then the Peach Melba. I can't say I wanted to share in that because I then became incredibly place bound, barely moving out of Seattle.

Well, you can watch all the people coming and going.

Exactly. But then subsequently I've sort of lived in Seattle as if it was a fate, which is a rather English thing to do.

How do you mean that?

It doesn't occur to me to move anywhere else. And of course there are practical things that bind me here; my daughter, who's with me three and a half days a week. So I spend half the week being a single parent, and single parents don't get to casually travel around very much. I do book tours and stuff like that, but I don't feel any great impulse to travel, partly because I feel as if I'm still traveling. I'm very aware of the rub of difference between my own Englishness here and the slight but distinct strangeness of the world I inhabit. It's not at all like an explorer among the native tribes, but I am aware that Americans are a different tribe.

Were you especially aware yesterday as more than one hundred million people tuned into the Super Bowl?

The truth is that the Super Bowl passed over my head completely. In the supermarket about three or four days ago, I got a hundred bucks back with my groceries. As the girl behind the till was counting the money out, the guy behind me said, "Don't bet it all on the Super Bowl." I said, "Look I don't even know who's playing in the Super Bowl."

When you spoke in Berkeley, you said you had a bumper sticker on your car reading, "Somewhere in Texas a village is missing its idiot." I'm curious, as someone who is not native to this country but who has lived here since 1990, what do you make of what's going on right now?

Well I think this is one of the worst periods American history has ever known. I think America is currently stuck with a terrifying administration, and I don't understand why more Americans aren't as alarmed. Actually I have to say that in Seattle most Americans are at least as alarmed as I am by it.

That's true where I live, too, the San Francisco area, but sometimes I think that we live in these oases of sanity.

I think the Seattle area is an oasis of sanity, an oasis of liberalism, and thank God for that, because I could not bear it if I were not living in an oasis of liberalism right now. I think that the Bush administration stands for something completely terrifying, particularly in relation to the rest of the world. Yes, its domestic policies are ghastly, the consequences of the Patriot Act are ghastly for Americans, but what is much, much more worrying is the emergence of America as the most loathed country on the face of the Earth, the country that's seen as the dangerous bear, that's distrusted by most countries, that appears to behave with a kind of petulance, a sort of adolescent quality about it that you wouldn't believe a major power, the world's last superpower, would be capable of. One feels that the whole psychology of this administration is the psychology of a rather brutish fifteen-year-old dominating the school playground. And that's terrifying for the world.

You've said the U.S. is "the most hated country in the world for all its good intentions." That's an interesting mix of sentiments—could you say a bit about that?

I think the good intentions are there—there's a kind of idealism about the way in which America is prone to act. There's a sort of corrupted idealism about the insanely innocent Wolfowitz plan for the Middle East, the domino theory in reverse, the spreading of democracy like a germ across the Middle East. Just invade Iraq, lop off the monster's head, and the people of Iraq will want to create a democracy. It'll be like Connecticut on the Euphrates, and this germ of infection will spread to neighboring countries, irresistably, because everybody really wants to be Americans. Everybody wants the dream of democracy.

And there's a germ of truth in that, too. But the way in which it was conceived by Wolfowitz and those guys: They knew nothing about the history of the country they were going to invade. They knew nothing about its culture; they knew nothing about its political divisions, its religious divisions. They went blind into this place, simply seeing it as a bunch of people under a dictator—take the dictator away and then there would be some sort of natural reversion that would take place to democracy, as if that were what people reverted to. Actually, as it's becoming plainer and plainer, if you had a democracy in Iraq, what the democracy would almost certainly be, with the majority of Iraqis being Shiites, would be a theocratic state, with close ties to Iran. This completely seemed to evade Wolfowitz's thinking—it's extraordinary. But it was presented as a kind of idealism: America doing good in the world.

Isn't history a form of intelligence, too? Shouldn't they have known something of the history and culture of this country that they were about to occupy? My favorite quote of the moment is from Ambrose Bierce: "War is God's way of teaching Americans geography." To which he might have added: history, religion, culture, and everything else. I suspect that some good may eventually come out of this simply because you cannot occupy Iraq for a year and more without learning something about it, and perhaps learning that you should never have invaded it in the first place. But it is a hell of a situation— what they have created is a failed state, another failed state.

Instead of fighting the war that they wanted to fight, the war of the nation-state against something that isn't a nation-state, the so-called war on terror, they fought the only war they could fight, nation-state against nation-state, our military against theirs.

Would you say that was calculated because that was the war they knew they could win?

I suspect that all the talk of Al Qaeda is another way of trying to make it thinkable, because what they're actually dealing with is militant Islam. And militant Islam is spread over such a multitude of places, not least inside America itself, that there is no way of treating it as an enemy. What they need is a good old-fashioned enemy, and Saddam Hussein provided them with a convenient one. So at least you could teach those buggers an example.

On September 13th, 2001, Le Monde had a headline reading, "We are all Americans." It seems as if there was an enormous amount of goodwill towards America at that time.

All squandered, all gone.

Do you have a sense of how people in Europe or around the world view the U.S. at this time?

Even in Britain, I think America has become greatly feared since 9/11 and feared, funnily enough, not for its military strength at all but for its apparent complete irrationality. There's a fear that this country is mad, and there's deep mistrust. I mistrust the use of security, for instance, over Christmas we went to orange alert. My great worry is that once you have a Department of Homeland Security you can use it for almost anything. You can up the alerts to orange or to red—you can do what you like with it. What happens if Bush is falling behind in the polls in October and the temptation comes to put the nation on high alert to protect it from terrorist attack? Well, of course, an American administration couldn't do anything like that.

In the 1970s you wrote Arabia—*is there one thing you learned during those travels that, if you had a half-hour with the key U.S. policymakers, you'd say, pay attention to this—you need to know this about the people in Arab lands?*

One thing: the Arabian Peninsula is probably the most memorious place in the world. It's where ancient events still rankle, for instance, relatively recent ones like the Balfour Declaration (1917), like the Sykes-Picot agreement (1916). As far as America is concerned, and to a lesser extent Britain is concerned, events that are already lost in the mists of the past. They might have happened yesterday as far as most Arabs are concerned. I get into a cab anywhere on the Arabian Peninsula and the cab driver trying to suss up my position will say,

"What do you think of Sykes-Picot?" Or, "What do you think of the Balfour Declaration?" The cab driver's a Palestinian and lots of Palestinians drive cabs all over that part of the world.

These events are recent. It's as if history all takes place in one awful moment as far as most Arabs are concerned. Injuries are felt and carry on from generation to generation. And the intensity of the injury does not diminish with the passage of time. Anybody trying to understand the feelings of Palestinians, the sense of Palestinian grievance, has got to understand something about that sensibility, in which Israel was created five minutes ago. They still have the keys to the houses from which they were evicted. You go to a Palestinian refugee camp and all the muddy streets between the tents are named with Palestinian villages, Bethlehem Road and so on.

The sense of *fait accompli*, which Americans take for granted with their sense of history, is absolutely not felt or recognized by Arabs. The grievances in Iraq, of Kurds and Shiites and Sunnis being amalgamated by the British into a single territory in 1915, is still felt as a personal affront by Kurds and Shiites and Sunnis in 2004. And that is why talking about respecting the territorial integrity of Iraq is insane in Arab terms. They see no integrity: they are Kurds; they are Sunnis; they are Shiites. They don't recognize Iraq, particularly the Kurds don't. They don't feel themselves to be Iraqis—they never felt themselves to be Iraqis—that was a colonial arrangement cooked up between the British and the French in the ruins of the Ottoman Empire, which was another imposition that they remember as if it happened yesterday.

Shifting to a different geography, Bad Land *explores the roots of Montana's settlers almost a century ago. In 1909, an act passed that would give 320 acres to anyone who wanted to settle in Montana. Brochures extolled the virtues of how beautiful and fruitful this land was, and then these people would get there and they had to fight for their lives. When you researched this period and place, what did you find most surprising about these people—what struck you?*

What I felt all the way was this was like a scale model of immigrants to America. It was the story of America written in one particular landscape. I mean, I could have written about the Mayflower pilgrims who found a land that was about as inhospitable to the Mayflower pilgrims as it was to the settlers in eastern Montana.

But there was something about this—they were sold a bill of goods.

They were sold a bill of goods—you're right. It was a great story of American enterprise and American commercial exploitation. The railroads had to make a living and they did. I did feel it was an American story—it wasn't a Montana story—it wasn't a piece of local history I was writing. It was sort of emblematic of immigrant experience in America. It all had a kind of rawness of somebody's confrontation with a landscape so extremely different from anything that they had expected. That's always, I think, true of immigrants coming to America.

I started a Ph.D. about immigration as a metaphor in the Jewish American novel from 1874 to the present day, the present day was then about 1965. I was then thrilled by the novels that were coming out in the United States, the young Philip Roth, the middle-aged Saul Bellow, the young, middle-aged Bernard Malamud. It was in Roth's first novel, *Goodbye Columbus*...have you read it?

Yes.

I remember how Neil Klugman makes this kind of migration from downtown Newark to the world of the Patimkins, who live up the hill in suburban Newark. Reading that, I thought, Jesus this is an immigration story. This is a story about being confronted with a brave, new world. You come from the old world; you find yourself at a loss in the new one. And I thought, Hey, what about Herzog? All that traveling that Herzog does trying to find himself in the world. It's a novel that zigzags all over the East Coast and a lot of it takes place in cars. And I began to see Herzog as this kind of immigrant.

So I went back in the thesis to try and do a kind of map from the first immigrants' memoirs of the Atlantic crossing to New York, usually to the garment district, living in tenements in New York, having been transplanted from *shtetls* in central Europe. I absolutely soaked myself—the earliest novel, I think, is *The Rise of David Levinsky* by Abraham Cahan, published in about 1890. It's the story of somebody who grows up in a village in Russia and makes his way to America and becomes a major millionaire owner of six garment factories. At the end of the novel he's found listening to the hum of his money-making machine, realizing he's lonely and desolate in the midst of all his wealth. Not a great novel.

But that's a contrast to Goodbye Columbus, *which ends with Neil's repudiation of the Patimkins and all they stand for.*

You can do that with Newark, but you can't go home again if you're an immigrant who has gone by steerage, three weeks voyage from Hamburg to New York and you've had your name changed and all of that. So this experience of immigration which started out in the Ph.D. thesis that never got finished because I got a offered a job in a university, and I thought, Fuck it, I'm not going on writing this Ph.D. thesis. It was a good time for higher education in Britain then. And there was a certain snobbery, too, among university teachers who didn't have doctorates. It was thought that only the relatively dim needed doctorates. Teaching on a B.A. was a sign of brightness. So I never finished that and instead started writing for money.

I felt that I was using all that old Ph.D. stuff when I was writing *Bad Land.* It was a classic immigration story of, yeah, being sold a bill of goods which shows up in the early accounts of Jewish immigration. There were lots and lots of wonderful letters home written by people who were starving on the streets of New York but who couldn't admit it. They had to pretend to their families back home that they were alrightniks, so they would sell America in their letters. More and more deluded people would come over, and they'd find the letter writer living in one room in the tenement having boasted of his wealth in America.

Speaking of the immigrant experience, the title of your book, Hunting Mister Heartbreak, *seems a conscious choice. People hear about unimaginable wealth and then they come here and it's so hard—they have to struggle just to get by. What I found most poignant in* Hunting Mister Heartbreak *is the generational experience, the unfulfilled desires of the immigrants and how those are thrust upon their children.*

The Seattle Koreans, the kids burdened with all the hopes of their parents…

As Jewish families did in New York eighty years ago, or fifty years ago, or twenty years ago (laughs). It's such a universal theme. Whether it's Jews or Mexicans or Koreans, it just seems that it's the responsibility of the children to bring redemption to the parents.

And the children, of course, become the parents to their parents because of the language problem.

Let's explore the notion of home. Do you feel at home here or does it still feel like a foreign place to you?

It seems like a very homely, foreign place but no, it doesn't feel like home. In many ways, I like this because one of the things that was happening to me living in London was I was canceling more and more parts of it out because I knew it so well. I wasn't listening; I wasn't seeing; I was going rather dead to it. I'd only become an observer when I came to America. The interesting thing is that after nearly fifteen years of living here I am still alert to the strangeness of it. I listen. I notice in a way that I would not be noticing in London. But that listening and noticing comes with a price, which is the continuous reminder that I am an outsider here. Just when I think I'm perfectly at home somebody says [putting on American accent], "Oh, you've got an accent—where's that accent from, Australia?"

Did having a child here make you feel more at home?

Oh, God no. But it gives one an immense stake in the place and so makes one feel more at home that way. If and when you do have children, you'll discover that there is nothing more alienating than being a parent, because you have to meet other parents and you get known as Julia's dad. People come up and introduce themselves. They say, "Hi, I'm Rachel's mom. Oh, you're Julia's dad."

This business of being Julia's dad and meeting Rachel's mom is for me one of the most alienating experiences I've ever had in my entire life. I think something in my shoulders naturally hunches as I approach the school. When I drive away from the school I feel an immense sigh of relief, as if I've escaped from jail. I always think that I'm masquerading at it, that I'm just pretending. I'm putting on a parent uniform, grinning and nodding, and trying to do the right thing but knowing I'm a complete fraud.

The other business, the private aspect of parenting, I think is what keeps me alive. I find it utterly interesting, just to be with her at this age watching her grow up, and having, I hope, some contributory part in her growing up. And it's totally enlightening—it also makes me feel warmer to and angrier toward this country because, although she has dual nationality, she is quite transparently an American child culturally.

She goes back with me to England once a year, but that doesn't make her English. I find myself as this outsider to America, having this all-American kid, and it makes me fear more intently what this country is doing right now because of her rather than because of me. If I really didn't like it, I could theoretically leave. But this is her inheritance. Are you aware of the kinds of exercises that we had in Seattle in May of 2003?

When they enacted a fake terrorist event with bodies strewn all over the streets.

Played by actors.

Well, it gave them work.

I don't know how credible and real the threat of Islamist terrorism is. Obviously it was real in the case of 9/11. Whether it continues to be real and how widespread the support for it is…it seems to me that America has done everything since in order to make terror spread wider. There must be a whole generation growing up in the Middle East and elsewhere who want nothing more than to inflict a further 9/11 on America, but that's largely because of what America has done since. But whether we're dealing with a bunch of mentally disturbed terrorists emanating out of a bunch of caves in Afghanistan, or whether we're dealing with some worldwide threatening people who are bent on a war between civilizations, who can tell?

My suspicion is that this administration is engaged in a vast exercise of exaggeration—it seems to be poisoning or potentially poisoning the life of children. Regarding strangers with suspicion, regarding foreigners as potentially hostile. It does seem to me that since I came to live here in 1990, there has been a revolution in the way in which America now looks at foreigners. Just as there's been a revolution, perfectly understandable, in the way that foreigners look at Americans.

There perhaps should not have been anything like a war between the civilizations but what is emerging really does look like one. And I'm appalled that my child should be growing up with all of this. Though I have to say, that what I'm saying now sounds pretty stupid when I think of her and her responses to it. Children are actually so much tougher than their parents ever believe them to be.

There's a quote in Hunting Mr. Heartbreak *about a woman from the South. You said she was, "kindly, intelligent, fair and trapped in the language into which she had been born." I think language is more powerful than we realize. Would you say a few words about how language colors our character or about how our dialogue says so much about who we are.*

I couldn't—it's just beyond me. It's such a gigantic subject, that. I totally agree with you, as I believe Wittgenstein when he writes, "the world we live in is the words we use." The cultural language that you speak, in French structuralist terms it's the *parole* as opposed to the *langue*, the *langue* being the entire language comprising all its dialects and the *parole* which is the particular speech. We are all prisoners of our own *parole* and that's dictated by history, by culture, by all those things that the Bush administration doesn't understand about Iraq.

I'm aware that I'm trapped inside the *parole* of somebody born into the particular class, in a particular country, in a particular year, and you fight against the limitations of *parole* but you know they're there—they're prison bars. They shape who you are and what you can think and what you can feel. If you've been born ten miles away, or even one mile away; if you'd come from a different class, a different background; if you'd had a slightly different personal history, you know you would think differently and feel differently. And an awareness of that relativism, of knowing that things could have been otherwise. That your own most strongly held feelings, thoughts, opinions could have been otherwise is important. And of course it makes one more attentive to the *parole* of other people listening to them speak in the dialect of their immediate culture, place, class, family, generation. You know that they could have been otherwise too.

In preparing for this interview, I learned that you had been an actor and a playwright.

A much longer time as a playwright than as an actor. I was an actor for about five minutes.

But it shows. When I saw you speak in Berkeley, it was clear that you take the spoken word very seriously. I think there's a way of speaking that's almost been lost. I visited my grandfather last month—he's ninety-seven years old—and the way he speaks has a rhythm and a cadence and almost a poetry.

Are you sure this is not a bit like the girl at the checkout desk saying, "Oh you have an accent," as if she didn't? I think we're probably more alert to other people's rhythm and cadence than we are to our own. I hear in your voice rhythm and cadence and particularity. Separated by a culture or by two generations, like you with your grandfather, you register his way of speaking as something different from yours. But you have such a thing, too, which would be recognized either by your grandfather or by people two generations younger than you as just as distinctive. We all have accents, as I keep on trying to impress on girls in supermarkets, who think that they don't have such a thing.

But I think it's something more. When you spoke in Berkeley, I could sense that you really cared about how the spoken word came across—it was more than a reading. Performance might be a little strong, but you very clearly wanted to engage the audience almost in the way an actor would.

That's probably true. I very, very much wanted to be an actor. And then I had a very brief taste of what it was like to be a professional actor, and I realized I was all wrong for it. I had the voice, but the body, the walk was all wrong. The height was wrong, too. I wanted to be a character actor. I was three inches too tall to be a character actor. Good character actors are five-foot-nine, five-foot-eight. Six foot is gangly, and I walk like a duck. You can't be a character actor if you walk like a duck.

You've written about "that small shabby independence, the freelance author's claim to standing in the world."

I think that was Dr. Johnson actually, the small shabby independence.

Have you achieved that, or gone beyond that? In Hunting Mister Heartbreak *you write about the prospect of earning $150 per article for a Seattle newspaper. And I'm thinking a writer of this stature should be making more than $150 a shot. We live in a society where we idolize our actors and our athletes, while people like you and Pico Iyer and Redmond O'Hanlon—you guys are among the top writers—and yet you don't earn what Tom Cruise earns—you don't earn what Barry Bonds earns.*

I was a university teacher and a lot of my friends have been academics. I have always paced my own earnings not in relation to writers—I mean who are you going to pace yourself against, John Grisham?—but rather, would I have been much better off as a university professor? No, I wouldn't have been much better off, in fact I would have been rather poorer. That seems to me to be a good shabby independence to have held on to. I've supported myself by nothing else except writing since 1969. I got a house, I got a car, no I'm not rich.

In Passage to Juneau, *you say travel almost always entails infidelity.*

Traveling with a companion, with a wife, with a girlfriend, always seems to me like birds in a glass dome, those Victorian glass things with stuffed birds inside. You are too much of a self-contained world for the rest of the world to be able to penetrate. You've got to go kind of naked into the world and make yourself vulnerable to it, in a way that you're never going to be sufficiently vulnerable if you're traveling with your nearest and dearest on your arm. You're never going to see anything; you're never going to meet anybody; you're never going to hear anything. Nothing is going to happen to you.

Whereas traveling alone, everything happens. And also traveling alone puts you in this position where you will do almost anything to make contact with other people. My experience of traveling with somebody else is that you just hang around with them. Half the point of traveling alone is that you get so lonely you need to talk to other people. And so you find yourself hanging around late at night in bars talking with strangers, which you'd never want to do. It would seem an insane thing to be doing.

You crave the company of people you might otherwise shun because you're so alone.

I remember a withering remark once made to me when I was in Syria traveling with a photographer, Dmitri. We were doing this job for *Radio Times*, following Freya Stark on a raft going down the Euphrates River, which was my first introduction to the Middle East. I got into a cab and Dmitri said to me in this rather weary way, "It seems to me you have the most extraordinary appetite for talking to bores." I think that's kind of essential, to be happy to spend one's time in the company of bores. Which you'd never do if you were traveling in a couple. But I think coupledom is the enemy of travel.

Or travel writing, maybe.

Well, I don't know. If travel is peeling off a skin, exposing yourself to the world so the world can expose itself to you, then I think it's the enemy of travel.

So where does the infidelity come in—do you have to leave your partner to see the world?

It means saying this domestic world which we count so valuable is a world that I am utterly prepared to leave for the next three or six months. And therefore you betray it. No, I don't know where I'm going to be—you won't be able to contact me on the phone. I'll call in. Every time you go away, it's like having an affair with somebody else.

What I found most poignant in Passage to Juneau *was the interaction with your daughter, who was three and a half. As you're leaving you tell her, I'll see you in twenty-one days; that's an eternity to her. And I sense that you don't know if you can keep that promise. It reminded me of Peter Matthiessen's* The Snow Leopard, *when he promises his son that he would be back by Thanksgiving. He can't keep that promise. And I think even when he made the promise he knew it wasn't going to be possible. Imagine this young boy whose mother died the year before, his father is off in the Himalaya and he's by himself at Thanksgiving. Would you like to comment on the sacrifices you've made to pursue this career as a writer who travels?*

For every month I've spent traveling in my life I've spent a year and more sitting at a desk boringly, alone, tapping away at a typewriter or a computer. The journeys are very short and the writing is very long. I don't suppose I've made any more sacrifices than any writer does. The essential sacrifice that every writer makes is that they give up the enormously attractive sociable world of communal work. Office politics, hanging out by the cooler, all of that stuff, for sitting alone in a room with their own thoughts. That's the sacrifice.

But traveling, and I haven't traveled for a book since 1996—that was *Passage to Juneau*—and I don't know when I'm next going to travel because I have two novels to write. The great advantage of travel is that it does get you out of the house. It gives you a social life, even if it's a sort of intermittent, serial social life. Every few years you suddenly have this life in which you do nothing all day except meet other people and blamelessly so. The more people you meet, the better for your book, the better for the writing. So you spend three or four months guiltlessly hobnobbing and being gregarious and having fun and hanging around.

What have you been proudest of, or what do you feel have been your most important literary contributions?

That's like asking me to be my own obituarist.

Well, do you feel you have a unique perspective or take on things?

I guess it would be, boringly, the immigrant thing, the sense of the novelty of living in a world that is not your own, which is a condition that we all experience all the time. But in some ways being an actual immigrant helps you get a grasp on being a stranger in the world.

As somebody who has left his home country and traveled extensively—

This is complete illusion—I haven't traveled extensively. I've done far less traveling than most Americans I know have done. It's just that every single journey I've taken, I've written about. I haven't really been anywhere. I went around the Middle East, that was the furthest serious traveling that I've ever done. And I've been around America quite a bit, and a little bit of western Canada. And that's about it—I've never been to Asia; I've never been to India; I've never been to New Zealand; I've never been to Australia. I hate long plane flights. I revere Philip Larkin who once remarked of China, "Yes it would be very nice to visit China if you could go there for lunch and be back in time for tea." Which is precisely how I feel.

But I think travel is leaving the mainstream. When you get in a boat, you've left the mainstream, ironically, because you're not in a society that the majority of the people inhabit.

Well, that's how I feel about going up to the supermarket just up the road. I only have to go there and I'm traveling, so in a way this is rather a good berth for me.

The Redmond O'Hanlon Show

Redmond O'Hanlon
OXFORD, ENGLAND

R EDMOND O'HANLON SEEMS TO HAVE STEPPED OUT OF NINETEENTH-
century Britain and into the jungles of Borneo, Africa, and the
Amazon. An intrepid explorer who's enraptured by knowledge, O'Hanlon follows the trails blazed by Darwin and Conrad, seeking to understand the natural world and human nature. A tireless
scholar, O'Hanlon served for fifteen years as natural history editor of
The Times (of London*) Literary Supplement* and is fascinated by the
habits of creatures ranging from prehistoric-looking fish to crippling
parasites. He's also riotously funny, and can make you simultaneously
laugh out loud and wince in pain when he's describing, to cite just one
example, the tiny South American fish that can swim up a man's urethra and porcupine its spines inside his penis.

O'Hanlon's first book, *Into the Heart of Borneo*, chronicles a river
journey with the poet James Fenton to the interior of Borneo. The goal
of the trip is to find a rare rhino, but like all of O'Hanlon's expeditions,
it's a journey into the human spirit. O'Hanlon confronts the helpless-

ness he feels, for example, when he doesn't have enough antibiotics to save an elderly woman with gangrene. His next book, *In Trouble Again*, takes him deep into the Amazon jungle, where even the bugs are called assassins and where piranhas can devour a man before his companions notice he's missing.

His masterpiece, though, may very well be *Congo Journey* (called *No Mercy* in North America), a Conrad-inspired trek into the depths of central Africa. The book begins with a visit to a *feticheuse*, a medicine woman, who warns O'Hanlon and his traveling companion Lary Shaffer that if they stay no more than two months, the forest spirits won't harm them. But if they remain in Africa just one day longer, she says, they will die. "But, I'm staying for six months!" O'Hanlon exclaims. "Then you will die," says the *feticheuse*, turning away.

The journey proceeds by ship, by truck and, ultimately, by foot, as O'Hanlon approaches Lake Télé, where a legendary dinosaur is said to dwell. Naturally, he doesn't take the most direct route to Lake Télé, instead trekking to interior villages, even to one settlement whose leaders have sworn to kill Marcellin, the leader of O'Hanlon's expedition. Much more than a story of adventure, *Congo Journey* is a tale of the heart. O'Hanlon is deeply sympathetic toward the members of his party and feels confounded by his inability to rescue them. He even falls in love with an orphaned baby gorilla, risking his own well-being to try to transport the gorilla to safety. The book culminates in a riveting crescendo of dreams, visions and revelations, and lodges in the reader's memory, its meanings growing and deepening over time.

O'Hanlon's *Trawler*, published in Britain in 2003, recounts a voyage on a Scottish fishing boat "in the worst weather at the worst time of year." O'Hanlon has to face his fear of the sea, his powerlessness on a trip he can't control, and the demons unleashed on a crowded ship manned by a sleep-deprived crew. *Trawler* is a tribute to the bravery of the rough men who sleep for three one-hour shifts every thirty-six hours and who have to employ strength, dexterity, and agility in the most challenging conditions.

O'Hanlon and his wife, Belinda, invited me for dinner at their home, called Pelican House, near Oxford. "Redmond's not well," Belinda said when I called from Oxford. "Where are you?" When I told her I was twenty minutes away and leaving England the following day, she invited me to come over but said Redmond might not be able to see me.

Stepping into the O'Hanlons' home felt like a time warp—I could well have been back in the 1880s. A giant stuffed white pelican guarded the entryway and sepia photographs covered the walls. The dining room was surrounded by bookshelves with musty biographies and volumes on arcane scientific subjects. An antique microscope stood in one corner. Adorning other shelves were specimens—a wild cat's skin here, a stuffed giant lizard there—collected during O'Hanlon's far-flung journeys.

Just moments after my pupils dilated to take it all in, the powerfully built and bespectacled O'Hanlon bounded down the stairs, saying he was feeling a bit better, and popped open a bottle of champagne. We talked over Belinda's beautifully prepared dinner, as Redmond's resonant voice leapt from the Scottish accents of the trawlermen to the soft affectations of his old friend Bruce Chatwin. Redmond often let loose with a booming laugh, clearly relishing the chance to escape his study and talk about the wonders he's encountered during his travels.

You've just come out with this new book, Trawler, *and you had the launch party here in your home. I heard the captain of the boat came and he was standing right here chatting with Martin Amis.*

I was so pleased he [Jason, the captain] came, and also that he looked very much like his description, standing there in the middle of the room with his massive thighs and huge hands and shoulders. And Martin went up to him and said, "I would just like to shake your hand, Jason, because I've read all about you. I am Martin Amis." I was passing with a bottle and Jason had no idea who Martin Amis might be. So he looked at this little chap and said, "Uh-huh." (Laughs.)

Mart said, "I just want to know if it really is dangerous or if old Reggie is exaggerating." Jason said [O'Hanlon puts on a Scottish accent], "Aye, it's no dangerous at all—the sister ship of the Norlantean sank last week, five members of the crew, not a man lost. Helicopters got there just in time."

What was the Trawler trip like for you compared to your other journeys?
In the Congo, South America, and Borneo, you could set a course and go.
Here you were at the mercy of the skipper and the ocean.

Very good question, no control whatever. That was part of the horror. You plan it like a novel and then people walk right out of your plot. But if somebody has got a six-foot long arrow pointing at you, the immediate reaction is to think, Jesus Christ, these are the real people at last. And I looked up the shaft of this arrow to see this impassive-looking, expressionless face, and then I thought, Shit, he's going to kill me. But then I thought, What a classy way to go. And then you sort of panic but after that of course it's all right.

But that's wonderful in a way, and romantic, and plugs into a long tradition and you just cannot help feeling flattered: this guy is taking the trouble to kill you. It's man to man. It's thoroughly personal, whereas, even the tail end of a hurricane is terrifying, a vast, indifferent ocean out there that couldn't give a damn about anybody. It all seems to be coming for you, though you know it isn't. And you don't think, What a classy way to go, you think you might get a couple of paragraphs in *The Times* (of London) if you're lucky.

It happens to them all the time, twenty-six vessels went down in '98, the last figures I've got, which is astonishing. And just a freak of statistics: twenty-six people drowned. There were 388 accidents, and that's interesting because after I left, Sean, the youngest one on the boat, he cut the top of his thumb off with a gutting knife. Now you don't stop for that—not just that, but it doesn't register as an accident. I heard three weeks ago that Jerry Thompson, the cook—they have no sleep so he was probably steadying himself with a winch, and the winch took off and he lost several fingers. So I rang Robbie and said, "How many is several?" and he said, "Four and three-quarter fingers." But you don't stop for that either, you just bind the stump up. And they carried on fishing, but that does qualify—just—as an accident. Grim, but they're all self-employed so they have no industrial compensation or anything. The community absorbs the injuries as it were. The rest of them carry on.

Trawler was meant to be *The Wild Places of Britain*—it was going to be a tour all around the wild places—and then I realized there certainly were some proper wild places, even in European terms, but they're all off the 200-mile limit in the Atlantic, so that was terrifying. And then this recurrent fear that I've had since I was a kid…I grew up in a vicarage so there was never any money. You could always have a holiday—the Anglican church here had an arrangement with the Church of Scotland—so my dad would swap his parish with a minister and we'd go up to Orkney and have a wonderful time.

I remember when I was eight years old—it's not in the book—my dad passed down his binoculars. We were standing on a little cliff on Shapinsay, one of these islands; it was August but there was a big swell running. And it was pretty special, first time he'd handed me his binoculars, and he said, "I want you to look at this." There was this small Scottish trawler and she was blue, very blue, on the top of a wave one minute and in the next disappeared, couldn't even see the masthead. So naturally, as an eight-year-old, I thought, Christ they've sunk. And then, they popped up again, as if she had come from the bottom of the sea.

And he said, "I want you to remember that because those men, they don't know it, but they're brave. That's what bravery is, really courageous men, they don't know that they have this gift of courage." The only other group of men that he admired as much were the Spitfire pilots, the hurricane pilots that he'd known in the war. At the height of the battle, the life expectancy of these twenty-year-olds was three weeks. So, my god, did they fill his chapel on the base every Sunday. God they prayed, whatever they actually believed.

Anyway it was just Spitfire pilots and trawlermen that he thought were brave, and it must have gone into my subconscious. It was an image of fear, that's what fear was, to be out on a trawler in bad weather. When I get these recurrent nightmares: you're on a trawler, the world suddenly goes green and there are the bubbles in front of your face; then oddly enough it's also cold. You wake up covered in sweat. I had that recurrent dream for years. After the Amazon it was added to, when we were there and rivers rose forty feet which added a bit to the dream. In fact you can't see her rising, the river is so big. But in the dream the Amazon keeps rising—it doesn't stop so there I am clinging to a log and then I wake up. Death by drowning. But since writing this book I haven't had that dream at all.

Was it cathartic in a way?

It must have been, but I didn't realize it as I was writing. I was writing it for Bill Buford at *The New Yorker* and it just took off and grew. It wasn't until halfway through that anyone told me it could be a book on its own. But the trouble with it all was: I am an evangelical atheist; I can't bear the thought of any religion. I can't get rid of the idea that it can't be real unless you're suffering. I think that's part of the problem—it's a really Protestant feeling.

So this book, what the fuck was I doing? It was 1998, one of the most beautiful summers we had here in the U.K. Even up in the outer Hebrides, it was just so beautiful, the sea was flat, calm, and all the wonderful birds there. It was sort of paradise. No one was nasty to me—no one stuck a Kalashnikov in my stomach. I was having such a great time on the coast before heading out to sea; I should have had my wife and family [two teenage children] with me. So it wasn't until I actually got aboard a trawler that I realized this was going to be the real thing.

Your dialogue sounds so accurate—did you use a tape recorder?

No, no, you can't use a tape recorder—nobody lets you and also the wet gets to it.

Belinda: He has a phenomenal memory.

Redmond: But that's the first thing that happens in the travel book. You have to compress conversations—that seems to me not just all right, but you have to, to make it any kind of work of art. Some of those conversations in *Congo* could have been put together from bits over a period of six months. *Trawler* felt like six months but only because you have these sleeps that just last an hour—well, you get three of those in thirty-six hours so the brain never has time to complete a sleep cycle.

Belinda: Redmond needs of lot of sleep in normal circumstances.

Yet on your trips it seems like you get up at four or five in the morning.

Yes, but in the jungle you can do that because you go to bed around four in the afternoon. The jungle really suits me 'cause you can't afford to waste your batteries. On the equator you get twelve hours of darkness and then, *bang!* the sun comes up and the sun goes down so fast.

On your trip to Borneo, were you going with the intent of writing a book about it?

Very much so. The trip was Fenton's idea entirely. But then he said I couldn't write about him unless it was done through his brother who had a tiny press in Edinburgh. Borneo was entirely sold by word of mouth because it had to be Tom Fenton publishing it.

So you just kind of took over the trip and said, "Let's go inland."

James just wanted to go snorkeling off the coast of Borneo. He just wanted a holiday. He was such an amazing companion.

Has he invited you on any other trips since?

No, I invited him, but he really did say he wouldn't go with me to High Wycombe.

Are you still friends?

Oh yes. I see a lot of him. He is a great poet, but he also has this incredible ability to reinvent himself.

As a person or a writer?

Both, really. It helps to be very rich, but equally that could be a terrible disadvantage. I admire him for all sorts of reasons—imagine if you've suddenly got 3 million pounds and then it rises to whatever it is now, 20 million or something, and you go back to doing the work that you love and you do best. He's an amazing art critic for *The New York Review of Books.*

    Belinda: Do you know that the millionaire thing is from *Les Miserables?*

I remember that in Into the Heart of Borneo, *Fenton was reading* Les Miserables. *I was going to guess that he didn't make his millions by selling his poetry.*

No, absolutely not. But when he was a professor of poetry at Oxford I could see young would-be poets going up to his vast estate thinking,

Jesus, if I could just write a sonnet, all this could be mine. (Laughs.) But in a way that's true, because it was his lyrics that made the money. He got 1 percent of the gross [from writing early versions of the lyrics for Andrew Lloyd Weber's play *Les Miserables*]—the gross was the stroke of genius on the agent's part.

[We start to eat dinner and the conversation leads to O'Hanlon's visit to Sa Francisco in 1997.]

I thought it was such a wonderful, liberal place—I fell in love with it. It just seemed so vibrant. This young bloke said, "San Francisco is really famous. Do you realize rollerblades were invented here? This is where rollerblades come from."

That did seem rather wonderful, that there's enough energy to invent things like that. But then, that's youth. And no national health—that's bad. All the taxi drivers there said they can't afford health insurance. I said, what the fuck happens if you get really ill? They said, "We go home and die." That's the sort of black underside of the great country of liberty.

All over the Congo, everywhere we went, I'd say this is Lary Shaffer and he's an American professor—they could tell at once he was American by the clothes, and they'd ask him, in all seriousness, can people die in America? He'd get so embarrassed. But politically he got it all right—and he cared so much in that New World way. He would just burst into tears; this big tough guy—he couldn't fucking bear it. Why wasn't American aid flooding in?

But actually, the power to change things in the U.S. is great—it's called television. I just said all this on *Letterman*—luckily I didn't know what *Letterman* was, I thought his name was Leatherman, like the knife, so it sort of dawned on me the way everyone was so tense that this was sort of a big telly show.

Someone told you that you were doing the Letterman show and you had no idea who he was?

No idea, which isn't a good thing—it's just sort of Oxford out-of-touch. But being picked up by this car that was 100 yards long, I knew it couldn't be the BBC. And I just happened to say—it was after *In*

Trouble Again, the South America book—I said Brazilian gold prospectors are coming up from the south and they're hunting these people down with shotguns like animals in the forest. *Bang!*—next day—questions in Congress. The Venezuelan army was told they got to fucking well get in there and protect these people or American aid would be cut off. I couldn't believe it. That really impressed me.

That must have felt good.

Yes, it did, but not for me. It told me what a great country the U.S. really is, 90 percent of the time all those ideals and the Statue of Liberty, it's all fucking true—it really is. It's extraordinary—the speed at which things moved. The Venezuelan army did go in and they do now have posts on those rivers. Whether they do anything or not…anyway, trivial story, but the power of television. And Letterman was magnificent.

[O'Hanlon gets a little vial off the shelf.]

Here's the little fish that swims up your dick. In fact it's a pregnant female so it's too big for me but it will probably fit you, you young bloke.

Should you have too much to drink, say, and inadvertently urinate as you swim, any homeless *candiru,* attracted by the smell, will take you for a big fish and swim excitedly up your stream of uric acid, enter your urethra like a worm into its burrow and, raising its gill-covers, stick out a set of retrorse spines. Nothing can be done. The pain, apparently, is spectacular. You must get to a hospital before your bladder bursts; you must ask a surgeon to cut off your penis.

—REDMOND O'HANLON,
In Trouble Again

I didn't realize they were that small.

Well, they fit right in the urethra—they're bloody everywhere.

I worked as a white-water river rafting guide…

Did you? Good God…

...and the first time I heard about the fish that swims up your dick, I thought, that's a nice myth.

That's right, just what I thought. But it's not nonsense—if you pee when you're swimming in the river you might very well get one of those. Theoretically—they've done it in the lab at Johns Hopkins or somewhere—the muscle, the filaments, *bang!* It's extraordinary. It theoretically can get up a stream of piss—they did it in lab. That was one of the first ones to reach Europe because these young scientists thought it was a joke. So they took these fine filament nets out and put them across the river and it's just packed, packed with these little catfish.

Didn't you do The Today Show *too?*

Yes, yes I did. But I got pulled off of the fucking show. Jane Pauley was stroking my…she was rubbing my knee, and she does it to everybody I'm sure, she's lovely. She asked me what's the biggest fear in South America, apart from that. [Points to the fish.]

I said it's a bug that gives you Chagas' disease. Anyway the parasite, no it's a trypanosome, gets into your bloodstream, that's it, the trypanosome comes out not in the bite but in the shit of the insect. It was exactly like this, I was trying to think, instead of saying "the feces" and that was it. You die from degeneration of the heart between one and twenty years later—it just eats the heart muscle. But there's no money in it. It only happens to poor Indians in the Andes and in the jungle, so eradicating Chagas' disease wouldn't bring you in a dollar.

So you said "shit" and that was it? You were off the show?

Yeah, off the show. It's a pity because it would've been the first time that Knopf had ever had anybody on *The Today Show* and on *Letterman*. They should have bloody well told me you can't say "shit" on American television. I'd read a bit of Saul Bellow and all the boys and girls, so I just assumed you could say anything you wanted.

TV's different; there are seven words you can't say.

Well, it's the fundamentalist Christian South, scary as hell.

One thing that seems clear about your work: each journey has a focal point, whether it's a mythic dinosaur or a rare rhino.

Well, I was naïve enough in Borneo to think we really might find this rhino. We might wind up in a clearing and it would be full of rhinos. (Laughs.) But of course with the noise we made, no rhino's going to hang around.

In Congo Journey *you could have taken a more direct route to Lake Télé.*

Yes.

But you chose not to.

It was perfectly obvious, *mokele mbembe* (the dinosaur) was like the Loch Ness monster but more interesting because I knew that every village had sort of a protective animal. It's one thing to read about that in anthropology and another to find out they actually fucking well do. And that it must be some creature of myth, which it is. But of course no biologist wants to hear that. I said so on a natural history program and it was edited it out. Those guys go there every two weeks. They know perfectly well what's in their lakes: no dinosaurs about.

So I suppose that sort of changed me, realizing the power of religion, having been an evangelical scientific atheist, as it were, and angry with everybody simply because I grew up in a vicarage. But Jesus Christ, what a stupid way to look at the world. How could you possibly get through life without a really powerful narrative structure of some sort? It doesn't matter what it is. Tolstoy could only write those great books because he had this absurd theory of history—it's what sustained him.

And you need a story that tells you why you're here, what you're doing, and then it becomes a background, and you need never ask about that again. So you can get on with life—that's the point of religion. You know, if you can't go to some unbelievably expensive institution and you haven't got hundreds of years of scientific tradition, that great communal effort is not accessible, what are you supposed to do?

When you were in the Congo, you had people looking at the Western system as just a variation of what they have. Jesus is your story as you've just put it.

Yes, quite right. No, Jesus, not a great hit really in Africa; any more than Allah. Both were slavers. Anyway, the thing that's good about both of them was stolen from Judaism, even the rituals, the whole bloody lot was pinched without acknowledgment. You go to a Jewish wedding and there it all is. The wine, there's no hint of a fucking cannibal ritual; you're not drinking the blood of the God; and the bread, you're not eating the flesh of the God. You're not back in Africa. The wine is there so that you can share a bottle at the end of the day and discuss your problems. Judaism is so bloody rational, I wouldn't mind joining a faith like that. In fact, all middle-class Englishmen of my generation are circumcised.

Right, you wouldn't have to go through the initiation ritual.

No, there's nothing left. (Laughs.) You can't do it now—it's barbaric. In the Amazon I had to go take a pee fifty yards away because I didn't want anybody to see that I'd been mutilated.

And yet what we think of as superstitions and crazy beliefs, they work in the interior villages of Africa; they make sense in the Amazon jungle, whereas what we believe makes absolutely no sense. I remember a couple of times in Congo Journey, *people would say, you and your white man's beliefs—can't you see what's really going on here?*

"I've been thinking," said Lary… "Why bother to go way up through the northern forests when all you really want to do is check out Lake Télé? Why not just go west? Get it over with?"

"I don't know," I said, caught off-guard. "I just have this feeling, I have an idea that once we've moved through those villages, found the pygmies in the forest, seen gorillas and chimps and guenons and elephants, when we've caught a glimpse of how people think—we'll *know* what's in Lake Télé before we even get there."

—REDMOND O'HANLON,
No Mercy

They really work, and they really adapted. If you have six children, say, you can be sure two of them will die. So you have all these big fears waiting for you and the main one is: we're all going to die. You deal with that by making everything into little fears, so if a *samale* [a spirit] proceeds through the village and you look at it through a crack in the hut wall, then something terrible will happen. If you don't, if you just carry on with your gossip, you'll be fine.

Now that's just the same as all the taboos on a trawler, how you really must not say sheep or pig, or rabbit or even salmon. And above all you mustn't wear green. But that tells you, the spirits of the sea, they not only care about your speech, they care about your fucking dress sense, your sense of fashion. It becomes personal—that's the way to get it down to human scale. And it's immensely comforting. But if you say "rabbit fish," everybody's touching cold iron. Cold iron's everywhere—that's what it's about—it enables you to cope with this horror out there. It seems to me that's the basis of religion. That's what ritual is about, to make things human, to make you forget the vast, indifferent 3.2 billion years of evolution that have gone on. They must have looked at the night sky and thought, Jesus, that's just too big, so you make those stars into angels, you transform it.

When you're in those villages and a child dies and it's because a woman has crossed a spirit, wouldn't there be guilt or shame or remorse? That would be horrible, I think.

Yes, but it seems to comfort everybody if somebody's got AIDS, that they've done something bad and the sorcerer is taking his revenge.

Belinda: Is that why AIDS, do you think, has taken such a hold?

Redmond: No, I'll tell you exactly why in Western terms that AIDS has taken such a hold: because everybody has chronic long-term syphilis and gonorrhea so everybody's bleeding in intercourse—so HIV just piggybacks. And the reason for that is the only way to cure syphilis, if you're the chief or somebody powerful, is by fucking a virgin. So they're fucking eleven-year-old girls. And syphilis can take thirty years to drive you mad and kill you as we know from the nineteenth century. But actually it's a lot shorter when you're not fed very well.

Belinda, what's it like to have your husband going into these life-threatening situations?

Belinda: When he goes, I just shut off and I assume that he's fine because he's happy doing what he wants to do, and everybody loves him anyway, everybody who comes across him, so he'll be all right. I just assume he's fine. And I'm not going to worry.

Redmond: You clean up my socks, don't you, first thing; stop them running around the place.

Belinda: He's very, very messy in everything except his writing.

I remember that comment Lary makes in Congo Journey *where he says, "Could you get your head out of your books and put your damn socks away?"*

He really meant it. Lary's a wonderful guy.

Belinda: Lary came back early, he came and stayed and said, "Don't you worry—if we have to send a search party out for Redmond, we'll just follow the trail of black socks.

Redmond: Is that what he said, witty bugger? When he came back he said to Belinda, "Well, one of us survived." Belinda took him down to see her parents, and he needed therapy apparently because he couldn't stop talking.

Is it true he couldn't bring himself to read the book?

It's true, he still hasn't, I think. He said [puts on American accent], "I'm not a fuckin' hero—can't read about myself."

So he doesn't want to relive it, but you had to relive it to write it. Even the darkest parts, you have to go through it again, don't you?

You have to be there more intentionally than you were at the time, really. So I can only write when it's dark and the world's closed in. I have to go to sleep straight after writing or otherwise the world just goes black, which must be how they (the trawlermen) feel. Working on a trawler is just really intense, a terrible way of life, it really shouldn't happen to anybody over thirty.

Well, the captain is thirty, and he's older than anybody right?

Yeah, but I think he's saved perhaps by the fact that his world is so big, even in terms of his bank balance. He is looking at other horizons and also feeling his way towards these fish. All that mystical stuff, he loves that, but he has a locker room that's filled with all the latest scientific papers—it's done by science. Jason is very bright—he's read everything.

How did he and the crew like the book?

He loved it. And Sean rang up last week and said [Scottish accent], "Sean, here, d'ya remember me? I read the book but I give it to me nan (grandma) first to read. I've never seen me nan in tears. Terrible. Nan came to the door and I said, 'Christ, is the house on fire, what the fuck's wrong?' She said, I've been reading your book and look here, at the end it says, I'm going home; I'm going to see me nan.' I've never seen her cry before." And she put her arms around him—he was brought up by his grandma you see. She was in floods of tears.

[Sean went on,] "It's a fucking classic, and my friends say, you got me to a T. And besides, I read your other fucking books and I've been traveling. I've been away for six months. Me friends, they call me international." So he'd been off smoking dope in Thailand and things. And he's what, twenty? I think he's twenty now.

I'm sure they were very happy about you showing how challenging their lives are out on the sea.

Really, that's all they wanted, so that they could give it to their women. It's an absolute runaway bestseller in Aberdeen. And booksellers never have seen such people in bookshops. They're coming straight up from the harbor still in their sea boots, and the line goes apparently, "I want a fucking book." And the bookseller says, "Well, what book." "It's fucking called *Trawler*, it's a piece of shite, it's about trawlin'. And don't piss me about, here's the cash—I want the book." They don't really want to come in this girly, shitty place—they just want the book.

I think one Aberdeen bookshop will have sold 500 by Christmas. I did this talk; there were these huge blokes in the audience—you don't know: Are you going to have the shit beaten out of you afterward? That's just such a wonderful, different world.

Your books almost have the feel of the novel—I wonder if you ever create characters or dialogue?

In my case, my books are compressed but the characters absolutely fucking well would have said those things if they'd thought of them at the time and if they'd had the energy to put it all together like that. But to move events around, you can't do that. Why not write a novel?

There was a big temptation in Borneo to say that Wallace's bird-wing, this incredible butterfly...I needed something wonderful to happen after James's near-drowning. I needed an interlude—it would have been great to have had those butterflies on the river beach then. But then I thought, no, it didn't happen like that; I never saw them again. I'm bloody lucky too because you only find these fantastically rare butterflies in that twenty-mile stretch above the rapids where James nearly drowned and nowhere else on earth—isn't that weird?

[Redmond opens the bottle of wine I brought and gets two rare first editions of Into the Heart of Borneo, *gifts for my editors.]*

When Tom Fenton went bankrupt, these Borneo books were seized. In comes this baldheaded guy and says "How much to release Tom Fenton from bankruptcy?" And they say 75,000 pounds. He says, all right, and Jesus Christ, this check does not bounce. And that's James. So a lorry arrived and delivered all these. He did it all without a word to his brother.

Time after time in your books you encounter misery or suffering that's beyond your ability to help—sometimes there's nothing you can do. In Borneo, there's this woman who has gangrene on her foot...

Oh, that was terrible. I took all I could afford: 2,500 pounds worth of medicines to Borneo. To the Congo, I took all the wrong things; I took the wrong antibiotics. I didn't know about yaws—I took 6,000 pounds worth of medicines to the Congo—maybe they did help, mostly antibiotics, and things like Savlon cream and bandages and a huge amount of anti-malarial drugs. I'm sure that helped, but you don't know if they've taken the right numbers of the right pills at the right time.

And if it does help, they thank the spirit, not you.

Right, it couldn't possibly be you. But that gangrene was terrible—I didn't even have the right antibiotics for that. And she needed vast amounts. And in the Congo these tropical ulcers, they are really difficult to deal with apparently.

Western medicine can't fix everything—there's a helplessness in that.

Yes, and Western aid can't fix everything. That tormented Lary, still does. The particular village where I think they probably did really want to kill us, Lary wanted to call in the U.S. Air Force—he thought that village could be sorted out. You take out this mad militia man. You just take control and put the schoolmaster back in his fucking hut and give these people a new chance at life—you give these people a school. He really thought this could be done. And then he wrote to his congressman and they weren't into a bit of it. He went into a depression; some things a man shouldn't see in life if he wants to stay happy. He still feels that way, that somehow that bit of the Congo should be detached from Africa and anchored off New York and given help and then schooling. Maybe it's the mix of genes in North America—it's utterly wonderful.

It's far worse there (in the Democratic Republic of the Congo) now because everyone has pulled out, the Russians, the Americans, the Chinese. This is not the real Congo south of the river—this is Congo Brazzaville, the old French bit, which was a model for all African states because it was tied to the French franc so the economy was O.K. At the same time it professed to be Marxist so Russian money came in, and Chinese money, and Cuban money. If you don't want people to report your war and massacres… anybody landing at the airport with a camera around their neck either goes to prison or is shot at once or at least his film stuff is taken away and sold south of the river. So funnily enough, no pictures, no news reports, no filming—it works. Also it doesn't help if you're white.

You hear, they cut you down to size—it's a metaphor. And Lary said no, it means they're going to take your legs off with a machete. And he was absolutely right—that's what they do. Once you've done that, it means that the corpse can't run after you. So you cut the legs off to stop that happening—and if you have time on the battlefield, you take the arms off so the dead body can't strangle you.

So it looks like completely random, crazy mutilation—it's not that; it's fear. I said that in the studio in New York at CNN about the

Congo, straight to camera. Again it was pulled—someone should've told me. I was just making this point that it wasn't mutilation for its own sake—it was fear from the soldier who'd killed this other soldier—it's not mad rage.

Belinda: Why was that pulled? Did you mention penises and things?

Redmond: No, it was just too vivid, I suppose. It was the morning news.

American television journalism has become so constricted that anything seen as too graphic is not shown. On a lighter note, you seem to take great pleasure in scaring the crap out of your traveling companions.

Not really…

What about rubbing that little fetish on Lary's face or sneaking up behind poor Fenton pretending you're a headhunter in Borneo.

The reaction was so extreme and wonderful…

Belinda: Show him the fetish. Does he need to see your room where you work—it's only fair. He's come all this way from San Francisco, he should see the chaos that Redmond works in. I never go in there.

Redmond: No, nobody's allowed in there.

Poor James was peacefully reading, his back to us, in the shade of a large boulder. He just happened to be opposite my position in the assault. I edged forward across the shingle until I crouched behind the rock and then, with what I imagined to be an Ukit-cum-Clouded leopard assassination howl, I lightly touched his neck. The Iban yodelled a particularly horrible battle cry. I can't say that James's hair stood on end, because the sample is not statistically significant, and he only emitted a smallish scream; but his legs went convulsively stiff and shot up in the air, and he threw his arms wildly over his head.

—REDMOND O'HANLON,
Into the Heart of Borneo

Should I carry a string with me so I can find my way out?

Belinda: I'll come and rescue you. Go ahead, good luck.

Wow, so this is where you work, really?

I don't have a computer or anything. This is where I've written all of
them. These are the maps, not for the jungle—these are the ones I use
here. I might be able to find you this assassin bug.

Belinda: I haven't been in here for years. Could anybody work in
here?

Somebody does.

This is the assassin bug—its legs are enormously long. [The reddish
bug, with a hooked beak used to pierce and suck out the tissues of its
prey, is about an inch long with gangly legs.]

Belinda: And all these obstacles…

Redmond: …it's to keep my mother out. She used to be really dangerous. She got in and burned everything.

This cat sits like Buddha in the middle of everything.

I talk to him all day long.

Do you bounce ideas off him?

He agrees with everything. That's what you want. [He gets the fetish.]
It used to be completely covered with colobus monkey fur.

So what's your attraction to the indigenous fetish?

Oh, it really works—it plugs into the subconscious.

Belinda: Oh, he goes berserk if he loses it.

R: That's true.

So you carry it for protection.

Of course I don't. [He pauses and shouts…] Get back! […and throws
the fetish at me.]

Belinda: For someone who is so skeptical about religion, he is so
obsessed and interested in this, which is another form of religion, isn't
it? We were in Rotterdam with his Dutch publisher, in this wonderful
hotel and we were having dinner. Redmond was bringing this out—

there was too much to drink. And I said put it away—you're going to lose it. In the morning, we were packing up to leave and suddenly Redmond was ripping the furniture apart in our hotel room. I said, "What's the matter?" and he said, "Have you seen my fetish?" I said, "No, I last saw it with you down in the dining room." He couldn't find it, and he went berserk. He started to shake and sweat and everything.

So we had to ask the people in the hotel and everything had been cleared out by then—they clear up restaurants late at night. But we had to stress it was really important that they find this thing. Anyway, they went into every bin bag—they obviously had thought it was a dead mouse, and they had thrown it out. But they found it. They sent it by courier on a motorbike to Amsterdam and delivered it to the hotel. So I went round to the bookshop and I did a tickling behind his ear. He was very relieved—it was amazing. He was thrilled—he'd really thought he'd lost it. It's pretty manky; it's a bit worn bald. He does take it around with him on all the publicity tours. He had it X-rayed in the Heathrow machines—I don't know what's in it. He says it's a monkey's finger.

Monkeys share a lot of genetic material with human beings and yet you eat their flesh, even their eyes…

R: Yes, absolutely their eyes! The skull's there. [Points to the shelf.] That's a howler monkey's skull.

So is there any queasiness…

The immediate emotional answer to your question is that when you boil a monkey up and the skin is white and the fur comes off, it looks exactly like a baby, except the limbs are a bit too long—it's horrific. The other thing I saw that I wish I never had, is that a wounded monkey, when you go to kill it with a stick, it puts its hands over its head—it's exactly like a child. It's just as grim as could be. And you're right, we're so closely related it feels just like cannibalism. It's a real taboo, but not just that: they eat chimpanzees and pygmy chimps, and they share not just a large amount of genetic material—they share 98 percent of their genetic makeup with us.

I said this to an absurd, stuck-up, appalling French structuralist and he said, "Well, that just shows you how important 2 percent is.

What a difference 2 percent makes." This gorilla baby I fell in love with was just so human.

Chimps are much more like us, run by males. They can be really aggressive and are great meat-eaters, which nobody really knew before Goodall. They rip colobus monkeys to bits. But then south of the river, it's fascinating. Our very closest relatives, the pygmy chimpanzees, are entirely run by women: an immense amount of sex, lots of parties, they actually fuck 3.5 times a day—it's just social bonding. But any guy who forgets himself and loses a load of sperm is in trouble because if he can't produce an erection again that day, the females chase him up a non-fruiting tree. He'll stay there all day—he gets no food.

Imagine, that's how the girls run a society. This is the worst thing that happens. In other chimp societies where males dominate, you get killed, you get banned from the society, you get ripped to bits by the dominant male. None of that happens in this society. It's all to do with sex—you just have to keep performing—it's really lovely. The orphans don't get killed by an incoming male; they get pampered by every female who hasn't got a kid. They have a wonderful time—they bring up all their children. It's a real female-run community. The only thing you have to do is fuck every girl who asks you.

I could live with that—

—without ejaculating.

Well, that's the hard part.

But if you do get punished, it's just a day. But that seems like a long time if you're up a non-fruiting fucking tree. There's no cruelty. There's no record of any murder, of any cannibalism. Just these poor young blokes up a non-fruiting tree all day. And there are females all around the bottom to make sure he stays up there. The next day, he is completely forgiven.

It's like being sent to your room.

For not being able to maintain your erection (laughs). There's no cruelty. It's a bit of the same sort of thing with the Iban of Borneo. All the old men said, "If there's a really important decision we take it—the women make all the small decisions." Somebody said, "Well when was the last big decision?" And they said, "Oh, in grandfather's time." (Laughs.) You express your power by the size of the party that you can provide once a year. And as a kid, if your mom and dad die, then the couples on either side adopt you.

That's the Iban; it's not hierarchical. Whereas the Yanomami (in South America), my God, if the wife doesn't produce the food on time you're allowed to take her thumbs off—it's just brutal beyond belief and entirely run by men. It sounds like the nineteenth century.

Speaking of the nineteenth century, it almost seems you were born 150 years too late, that's what Lary says, that you're like a nineteenth-century explorer.

I would have loved to have been a nineteenth-century explorer, but I would have been terrified. They had nothing to protect themselves from crotch rot.

Belinda: He's a little obsessed with crotch rot. He still thinks he's going to get it, even here at home. He uses Savlon every day.

Walking through the heath…

Belinda: (Laughs.) He's just obsessed with Savlon—if any of us needs Savlon, which is our antiseptic cream, it's all up in Redmond's room. It's all tucked away.

Maybe you should do the adverts for Savlon.

Yeah, I could put it on personally. It really works. So I wouldn't have liked that about the nineteenth century but then…80 percent of the white guys sent out to the west coast of Africa died—it was called the white man's grave. They died within three weeks or else they had a chance—some people's immune system could cope with vivax malaria. The rest just died. The only people sent there were the third or the fourth sons of these families. Number one would inherit the estate— number two went to India. The last poor little sod, the nanny's darling, he was sent to west Africa and never came back.

So what's the appeal of the nineteenth-century ideal for you, is it that there was so much more to discover?

Yes, and also the way they went about discovering it. It was the excitement of biology.

Belinda: When he did his degree in English, all the time he really wanted to be a scientist or a doctor, so he researched all the nineteenth-century science and Joseph Conrad and everything.

Redmond: But it was powered, you see, by natural theology, this Protestant idea, that's why you don't find any good early Roman Catholic biologists anywhere. That was a vertical world based on revelation, so God talked to you directly. You went to confession. Luther and Calvin and all the boys and girls, they said absolutely not, it depends on grace, but grace was demonstrated to you by what happened in your own life. Without knowing it, they produced a new structure which must lead to great success in life because these guys were straining to make themselves successful as God would have wanted.

They'd be praying not for the purity of soul but for the next cotton works. That would mean God was blessing them. So the Protestant world was bound to completely rub out the Catholic world in the South if you had that belief. And with it went this idea that God had made everything. The only way to really get to grips with his work was to look at what he had done in nature.

So you are glorifying the works of God just as much by laying out a perfect theory of earwigs, each one made by God individually, or lice even, anything, especially birds' eggs, ferns, orchids. So every vicarage had those marvelous cabinets, the oak butterfly cabinets. That wasn't a trivial business—that was telling you how God thought and worked. And that was so much more fun than visiting the sick in the parish, and you got just as many good marks from your bishop.

The only bad thing came in 1859. The only people really well qualified to understand Darwin's flippant argument: God hadn't made all these things to fit into the world perfectly. Just a little example: the eye spots that are like an owl on the back of a particular butterfly's wings. God didn't put those eye spots there for our delight. They're so beautifully done, so like the eyes of an owl. Darwin realized that when the butterfly flashes its eyespots, the poor little sparrow that's about to eat this butterfly thinks it's a fucking owl, wets itself, and falls off the branch. That's the tiny difference in the explanation.

How about Conrad? Do you see your trips as inspired by Conrad?

Yeah, but I didn't want to think about or talk about that. Even in Africa, I'm always conscious of Conrad wherever I go. I'm not sure where I read this, maybe it was André Gide, but during the day, the heart of darkness seems to be quite extraordinarily well lit. But my God, those twelve hours of darkness—Conrad is just so right. He's the most wonderful writer—I adore the guy, of course.

But it's not just these small books like *Heart of Darkness* that grow in the memory. Like Hardy, you mustn't read Hardy twice, just let him rest in the memory and the scenes grow. Whereas a great, great novel like Tolstoy, you've got to re-read it because everything shrinks; you can't remember such detail. But the kind of subconscious, primitive myth quality in Hardy which is under all the crap if you read it closely, my God it grows.

Conrad, wonderful writing and amazingly powerful myth, and the really weird thing is, I promise you actually, *Heart of Darkness* must be as long as *War and Peace*—it's just an essay, but God it grows. It's marvelous, wonderful.

When you're in Africa, you say the white man's time is the day, but the night…

…belongs to Africa. It's awfully difficult after six months not to think that they may be right about the spirit world. I mean I know perfectly well that they're not, but it's the dream, it's the subconscious that plugs into the brain. It's the way the brain works and organizes itself. And also just to put that in context, there are more sorcerers, more astrologers in France than there are priests. They're both absurd, but Jesus Christ. Then you've got to think of Nancy Reagan (who relied on astrologers for advice), and there is a deep connection with Africa in all of us. Which makes sense because we've just moved a few miles north, all of us, all the people of Europe, and that includes America.

Whereas in South America, the Yanomami, they just look through you; they feel so utterly different. They only got there perhaps thirty or forty thousand years ago. They'd come up from Africa along the coast right through unbelievably different geographic pressures, right down to North America into the South. They even look different—they've had all their European/African diseases bleached out of them. No wonder they feel different.

Whereas there's absolutely no theological gap in understanding when you go to Africa—you fucking know. I'm glad I went there last, as it were. It's immediately familiar. You could say that's just because I've read a lot of African ethnography, but you know what this great drumming is about. It makes all that tradition seem like a vicarage tea party. They're eight-foot tall, these drums, with these huge guys playing them on a platform. And the earth moves. And as for going ashore for a howl and a dance, Conrad got that wrong because it's an understatement—it's just wildly exciting. You understand exactly what's going on, even with a protective animal, like *samale*; it's all part of our dreams. It sounds ridiculous but I'm sure it's simply because the geographical distance, therefore the natural selection distance, the pressures, fuck all, skin color is twenty or thirty genes in as we now know 30,000; most think it's 100,000.

I defy anybody to go to Africa and not know what's going on, but also to be terrified, because you know perfectly well you could be hacked to bits by a machete for the very best of reasons. And as it was happening, they'd be laughing because you're going to the next world and they're going to see you again, and everything will be fine. You'll have a party. It's just here you're not wanted anymore. It's scary as shit (laughs).

Whereas in South America, these guys have only got there twenty or thirty thousand years ago. In terms of nature and the forest, these guys are fantastically advanced and complicated. Their cosmology is very like Christianity. It's full of bullshit. It's not good and rational like Judaism. It has a three-tier universe: Heaven, limbo, hell. In hell, there are people there who, all they do is wait for souls to fall down, who have been condemned by the shaman. It's universal.

What's the most profound insight or discovery you've made by trekking among indigenous peoples?

Very profound, because it's perfectly obvious that we're all exactly the same race, let alone the same species. As hunter-gatherers, sure they've been heavily selected, but they come up to you with their bright eyes and their wonderful, intelligent-looking faces and you think, This guy got a first at Oxford. And then I come back, and you actually do, as Lary said, want to get down and kiss the tarmac at Heathrow. And then you come back to Oxford, it is a celestial city, it's as near as we'll ever get to paradise, a university town.

It's just extraordinary: all this evolution, all this social work, all this quiet effort by intellectuals, it shouldn't exist at all, by the way. There is this place and you walk around and you think, My God, it's so impressive all these buildings, but the real feeling that's very, very disturbing, is you think this is so advanced, so fragile, so extraordinary, it could be swept away tomorrow. That's religion to me.

You just think it could all be swept away, and it's so precious, and the West seems so tiny, I'm afraid to say, in terms of population of the world. Jesus, I feel so privileged, such honor, so lucky to have been born in this particular part of the world. It was all given to me on a plate—all I had to do was work at school. Ridiculous, ridiculous.

Then you think after about a month or so, it goes, you forget all that, but luckily that feeling really has lasted. Imagine, everybody in the south, all the millions, somehow we have to give them universities, God knows how, but what else is there to hope for? Manou was saying to me [in *Congo Journey*], I just want a book. So I said, "Well, what book?" He said, "I saw one in the market last year."

At Home
with the
Spirits

Isabel Allende
San Rafael, California

L IKE THOUSANDS OF OTHERS, ISABEL ALLENDE LOST A LOVED ONE
in the September 11th attacks. Her father's cousin, Salvador,
was in one of the buildings shattered by terrorism that
Tuesday morning. Beyond the loss of her beloved "uncle," Allende says
she lost her innocence on that fateful day, and she has viewed the
world in an entirely different light ever since.

The year was not 2001—it was 1973. On September 11th of that
year, Salvador Allende, a democratically-elected socialist, was president of Chile. He died in a CIA-backed coup, which placed General
Augusto Pinochet in control of the country, a sixteen-year dictatorship
that led to the disappearance, torture, and murder of thousands of
Chileans, and the exile of many thousands more.

One of those exiles was Isabel Allende, who fled with her family to
Venezuela. Though born in Peru in 1942, Allende's family had been
prominent in Chile for generations. When she was three, her family

moved back into her grandparents' home in Santiago, the setting for Allende's breathtakingly successful first novel, *The House of the Spirits*.

That novel began as a letter to her grandfather, one of the central figures of her early years. She kept writing after her grandfather died and when she finished, she gave the manuscript to her mother. Though horrified about revealing the family's secrets, her mother encouraged Allende to publish the novel, which has sold in the millions and has been translated into dozens of languages. Allende's success continued with such novels as *Of Love and Shadows* and *Eva Luna*.

In 1987, while on a book tour of the United States, Allende met William Gordon, a San Francisco attorney. She thought she'd have a passionate affair with him for a week, but that week has stretched into sixteen years and counting. Willie, whose life was the basis for Allende's novel *The Infinite Plan*, now lives with Isabel in a tasteful home on a hilltop in Marin County, overlooking San Francisco Bay. Next to the main house is a cottage where Allende creates her wondrous works.

Naturally, the question arises: Why include Allende, a renowned novelist, in a book about the world's leading travel writers? First, she has been a traveler all her life, though often by not by choice. "I travel in spite of myself," she told me. "I'm not a good traveler, or a happy one." Second, she's written brilliantly about travels ranging from a trip to the Amazon to her most difficult trip, flying from Spain to California with her comatose daughter. Third, her travels are often the impetus for her novels, providing her with characters and settings. And finally, because, like many authors who travel, she's an outsider, both in the U.S. and now in Chile, and thus has a sharp view of her adopted and ancestral homes.

One of Allende's most recent books, *My Invented Country*, published in 2003, is a wistful look at Chile sparked by a question about nostalgia at a travel writers conference. Held annually at Book Passage, a San Francisco-area bookstore, the conference has been graced by Allende, who engages audiences with her insights into travel and writing. She also brings humor to her talks: Relating an anecdote about a dentist who said he'd like to be a novelist when he retires, Allende shot back, "And when I retire, I'm going to do root canal!" Next came her jaw-dropping advice to the 100 aspiring travel writers in the audience:

"Write stories that no one can check," she said with a smile. "Just make it up. If you go to Morocco and nothing happens, that's not a story. But if you're kidnapped…"

In her book, *Paula*, about the loss of her daughter to a rare disease, Allende says that whenever she was having a difficult time in a relationship, Paula would ask her, "What's the most generous thing you can do?" Since then, being generous has been Allende's guiding principle, and I've had the good fortune to witness that. During the Book Passage conference, the bookstore's café was short-staffed so Allende volunteered to serve espresso and cappuccino. Later during the four-day conference she invited the thirty or so faculty members to her home for a sumptuous dinner. I complimented her on the *empanadas* and she told me she had made them herself. As I was leaving she rushed towards me with a bag, saying, "You must take these home," and for the next few days I savored Isabel's cooking, reliving the enchantment of that magical evening.

For the interview, I met Allende at her home on a brisk November morning. The sand-colored house, built just a few years ago, was blasted with treatments to make it look like a century-old Chilean home. The wrought-iron balconies around the windows lend it colonial elegance, while the sage and rosemary that border the walkway add a distinctive California touch. Affixed to the house was a thick wooden sign reading, "La Casa de los Espiritos."

The bay glistened in the scattered sunshine and the living room windows offered sweeping views of three Bay Area bridges. Inside her home were museum-quality pieces that Allende has collected during her travels: an alabaster Buddha from Burma, a Tibetan trunk bought in Nepal, a blowgun from the Amazon jungle. "This tribe had been contacted (by outsiders) for the first time just five or six months before we arrived," she said, "and they were already selling their stuff. It was very sad and I feel terrible that I have it, but I'm glad that I have it and not somebody else."

Isabel and I conversed at a sturdy wooden table that once belonged to her grandfather. The table's foundation arabesqued into four gargoyle-like heads that looked like a cross between lions and dogs. "It comes probably from Spain and was in my grandfather's house forever," she said. "It was where my grandmother held her seances, but it was lost for years during the time of exile. Then my mother found it in the house of relatives and sent it to me."

$$\approx \approx \approx$$

I saw the sign on the way in: La Casa de los Espiritos.

That's a sign that my son made and I've had it hanging in my house for more than ten years now. In a way I think it represents not only my first book and the fact that I have made my life in the last twenty-two years writing, but it has a lot to do with how I see my life and my home—it's full of spirits.

Just a moment ago we were talking about the travel in your life and how much of it has not been of your own volition. You've been a refugee—you're now an immigrant here—and I wonder if you might say something about how those travels, whether voluntary or involuntary, shaped your life.

Oh definitely, my life has been shaped not only by the places I have been but by the fact that I have had to carry my roots with me. It's different from the experience of travelers who go to places and come back. In my case I have been propelled to different places without much choice. As a child, as the daughter of diplomats, I would have to follow my stepfather wherever he went, places that they could not place on the map often and that forced me to learn new languages and make new friends, start a new life. Then after a year or two, we would be uprooted again and we would go to another place.

And every so often, we would go back to Chile, every three or four or five years, and find that we didn't belong there at all. We spoke with an accent. The other kids had grown and things had happened in their lives that we didn't share, so we were always the new kids in the neighborhood, even in Chile. So finally when I went to Chile, I decided I was never going to leave again and then I married. I became a journalist, and I was a very happy one for a while until we had the military coup in Chile. I was again forced to leave. And there wasn't much choice of where you could go because at the time I left Chile, Chilean refugees were not accepted in many places, especially in Latin America.

Latin America in 1975 was living under a wave of right-wing military dictatorships. There were masses of refugees moving all over the continent. Chileans, Argentinians, and Uruguayans were less welcome because they were middle-class and usually educated and would take jobs from people in other places. We were not welcome.

So my life has been about those unwanted trips. I married my first husband, and now my second husband, who both love to travel. So I have had to travel with them for pleasure, supposedly for pleasure. And I go places and I don't want to go. I want room service—I don't want to be on a boat in the Amazon. I don't want to be walking in India in the market and it's terribly hot and there are flies all over and people look threatening—I don't want to be there.

And yet when I come back, that is what really shapes the writing later. I say I am never going to write about this place because I don't understand it and I have nothing in common with it. And then suddenly, years later, I find myself writing a story that is either placed there or inspired by the place.

As somebody who has been on the move so much, do you feel you have roots in a certain place or do you keep them inside?

I don't know. To be quite honest, I think that I have planted my roots in my family and in my writing. Therefore, I can move to another place and start anew if I have those people I love with me. But you know I've lived in the United States for sixteen years and I'm beginning to feel comfortable here, which is not good (laughs).

I must make clear that I do not belong to that weird group of people who travel to remote places, survive the bacteria, and then publish books to convince the incautious to follow in their footsteps. Traveling demands a disproportionate effort, especially when it's to places where there is no room service. My ideal vacation consists of sitting in a chair beneath an umbrella on my patio, reading books of adventures I would never consider attempting unless I was escaping from something.

—Isabel Allende,
My Invented Country

Not good for a writer or for your sanity?

For everything—it's not good because I don't like the way the United States is going. I am a dissident. To feel comfortable in a place where I don't like what's happening...

Politically?

Politically, but not only politically, culturally, too—the fascination with violence shocks me, the vulgarity, how everything is geared to the intellectual level of a thirteen-year-old uneducated kid. So all that shocks me. But at the same time I'm very comfortable here, and there are things in this country that I like. I feel I can work with those things to make changes in my life, and maybe in the world. Which is a very arrogant attitude. On the other hand, as a writer it's good not to be comfortable, you know that. When you are too comfortable, what are you going to write about?

And also when I think of my life, I think that one of the good things I have learned is to be detached. If tomorrow my house burns, I would be sorry but I would not be devastated because I'm not attached to anything in here. I would try to save from the fire my mother's letters or the photographs from the past, but maybe I wouldn't, because in a way I can always write about it. I carry it inside in ways that are wonderful.

That's interesting. When I spoke to Pico Iyer, we started our conversation by talking about his family's house burning down in a forest fire and that a Buddhist symbol of freedom is the burning house. He lost everything, he lost manuscripts. He spoke to his editor and his editor said, "Great, now write what you want."

I have had that feeling, too, of things lost in the traveling, lost in exile, lost in having to run away. You leave everything behind, always with the idea that you'll come back and that you'll find everything untouched, and it never happens. So then you come back and it's not there—you don't even remember what you left behind. So that is how little importance it really has.

You've written that your earliest travels were with your grandfather around Chile—that seemed to be something you really enjoyed. Some of your later trips, for example to Lebanon, seemed very isolating. Was your first sense of travel exciting and exhilarating or was it, "Oh, I'm getting dragged all over the place."

First of all, I was born in Peru, and we traveled back to Chile when I was around three. I was totally uprooted from whatever I had known and dumped in my grandfather's house, which very soon became a house in mourning because my grandmother died.

How old were you when you're grandmother died?

Around five. The house was devastated by…first of all it was a house of males. There was no sense of having a comfortable and nice home. But I had a very complicated relationship with my grandfather. My grandfather would have loved to have had a grandson instead of me. And then he had two grandsons, but I was the oldest. I was probably smarter than my two brothers at the time because my grandfather eventually came around to consider me someone he could talk to. I learned to read very, very early and when my grandfather would see me reading the newspaper at a very early age, he started talking to me.

Those trips with my grandfather were not only trips into nature—you can't imagine what the south of Chile looks like, and how it looked then. We would go by train all the way south and we would take a car, and then we would take horses and mules across the Andes. We would go to Patagonia in Argentina and then there were 600 kilometers in a car to get to the haciendas where the sheep were.

So the distances, the beauty, the variety of the landscape, the people, the extraordinary people that lived isolated, those Indians—it was such a fascinating thing. But what made it most fascinating for me was the fact that I had been selected by my grandfather in this silent trip. Because we didn't talk, it wasn't about talking or my grandfather saying, "Look at the mountains." He would just sit on his mule and I would sit on another mule and we would just go. And then I would hear the stories of the men in the evening when they would light a fire and cook a lamb, and pass around some liquor and some *maté*. They would talk and I would listen quietly to the stories without interrupting.

My childhood at the time with my grandfather was about silence, a very introverted experience, and the extraordinary impression of the world around, with this man who projected total safety. He was a patriarch, respected. To me, huge.

In My Invented Country *there's a quote that makes me wonder if the best travel writing comes from the story, which might not be totally bonded to the facts. You write, "If I had never traveled, if I had stayed on, safe and secure in the bosom of my family, if I had accepted my grandfather's vision and his rules, it would have been impossible for me to recreate or embellish my own existence because it would have been defined by others and I would merely be one link more in a long family chain. Moving about has forced me, time after time, to readjust my story, and I have done that in a daze, almost without noticing, because I have been too preoccupied with the task of surviving." So is your individuality and the person you've become in large part due to this life of travel?*

I compare myself with most women my age and the men my age that never traveled or traveled very little and stayed in Chile. And we are different—there's no doubt that I have had to tell my story and they haven't, because they have witnesses all over.

Their community?

Yes, they belong in a place where their lives have been witnessed for sixty years by their community, by their family and friends and by acquaintances, and by a country that in one way or another has grown up with them and developed with them in the same direction. That has not been my case because in every place I go, I have to tell my story.

When I met Willie for the first time he told me his life and I told him mine, but I didn't tell him the truth. Basically the facts were true, but I invented a character, a person that I wanted him to like. And in time, of course, that doesn't work and he finds out who I really am.

But every time when you tell your story you change it: you add adjectives, you add color, you end up forgetting all the grays in between and you only remember the highlights and the darklights. People who don't tell their stories, who don't have to reinvent themselves, have, I'm sure, a different memory of their lives than a person who only has to grab the big moments, good or bad. Those are the ones you tell. Those are the ones that end up defining you.

So I think that for a traveler, a person who spends a month in a place, what does that person bring back? The person doesn't bring back the month; the person brings back the big strokes, the brilliant colors, the intense experiences, and in a week you have forgotten how uncomfortable you were and the mosquitoes. You only remember those things that eventually you might write about, and I think that's what happens with my life.

I think that's how everybody remembers—it's selective—there's no way you can remember everything so you remember what makes the deepest impression on you.

But in my case I remember what makes a good story, not necessarily what makes the biggest impression, but what makes the best story.

Whether you're writing travel stories or novels, one of your many strengths is creating a sense of place. I wonder what you think is most important to create that sense of place. When we read your books, we know where you are—we feel it. What are your keys for doing that?

I would say that most important is to describe it with the senses. So I describe the smell, the color, the temperature, the texture, how you feel time, because time varies in every place. If I'm writing a novel, I try to understand the history of the place because the history determines much of the character of the people in that place. A country like Armenia, for example, that has suffered so much persecution and violence, and has been invaded, is quite a different place than Switzerland. And when you talk about the senses and know the geography of the place, the topography comes alive because a place of mountains is quite different than a plain.

Often I have written books in which the place is not mentioned and the reader guesses where the place is, like *The House of the Spirits* or *Of Love and Shadows*. It could be any Latin American country, but everyone knows it's Chile. Some people have thought it might be Uruguay, but there's no doubt that it is one of those.

Clearly you've been an outsider for most of your life. When you write about travel or destinations, does that outsider perspective help you see a place with fresh eyes?

I think the thing that being an outsider gives you is that you don't take anything for granted. You start questioning what you would never question if you really belonged. I find myself asking Willie stupid questions about the United States because I didn't grow up here. They say that in order to understand America, you have to spend the first twelve years of your life here, because in those first twelve years you acquire everything that defines this nation. Everything else you add, but that is really essential—and of course I wasn't here then.

So I find myself asking questions because I don't take anything for granted. For example I said, "Willie, why is everybody talking so much about Michael Jackson right now when they just bombed Istanbul and when Bush is in London? I mean, who cares?" And Willie says, "You don't understand—he's a celebrity." I said, "He *was* a celebrity (laughs). He's a freak and he was a celebrity. What's the point?" But Willie says, "You don't understand. In the United States once you are a celebrity, you are a celebrity forever." And that is different from other places in the world, but for him it is just a given. And I need to question it to understand that that's the way it is here.

I always believed I was different; as long as I can remember I have felt like an outcast, as if I didn't really belong to my family, or to my surroundings, or to any group. I suppose that it is from that feeling of loneliness the questions arise that lead one to write, and that books are conceived in the search for answers.

—ISABEL ALLENDE, *Paula*

What happened to you on Tuesday, September 11th?

Which one?

I was going to let you decide.

For me, when I think of September 11th, it's always 1973. It's the day of the military coup in Chile and I think of that because it changed my life in ways that the other September 11th did not.

What happened? I lost my innocence. Until then—I was thirty-one years old—I had been like an eternal teenager. I had a preconception of the world as a place where if you behaved according to certain rules of honor, dignity, and responsibility, and showing up on time and working hard, things would work out for you. Because I was supported by a family, a tribe, a set of rules, and connections that sustained everybody in Chile at the time and probably still does.

But then we had the military coup and everything that I believed was challenged. First of all, the vocabulary: there were words that you could not say anymore. It was forbidden to say the word *compañero*. You could be arrested for that and that had been the word that we had used for three years as a greeting word, instead of saying *amigo*. It was forbidden because it was a leftist word. You could not say the word *democracy*, or the word *people*, without an adjective. You could say for example *conditioned democracy*, or the oxymoron of *totalitarian democracy*. You couldn't say *people* because *people* was a word that was linked to the guerrillas and the leftist movement.

The vocabulary changed, the way you related to people changed. Everybody felt that anybody else could be a hidden enemy, even in your family. You didn't trust anybody anymore. Violence became institutionalized. Before, in Chile, you could be afraid that you would be mugged, but we were never afraid that the police, without uniforms, could break into your house, arrest you, and your family would never see you again, that your children would be tortured in front of you, that at night during the curfew if you heard a car you prayed that the car wouldn't stop in front of your house.

That state of mind was so sudden and so brutal and so profoundly intense that it changed my character, my life. My youth, not my youth, but my innocence just ended and I started realizing that the world is a very nasty place and that I had to be aware of it and be cautious and be alert and protect my family, do anything to protect my family.

How did you feel about the U.S. then and how do you feel about it now that you're a resident?

I felt very angry then because the United States was involved, as it has been for a very long time, in supporting dictatorships, tyrants all over the world, especially in Latin America. Kissinger's policy toward Latin

America was to support dictatorships because he had the idea that it was much easier to have a relationship with a corrupt government where there is no public opinion, no free press, no parliament, and you can just deal with it by bribing a few military men and the government. That is not always possible in a democracy. It didn't work.

Also, it was the time of the Cold War when they thought that strong military governments could eliminate any possibility of communism in Latin America, which happened. That was successful—they destroyed all leftist movements, and there was a generation that was wiped out, an incredible number of people who died or were expelled from their countries. So I was very angry because the United States represented for me everything that was wrong with politics.

Then I went to Venezuela—there were many years in between—and when I ended up coming to the United States, I came on a book tour. I was not planning to stay here. And then I met Willie and I came to be with Willie for a week, and then and I stayed for two weeks, and then I stayed for sixteen years. Things changed.

I have traveled all over the United States—I've been in Alaska and the Midwest. I've been in the north and south and everywhere. I see that there are many nations within this nation. I see that there is a vast number of dissidents. There is also a vast, silent, fascist minority that is really scary. And it's always there, lurking in the shadows. There is fundamentalism. The same people who were burning blacks in the South and burning crosses could do it again if given the chance. They would have women in *burkas* if they could, because the fundamentalist Christians aren't at all different from the fundamentalist Jews or the fundamentalist Muslims. They all come from the same place, from the place of knowing the truth and having a direct line with God.

It's a very anti-intellectual approach.

They don't want women to know anything; they don't want people to be educated because reading books is dangerous. And this is a country that reads very little. The average American reads one book a year and that includes the telephone book (laughs). It's pathetic.

And yet there is this incredible young energy in this country; this arrogant, almost childish energy that makes Americans believe that they can do anything. They can open a canal in Panama—they can go

to the moon. They can transform the Muslim world into a democratic America that buys McDonald's. That's the mentality, and in spurts
they achieve lots of stuff—they have a great capacity to penetrate and
change the rest of the world. And that's why for me it is so fascinating
as a foreigner to live here, because I see the possibilities.

If I tried to make a change, impose an idea of any kind in Chile, it
stays in my backyard, it doesn't go anywhere. If you make the change
in the United States and you start influencing people, you change the
world. A mother who decided that drunk people should not drive has
created a movement that has changed laws in the United States and
eventually will change laws in the world.

So that's what you can do from this country. You can do a lot of
good and you can do terrible things, and we do terrible things. When
I watch a movie and I see that everything we export is violent and vulgar, I'm devastated. Because I know that with the same technology and
the same means, the same resources and the same people, we can
export something that would change the way people relate to one
another. And that is possible. So I feel that there is an empowerment
just by being here.

*When I traveled in Chile, I was struck by how much it felt like California,
the length of the country, the ocean, the coast, the mountains…*

The vegetation is similar.

I wonder if this, California, is your inverted country?

I didn't think that way for a long time, but one day I went on a long
book tour to Europe with Willie. We were coming back and the plane
was landing in San Francisco and I said, "Whew, finally home." I hadn't
said that, I don't know, ever. I don't think I ever said it in Chile either,
and I realized that it was more than that we were finally ending that
tour and coming back to our house. It was about the landscape—it was
about something very familiar that I feel in California. But the lifestyle
is different. When I go back to Chile, I'm shocked at how traditional
and conservative and Catholic and backward it is, because I live in San
Francisco.

And so when we are discussing gay marriage, in Chile people don't talk about gays—it's shocking. We are talking about abortion today because they are chipping away at the rights of women. In Chile we are not beginning to have anything to chip off—it's just not discussed.

Is abortion legal?

No, it's not legal—it's done everywhere, but it is not legal. And it's not discussed openly, and no one is going to legislate about that for a long time. This is a country that has no divorce—they are legislating about divorce at this point. So can you imagine gay marriage or abortion.

In terms of all your writing, all your work, what do you feel is most significant, either for your readers or for you?

I don't know for my readers because I think that people read differently, and sometimes the translation will make all the difference. But for me the most important book was *Paula*, because it forced me to go inside. I'm a very out-there person—I'm into the story. The whole experience of the death of my daughter and writing a book forced me to go on a journey into the past, and into myself which in a way was a threshold for me. I left behind my youth with that experience. That was the year that I turned fifty. It was more than just the hormonal thing and the fact that at fifty you're not young anymore. It was much more than that. It was like throwing everything overboard in very deep ways. In that sense, the book helped me very much.

I remember reading Paula *thinking that writing about your daughter and dredging up all your memories, it was keeping her alive in a way. You wrote that after your daughter had died you went to Nepal and India, and that seemed to open you up and perhaps bring you back to life.*

It opened me in many ways because it took me out of my comfort zone. I was comfortable in the mourning, in the sadness, in the loss. It wasn't nice, but it was comfortable because I got used to it. And then that trip sort of threw me in the middle of the crowd. First, your personal space disappears and you're always touching somebody. You're shoulder to shoulder in a crowd that is almost always poor. You don't understand what they speak; you don't want to eat what they eat; you don't understand the rules. You feel a little threatened, but then you realize after a while that there's nothing threatening. These are peaceful people—they're not going to do you any harm, ever. But it takes a while to adjust to that.

There is no space between the notes. Music is about silence also. Life is about pause. In India, in the cities, everything happens in an intense way and there is no respite: the noise, the crowd, the things that happen, the images, the color, the textures. One pattern on top of another pattern on top of another one. So there's never a blank space. That was a shock, a wonderful shock, because it made me feel like a fly, totally unimportant, totally…who cares if your daughter died? You think that my daughter didn't? Who cares if you're in pain—do you think that we are not in pain? Life is pain. Life is about loss, life is about decadence, and this rotten cow in the middle of the street and the vultures eating the cow, that's what life is about. And get up, come on, get a life. But that was wonderful, the shock of that.

And I think I learned forever that lesson. I also got in touch with Buddhism. I'm not a Buddhist, but I love many things about Buddhism. And one of them is the detachment, the fact that life is change. You can't cling to anything, to people, to memories, to anything. Everything changes. Everything is transient, just pass, pass, fly, let it go, let it go. Ah, that was wonderful.

Let's say, hypothetically, your grandson came up to you and said, "Grandma, you have a good long time to live, you have three more years." Would you spend them here or are there any places you'd like to go see?

(Laughs.) Look Michael, if I thought I had three more years to live, I would give away everything; then I would leave enough money for my children and grandchildren to have a good life. I would take them all to Africa to see the animals and see the people in Africa. And then I would live for the last few months in a cell, in a cell with a view if possible, a cabin or someplace where I am alone and where I can really go inside. I think that what happens with aging is that we start closing down. We hear less, we see less, we can't smell, and we can't remember. We are tired, we have pains and ailments. We start staying more and more at home, and then more and more in our room, and then we end up in our bed, and then we die.

And that's the natural process. If it were speeded up in some way for me, and I had three years, I would try to give myself the time to go through that process of shutting down. The place I would like to go right now would be Africa. It's a place of violence and death and beauty, and everything comes from Africa.

I just wrote a book that is placed in Africa, in equatorial Africa. It's the last volume of a trilogy for kids. The first one is placed in the Amazon, the second one in the Himalayas (and that comes from the trip to India, Nepal, and Tibet), and the third one is in Africa. I didn't go to Africa, to that part of Africa, so I researched a lot and I saw innumerable films and photographs, and I'm in love with the idea. I hope I won't be too disappointed when I get there, but I'm in love with the idea of Africa.

It seems a very happy place despite all the sorrow.

Have you read those books, *The No. 1 Ladies' Detective Agency*? They're placed in Botswana—they're written by a British guy, Alexander McCall Smith. He lived in Africa and was born in Botswana and there is such delicacy in those books. They give you the spirit of the people, how polite the relationships are, and how they can hack your head off. All that is in those little books.

Are you familiar at all with Malidoma Somé? He's from the country that used to be called Upper Volta, now Burkina Faso. When he was a young boy, maybe four or five years old, he was captured by missionaries and taken to a Jesuit school and educated in the Western ways. He finally escaped when he was twenty and returned to his people, but he was a foreigner in his own tribe. And then he came to the U.S. and wrote a book, Of Water and Spirit, *about what it's like to be from two worlds. He talks about flying back to Africa and how he crossed the ocean and got there in a few hours. He told his community that he was very tired from it. The elders said, "Of course you're tired; your soul hasn't caught up with you yet."*

(Laughs.) That's jet lag.

In your talks you mention nostalgia as an influence. How does nostalgia affect how you approach the world or your writing?

I think that nostalgia is a sort of bittersweet sentiment that forces you to reinvent the past in better terms most of the time. It's deceptive—nostalgia is very deceptive because you end up thinking that things were in a way that they never were. I have a very nostalgic feeling for my grandfather. I have totally invented my grandmother. I am sure that she could not have been the way I think she was. But my grandfather I knew very well because I lived with him many, many years. And then I visited him every single day of my life until I left Chile in 1975. So every day I would sit with him in silence, or talk with him and he would tell me things. And I have a very nostalgic feeling for what he represented. And he represented a world of clear rules, a world where things were a certain way and they were not questioned.

It was all about dignity—and respect. It was very much like the Mafia, you know (laughs). It's like *The Godfather*. There was something about things a man does, and things a woman does, how you never whine, you never complain—you take whatever comes and you confront it. And you have the certainty that you will be on your knees a thousand times and you will always get up, and there is no whining. I have a longing for that because I live in this culture where I see my grandchildren whining, and it makes me crazy (laughs). I see them pampered, and I see that people have time at eleven o'clock in the morning to be having coffee and biking in Marin County. These are young men, and I ask Willie: "They don't work?" Willie says, "They're all therapists." (Laughs.)

So I have a longing for that sort of rough world that was primitive and must have been awful. I know I could not possibly live there anymore. I questioned it then and I would question it again. It's this nostalgic thing that makes you crave something that wasn't even good. That's why I say it's deceptive.

With time and distance the elements that are appealing come out...

Yes...

But that's authoritarianism.

Of course, and patriarchy and classism and racism and male chauvinism. And I fought all that desperately—I had terrible fights with my grandfather. I don't remember the fights, I remember what he represented. I can't say what it is, but it was very much about honor and that you wouldn't be caught dead lying, because lying was cowardice. All those things that don't exist anymore and maybe it's good that they don't.

I think like everything it's a mixed bag; there was an integrity in that and an honesty and a strength, but the shadow side of that was everything you just said.

For example, my grandfather was a patriarch in the old nineteenth-century style, so he was the head of the family. His authority was never questioned, his desires were orders, and he protected everybody around him, fed everybody around him. But he would be extremely gentle and polite with women because women were weak creatures that needed to be protected by the males. So the fact that his granddaughter would stand up to him and defy his authority...I would ask why can my brothers go out at night and I can't? Why can my brothers have sex with the maids and I can't have sex with the gardener? (Laughs heartily.) I was fifteen, so my grandfather just flipped out. He couldn't take it. So there was, as you say, the shadow which was also part of it.

It seems clear that you've lived in interesting times. I think it's a Chinese curse, actually, when somebody says, "May you live in interesting times." Do you ever long for less interesting times?

No, no, no, no, not at all. There's not one thing—except of course the loss of my daughter; no, not even the loss of my daughter—for which I would rather not have been present. I'm happy that I was present in the military coup, that I was present in the terror that came afterward, that I lived the exile, and that I was present when my daughter was sick and when she died. Nobody told me about it; I was there. I would not like to have missed any of the pain or the losses because I like interesting times very much, and I hope that the rest of my life will be interesting, too. I don't want a happy, comfortable life.

I have a character in one of my books, I don't even remember which one, either *Portrait in Sepia* or *Daughter of Fortune,* in which someone says, "I want you to be happy," and the person snaps back

"That's the last thing I want!" The last adjective I would use for my life is happy. I want an interesting life, I want a passionate life, I want other things, but not a happy life. I'm not against happiness. I love that things are working well for me right now. But I'm not afraid of the fact that my life is all about ups and downs. I know that right now it's a great time and it won't be great in a year.

Does that help you enjoy it even more?

Oh, of course, of course. Every hour I spend in my little *casita* writing, I realize that I have this incredible freedom to write about what I want. I have no pressure—no one is knocking at my door asking for a manuscript. No one is telling me what to do. I do it on my own terms and then at seven o'clock Willie calls me and says dinner is ready. And he has a glass of wine and we are going to eat alone, and there's music and the bay, and the full moon. And I say, Wow, what a privilege—it can't last because it's not fair.

A Hop
Across the
Pond

Bill Bryson
HANOVER, NEW HAMPSHIRE

A COLLEAGUE WHO EDITS HUMOR BOOKS FOR TRAVELERS' TALES HAS a system for deciding whether a story is funny. She reads it aloud and writes "LOL" next to every passage that makes her laugh out loud and puts a smiley face next to every phrase that makes her grin. Apply this technique to Bill Bryson's books, and the pages would be so full of LOLs and smileys they'd be hard to read.

Yet Bryson does much more than make readers laugh. The Iowa native has a knack for imparting knowledge without lecturing. Reading one of his books feels like visiting with an old friend who spins the most amazing tales: you laugh, you learn, you long for more. Whether he's in an upscale restaurant musing about ordering "a crepe *galette* of sea chortle and kelp in a rich *mal de mer* sauce" or wondering how the prime minister of Australia could go for a swim and just disappear, Bryson's books are engaging and hilarious—especially when read aloud.

Bryson has a political side as well. In *I'm a Stranger Here Myself*, a collection of columns written for a British newspaper, he says "the more recklessly we use up natural resources, the more GDP grows." Yet even when pointing out a country's flaws, Bryson is congenial. Whether that's his American optimism or the politeness endemic to his adopted home, Great Britain, seems a moot point.

As a young man, Bryson traveled to England, fell in love, and spent a couple of decades in the Yorkshire Dales. His wife, Cynthia, and four children are British subjects, and today even Bill has a touch of a British accent. The family moved to the U.S. in the mid-1990s when Bryson was a literary light in Britain but not as well known in his home country.

That all changed in 1998 with the publication of *A Walk in the Woods*, which rocketed Bryson into the hearts and minds of American readers. Two years later he followed up with another hugely successful and entertaining book, *In a Sunburned Country*, a stylishly quirky book about Australia released just before the 2000 Olympics were held in Sydney. In 2003, Bryson published *A Short History of Nearly Everything*, in which he explores the scientific mysteries of the universe in his typically accessible prose. The book hovered near the top of bestseller lists for months, on both sides of the pond. He has also written several books about the English language, including *The Mother Tongue* and *Made in America*.

I traveled to Hanover, New Hampshire, on a snowy April morning and met Bryson a block from Dartmouth College, at a convivial café called Lou's. It was too loud to tape an interview there, so we walked through six inches of powder to Murphy's on the Green, an Irish pub that hadn't yet opened for the day. Bryson is a friend of the owner, who brought us coffee. Next to our table I noticed a small brass plaque reading "BRYSON'S BOOTH—Dedicated 5/5/99." I noticed that the date, with month and day the same digit, would be written identically in England (where the day precedes the month) and in the U.S. So it seemed appropriate that I was interviewing Bryson on April 4, which also would be written 4/4 in both countries.

I'd heard from several colleagues that Bryson is astonishingly gracious, but I didn't realize how generous until he told me he'd returned from a weeklong trip the previous day and was leaving the following day to find a house for his family in England. Eight years after moving to the U.S., the Brysons had decided to hop back across the pond.

After patiently fielding questions for an hour and a half, Bryson stood in the snow in front of the Dartmouth Green so I could take his picture. As he bade me a warm farewell, he invited me to visit him in England once he got settled. A few months after Bryson, his wife, and their four children returned to England, settling near Norwich (about a hundred miles northeast of London), I spoke to him by phone. He was happy to have his family back in England and said he'd just returned from the Yorkshire Dales where he'd seen old friends. He told *The New York Times* that returning to America was like "moving back in with your parents in middle age" and that he felt he had "stopped being distinctive" in the U.S.

As he turned towards home that day in New Hampshire, I stood there in the snow, gazing at the steeple across the green and said, out loud, "Wow, what a nice guy."

≈≈≈

I'd like to start with why you decided to move back to England.

Well, we find ourselves in this position that's both delightful and slightly discouraging because we're attached to two different countries. We moved to Hanover originally with the idea of staying five years—we thought it would be a good thing for the kids to divide their childhoods between two countries. I've always felt very lucky to have had that chance and thought how much better it would be to give that to children at a younger age. We never came here with the intention of it becoming permanent.

It's now been eight years because we've been so happy here, but ultimately, and this is something you'll understand today, it's the weather that's driving me away. My wife is homesick; I miss a lot of things about Britain that I really liked, but the decisive factor is the weather: the New England winters are too long. It's very pretty—I enjoy it, but I work at home and I'm cooped up. I go all day without breathing fresh air and it gets to be three o'clock in the afternoon and I really want to go out and do something.

On a day like this you're extremely circumscribed in what you can do. You can go for a kind of walk but it's not much fun. I tend to take along work and read it as I'm walking along, but I can't read while I'm walking through snow. And also you freeze—you don't want to go too far and get wet and cold and find yourself three miles from home. In Britain the one great virtue is that the weather is very mild. Even though it's not terribly sunny you can pretty much go outside any day of the year.

So will you be moving to a place where Cynthia can get her pizzas delivered?

(Laughs.) We're sort of sated on all that type of American stuff—the pendulum is swinging back the other direction. If we never see another Kmart again life will conclude very happily. But eighteen months from now we could be feeling very envious of anyone who has access to a Kmart. We're completely, happily filled up with the American experience at the moment. What we want is a quieter existence.

What part of England do you expect to return to?

We don't know—part of the curse of what I do is that we can live anywhere. I don't have to get to an office every morning so we have greater flexibility about where we go. My thinking is that we would be outside the commuter zone of London. There's no reason for us to pay London prices, but we'll still be in the south of Britain.

I know you had a long career working for newspapers in London. I'm wondering how you got started as a travel writer.

All the time that I worked on newspapers I was always just a copy editor—I never wrote. In 1977, when we first settled permanently in England, I got my first grown-up job working for a paper on the south coast of England. I started writing freelance articles, mostly travel articles for Sunday newspapers about British destinations, simply as a way of supplementing my income. It was a way of paying for a washing machine or a stroller for the baby. It was travel not because I was particularly drawn to travel—in fact I couldn't really afford to go anywhere much either in terms of time or expense—but it was easy to write travel pieces for Sunday papers about areas in Britain that I could get to quite easily. The great thing about Sunday papers was you could sell the same article over and over again.

After you got more established how did you pick your destinations or subjects?

In 1987 I realized that being self-employed and writing was what I wanted to do. I had no desire to become a travel writer, in fact it never occurred to me to think of myself as that. When I went freelancing I was putting out and submitting all sorts of ideas to publishers in both Britain and the United States. A British publisher picked up on the idea of me coming back to America and traveling around the country and that became *The Lost Continent*. It didn't occur to me that it was a travel book—it was more of a memoir, about growing up in America and looking at how America had changed and how I had changed in the years since I had moved away. That book didn't sell in large numbers but it got a reasonably encouraging critical response.

Some weeks or months after it had come out, I went to lunch with my publisher and he asked me what I wanted to do next, and I gave him a whole bunch of new ideas, none of which were remotely travel related. He told me, "You have to follow this up," and it was the first indication that I'd become pigeonholed. They want you categorized in the publishing world.

So I thought, the next thing I did in my life after growing up in Des Moines, I came to Europe and hitchhiked around and essentially didn't go home—I stayed on. So the idea was the next book that would become *Neither Here Nor There,* about traveling around Europe. And it's really based on the next phase of my life. That did even better. By the time *Neither Here Nor There* came out, it was pretty well established that the publishing world's expectation of me was that I would write travel books with a humorous bent, even though I was trying very hard to write other types of books as well. I was doing these books on the English language.

It almost seems like writers today are pigeonholed as brands. The Bill Bryson brand is humorous travel and Tim Cahill is adventure...

And it's very, very hard to get out of that. Partly the reason Tim Cahill is adventurous is because he's an adventurous kind of guy. He's more inclined than the rest of us to do adventurous and brave things, partly because he knows he can write it very skillfully, but also because he's drawn to those types of things. He's in his element in those situations. It's sort of the same with me: I have a kind of travel I do which is very limited. I'm a motel traveler. And if you have a really successful book, then you really get pigeonholed because publishers want you to do the exact same book, part two.

Did anyone ask you to go on another hike?

Black bears rarely attack. But here's the thing. Sometimes they do. All bears are agile, cunning, and immensely strong, and they are always hungry. If they want to kill you and eat you, they can, and pretty much whenever they want. That doesn't happen often, but— and here's the absolutely salient point—once would be enough.

—Bill Bryson,
A Walk in the Woods

After *A Walk in the Woods*, I said to a publisher in New York that the next thing I'd like to do is a book on Australia and they were sort of in dismay. They wanted me to go out and do the Pacific Crest Trail, to do another long-distance trail with Stephen Katz.

Other authors come under the same kind of pressure. That's why you get *A Year in Provence* and then *Toujours Provence* (laughs). I don't think it's a very wise thing to do, but you can certainly understand why it happens. Publishers will waft a great deal of money in front of you if they think you can cash in on the fol-

low-up. And there is this sort of ready-made market—it is an amazing thing that readers do want the same book again when they like something. There is a kind of comfort factor.

I get clobbered a lot, in Britain in particular, and increasingly accused…they'll say this book is funny in parts but a lot of it is really boring—you know, there's too much serious stuff. Some people just want jokes. They want me to be Dave Barry and not be serious about anything. As a reader if I'm investing money and several hours of time in something, I want to come away with more than just yuks; I'd like to actually learn something. In the U.S. I haven't had that complaint at all—people do expect there to be a serious side of things. In Britain they say, "Bryson's run out of jokes and now he's trying to pad it out."

*When I think of some of the passages in your work that I've most appreci-
ated I think, for example, of your heart-rending description of the chestnut trees in* A Walk in the Woods. *To me the humor has more impact
when it's spread out—it almost pops up at you.*

I agree. It can be a lot more effective because you can sort of surprise
people with it. But also the one thing I've learned is that reading a
book is a stretched-out process—you're not going to do it in one sitting—and so it's a mistake to go at it as though you're doing a stand-
up routine. People just can't handle that many jokes, so I try to be
more selective with humor. When you first start out you have this feeling that you have to provide a joke every paragraph as you would if
you were on stage in front of an audience. But in a book I don't think
you need to.

*Could you discuss how you research a book? Some of the stats you come up
with are amazing, for example, your comments about the U.S. Forest
Service in* A Walk in the Woods.

Overwhelmingly that stuff was learned afterward. I went out and had
the hike and it was while I was out there that I was thinking about
these things. How did these mountains get here and why are they not
craggy? Essentially it was just going and realizing I don't know a thing
in the outdoors and I don't know the names of any of these trees.
There was nothing I could do about it at the time, being out in the
woods. After the trip was over I started going to the library, and in the
course of trying to find out a particular fact your reading becomes
more general. You find, this is all interesting. So in that case I was just
propelled by curiosity.

In other cases like in the book about Australia, I was curious about
Australia from the outset. I was traveling around in different circumstances. I was mostly driving rental cars. I had an empty back seat and
a trunk so I could go into a secondhand bookstore and just load up
with books. I was learning and having the experience at the same time.
One of the things I find most gratifying about what I do is once you
really get into a subject you reach a point where you're almost insatiable in your curiosity. You just want to know more. For a little while
there wasn't a fact about Australia that wasn't of interest to me.

You take the reader on that voyage of discovery. It's like you're talking to a friend and saying, "Did you ever hear about this prime minister who disappeared?"

There's a natural human instinct: Whatever experience you have, as soon as there's something amazing to you, you want to find another human being to share it with. It's nice when somebody like you says you appreciate that—that's just the greatest thing. Those stories that are so interesting you think: Why have I never heard this? How did the prime minister of Australia drown and I don't know anything about it? They lost the body—that's just the most amazing thing. I just love that story.

A question about guidebooks: I remember that line where you referred to a guidebook series as "Let's Go Get Another Guidebook." I notice you don't seem to rely too heavily on guidebooks.

I do use guidebooks to get a general idea about things—they're useful for addresses and hours. But as a traveler, quite separate from writing about places, I love that sense of arriving someplace and you don't know a thing about it and it turns out to be really delightful. Where, if someone says Sausalito is the most charming little spot, you get there and think, Well, I was expecting more than this. But if you just stumble on these places...

If you read the travel books too carefully they are going to rob you of that sense of discovery. But if you don't pay some attention to trav-

[The Forest Service] casually announced that it would allow private timber interests to remove hundreds of acres of wood a year from the venerable and verdant Pisgah National Forest, next door to the Great Smoky Mountains National Park, and that 80 percent of that would be through what it delicately calls "scientific forestry"—clear-cutting to you and me—which is not only a brutal visual affront to any landscape but brings huge, reckless washoffs that gully the soil, robbing it of nutrients and disrupting ecologies farther downstream, sometimes for miles. This isn't science. It's rape.

—BILL BRYSON,
A Walk in the Woods

el books, you could very easily just buzz past, which is something I've done many times, you know, missed the real charming places.

You almost seem like an outsider even here in the U.S. where you were born, and in England, your adopted home. Do you feel the best travel writing comes from that outsider perspective or do you get the good stuff when you're more of an insider and really know a place?

That's a very good question and I suppose the answer is both. If you know the place, you'll understand a huge amount more. I can write with some authority about the United States because I'm intimately acquainted with the education system, history, politics, and all that because I grew up here. Equally, I can claim to write with some authority about Britain—nobody can call me ignorant. On the other hand, I didn't want to spend my whole life writing about Britain and the United States.

So when I go to a place like Australia, I try to make a virtue of knowing nothing about the place. There's a certain value in both of those. Even when you're writing about a place that you know, I think it helps to be an outsider. And I think overwhelmingly travel writers are in that position.

Clearly travel writers are storytellers—where's the line between enhancing a story and straying too far from the facts?

(Laughs.) The problem is sometimes I'm trying to impart information and other times the reader can see that I'm not anywhere near the truth, the literal truth. When I'm being comical I'll take an awful lot of license. I make no secret of it—I think the reader can tell that I'm exaggerating for comic effect. The thing I wouldn't do is pretend to be someplace where I wasn't. All the things I've written are based on reality and things I've actually witnessed. But that may have been only a starting point.

When you say that I think of that scene in Neither Here Nor There *when you're in Yugoslavia and you've rented a room from an elderly woman. Then you go and have a few pints in the local pub and can't find your way back to the room.*

That's a perfect example, Michael, because that's exactly the sort of thing that actually happened. I didn't know where I was and I did take a taxi and I remember him going all over the place and having great trouble finding it. The house was being reconstructed a little bit—an extension was being built—I did have to walk across a plank and it did turn sideways and I did whack myself, so all of those things are real. But then there will also be free exaggeration in terms of how lost we were or how much confusion there was or how much pain I felt. But you do it with the assumption that the reader will realize that this is exaggeration for comic effect. Five pages later I might be telling you about the geologic history of the region and there'd be no reason to exaggerate.

What's it like to return to destinations you visited long ago, for example, returning to places you traveled to fresh out of college?

It's weird in the United States because it's all changed—three years later it's not recognizable. There's a mall there now or some big-box store. It's so hard in the States to find anything the way it used to be. In Europe it's exactly the opposite—you go back and nothing has changed. It's the same café and still the same old waiter.

On an emotional level, people say you can't go home again. Can you go back to your favorite places?

Yeah, I think so. My favorite thing in the world after I've had a great travel experience is to take my wife there. I've experienced that a number of times in Australia—I go back and it's so much more fun when you don't have to write about it. You can't re-create an experience, but you can certainly revisit the site.

In Neither Here Nor There *you say you could spend your entire life waking up in a new city—do you still feel that way, or do you now enjoy being more settled?*

Well, both. There's always been this irreconcilable conflict since I started writing for a living: I have a very happy settled home life, and I love to be at home with my family. My prospect for this evening is a nice dinner and then I'll watch the Red Sox on TV, and I'll be very happy. And I'll feel as if I could do this every night forever.

At the same time I really love to go places and see new things. What does amaze me after all this time is that it hasn't palled as much as I expected it to. Even opening the door to a hotel room, that feeling of anticipation: What's behind this door? I still get that kind of rush. And I certainly feel that if you put me down in a fresh locality or city, particularly if it's an attractive place with a nice climate or good-looking cafés, a nice city to wander round in, San Francisco as opposed to Peoria, I really like that business of setting off and just walking. I'm pretty sure that I'll never tire of that.

What are some of the sites that have moved you?

One that leaps to mind is Mt. Rushmore. I was just knocked out. It was impressive, the scale, you sort of don't know what you're going to really see. You think maybe it will be kind of small and in fact it was really neat. Baseball parks do the same thing to me, every time. That feeling when you emerge at the end of the runway and there's all this green field in front of you. And when they play the "Star Spangled Banner" and sing "Take Me Out to the Ball Game." It always makes the hair go up on my neck. I'm not usually very much amused by these sorts of patriotic gestures. The Grand Canyon is another—you know you've seen it so many times. I saw it when I was a kid, so you know what to expect, but when you get back it's even more fabulous.

Is there anything, apart from a really good chocolate cream pie and receiving a large unexpected check in the mail, to beat finding yourself at large in a foreign city on a fair spring evening, loafing along unfamiliar streets in the long shadows of a lazy sunset, pausing to gaze in shop windows or at some church or lovely square or tranquil stretch of quayside, hesitating at street corners to decide whether that cheerful and homey restaurant you will remember fondly for years is likely to lie down this street or that one? I just love it. I could spend my life arriving each evening in a new city.

—BILL BRYSON,
Neither Here Nor There

*Have you ever had the opportunity to see it from within, on a raft trip
down the Colorado? It's remarkable—you're traversing more than two
hundred miles of canyon. The beauty within goes beyond what you can
see from the rim.*

I'd really, really love to do that because I've only been there twice and
both times have just been looking over the edge. And both times in a
hurry to move on. The first time was a family vacation when I was
young and the second time was when I was doing *The Lost Continent*
and I had to go. I'd love to go back. Zion National Park was another
place that I was really knocked out by and I'd love to go back there and
have a better look. If there's a part of the world that I haven't done justice, it's that little corner.

What strikes you most about a place? The people? Aesthetics?

Aesthetics, I guess. I think what I've always been looking for and what
I set out looking for in the beginning was a place that was better than
Iowa, that wasn't Des Moines. What grabbed me when I was a kid was
looking at pictures in *National Geographic* and thinking these places
look so much more interesting and colorful—they were sort of
drenched in color. A picture I remember perfectly was some kid in
France who was ten about the time I was ten and he had a couple of
baguettes on the back of his bike. And I just wished that my mom sent
me out to get bread that looked like that. What I've been hankering
after is some sort of perfect place. It's become more complicated now,
but I'm still looking for that.

All human beings do essentially the same things everywhere on
the planet. We all eat and drink and procreate and watch a little TV in
the evening. And yet there's such a variety of ways in doing these
things. And I love that.

What do you feel you've accomplished with your books?

I've put the kids through college and paid the mortgage. I started writing as a way of supplementing my income and then eventually started
writing as a way of making my income. All I ever wanted was to be able
to pay the bills through writing. I have no greater wish than that.

Nothing loftier?

No, nothing loftier at all. None of us are judges of our own work, but also it's impossible to judge somebody's work in his own lifetime. In terms of what I've achieved, it's just pay the bills and I'm very pleased I've been able to do that.

Any thoughts on how frequent travel has shaped your outlook as a citizen of the world?

Nothing too profound, but it has made me appreciate that we are all one. When something like the war in Iraq is going on, it does bother me that people can be so blind to the fact that Iraqis are also human. These people we're killing are not characters in some sort of Nintendo game. These are real lives that are being snuffed out—they have as much right to live as we do. An appreciation of that is the one real bonus of having traveled. You realize the world is just full of other human beings who are exactly the same as us. We're not superior, or different, or inferior.

When I see the "God Bless America" bumper stickers I think, Well, why not "God Bless Everyone"?

Yes. I've never been to Iraq but three or four years ago I was in Damascus, Syria, a very beautiful, very historic city which I imagine is very similar to Baghdad. I don't want the people in Damascus to be dead and I don't want their buildings blown up; it's a very beautiful city, and I feel the same about Iraq.

I wonder, if Americans traveled more, if they met people who were living on $2 a day, whether the country might be more compassionate.

Well, I don't know. I don't think travel is the least bit broadening unless you want it to be. I think it's very easy to travel and not become the tiniest bit broadened by it. To me it's a miracle that people could go places and come away and not say this is really beautiful, why don't we try this back home.

Your new book is called A Short History of Nearly Everything—*that sounds ambitious!*

I promised my wife I would take a break from traveling and do something that was based on library research. And also I just wanted a break from traveling myself, and traveling for writing purposes. I've been fascinated for a long time by the whole universe. As far as we know, this is the only place where this kind of thing happens, where atoms come together in animate forms. The one thing we can guarantee is that our entire experience will be on this planet. We will never know another world.

When I started thinking about that it made me blush about how little I knew. If aliens did take me away, I couldn't tell them a single thing about the planet, how it works and operates. So my idea is that I would just try to understand how the Earth works and why I'm here and how we got here and what were the necessary steps that got us from the Big Bang to now. The title of the book was kind of a joke, but it really does feel as if I've done a history of nearly everything. If you were to ask what's in the book I'd say, "Nearly everything."

There's a whole bunch of people who science has missed in school, me most of all. I didn't understand what was remotely interesting about chemistry or physics, but all that stuff is inherently interesting because we're all chemicals. We're all governed by the laws of physics. So that's the idea: to try to understand it and to write about it in a way that people like me might find it interesting.

If you hadn't been a writer, what do you think you'd be doing with your life?

No question, I'd be a copy editor on newspapers, presumably in London. I had a very happy career as a copy editor and enjoyed being an editor. That amazes a lot of people who are writers because they think that editors are somehow people who have failed. I enjoyed the process of editing. I liked sitting around the table with people and having a kind of camaraderie about being in an office. I thrive on routine. Part of me enjoys being at the same place at four o'clock every day. You get all that comfort in newspapers but also the work every day is different, what's happening in the world is different every day. I really enjoyed that.

What impresses me about you is that you did it in England, and British English, as you've written about, is so different from American English.

I had to spend two years working on a small paper and I really applied myself during those two years to understand British politics, British history, and familiarize myself with a lot of aspects of British culture. And on top of all that, usage. But it was interesting and I wanted to do it. It wasn't like a trial or a hardship. Again, because you're living there and it's going to be your life, you are very interested in knowing all these things.

Are you familiar with the show Seinfeld—*I ask because I see some similarities, with the strength being the writing, the humor and punch, but the other thing is that* Seinfeld *had a bit about the show being about nothing. Now I mean this in the most complimentary way: Is there a similar thread in your work?*

I like the business of just going somewhere. The only thing I can do is spy on the world. I sit there and watch what's happening. When I read someone like Paul Theroux, who's very good at bringing people out and getting conversations going, he sits in a railway car with somebody he's never met before and this wonderful stuff comes out, and he gets these great stories. I wish I could do that but I cannot interact with people; it's against my nature, and so what I do is I spy. It means that you pay attention to the little things in life.

Iowa women are almost always sensationally overweight.... I will say this, however—and it's a strange thing—the teenaged daughters of these fat women are always utterly delectable, as soft and gloriously rounded and naturally fresh-smelling as a basket of fruit. I don't know what it is that happens to them, but it must be awful to marry one of those nubile cuties knowing that there is a time bomb ticking away in her that will at some unknown date make her bloat out into something huge and grotesque, presumably all of a sudden and without much notice, like a self-inflating raft from which the pin has been yanked.

—BILL BRYSON,
The Lost Continent

On another subject, I share your passion for baseball, so I have to ask: Why are you a Red Sox fan? As a Midwesterner, why not root for the Cubs?

If you're my generation or older, you were either a St. Louis Cardinals fan or a (Chicago) Cubs fan. It depended a lot on which part of the state your elders grew up in. People from southern Iowa tended to favor the Cardinals. I grew up as a Cardinals fan—it was the great days of the Cardinals with Bob Gibson and Lou Brock—supporting the Cardinals meant you were following a winner.

The Red Sox came later. Once you move to a new region of the country you have this new team imposed on you. You can't live in New England and not be interested in the Red Sox. Also, I'd been disconnected from baseball for twenty years—it's like a second marriage. So it wasn't like I abandoned the Cardinals and ran off with a mistress or something. You know, it's a sickness, you become completely obsessed. Even at the end of the season when they're twelve games out with only eight games left to play, I'm still watching. It doesn't matter whether they win or not, you just hope Trot Nixon gets a hit.

I read the piece you wrote in The New Yorker *(April 9, 2001) about your dad being a sportswriter. I found that really interesting because the portrait you paint of your father in that story was quite different from how you portrayed him in* The Lost Continent.

Well, it was an attempt to make amends. Both of those portraits are absolutely true and both are very much incomplete. My dad was a lot more than those added together. He was a lot more difficult than comes across in either of those. In *The Lost Continent* he was Dagwood Bumstead, the guy who was behind the wheel of the car and was lost. All dads were that man. And he was just sort of this one-dimensional cartoon figure who represented all fathers in the 1950s. And it was entirely accurate—all those places where I said he got lost, he actually did. We spent so much of our vacations driving around the perimeters of things or just seeing where we wanted to go on the other side of a bunch of farm fields. We were always within sight of it but could never quite find the way to the front gate. So all of that was true.

But of course there was a great deal more to it than that. My dad really was a remarkably gifted sportswriter. He could have been nationally recognized and highly respected by his peers if he had worked in a big-league city. And yet he chose to stay in a minor-league city with his kind of talent, so he was always a mystery to me.

Given your love of language I'd like to ask you about some unfathomable English words. Where do we get words like "invaluable" which means more valuable than valuable?

English is peculiarly peculiar in those ways. I don't speak another language so I can't speak with authority, but non-native speakers go on about all these oddities—it does seem bizarre. Part of the reason English is such a great language for humor is there are so many opportunities for puns. Words have so many different meanings and how you arrange them is particularly fruitful in that way.

Do you have any advice for aspiring travel writers? What are the qualities and talents that led to your success?

Luck. Luck is such a crucial factor. I get sent a lot of advance reading copies and books in manuscript form—you read it and think, This is pretty good. Then you never hear of that book again because more than ten thousand books come out every month, so the chances of any one or two or three of those being noticed by the world at large is…that's all that the world is going to notice because most of the books that get attention are by people who are already established. So luck is a huge factor.

But on the other hand I think it's a myth that writing is really, really hard to succeed at because you've got to be more talented than at least some of the people who get books published. So it's not impossible. Travel writing is a particularly good area because there are so many outlets: magazines, Sunday newspapers. I'm not very experienced at this but I imagine it's a lot easier to sell a travel piece about hiking in the White Mountains for the weekend than it would be to sell a short story. So in that sense I think travel writing is a pretty good market. If you're writing fiction you could be really good, and it could take years before you sell a story.

People think there's some trick to getting published, that all publishers just reject everything that comes to them and that there's no way you can break in, as if the people who are published are pre-ordained, that they were given the secret. All writers were once aspiring writers—we were all in exactly that same position and it wasn't some magic trick. All the time I get letters from people asking, what's the secret, like there's some incantation. The secret is you just pound a path to the top of the mountain. You don't just sort of levitate your way up.

Writing is hard work—but it's a myth that earning money and succeeding at writing is hard work. Becoming Stephen King or John Grisham takes a lot of talent and hard work and luck, but just getting stuff published and earning an income, I don't think is that hard for the simple reason that there are so many outlets now. It's not easy, but it's not nearly as impossible as a lot of aspiring writers think. If you apply yourself and become specialized in an area and create a little niche for yourself it's not that hard. It might be hard to make a really good living at it, but it's not that hard to generate some kind of an income.

You recently wrote a small book about Africa, Bill Bryson's African Diary. *What a nice thing for you to donate all the proceeds to CARE.*

Thank you—it was very inspiring. The people there and the CARE staff are so much more heroic than the rest of us could ever be. They face discomfort and danger, the most thankless work in the world. And they do it because they're good people. They work really, really hard for nothing. The Kenyans, I thought, were unusually wonderful people—they just seemed friendly and cheerful, upbeat, indomitable. These are people who've got nothing, really very close to nothing. It was thrilling, moving. The worst part about it is that you come home and feel guilty about everything for several weeks afterwards. You and I can have anything we want—other people have never been as comfortable as we've been in the past hour.

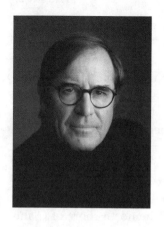

Dark Star Shining

Paul Theroux
O'AHU, HAWAI'I

"WOULD THE REAL PAUL THEROUX PLEASE STAND UP?" I have a vision of the 1960s game show *To Tell the Truth* with Theroux, one of the world's leading travel writers and novelists, as all three contestants. One is holding *My Secret History*, a second cradles *My Other Life,* and the third leans on a stack of his thirteen travel narratives. As hard as they try, the audience, his readers, are never quite sure who is the genuine Theroux.

This much we know: Paul Theroux was born in 1941 in Medford, Massachusetts, into a Catholic family that would grow to seven children. He later became an Eagle Scout and volunteered for the Peace Corps, serving in Malawi as the country gained its independence. After almost two years there, Theroux was dismissed from the Peace Corps in 1965 after allegedly taking part in a coup. When asked about this during a 2004 address in San Francisco, Theroux said he was just taking the mother of Malawi's ambassador—and her dinner service for twelve—to Uganda. On the way back he was asked to deliver some money and a message, which, though he says he didn't know it, was part of a plot to kill Malawi's president.

From 1965 until 1968, Theroux taught at Makerere University in Kampala, Uganda, where he wrote his first novels, met his first wife, and introduced himself to the writer who would become his mentor, V. S. Naipaul. Theroux and Naipaul later had a falling out, a tale recounted in Theroux's bittersweet 1998 memoir, *Sir Vidia's Shadow*, which Theroux said is one of his favorite works. While traveling in the Pacific for his lighthearted 1992 book, *The Happy Isles of Oceania*, Theroux became enamored with Hawai'i. He now lives much of the year on the north shore of O'ahu with his present wife, and spends summers in Cape Cod near his boyhood home.

Theroux's 1975 travel narrative, *The Great Railway Bazaar*, set the tone for a new generation of traveling writers. He eschewed florid prose in favor of unvarnished observations, peppered with abundant dialogue. Two other rail narratives, *The Old Patagonian Express* and *Riding the Iron Rooster*, followed, revealing Theroux's penchant for rough,

Naipaul to me is an interesting monster, but his books, generally speaking, are wonderful. Books are not written by angels—they're written by human beings who have problems. If we were normal, balanced individuals, we would not write books.

—PAUL THEROUX, interviewed on KQED's *Forum*

overland travel. "Rattling through the middle of China on the so-called Iron Rooster, gathering notes for my book of China travels, I used to think, 'This is heaven!'" Theroux wrote in a 2002 *Time Asia* essay. "I had people to talk with, a bed to sleep in, ethnic food in a dining car, plenty of room for walking up and down, a place to write and a great deal to write about."

In 2003, Theroux released his ambitious *Dark Star Safari: Overland from Cairo to Capetown*, a riveting account of his return to Africa almost forty years after serving in the Peace Corps. "This trip was special to me—because the road was in part Memory Lane—and because I loved the challenges," Theroux told *Peace Corps Writers*. "There is nothing in the world more vitalizing to me than traveling in the African bush."

Some criticize Theroux for what they view as his merciless treatment of people he meets during his travels. In *Dark Star Safari*, he calls the Nile cruise passenger "someone in the process of becoming a licensed bore" and skewers one couple: "the hard-faced woman and her bosomy husband, each seemingly midway through a sex change." But he can also be sympathetic, particularly to the impoverished Africans he meets. "On my trip, the best people I met were bare-assed—they had nothing," he said during a 2004 radio interview on KQED's *Forum*. "One-on-one in a dugout canoe with some barefoot person, I got the truth."

Though he's made no secret of his distaste for being interviewed, Theroux conversed with me via e-mail and replied to follow-up questions. A week after we concluded our e-mail volley, I met Theroux in San Francisco at the Commonwealth Club where he discussed *Dark Star Safari*. He was genial and friendly when we spoke for a few minutes after his appearance. He even posed for a picture.

So who is the real Paul Theroux? Not, he says, the protagonist of *My Secret History*, nor the character named Paul Theroux in *My Other Life*. "I thought that *My Secret History* was very artfully constructed, and most of it was made up. And people said, 'Well that's your autobiography.' So I thought, I know what I'll do. I'll write a book and call it an autobiography. But it will be all lies," Theroux told *Salon*. "And in fact *My Other Life* is a pack of lies that looks like it amounts to a sort of truth. And I suppose it does. Because even when you're making up a lie, *you're* making up the lie. The writer is making up the lie. It's his or her lie. So it's a very individual thing, lying. And if you tell enough of them, I suppose you reveal a great deal."

Ultimately, Theroux's most self-revealing books may be his travel narratives. "Travel is a form of autobiography," he said of *Dark Star Safari*. "This book is not about Africa—this is a book about my trip through Africa—this book is, I suppose, about me."

~∾~

When I spoke with Jonathan Raban in Seattle, he said he views you, along with Bruce Chatwin and Redmond O'Hanlon, as someone who has given the travel narrative a new shape based on the novel. Would you agree? If so, would you describe how you've applied the novelist's techniques to your travel writing and why you feel that's a more interesting approach?

I did not set out to give the narrative of my journey a new shape, but I certainly made a conscious effort to avoid everything I disliked in the typical travel book. I hated the way trips were truncated and summarized ("Then we went from Colombo to Calcutta, where we found…"). I hated the "we" of the husband and wife, or traveler and friend. I hated condescension ("Then Abdul loaded the car with our luggage").

I wanted to avoid sightseeing, museum scrutiny, church-going, and the veneration of graveyards and monuments. I most of all wanted to avoid the traditional tone, which might be summed up in Erica Jong's assertion [in *Fear of Flying*, a travel narrative disguised as a novel], "Vienna. The very word is like a waltz." And dialogue—travel books seldom had much. I wanted lots of voices.

In your travel books, your characters are highly developed and you often recount pages of dialogue. In my interview with Raban, I asked him about dialogue in his work and he said, "I think that sometimes total recall is not as suspicious as it may look. Writing in a state of almost trance-like memoriousness, you are able to recapture things that you ought, by all the sort of normal laws of memory physics, to have forgotten." Can you discuss how you recall dialogue and translate it to the page?

I agree with Jonathan about the trance-like state of the engrossed and memorious writer. I also think fear and anxiety help one remember—we are, after all, animals and are most alert when we are nervous. Funnily enough it was V. S. Naipaul who suggested to me various methods for sitting po-faced talking to someone and remembering everything the person says. In traveling, I have never sat in front of someone taking notes unless the person happened to be blind—Borges comes to mind. Making notes and sticking a tape-recorder into the person's face just puts them off and makes them evasive, if not mendacious. I write down the dialogue as soon as I am out of the person's sight.

You shun official travel to go incognito, usually overland. I've especially enjoyed your books based on train journeys. Would you discuss the allure of locomotive travel?

Going overland is the only serious way of traveling, and the train is the simplest way of going overland. I am speaking of very bad trains. Super high-speed trains (in Japan, France, etc.) are not much use and aren't much different from planes. The first memorable journey I took in my life, aged seven or eight, was alone in a train from Boston to Hartford. Maybe that helped to shape me. Also, ideally, a train is a cultural artifact, a big wheezing thing that represents the country and contains its citizens, their chickens, their children, their eating and sleeping habits.

In your most recent travel book, Dark Star Safari, *you revisit Africa almost forty years after serving in the Peace Corps and teaching there. I know it's hard to sum up almost five hundred pages in a few sentences, but could you say what made the biggest impact on you?*

The sense that forty years of volunteers, aid, money, charity, World Bank and IMF efforts had made no impact at all—indeed that such efforts had been harmful.

Travel is transition, and at its best it is a journey from home, a setting forth. I hated parachuting into a place. I needed to be able to link one place to another. One of the problems I had with travel in general was the ease and speed with which a person could be transported from the familiar to the strange, the moon shot whereby the New York office worker, say, is insinuated overnight into the middle of Africa to gape at gorillas. That was just a way of feeling foreign. The other way, going slowly, crossing national frontiers, scuttling past razor wire with my bag and my passport, was the best way of being reminded that there was a relationship between Here and There, and that a travel narrative was the story of There and Back.

—PAUL THEROUX, *Dark Star Safari*

What were the most significant changes? Did you have expectations or preconceptions shattered during your travels through Africa?

I think in one respect the whole book is a record of disillusionment and that is why it meant so much to me. But I can't summarize the book. It was an enormous physical and mental effort and ought to be read by anyone who has a question about it. I have done my best in writing it.

Given the desperation in Africa today, with poverty, corruption, AIDS, and other diseases, isn't aid essential—wouldn't there be greater suffering without it?

I don't know. It is a demonstrable fact that aid has not made much difference except to line the pockets of plutocrats. So why not try something else—or try nothing at all? The majority of Africans live without any aid at all, as subsistence farmers.

Now that you're over sixty and you've sold truckloads of books, why do you keep embarking on such challenging trips?

Even if I were not a writer I would be a traveler, perhaps more of a traveler. I stopped writing for money many years ago. I never traveled strictly for the money. The only worthwhile trip is what you call a challenging trip. I have no interest at all in European travel, or sunshine tourism, or even traveling with another person.

May I add that Bruce Chatwin (see the excellent biography by Nicholas Shakespeare) never traveled alone—never, ever. Graham Greene usually went with a mistress or a male friend. Naipaul's "solitary" journeys of discovery were always made with a woman in tow, never his wife—someone to rent the car, pack the bags, do the fussing. Two-thirds of the way through *Tristes Tropiques*—a book I love—Levi-Strauss lets it drop that his wife has always been in his wagon train. Traveling with another person is not my idea of travel. I am amazed by what fussbudgets most so-called travel writers are.

What sacrifices have you made to pursue this life of extended journeying—are there personal costs?

In my case, malaria, intestinal parasites, malabsorption syndrome, dengue fever, gonorrhea, cataracts from excessive exposure to sun, gout from kidney damage owing to severe dehydration, putzi fly infestation (the flies laid their eggs on my damp shirt and the hatched larvae burrowed into my flesh), amebic dysentery, and the usual ailments. But I was divorced for other reasons, not travel. I have been lucky in having married a succession of Penelopes.

I assume this is a reference to the wife of Odysseus. Would you say a bit more about this? How have the women in your life been supportive of you? Has it been difficult for them or for you to have such prolonged separations?

In general very supportive, but it is never easy for any traveler's or writer's spouse. I don't think I am alone as a writer and traveler in needing a great deal of solitude, privacy, and freedom. The women in my life (as you put it) have been strong independent people who have had their own careers. Four wonderful words I have seldom heard in my life are, "Your lunch is ready."

You seem especially interested in border crossings—what is it about traversing frontiers that engages you?

The border is drama, misery, real life, strangeness, and the actual sight of the dotted line one sees on a map. But it is usually the farthest distance from the capital, and so highly revealing of what a place is like. Also somewhat lawless—people trying to get out, others struggling to get in. The international airport in the capital is the place to avoid if you want to know how the country works.

How do you prepare for an assignment—how much do you research a destination?

Lots of map reading. Practical reading and research, often to do with border crossings or transitions—how to get from K to Q. But I resist trying to find out too much, because I wish to make my own discoveries.

You don't travel with a camera or tape recorder—why not?

No electronics at all. Can't stand them as items in luggage. They break. They get stolen. They are heavy. They are extremely distracting. I do have a little shortwave radio—often stolen. On my Africa trip everything I owned was stolen towards the end of my trip—I mean, my entire bag and its contents. Where would I have been if I had had developed film, tapes, cassettes? I write in a notebook and when I have a chance, every fifty pages or so, I photocopy the story so far (photocopiers aren't hard to find) and mail it to Penelope for safekeeping.

Why have you chosen to live on Oʻahu and spend your summers near where you grew up in Cape Cod?

Why do I live in rural Hawaiʻi from October to May, and on Cape Cod from June to September? Is this a serious question? By the way, I have often remarked in my books on the nastiness of urban life.

I know you've commented on the unpleasantness of urban life, and yes this is a serious question. Oʻahu and Cape Cod are lovely places, but the world is full of lovely places, why these? I know you enjoy kayaking—is this why you live near the sea? Have you kept a place in Cape Cod because it's close to where you grew up—is it important for you to be close to your roots?

I like being near where I grew up, especially in the summer—I know and love the weather. I could only live near the sea—not just for the boating and the swimming. There is something magical about marine sunlight. I also subscribe to the ancient Phoenician belief that a day spent on the sea is a day that is not deducted from your life.

In The Happy Isles of Oceania, *the writing seems to get sunnier as the book progresses from the gloom of your divorce to the bright prospect of new love. How much is your travel writing colored by your mood?*

Quite a bit, I think—or more than quite a bit. But if I am in low spirits I avoid travel and stay home, since travel makes my low spirits lower. It took years before I felt properly psyched up in the right mood to return to Africa.

Do you feel that travel writing today is constrained by political correctness, that some writers hesitate to write critically about people in developing countries? In reviews you've been taken to task for belittling people you meet during your travels.

Reviews! Ha!

But do you ever feel that reviews and critics serve a useful purpose, or are they just an irritant that you ignore? Have you ever cared about reviews, perhaps early in your career?

I often seriously wonder whether some reviewers actually read my books. I think of any new book of mine as related to all my earlier work, but I seldom see reviewers doing any homework. When I was a weekly reviewer for *The New Statesmen* and *The Times* in England—in the 1970s and early 1980s—I was very diligent. There is also the fact that many reviewers begin from a prepared position, having decided in advance what I am like, what my book will be.

Do you ever worry that you're too harsh in your writing?

No. I have written as my inner voice has directed me to the truth.

I think that what people call grumpy, prickly, or dyspeptic is really a misunderstanding of irony. Because a lot of irony looks like dyspepsia. Irony looks like prickliness. But actually it's just another form of humor, isn't it? It's veiled sarcasm. I think that the people who read my books and like them, and there are plenty of them, wouldn't read me if I was merely a bad-tempered person.

—PAUL THEROUX, interviewed on Salon.com

Have you ever looked back at a characterization and felt you were a little too hard on that person?

Not at all. I find these questions meaningless and irrelevant. To people who find me a teeny bit too critical I urge them to read Graham Greene's *The Lawless Roads*, a book which is a long rant about how awful Mexico is ("I hate Mexico and Mexicans"), and so forth. Waugh's *Labels* is a mockery of the Mediterranean. Malinowski's *Diary* is full of racial slurs. Even Levi-Strauss howls from time to time.

Is there a place you haven't been that you'd like to visit?

There are many places I would travel to, and just as many I would like to return to. I published *The Great Railway Bazaar* almost thirty years

ago. I could take that trip again and write a different book. I often
dream about traveling in Angola, where I have never been.

What's the best thing that has happened to you during your travels?

In Africa as a traveler, a writer, and a teacher in 1967, I met a woman.
We were married in Uganda where our first son was born. Later we
moved to Singapore where our second son was born. Nothing can
compare with that.

The worst?

There are no "worsts" in a negative sense. There are only experiences
which are the very stuff of my books.

*Fair enough, but could you say if there have been any calamities, threats,
or diseases that have caused pain that far outweighed their value to you as
a writer?*

The worst thing? I would say having a nervous teenaged boy pointing
a very old and unreliable looking rifle into my face, with his finger on
the trigger. He had nothing to lose. I had quite a lot. On two occasions,
both in Africa, I have been shot at. These are situations I would like to
avoid. The worst thing is to be perceived as weak, an easy mark. This
happens everywhere: "Let's get that old geezer" is a cry heard from
New York City to Cape Town. The main thing is to be anonymous.

Who do you like to read? Would you cite a few of your favorite books?

The inevitable question but the hardest to answer. I read one or two
books a week, seldom are they new ones. For example, yesterday I read
a volume of Nabokov's short stories—he is pedantic and his work has
not held up for me. Today after lunch I reread most of V. S. Pritchett's
Midnight Oil. Wonderful. Last week I labored over some late James
stories and Camus' *The Plague*—by the way, all the characters are men,
all French. A novel set in Algeria with no women or Arabs! Ha!

Last month I wrote an introduction to Thoreau's *The Maine
Woods*, which necessitated reading lots of books about Thoreau and
Maine. This month I wrote an introduction to Greene's *The*

Comedians, which meant having to read a lot about Haiti and Greene. I just got a biography of Havelock Ellis out of the library and am intending to read Marjorie Bowen's *The Viper of Milan*. As far as new books, I always read books written by my friends.

Would you name a few of these friends?

One of my oldest writing friends is Jonathan Raban. I think I have read most of what he has written. I think he is brilliant. Other friends in this field for whom I have enthusiasm: Redmond O'Hanlon, Pico Iyer, Geoffrey Moorehouse, Ted Hoagland, Bruce Chatwin, Sara Wheeler, and so on.

I was proud of being a travel writer in Oceania. I stopped seeing it as a horrid preoccupation that I practiced only with my left hand. But when I got to Hawai'i I changed my mind. I was not sure what I did for a living or who I was, but I was absolutely sure I was not a travel writer.

—PAUL THEROUX,
The Happy Isles of Oceania

Specifically, who have been your favorite authors who base their work on their travels throughout the years?

I always answer this question with *The Worst Journey in the World* by Cherry-Garrard. I could add Levi-Strauss, Pritchett's *The Spanish Temper*, early Naipaul books, Waugh, and Greene, of course. Lots of others. But these are for amusement. I have read all the obvious books too: Flaubert in Egypt, Gobi Desert chronicles, Charles Waterton, Darwin, but I am not a great reader of travel literature, especially the felicitous kind. I am quite an avid reader of ordeals, life-threatening experiences, and harrowing diaries of near escapes. I see *Three Months in a Rubber Dinghy!* and my hand leaps to the shelf.

What are the most important components of compelling travel writing?

Only one. Seeing a place as though for the first time and truthfully describing your experience of it.

Would you cite one or two overarching things you've learned about the world through your travels? What have you learned about yourself?

That life is very short, but that it is shorter and so much worse for other people.

By other people do you mean, for example, people in Africa with very limited access to basic necessities? Or people stuck in menial jobs in the developed world? Or do you simply mean anyone without the curiosity to explore?

I mean the people I have traveled among, who because they aren't working in sweatshops making widgets don't count in today's GNP-obsessed world. And in general they are hounded to death by Christian evangelists.

You've said that you wrote The Mosquito Coast *in lieu of taking your family there. What other roles does fiction serve for you and do you prefer writing fiction to travelogues? Do you enjoy going back and forth between the two forms? Or, like Raban, do you see them as not really different?*

I know Jonathan's views on this subject, but speaking for myself: I do see travel and fiction as arising from different sources, even though both are creative. I am a slow fiction writer but find the process satisfying—it is fantasizing in my case. I want to think that I go to a place, try to enter into its life, and record my impressions. But deep down I suspect I am inventing the place—a suspicion I try to resist.

Do you feature a specific aspect of yourself in your travel books? Have you crafted this persona of the sometimes cranky, irascible traveler to serve your literary aims?

A cranky, irascible traveler I am not. I am good-tempered and optimistic and perhaps a little strange—blame my profession. I have chosen difficult journeys among, in general, remote people. I have not chosen a persona—how could I, and what would that accomplish? I am usually just grinning like a dog and wandering aimlessly.

Did growing up in a large Catholic family influence your decision to become a writer?

The large family of seven might have had an effect—certainly it made me want to leave the house and live on my own, as well as provoking in me a desire for solitude. But Catholic—I don't think so. My faith lapsed early—see *My Secret History*—and my more recent "A Judas Memoir" in *The Stranger at the Palazzo d'Oro* for fictional representations of my feelings. Catholicism seemed to me a crock because I did not believe in transubstantiation (wine becoming blood, bread becoming flesh), nor in Hell, nor the Devil, and so forth. I have no belief in a personal God and I felt that religion was an obstruction to my wishing to be a writer.

What advice would you give a teenager in Nowhere, USA about the importance of travel in the formation of a good person, a strong person, a better citizen?

Dear Teenager, Leave home. Go to college if you can, but in any case, keep going and be self-sufficient.

What would you like written on your tombstone?

No tombstone, no monument for pigeons to shit on. Scatter my ashes in the deep sea.

The World for a Song

Arthur Frommer
NEW YORK, NEW YORK

A
S I COMPLETED MY FIRST BOOK ABOUT USING THE INTERNET FOR
travel, in 1996, I decided I wanted a pioneer to write the foreword. I wanted someone who had foreseen great changes in
the travel world and helped travelers make the most of those changes.
Though *Europe on 5 Dollars a Day* appeared several years before I was
born, it reflected the spirit I hoped to capture in my Internet book. I
didn't know if I, a young, yet-to-be-published author, could entice a
luminary like Arthur Frommer to help me, but I thought I'd try.

To my amazement, I found Frommer listed in the Manhattan phone
book. I contacted him, described my book, and agreed to meet him the
following month at a book event in the San Francisco area. When I
introduced myself, he greeted me like an old friend and immediately
agreed to write the foreword. As I stammered that neither my publisher nor I had much of a budget, he shot back in his deep, sonorous voice,
"Well, I will require payment: one signed copy of the book!"

Frommer's foreword presciently predicted the enormous growth of the Internet for travel, which was by no means assured in 1996. He accurately forecast that online discounts would drive the adoption of the Web as a tool for purchasing flights and hotel rooms. But his intuition about the Internet wasn't surprising given his vision in travel publishing.

As a G.I. stationed in Germany in the mid-1950s, Frommer had traveled on a shoestring whenever he had a couple of days off. Early on, he realized an essential truth pertaining to intrepid travelers: the less you spend, the more you enjoy. After traveling widely throughout Europe and self-publishing a slender guide for G.I.s, Frommer wrote his seminal *Europe on 5 Dollars a Day*.

Until that book's 1956 publication, overseas travel had been the province of the wealthy, and guided tours were the norm. *Europe on 5 Dollars a Day*, along with the innovation of the jet engine, propelled a new wave of independent travelers across the Atlantic. Though the title has changed to reflect inflation, the book has sold about 3 million copies, and the Frommer's series has grown to hundreds of titles.

After four decades in travel publishing, Frommer turned his seemingly inexhaustible energies to the creation of a web site called Arthur Frommer's Outspoken Encyclopedia of Travel, which launched in early 1997. The next year he began publishing *Arthur Frommer's Budget Travel* magazine, which filled a gaping niche. I was proud to write an article for one of the first issues of *Budget Travel* ("Hostelling the California Coast"), and developed a working relationship with Frommer. Every year or so, I'd stop by *Budget Travel*'s office while in New York and Arthur would welcome me like a member of his family.

Despite his mainstream successes, Frommer hasn't sacrificed his principles. In the 1990s, he quit working for a New York radio station after it hired a racist talk-show host, and while editor of *Budget Travel* magazine advised his readers to boycott travel to the Cayman Islands, which had refused entry to a gay cruise tour. He even once wrote a guidebook, to Branson, Missouri, that almost advised travelers not to visit, because Frommer found the place so distasteful.

To interview him for this book, I met Frommer at his New York City apartment on a frigid January day. Two things immediately struck me: first, that entire walls had been converted to bookshelves holding more volumes than many small-town libraries; and second, the jaw-dropping view of the Hudson River, twenty-seven stories below. "You can see that half the river is frozen," Frommer said, displaying a keen interest in the world from his lofty perch.

The next morning Frommer, who was seventy-four at the time, and his wife Roberta were jetting to Maho Bay Camps on St. John in the Virgin Islands, to stay in a canvas tent for a week. Not many of their peers would choose to stay in a tent with bathrooms a short hike away, but for Frommer this was enticing. "The last time I was in the Virgin Islands I thought, Why not stay on a cot on the beach under a canvas awning—wouldn't that be a wonderful way to live?"

If I were not to mention the wholesale destruction of the ecology by certain Branson developers, the ugly racism that—to my eye at least—is so painfully evident in the casting of most Branson shows, the overly vulgar commercialization of some (not all, but some) Branson theaters, the violent jingoism of certain Branson performers who themselves have never served in the military, I'd be writing a puff sheet, not a travel guide.

—ARTHUR FROMMER,
Arthur Frommer's Branson!

Maybe you could start by telling me about your early life, where you grew up and how you got to New York.

I was born in the year the Depression began, 1929. My father and mother were both immigrants to the United States without any resources or family wealth. My father got a job in the apparel industry and throughout the 1930s moved from one city to the next with various clothing factories until they'd go bankrupt. He was proud of the fact that he was continually employed throughout the Depression—that he always had a job and was able to support his family.

I was born in Lynchburg, Virginia. When I was four or five, we settled down for a time in Jefferson City, Missouri. I grew up until the age of fourteen in this idyllic Mark Twain-like setting of Jefferson City, a town of around twenty thousand people, the capital of the state of Missouri, and to me the Athens of the world. I had an idyllic boyhood even though I was probably the poorest young boy in my entire public school. My father had a very modest job—at a pants factory called Oberman's—we didn't have any luxuries. I believe I was about sixteen or seventeen years old before I once went to a restaurant. I grew up at time when some children would come to school barefoot because they had no money for shoes.

Of course, I grew up worshiping Franklin Roosevelt and the New Deal. I remember, because I recently sang it for my daughter, that when Irving Berlin composed "God Bless America," we immediately put words to it that went "God bless Franklin Roosevelt, our native son, stand beside him, and guide him, till his fight for the right will be won; for a third term or a fourth term, put your shoulders to the wheel, God bless Franklin Roosevelt, that's how we feel." That's how I grew up, in a liberal Jewish family, living very modestly in Jefferson City, Missouri.

In 1944 my father got a better job in New York City. He announced to us one day that we were moving, and it was the darkest day of my life. I couldn't understand how any human being would want to live anywhere else but in Jefferson City, Missouri, where I was already dreaming of becoming governor someday. In any event, I got picked up and moved right to the heart of Brooklyn—it was the most incredible culture shock any human being has ever gone through.

That's a tough time to move—in the middle of your teenage years.

Right in the middle of my teenage years, with all my friends and associations in Jefferson City. I got to New York City still imbued with all the American values of success and nothing being out of your reach. The second day that I was in New York City, I got on the subway and I went to Times Square to look around at the various newspapers there to get a job as a copy boy. I went to the *New York Herald Tribune*; I went to the offices of *The New York Times*—there were no such positions. And then I saw the *Newsweek* building and I got a job initially as an office boy.

I was fourteen years old. It was only because the war was at its very peak—this was 1944—that a fourteen-year-old boy could get a job. I was so incredibly proud of the fact that I worked after school as one of the two office boys in the editorial department of *Newsweek* magazine.

I was there no more than a week when I typed out a memo to the editorial director of *Newsweek* suggesting to him the publication of an edition called *Newsweek Jr.* I felt that there should be an edition of *Newsweek* written in clearer and more understandable language that would replace *Scholastic* magazine. I got a response that the idea had been advanced by others but that they were grateful.

For the rest of my high school—I was enrolled at Erasmus Hall High School in Brooklyn—I became the editor-in-chief of the *Dutchman,* which was the school newspaper. When an issue would come out I would grab fifty copies, take the subway that afternoon to my job at *Newsweek,* and circulate the copies to the editorial department so they saw that their office boy was an editor-in-chief.

It was so unbelievably fortuitous and coincidental that just a few years ago my magazine, *Budget Travel,* was bought by *Newsweek.* In my first meeting with the officials at *Newsweek,* I told them that I was *Newsweek's* oldest employee. Sure enough, they went into the archives and found a copy of the in-house newsletter published in 1944 with a picture of me at an office party. There I was, little fourteen-year-old Arthur Frommer at *Newsweek.*

In any event, when the time came to go to college I was absolutely hell-bent on going to the journalism school at University of Missouri. That was what I dreamed about and already I wanted to be a journalist. My mother got very ill at the end of my first year at the University of Missouri, and I had to move back to New York and finish up college. I transferred to New York University, Washington Square College, where I majored in political science but minored in French.

Even though I wasn't thinking of travel writing, somehow or another the international world still attracted me. I graduated from NYU in 1950 and won a scholarship to Yale University Law School, an exhilarating place. I was one of the editors of the *Yale Law Journal* and graduated with honors in 1953. I had my mind set on getting a clerkship with a judge in one of the federal courts but by that time the Korean War had broken out.

Immediately upon graduation from law school I was drafted into the Army in 1953. To my amazement at the end of basic training, I was placed in Intelligence rather than being shipped out in an infantry unit to Korea. It was the most fortuitous thing that ever happened to me and subsequently I was sent overseas to Germany.

Were you sent to Europe rather than Asia because you spoke several European languages?

That was one of the reasons: I spoke a little bit of German; I was fluent in French; I was quite fluent at that time in Russian. My mother was from Russia and I had studied Russian at NYU.

But some office in the Pentagon found me when I finished basic training and yanked me out and sent me to Europe. I served in Europe in two places primarily: with a unit engaged in various forms of covert intelligence that was headquartered in Berlin, and later in the U.S. Army Europe Intelligence School in Oberammergau, the famous Passion Play town. They had a barracks high on the hillside in the Alps overlooking the town and it was the headquarters of the U.S. Army Europe Intelligence School.

When I arrived in Europe, I wanted to pinch myself for my good luck. I had never dreamed that I would have the resources or the money to travel in Europe. At that time hardly anyone ever considered themselves able to do so. Here I was, a French language student, dreaming of sidewalk cafés, of Hemingway and all the rest, but I never dreamed I'd be able to get there. And suddenly I found myself in a little town in Germany with the U.S. Army.

The first three-day pass that I was able to wangle, I was shooting onto a train headed for Paris. We crossed the border at Strasbourg in the middle of the night, and I got out of the train. I walked across the tracks to the French portion of the station and I ordered a café and a croissant in perfect French. I was having the dream of my life—I was in France! I could hardly believe it and subsequently re-boarded the train and had my first vision of Paris.

I lived like a budget tourist without thinking about it. Obviously I didn't have the money to stay in a normal hotel. It didn't even occur to me to stay in a normal hotel. I immediately took the Metro to the Left Bank and started looking around for all these tiny little hotels that I'd heard about. I went to the Rue des Ecoles and I stayed at the Hotel Claude Bernard.

For my two years in the Army—I worked hard in the Army and

they got their money's worth from me—but every weekend, every leave, every time there was even a day free, I got out of there and I went somewhere in Europe. There was one trip I made to Venice where I ran out of money at the end of the first day even though I had another day left. I had my train ticket to go back, but I didn't have a penny. And rather than go back, I existed in Venice without eating for an entire day because I just wanted to drink in every moment.

By the way, on that day that I had no money when I was starving, I looked down the street and there was another guy from one of my units, and I went running after him and I said, "Oh, thank god, you're like manna from heaven, lend me $5." And he looked at me with these sorrowful eyes and he said, "You know, I have never been with a woman. I have $10 and a prostitute costs $8…" And I said, "All right, that's it." I walked away. I could not take from him the money he had set aside for his first sexual act.

But I went everywhere. I was teaching myself how to use the Military Air Transport System, which gave you a free ride on an Air Force plane, space available, if you were a G.I. You'd say, "Where are you flying to?" and they'd say "Stockholm" and you'd get on the plane and you'd fly to Stockholm, free of charge, sitting in a bucket seat.

I never thought I was ever going to be a travel writer. I was just having a wonderful time traveling on the slimmest of funds but having an experience that was turning me upside down, this direct contact with the life of Europe, with people, seeing all sorts of strange ideologies and lifestyles and approaches and politics in sixteen different countries, just going every weekend, flying somewhere or taking a train somewhere.

But there was one particular trip that really caused me to wonder whether I should write about this. A sergeant in my unit told me about an island called Mallorca off the coast of Spain, a ferry ride overnight from Barcelona. He said he heard that Mallorca was cheap. I'd never heard of it at the time; this was in 1954 or 1955. I got on a train and went to Barcelona. I bought deck passage on the overnight ferry that went from Barcelona to the island of Mallorca—you didn't get a bed; you just lay down on the deck.

I arrived in the port of Mallorca in the morning to see the sleepiest little main town. There were bales of hay scattered around for donkeys and horses. But I could see that there was also a little hotel right on the square. In broken Spanish I asked them if they had a room for two dollars. And immediately I saw that I had made a terrible mistake because the man said "Yes!" unhesitatingly. I realized I should have asked them for a room for one dollar.

I proceeded to have the most glorious week of my life. Mallorca was just ridiculously cheap. I would go into restaurants and order all these famous dishes that I'd heard of all my life, breast of guinea hen under glass—I think I ordered caviar, I had wine. The entire bill would come to seventy-five cents. I would go to a beach in Mallorca and raise my hand. A waiter would come over with the drink and it would cost ten cents. I remember thinking, Someone should tell the public about this. This is really an extraordinary boon available to the possessor of the U.S. dollar.

The exchange rates at that time were so incredible. Europe was just recovering from World War II and it was just staggering how well you could travel on very little money. It was during that trip to Mallorca that the genesis of the idea of writing a book about how this travel was available first emerged. It was to be a book, I decided, for my fellow G.I.s. It was then I decided to write a book called *The G.I.'s Guide to Travelling in Europe*.

And in the barracks at night I started writing down what I had experienced on my own travels through Europe on my weekend passes and on my leaves. *The G.I.'s Guide to Travelling in Europe* was the strangest guidebook ever published because I had not taken any notes while I was traveling. I never dreamed that I was going to write about it. I had no addresses. I had to describe every hotel and restaurant from the mental picture that I had as to where it was located.

So it was almost impressionistic.

It was impressionistic, it was from memory. I had no notes. I said, when you get to Paris, take the subway to the Boulevard Saint-Michel station, look up the hill, at the very top of the hill you'll see a grocery store, if you turn left about twenty yards in, there's this big church building which will let G.I.s sleep in the basement for fifty cents a night. But I didn't know the name of the place, nevertheless the instructions were fairly good.

One chapter was called "Free Air Force Flights and How to Get Them." I sent a letter to the traffic officer of each of the major U.S. Air Force bases in Europe asking them to write back and to tell me of any scheduled flights. Every single one of them responded. The guy who was in charge of flights in Frankfurt said every Saturday at four P.M. we run a flight to Paris or we run a flight to London. When the book came out it caused a major security flap, because even though each one of them was entitled to give me that information, the totality of the information gave away the entire Air Force structure of Western Europe.

Anyway, I wrote this book, *The G.I.'s Guide to Travelling in Europe*, this tiny little book. I borrowed some money from a few sergeants in my law firm—I think I had $800 or $900. And I took it to a little printer in Oberammergau, Germany. We printed a small supply, 10,000 or 12,000 copies, which I sent to the *Stars and Stripes* system in Europe [which supervised all the PX stores at U.S. Army bases]. In late 1955, a couple of weeks before I was rotated home and was discharged honorably from the Army, the book went on sale.

I came back to New York, thrilled to be out of the Army, thrilled to be starting my legal career at last, put on my suit of clothing, went running to Paul Weiss, Rifkind, Wharton & Garrison and began working at law. A couple of weeks later I received a letter from the distributor that the book had virtually sold out the first afternoon. I had stumbled by absolute accident upon this urgent desire on the part of G.I.s for this kind of information. There were no useful guidebooks at that time. There was Fielding, but Fielding was written for high-spending, first-class American tourists.

How much did the book sell for?

Fifty cents. Prices in those days were so low. I've looked at the early editions of *Europe on 5 Dollars a Day* recently. A hotel room cost $1.90. A meal was 60 or 70 cents. But the *G.I.'s Guide* was a great hit and went through two or three printings which I would have to do long-distance. I was amused by the fact that I had written this very popular book.

In the course of those six years or so that I spent at Paul Weiss, from 1956 to around 1962, Adlai Stevenson joined Paul Weiss after his second defeat for the presidency. He was given the office next door to mine, and even though I didn't work with him, the nameplate outside my office was the last thing that he saw every morning before he went into his office. Which meant that I was the only associate in the entire firm whose name he knew. Shortly after he joined the law firm, I started getting phone calls from all sorts of socialites: "This is Mrs. Stuyvesant-Wainwright. I met Governor Stevenson the other night at a cocktail party and told him about this terrible problem I'm having with my landlord," and he said, "You call up Arthur Frommer and he'll take care of it right away."

There was a time at Paul Weiss, where if you had a very weak case and needed to present the court with a very colorful brief that opened with sensational statements, you would be asked to "Frommerize" the brief, because the briefs that I wrote as a young lawyer were known for openings that would capture a judge's attention. There was one brief that I opened with a poem: I quoted a classic poem of English literature.

Our firm represented Readers Subscription, which had the mail-order rights to *Lady Chatterley's Lover*, and was the smallest client that Paul Weiss had. The postmaster denied the use of the mail to *Lady Chatterley's Lover*—the postmaster general himself determined that the book was pornographic and could not be sent through the mail. Our client came running to Paul Weiss, and because there was no money in it, they assigned the youngest lawyer on the entire staff to defend *Lady Chatterley*.

It was the greatest moment of my life. It was so exciting. The trial, before a judicial officer of the post office, was held in downtown New York. We lost as we knew we would, he was an arm of the postmaster general, but then we won on appeal. We took it to the federal district court to Judge Frederick van Pelt Bryan, who freed *Lady Chatterley's Lover*. It was one of the great landmark decisions in the law of pornography.

In any event, I'm practicing law at Paul Weiss, working around the clock, and in the back of my mind I say to myself, maybe I should bring out a version of the *G.I.'s Guide* for civilians. Even then not really making a decision to devote my life to travel, I was up to here in law, but I thought, Dammit, I would never forgive myself, I really must do this. And during my first vacation, I got a one-month vacation during the summer, I went back to Europe and in thirty days I went running like a madman to the eighteen or nineteen cities that had been written up in the *G.I.'s Guide*, getting the addresses, filling in the gaps, working from morning till night, getting up at five in the morning in Brussels and just crisscrossing the streets until midnight, then taking a train at night to the next city.

And I brought out the first edition of a civilian version of the *G.I.'s Guide*, which I titled *Europe on 5 Dollars a Day*. Because I had not taken the *G.I.'s Guide* to a publisher but had published it myself, it never occurred to me to take *Europe on 5 Dollars a Day* to a publisher. Instead, I took it to a printer, Liberal Press at Fourth Avenue and 10th Street. I hired them to print 5,000 copies of *Europe on 5 Dollars a Day*.

The book was actually on the presses being printed, when it suddenly occurred to me that I needed a distributor. I needed somebody who would get it to the bookstores. I was thinking in such small terms—I learned about a tiny little company, a guy named Jay Greenberg, who delivered small literary magazines to bookstores in the tri-state area, and he took on the distribution. It no sooner reached the bookstores than it absolutely disappeared. There was such a reaction to that book. It became a giant bestseller. I was still practicing law and going back to Europe for a month every summer to update it.

And the book started growing. I'm working at Paul Weiss from nine in the morning until eleven at night and then going home and staying up until three in the morning—how I did it I have no idea. I then get to the point where I think, why not *New York on 5 Dollars a Day*. What's fascinating is that while working for Paul Weiss, I built the company up to five titles. I started hiring people to write other 5 Dollars a Day books. I was living a life of madness. Finally after five or six years of trying to juggle the two, in 1961, I had to make the agonizing decision between law and publishing. I decided to go into publishing on a full-time basis, and I reluctantly resigned from Paul Weiss.

I went into full-time publishing and soon after also became a tour operator. I rented a little office on Fourth Avenue to publish these five little guidebooks. Prior to 1961, the only eyes that ever saw the text of any book that I did were mine. These books were never edited, and it is to that that I attribute their success. I am absolutely convinced that if I had been made to give the manuscript of *Europe on 5 Dollars a Day* to some editor, to an English major who graduated the year before and is working for Simon & Schuster, that she would have squeezed out of the manuscript every bit of the color and the innocence and the joy that made it such a great success.

I wrote the first edition of *Europe on 5 Dollars a Day* in a white-hot, high-pitched fervor, almost in a fever of composition. I was so excited about what I saw as this magnificent opportunity to visit a sophisticated, ancient civilization and to derive lessons from it. I felt that what I was doing was beneficial to people, and I know that the kind of hyperbole and the kind of colorful metaphor that marks almost all travel writing that I do would never have survived editing, because too many publishers give a manuscript to some young kid who has to prove his worth by rewriting the whole thing. There are portions of *Europe on 5 Dollars a Day* that are extremely lyrical. The book is a practical book, but it is filled with all sorts of rhapsodic comments about the joys of traveling in Europe.

Let me just read you the opening of the Venice chapter. "To feel its full impact, try to arrive at night when the wonders of the city can steal upon you piecemeal and slow. At the foot of the Venice railway station is a landing from which a city launch embarks for the trip up the Grand Canal. As you chug along, little clusters of candy-striped mooring poles emerge from the dark, a gondola approaches with a lighted lantern hung from its prow. The reflection of a slate-gray church, bathed in a blue spotlight, shimmers in the water as you pass by. This is the sheerest beauty and a sight that no one should miss."

That was *Europe on 5 Dollars a Day*. It was not simply a compendium of facts and recommendations. It was a joyous reaction to Europe and written with personality in a way that guidebooks today are generally not written. You write a guidebook today, and it goes through the maws of a big organization that rewrites everything. That opening paragraph would never have been permitted in any guidebook published in the United States today.

I have been an implacable enemy of copy editors, not only in the publication of guidebooks, but in the publication of my magazine. Until I was pushed into doing it, I didn't want to have any copy editors. All of the books that I published in the early years were written like that. Each book was written by one person. Each book reflected the eccentricities, the judgments, the personal viewpoints of that one person, which were never censored by the publisher.

Our first edition of *Mexico on 5 Dollars a Day* was written by John Wilcock, who hates Mexican food. He spends pages telling you where you can find a decent tuna-fish-salad sandwich in Mexico City. He doesn't like Mexican food, yet he's the author of one of the classic guidebooks to Mexico. When you read the restaurant chapter you could tell that he is virtually holding his nose. I never changed that—what he wrote went into print. In my opinion, a copy editor's function is grammar, punctuation, consistent abbreviations, and the like—it is not style. A copy editor has no right to impose his or her style upon that of the author.

I've often said that editors should take the Hippocratic Oath: First, do no harm.

Of course. In 1961, I started publishing travel guides on a full-time basis in addition to writing my own travel guides. I wrote guidebooks to New York; I wrote a guidebook to Amsterdam called *Surprising Amsterdam*. That became the advertising slogan of KLM. I wrote *A Masterpiece Called Belgium*. That represents the purest reflection of how I think a guidebook should be written. *A Masterpiece Called Belgium* is not simply practical guidebook, it is an attempt to provide my viewpoints on the culture and art and politics and society of Belgium to give the reader a well-rounded picture of the country.

I wrote, in later years, *The New World of Travel*, [a guide to alternative travel, such as volunteer vacations]. I've also written a couple of political books: *The Bible and the Public Schools*, a defense of the

When we first wander through it, astonished and silent, we try to rein in our excitement.… Bruges is a medieval city perfectly preserved, a giant sprawling ancient metropolis once of world significance, and yet today almost unaltered in its former splendor, its awesome beauty and size. Suddenly, those people of the Middle Ages cease, in our minds, to appear a quaint and backward species, to be patronized. All at once we realize, if we hadn't before, that people have nearly always had aspirations and achievements equal to ours.

—Arthur Frommer,
A Masterpiece Called Belgium

Supreme Court decision invalidating compulsory Bible reading in public schools. I also did a campaign screed that was anti the candidacy of Barry Goldwater. When Goldwater got the Republican nomination I was in Europe, and from that far away I got terribly scared he might win. I cut short my trip, came back to New York and in thirty days wrote a book called *Goldwater from A to Z*.

But primarily I wrote guidebooks, although the supervision of their publication has slipped away from me now. When you sell the books, as I did in the late 1970s to Simon & Schuster, you start out actively supervising, but then they get removed further and further. They are now owned by John Wiley.

I've always felt that travel is a serious subject whose rewards go well beyond that of entertainment and recreation. The average magazine or newspaper editor looks upon travel as a subject of trivia, as something that you engage in to relax from stress, to reinvigorate you. I've never believed that.

We all tell ourselves that we're all stressed out, that we gotta have a vacation. We dream of going to a Caribbean island and just lying on the beach for two weeks and relaxing and getting away from the rat race. We go to the Caribbean and we lie down on the beach and after one hour we begin to fidget. We're already as well rested as we ever need to be, and then we're looking for something more profound to do. But of course by that time there is nothing else to do.

I believe that travel is one of the finest methods of self-education, that travel pursued properly expands your horizons. I have always tried to emphasize that goal and to make explicit that the best form of travel is a learning approach. That was the point of *The New World of Travel*. Though most people say that they travel to certain destinations for sightseeing, I think sightseeing is as inane an activity as the words entail. We travel thousands of miles to go look at some dead physical structure that we have seen thousands of times before in picture books or on television. We go to Paris; we look at the Eiffel Tower and we think we've traveled.

To me, if travel only consists of sightseeing, it is no longer worth the time or the effort or the fatigue. The only things that interest me are people and ideas. I love going on trips that shock me, where everything I believe in, my religion, my politics, my social outlook, is immediately challenged with diametrically different viewpoints. In that kind of context you reassess your assumptions and you gain from it. The reward of that is extraordinary.

You recently went to Cuba…

Certainly. No matter how many times you've read about Cuba in *Time* or *Newsweek*, there's nothing like going and seeing it with your own eyes. During the Cold War, you could read endless newspaper articles about East Berlin or about Moscow or St. Petersburg, but not until you actually went there and exposed yourself to it did you really get a full understanding of it.

I'm still engaged in that kind of learning—last summer for our vacation, Roberta and I went for two weeks to Ireland. But instead of getting onto a bus and engaging in such foolishness as kissing the Blarney Stone, we enrolled in a course in Irish civilization in University College, Dublin, and for three hours every morning heard lectures related to the history or culture of Ireland. This was an extraordinary experience. You didn't get the superficial tour operator's view of Ireland, you learned about the disquieting aspects of Ireland in some instances from specialists in the subject.

In one phase of my life I deliberately went to a whole series of New Age institutions and resorts, even though my own state of mind is not at all what you would call New Age. I'm a highly rational person. I am a skeptic, an agnostic. I do not yet believe that magic crystals will bring us understanding. And yet I regard it as part of the adventure of life to confront that type of speculation. I thought it was exciting to go to the Omega Institute or to go to Esalen, or to go to this place in Scotland, Findhorn, and listen to these outlandish theories about social relationships, about diet, about nutrition, that challenge you, that make you think.

All of us were skeptical at one point in our life about institutions that turned out to have been valid. When I first heard of acupuncture, I thought it was the greatest nonsense ever. I think it's important throughout life to confront yourself with opposing systems of politics, to people who stand for the opposite of your own most cherished viewpoints. I love conveying that experience in my writing about travel.

Roberta and I for New Year's went to Colonial Williamsburg. For some crazy reason I'd never gone to Colonial Williamsburg even though it was the first theme park. It's fascinating to see how the people of Colonial Williamsburg have been made to face up to the fact that many of our most hallowed founding fathers were slave owners, not just Thomas Jefferson, but Washington, Patrick Henry, and others. To go to Colonial Williamsburg and to see them grappling with this issue and trying to give an honest response to it and rearranging the whole presentation to show you slave quarters, to enable you to talk to an historical interpreter who plays a slave. You learn about American history, warts and all.

This is the kind of subject matter that I've tried to deal with in travel writing. In the publication of *Budget Travel*, which I edited for six years before I left it in September 2003, I tried to make sure that travel was dealt with not as a recreation but as a learning experience. Many of the articles that I ran incorporated that discussion, and I plan to write about that for the rest of my life.

Throughout your life you've said, the less you spend, the more you enjoy.

I still believe that. When you live lavishly you're really living a kind of life which only a small fraction of the world enjoys, and which is enjoyed primarily for reasons of social emulation. You want to impress other people. I have stayed at every kind of deluxe facility you can imagine. I've been sent on publicity tours by my publishers on arrangements they have made, and I stayed at Ritz Carltons and the great hotels of Europe.

I regard them as one more crushing bore after the next. When I was a tour operator and my business was very important to the airlines, I always used to be upgraded to first class across the Atlantic, even though I would never ask for it. I would just show up and miraculously they would put me into first class. I would come home puzzled and tell my wife that the people that I was seated next to were so incredibly right wing. Every one of them was for Nixon, it was such an atypical group of people. It took me a long time to realize these were rich people buying the first-class seats—they weren't nearly as interesting to talk with as the people that you ordinarily meet in tourist class or the breakfast room of a pension. I will go to my grave claiming that the less you spend the more you enjoy, the more authentic the experience it is, the more profound, the more exciting, the more unexpected.

When you started your magazine in the late 1990s, you were at an age when many of your peers had already retired. What was that like for you?

It was an exhilarating experience and somehow or another I was physically up to it. I'm still not stopping—I have no intention of retiring. I do plan to do a broader form of writing in the years ahead. I have started on a political work that I've been thinking about for twenty years which has nothing to do with travel. I've always believed that I owe to the readers of my guidebooks a frank view of my reaction to certain destinations and have never held back in exposing a liberal viewpoint politically in my guidebooks.

And in your magazine, too. I remember a cruise ship, a gay tour…

…that was denied landing rights in the Cayman Islands. We came out and said we would no longer write about the Cayman Islands— that any destination that will not accept all Americans should not be patronized by any American.

In all the years that I've been writing about vacations, I have dreamed—endlessly dreamed— of publishing a magazine called *Budget Travel.* And throughout that time, I have hurt—literally hurt—when I read what passes for the travel press in America. We hope to publish the first national travel magazine that is relevant to peoples' lives.

—EDITOR'S LETTER, *Arthur Frommer's Budget Travel*

Didn't you quit working at a New York radio station after it hired a racist talk-show host?

I resigned from a highly-successful, heavily-listened-to weekend radio program over at WOR because they hired a vicious racist named Bob Grant, indicating to me that WOR had made the decision to become a hate station with which I could not remain associated. Bob Grant is the man who had earlier been fired by ABC because he had openly rejoiced at the death in an airplane disaster of Ron Brown, then the secretary of commerce. He had earlier stated over the air that blacks were lower on the evolutionary ladder than whites, called African-Americans "savages," and said that Martin Luther King was a "scumbag."

Within days of his being dropped by WABC, WOR hired Grant. I immediately resigned, saying that I could no sooner remain on such a station than I could have remained in the 1930s on a Berlin radio station featuring the famous German broadcaster Joseph Goebbels. Though I hated to lose this program, which was also nationally syndicated and had an audience of hundreds of thousands, my resignation was the proudest act of my life.

Mainstream travel publishing today doesn't reflect many of the values and ideals you've espoused. Can you give me your assessment of the state of travel publishing today, guidebooks, magazines and the like?

It's become a big business and is operated on such cost-conscious principles by publishers trying to get the most for the least that there are very few people who can earn their living writing about travel. Therefore they do not devote to it the kind of attention that the few lucky individuals like myself were able to devote to the guidebooks that we wrote. When I was writing *Europe on 5 Dollars a Day*, I was spending months each year laboriously researching the cities of Europe. Today an author doesn't have the income to do that, doesn't get paid enough to justify that amount of effort. It's a terrible dilemma. I've often thought about what I would do today if I were publishing guidebooks again. Would I be able to compensate the authors sufficiently for the kind of effort that I would want them to put into the research and composition of their text?

Very early on you jumped onto the Internet with Arthur Frommer's Outspoken Encyclopedia of Travel.

I plunged into the creation of our first Internet site, devoting close to two years of my life to it. Originally the *Encyclopedia of Travel* was going to be a CD-ROM, but then the market for CD-ROMs disappeared. I spent two years in a little office collecting and gathering together everything I knew about travel and trying to organize it into an encyclopedia. It's been very exciting to create what I believe is a very good site that performs a service for the public. As you know my daughter (Pauline Frommer) is now in charge of that effort. It's astonishing to see the depth that she has created at that web site.

Would you have any advice for aspiring travel writers?

Many people tell me that they want to write about travel and ask me how they can go about doing it. I say a travel writing career is the easiest writing career in all the world. There is such a great need for good travel writing, and so little good travel writing being presented to editors, that talent is immediately recognized.

When a good manuscript comes into a travel publisher or a guidebook publisher, it is immediately spotted. It is not overlooked. Therefore I tell people who want to write guidebooks or magazine articles to simply perform an audition—make believe that they are writing about some aspect of their own community for a guidebook. If you live in Chillicothe, make believe that you're writing the hotel chapter of a guidebook to Chillicothe, and go out and do the research and write it up. If you are good at it, if you are truly talented, it will be recognized.

There are a great many people who write for Frommer's guidebooks whose work just came in over the transom, who had never written before and whom we contracted with based on reading a really great audition. A young woman named Beth Bryant called us many years ago—she lived in Washington D.C.—and said she wanted to write guidebooks. I said, write the restaurant chapter of a hypothetical guidebook to Washington D.C. in which you rate the government cafeterias. And she wrote this absolutely delightful comparison of the Justice Department cafeteria with the Commerce Department, all of which are open to public visits. We immediately knew that we had a star on our hands. She was sent to Ireland where she wrote the first edition of our Ireland guidebook which is a travel classic. It's one of the best ones we've ever done.

After all your world travels, do you have a favorite city or a place that still warms your heart?

I don't even hesitate, the city of Paris. People are always disappointed when I respond with such a familiar location—they're expecting something much more exotic from me, but I regard Paris as being on the frontier of every major subject, of literature, of art, of culture, of cuisine, of political thought. I am constantly invigorated by my trips to Paris. I'd love to spend more time there. I've often found that the French have become surprisingly courteous in their response to the American tourist recently, even more so now that there is such a vast political gap between our governments. But Paris is my favorite place in all the world.

When Worlds Collude

Pico Iyer
SANTA BARBARA, CALIFORNIA

"I F TRAVEL IS ABOUT THE MEETING OF REALITIES, IT IS NO LESS ABOUT the mating of illusions: You give me my dreamed-of vision of Tibet, and I'll give you your wished-for California," Pico Iyer writes in an essay entitled, "Why We Travel." Born in England to Indian parents, Iyer moved to California with his family when he was seven. He soon returned to England for boarding school, spending most of each year in an educational institution with roots stretching back to the fifteenth century. He may not have realized it then, but his unique background, a braid of Indian blood, English tradition, and American hopefulness, would provide an ideal platform for writing about the cross-currents and mingled dreams that course between cultures.

Whether it's a KFC in Beijing, baseball in Japan, or the comings and goings at the twenty-first-century city that is LAX (Los Angeles Airport), Iyer brings a keen eye and startling attentiveness to his subjects. He strives to venture into the world with beginner's mind, the

Buddhist concept of leaving preconceptions behind. His insights astonish us, yet his writing never feels preachy; typically he lets readers draw their own conclusions.

Iyer's first book, *Video Night in Kathmandu*, is a kaleidoscopic view of ten Asian countries that Iyer visited during the mid-1980s while on leave from his day job at *TIME* magazine. Next, he traveled to Japan to spend a year in a monastery, but after a week Iyer's curiosity about Kyoto propelled him onto its back streets. The result is an often-meditative book, *The Lady and the Monk*, which has the feel of a novel.

The Global Soul, a millennial look at our modern world, explores its new states from Toronto's "multiculture" to jet lag. In the book, Iyer considers today's amorphous conception of home, moving from the freedom that arose out of the ashes of his family's incinerated house in Santa Barbara to his "alien home," a two-room apartment in Japan that he shares with Hiroko, the "lady" from *The Lady and the Monk*.

Today Iyer spends much of the year in Japan, without access to English-language newspapers or TV programs he can understand. "I feel, more and more, that I have too much information in my life—not too little," he said, "and what I crave most is the chance to step back." He also spends a few weeks annually at his mother's Santa Barbara home and frequently retreats to a Benedictine hermitage in central California.

Iyer's travel stories appear in *Condé Nast Traveler*, his essays in *TIME*, and in 2003 Iyer published his second novel, *Abandon*. A recent work, *Sun After Dark*, is a set of linked trips into various states of mind, conscious and subconscious, triggered by journeys to some of the poorest (and least American) countries in the world.

I visited Iyer at his mother's rebuilt home, in the hills above Santa Barbara, on a foggy, late-spring day. When he saw the dancing-bear stickers on my truck, he told me he too had reveled in the bacchanalian exuberance of Grateful Dead shows. Knowing that he loved Van Morrison, I'd brought him a bootleg tape of a 1991 concert in Europe, for which he thanked me effusively.

As we walked into the house, we talked about the 1990 forest fire that leveled his family's home and destroyed two of Iyer's almost-finished manuscripts. As he discusses in the first chapter of *The Global Soul*, Iyer mentioned that a Buddhist symbol for freedom from illusion is a burning house.

"All the props of my parents' sixty years, all the notes and prospects I'd been collecting for fifteen years, all the photographs, memories— all the past—gone," he writes. "I'd spent much of the previous year among the wooden houses of Japan, reading the 'burning house' poems of Buddhist monks and musing on the value of living without possessions and a home. But now all the handy metaphors were actual, and the lines of the poems…were my only real foundations for a new *fin de siècle* life."

You've called yourself a born traveler with Indian heritage, birth in England, childhood in California and so on. Some people who have been schlepped all over the world as children just want to find a plot of land and stay home. Do you ever feel pulled toward a more settled life with less travel?

You're absolutely right that travel is in my bloodstream and to some extent I'm reconciled at this point in my life to the fact that I'll probably never get it out of my system. It is the essence of me as much as my height and the color of my hair. For somebody of my background, that makes it interesting. But even when I settle down, by my standards, most people regard me as being extremely itinerant. You're right to suggest that in some ways to me the great luxury now is staying put.

For example, when I live in Japan, as I do seven or eight months of the year, I spend three months without a car, without a bicycle, seldom leaving the immediate four square blocks of my neighborhood, and not even speaking English. In some ways it's a very intense form of stillness. Four times a year I go to a Catholic monastery in Northern California to complement the process of movement. Ultimately, movement is only as valuable as your commitment to stillness, and vice versa. I try to keep both poles going in my life. Many people who are shuffled around a lot when young hanker after a base in some ways. I decided, as I was being shuttled around, that my base would have to be inward and that it would be important to erect some solid ground inside myself that I could take everywhere, as a snail does. I never have felt a real attachment to a piece of property.

Would you talk a little more about your inward home, the base you've created for yourself inside?

That's probably made up of friendships, loyalties, interests, and the passions I take with me wherever I happen to go. I'll have certain Van Morrison songs I've listened to intimately for twenty years and to some extent they form a part of my home. Whether I'm in Tibet or sitting here in Santa Barbara, that is a place I can return to. I sometimes think that the English language has been a home to me, because it's the one thing that's kept me company every living breath of my life. For any writer, language and words are a kind of refuge and a kind of portable home. And those of us who are born to English are lucky, in that we can take our home everywhere we go because English is a lingua franca around the globe.

I've always had this sense of home being something invisible and portable and I think this was intensified for me when this house

I came from nowhere.... I'd never had a strong sense of departures (or arrivals); I'd grown up without a sense of place.... Someone like me, I figured, could (for worse as much as better) fit in everywhere.... Everywhere could be home to some extent, and not home to some degree. My sense of severences was less absolute.... I knew I could get anywhere very soon, and nothing was final.

—Pico Iyer, *The Global Soul*

burned down to the ground in a forest fire in 1990. I was caught in the middle of the fire for three hours and finally managed to escape down to a friend's apartment. I went to buy a toothbrush and the next day when I woke up and somebody asked me, "What's your home?" I, in a very direct sense, couldn't point to a piece of soil or point to anything except what I had on my person or inside my person. Life performed the happy task of making what had been a metaphorical truth a very literal truth.

In the aftermath of the fire, what was your greatest sense of loss? Did you feel the liberation initially or did that come later?

I probably told myself that I felt liberation—in reality the only thing I missed was all my notes and the many books that were in progress or that were close to completion that were reduced to ash. And yet at the same time I probably did quickly see that as a possible liberation. I think one of the good things about being a traveler is that you come to see every circumstance as a possibility. When any of us are traveling, especially in one of the difficult parts of the world, we know that in some ways the more things go wrong, the better the stories that we will bring back from it.

There's some degree of detachment you get as a traveler which means that in the midst of calamity a little part of you is outside that, taking a record of it and turning it already into a narrative that will be amusing or healing or whatever. The other way in which travel helped me is that most of my traveling has been to places where people would be desperate just to have one room in this little house. It's always a humbling process. I realized even the day after the fire, when I had no property I was still leading a life that would be the envy of 98 percent of the people on the globe. Traveling is a wonderful way of putting things into perspective.

In terms of liberation: the day after the fire I called up my long-time book editor in London and I told him that since all my notes were gone, all the books that I'd been promising him were gone. He said, "Well, that's great; you should celebrate! It's the best possible thing that could happen to you because now you're liberated from your notes." And it was good to hear that from him because it would have been hard to persuade myself of that. But I'm sure he was right.

When you're traveling with a view toward writing about a place it's a hard balance trying to decide how much you want to annotate it and how much you want to rely on intuition, even imagination. Once you've made that decision, when you get back home you have to decide to what extent you're going to be hostage to your notes. I was always very hostage to my notes. I probably was usefully liberated by the fire, especially since the previous year I'd gone to Japan with a view to living more simply and without possessions. I couldn't complain when I got the chance.

You mention perspective. Having seen so much of the world and how little materially so many people have, you might have that perspective whereas maybe 90 percent of Americans don't have that viewpoint. I've *read that only 14 percent of Americans hold a passport. When I have an extra $1,000 in the bank I'm thinking airplane ticket—I'm not making a down payment on a new car. It seems like travel is the priority in your life.*

Exactly—it's the only luxury I indulge myself in. My only car in the world is this rickety bottom-of-the-line Toyota that doesn't even have a mirror on the passenger side and doesn't have air conditioning and is pretty much on its last legs. I've never owned property in my life and to this day I don't have any place of my own—I go back and forth between my Japanese partner's two-room apartment and my mother's house where we're sitting now. The notion of having a place of my own is almost anathema or unthinkable to me. I literally live out of a suitcase and like the sense of light-footedness and the sense of freedom that it gives me.

The other part of it is that all of us can travel within our own hometowns. Some of the things you see in the farthest and most difficult corners of the world you can see today in central Los Angeles or Atlanta or Detroit. But we're less moved to do that. That's one reason I've always been inspired by the process of travel: it opens your eyes to things that are all around you at home but things that you take for granted.

I think as soon as some travelers get off the airplane somewhere they are more open, more approachable and more willing to meet new people— they're different people.

Absolutely, different people, and often better people, kinder people, more open and attentive people. When walking down the street in Santa Barbara, when I meet a stranger, as I do every three seconds, I'm very rarely moved to talk to him or to find out about his life. When walking down the street in Damascus or Ascunsión, I would find everyone interesting, and I would want to hear every story around because I wouldn't be walled in by the illusion that I know them. In Santa Barbara I tell myself that I know something about strangers' circumstances and can read something of them—which is, I think, an illusion.

I just wrote a novel as you know and I gave the main character the name of Ms. Jensen. That's because, as I understand it, there's actually a Ms. Jensen who's the crown princess of Thailand. She grew up in the Grand Palace, the eldest daughter of the king and queen of Thailand, but just happened to marry a Danish man and move to Los Angeles and lives as the somewhat anonymous Ms. Jensen. The reason that's always fascinated me is that it speaks to my sense that especially nowadays in America with so many immigrants all around us, we pass people in the street who have amazing histories and backgrounds unfathomable to us, but we see them as just another person who's arrived from Thailand or Rwanda.

In some ways our immediate surroundings in California are getting more interesting and more worthy of the travel writer's eye than ever because so many cultures are just round the corner here. A lot of what I've been writing about is the way you can travel without actually moving 2,000 miles because I think for me the main aspect of travel is simply forcing yourself to open your eyes and see the world more attentively than otherwise. I'd love to write a travel article about my hometown of Santa Barbara and walk through it as if I were just arriving for the first time. But it's hard to keep that freshness and remain genuinely open.

Would you talk about what you were first seeking when you started traveling on your own and what you're seeking now and how that's changed?

These questions are too deep. (Laughs.) Who's my favorite musician? Van Morrison, I can answer that one. When I first really began traveling through Asia in the mid-'80s, while I was working at *TIME* magazine in New York hoping to become a full-time traveler and writer, what I realized I seemed to have a special sensitivity to—not because I'm a sensitive person but just because of my background—is this whole new culture that's arising out of the mish-mashed collisions and collusions of East and West. When I would walk around Beijing I would take in the Forbidden City and the Great Wall, but what particularly engaged me were the places where these ancient, Eastern things met and assimilated and re-created something very modern from the West. So although it wasn't what I was seeking, it seems to be what often found me.

This confluence of cultures?

Yes, because I am a confluence of cultures myself, I felt an affinity with this new mongrel world. Also I felt it was something new and uncharted.

I felt I had nothing to contribute in the description of traditional China or the Great Wall or the Forbidden City, which people have been writing about more eloquently than I ever could for hundreds of years. But there was something new that no one had really stopped to think about and that I naturally found myself drawn to, and was changing almost as quickly as I was writing it. So my first few years in Asia, that's what I found myself gravitating towards.

I first really began traveling when I was seventeen. I went to India and at that time what I was seeking was to become the Indian Leonard Cohen. I was in a sheltered, fifteenth-century, English boarding school and all I wanted was the opposite of it: romance, adventure, everything that was forbidden. I remember when I was seventeen walking around India with almost nothing except a guitar and a very scratchy cassette of Leonard Cohen's first songs and the wish to turn myself into a romantic gypsy.

In those days, I think I was looking for solutions to certain questions—now I'm looking for questions that become deeper the more you investigate them. I'm looking for places that will shake me up and force me to question things that I take for granted. I want more and more to be unsettled by places. In some ways, therefore, the process of traveling has become more inward.

To take an example: I went to Tibet for the first time in 1985. Because Tibet had just opened up to the world, people knew very little about it, myself included. I just transcribed my days there and the interactions between the handful of Westerners who stumbled into what used to be known as the Forbidden City of Lhasa and Tibetans who had seldom seen the West before. That seemed to be the news coming out of Tibet: this new dance between East and West. When I went back to Tibet in 2002, all that was relatively old news.

So when I went back, although I was taking in the details as before, really what I was asking is the question that Tibet awakens in everyone who goes there, which is how much to believe, how much we're projecting our longings onto it, to what extent it really is a magical place—much more internal questions than before. I think that's a reflection of my sense that whenever I take a trip the point is to see things differently. So if I go to a place I've been to before, I want to ask different questions and make sure I'm not reproducing that earlier trip.

The danger attending any travel writer is that travel writing is generated by the excitement of discovery and the wonder of coming upon something unsuspected. If you travel a lot, as many travel writers do, there's a danger of losing that sense of freshness. You have to, perhaps artificially, keep it alive, always asking different questions of yourself and trying to come at things at a different angle so that you can have a quickened sense of discovery.

Do you select the angle and try to come up with questions before embarking on a journey, or do you go and see what questions arise when you get there?

I think both, and I think my method has changed a little, more toward agnosticism. Certainly, when I wrote my first book, *Video Night in Kathmandu*, because I was going to ten Asian countries and only spending two weeks in each, and because I had never studied any of them and didn't speak the language, and really was nothing more than a typical tourist, I thought I was in no position to say anything useful or novel about any of those places. The only way I could justify my writing was to take one specific aspect of each place and through that keyhole try to see the larger culture.

I chose a very specific focus that I could understand. When I went to Japan, because I didn't speak Japanese, I chose the theme of baseball, since I figured I could understand baseball even without speaking Japanese. By going to baseball games and following the lead of baseball, I could see something about how Japan was taking a quintessentially American thing and turning it into something Japanese, which is the heart of what Japan does with everything from the outside world.

In those days, I would pick a theme and use it as a center around which to collect my impressions. So when I went to Japan I wrote about Zen temples and the museum in Hiroshima but always brought it back to baseball because I think the first imperative of any travel writer is clarity: to take a reader and lead her by the hand through the adventures and discoveries that he's made. One has to use something simple that people can relate to, and baseball was that for me. Nowadays, I tend not to have such a specific angle. I think I'm more eager to be surprised by places.

When I went to Tibet last year all I knew at the outset was that I was going to register how Tibet had changed. It was my third trip and I hadn't been there for twelve years and I wanted to see how it was different. But at the same time this other question suddenly came to me: Although I've traveled a lot, I've noticed odd, intense dreams and strange coincidences and very powerful moments seem to happen much more in Tibet than most other places I've been—why is that?

Eight months before, I'd been to Bolivia, which is very similar in certain ways to Tibet, and in some ways these days more interesting. In Bolivia I'd experienced these intense dreams and lightheadedness and the power of being surrounded by something magical, partly because of the altitude. So with Bolivia fresh in my mind, I was looking at Tibet and saying how much is its magic due to altitude sickness and how much is it something intrinsic to the culture? I like those kinds of questions because they are fundamentally unanswerable. All I can do is travel deeper and deeper into the question. The more I travel into it the more it will open up into other questions.

In conversation once, Milan Kundera said to Philip Roth something like, "The purpose of a novelist is to encourage the reader to comprehend the world as a question," and I think I would extend that to a travel writer. So that's what leads me on these days—because I think the whole process of travel is fundamentally inspired by curiosity. Curiosity has to do with wanting to resolve something or know something more about a place, the longing to journey deeper into a question. Or to go to places in oneself that one seldom visits when encircled by the familiar stuff of home.

You had a pretty unusual path in that you had probably the best possible British education and then you found yourself on the road for Let's Go, living on a shoestring. Can you talk about your early career at Let's Go and at TIME and how that shaped you?

In terms of preparation for being a travel writer or a traveler, I think those British boarding schools are invaluable. It's no coincidence that to this day, although there are fewer and fewer of these schools, a disproportionate number of the travel writers that we read and enjoy come out of such backgrounds. Those schools are essentially preparations for empire—they're crosses between a military and monastic training, very rigorous and tough.

Really, what they're teaching you is to live very simply, on inedible food, in extremely spartan quarters, waking up at six in the morning, having cold showers, slogging through the mud on a drizzly November day, voluntarily putting yourself through a lot of hardship. In some deep way that was because most of the people coming out of these schools 150 years ago were going to go to Afghanistan or India or Kenya to slog through very, very difficult circumstances. Although the empire is gone, it's still really a training for that.

The boarding school was a very good training for being in very difficult circumstances—many of my friends from there, to this day, when they take a family vacation, will go to Ethiopia or Yemen or Haiti or places more difficult than not. The other important part of that training is that if you go to a private school in England you have a year off between graduating from high school and going to college—the assumption traditionally has been that that's a year in which you go and see the world so and live in a difficult place, work and really learn enough about the world that when you go to university you see some of the limitations of university. So that's what I did. When I graduated from high school I came here to Santa Barbara and worked in a Mexican restaurant for three months as a busboy, distributing water into people's laps. I saved up enough money to take a bus from Tijuana down to La Paz, Bolivia and then to fly up the eastern coast of South America and back through Trinidad and Barbados, then to Miami, and a Greyhound back across the country—three months of pretty strenuous traveling across almost the whole of the Americas.

To this day I'm very grateful to that educational system, not for the Greek and Latin it taught me, but for a certain familiarity with the world that I think it's expert at passing on to its victims. Let's Go was a great training in terms of learning to move fast, to take lots of notes, to write them up every night in great detail and to take the measure of a place. I worked on the Let's Go books for two years, 1981 and '82, and in my first year one of the places I was responsible for was France, about twenty-seven towns in twenty-eight days. In each town I was responsible for visiting all the sights, ostensibly visiting all the hotels and restaurants, and then every night writing up ten to fifteen pages of prose on carbon copy paper in those pre-computer days.

I had to learn to keep my eyes always open, not even to rest for thirty minutes and I had to get in the habit of waking up at dawn, taking a train, getting into a town and just walking around it for ten hours. And then, at the end of those ten hours, to sit down in a very clammy, rat-infested hotel and write it up. It was a good training in bearing in mind the readers' needs more than the writer's needs. When I went into a town my impulse might be to commit 2,000 words of flowery prose on the soul of Nice, but what a typical Let's Go reader needs to know is just how to get a cheap meal. Traveling on a shoe-string was a good training for almost everything—the cheaper the hotel I stay in, the better the stories that come out of it. And I think that's almost an unfailing law. At the time, I didn't think it was training for being a travel writer—I thought it was just a working vacation.

Or another cruel rite of passage?

Well, actually I liked it sufficiently that after one year of staying in rat-infested hotels I signed up for a second year, so clearly I realized that self-inflicted punishment was my second nature. A couple of years later I realized the great virtue of the whole process. I learned to write clearly and concisely and learned especially to keep the readers' needs in mind. If I were writing 600 words on the week's events in Lebanon, the last thing any of *TIME*'s 30 million readers would need is my wordplay or my rococo stylistic experiments. They just need a very succinct and simple description of what happened.

Working for *TIME* was a very good training in selflessness and in learning about places very quickly, because I was writing on world affairs in New York for four years and usually writing about places I had not been to. My editor would come in each week on a Tuesday and say, "This week you're writing on Paraguay, or South Africa or the Philippines," none of them places I knew. I had to learn a little bit about them very quickly and then have enough expertise to guide the reader through some of the simple facts of those places two days later.

It was also good training in not being cowed. For the kind of writing I do, I won't say that ignorance is an advantage but it's certainly not a deterrent. I found in working for *TIME* that it would have been almost impossible for me to write an article about England, because I had twenty years of experiences and mixed feelings and complicated ideas about the country where I was born. To begin to compress them into a small space and then to try to make them intelligible, even interesting was well beyond me. Whereas if I was asked to write something about Paraguay, I was that much closer to my reader in terms of how little I knew and my curiosity in learning about it. So when I came to travel I never felt inhibited by the fact that I didn't know very much about a place. I thought, well I'm probably similar to a typical tourist.

I remember when I went to Thailand in 1983 and wrote a chapter in my first book about it, a lot of my chapter had to do with hotel keepers, bar girls, and *tuk-tuk* drivers. They have nothing to do with the heart of Thailand, but they have a lot to do with the part of Thailand that a typical visitor experiences. A travel writer is in some ways a professional amateur. One of the advantages he has is that he's not encumbered by an agenda and not weighed down by twenty years of studying a place, but can try to bring some of the freshness to it that any first-time visitor would have or want.

So you're out of TIME *and take this four-week vacation to Asia and you realize this is real: the sights, the sounds, the textures, the emotions. What was that like and did it make you feel different about what you were doing, writing about the world from a little cubicle in the Time-Life building?*

It made me feel differently about how I wanted to write about the world. I joined *TIME* in October 1982, and I took a four-week vacation in October 1983. That was a trip that turned me around forever, because it was my first real taste of Asia. I can still remember, vividly, almost every moment of those first few days—the arrival at Bangkok's airport, the trip from the airport through the winding lanes, the overnight train to Chiang Mai and waking up to see the dawn and the cool mountains and the villagers working in the fields; and a few days after that, going to Burma which to this day is a magical and transforming place. Every day presented me with something completely outside my experience. I was twenty-six at that point, and I'd never stayed with a group of animists who were eating dogs and smoking opium. I'd never been in a place like Pagan, where there are 3,000 temples that are white and golden and clay-red everywhere you look. I'd never stayed in a fancy hotel as I ended up doing in Hong Kong. On that first trip I had a one-night layover in Narita, Japan. I'd never been to Japan before and I had one morning free before my flight back to New York. In that morning I walked around the town of Narita and in some ways that so changed my life that a few years later, I went back and lived in Japan and I live there to this day.

It all seemed so real and so wondrous and so exotic. Every person I met seemed to have a story that was so fascinating and so outside my experience. I thought that I was alone in a richness of stories and senses and sights unlike anything I could re-create in midtown Manhattan.

When I returned to New York, what I remember mostly was this feeling of homesickness, as if I'd met a girl on a holiday, fallen in love with her, and then had to fly back to my home on the other side of the world. All I could talk about was going back to that experience and that place, because it so excited me and so opened me up. I resumed my job and continued writing articles for *TIME* magazine, but I'd keep sneaking out to the *TIME* library and just open any magazine that had an article about Cambodia or Laos, which were not places I had ever visited, but were close to them and fragrant with the same feeling.

I would sit in my apartment and just look at my pictures over and over. They were very undistinguished snapshots, but I enlarged them and framed them and put them in my office so that when you walked into my office in Rockefeller Center, you'd see a temple in Burma and a side street in Chiang Mai, or a little girl from Indonesia. I just began to plot about how I could get back there. It didn't make me frustrated with the kind of writing I was doing, but it did present me with this alternative world that was very difficult for anything to rival. I did go back five months later to Asia and then again six months after that. So I took three holidays in the course of a year in Southeast Asia, and those three holidays gave me enough material to begin to write a book.

One advantage I had was that I wasn't traveling with a view to writing. I was just traveling on vacation, with a view only to experiencing and opening myself up to everything as much as possible. When you travel to write, to some extent you're in danger of limiting yourself. I just wanted to wander and take in as much as possible, and while taking these vacations, I was so excited that I was scribbling hundreds of pages of notes in my journal—and I don't even keep a journal the rest of the time. I was also thinking that if I'm going to all the trouble of writing all this down for myself, I might as well share it with other people.

It was an exciting time to be in Southeast Asia because although it was only twenty years ago, the area was still relatively undiscovered. Thailand in 1983 was to some extent the Wild West. For better and worse. You were often getting accosted by strangers with uncertain motives in the street—even when you got to the airport (it was a fairly rickety airport in those days), people would loom out of the dark showing you albums full of pictures of scantily clad girls or all kinds of places you'd never want to go to. Things had a lawless, open feeling that they'd lost in Thailand even by 1988.

But at the same time I don't conform to that comforting notion we often have that places get spoiled. I think it's more that our perception of them gets spoiled. After that first impression, when we go back to a place, what we're doing is not seeing the place naked but comparing it with the place we saw before and registering some fact about how we've changed or how we've lost an element of innocence. So I think corruption is in the eye of the beholder, more than in the place itself.

I know you speak of how each culture adopts other influences but it seems indigenous cultures are under siege. Is something being lost?

Indigenous cultures are often older than we are and to some extent wiser than we are, and to some extent more resilient than we are, too. So it's akin to the process of seeing anybody grow older. Somebody age thirty is different and a little more sober and less innocent that she was when she was fifteen. And when she's fifty, she'll be different still. But the heart of her character often doesn't change very much. And what was frustrating about her at fifteen and enticing about her at fifteen is often the same when she's fifty, even though she's going through that inevitable process of gaining certain kinds of wisdom and losing certain kinds of innocence.

Bali is an interesting example because when I first visited it in '84 and '85—and the chapter I wrote about it in my first book was entirely about addressing the question of how much it was getting spoiled—one of the things I discovered when I was doing my research was that every book on Bali, most of them from the '30s and '40s, said that Bali was about to be destroyed by the global megaculture. A book from 1939 was entitled *The Last Paradise*. There seems to be something intrinsic about Bali that has people always asking the same question about it.

And when my friends go to Bali today I hear them asking exactly the same questions I asked in 1984, which is exactly the same question that was being asked in 1930. I'm not convinced that the place has been spoiled or corrupted because I feel that the character of the Balinese people and the culture, which is the reason most of us go there, remains as interested in the outside world and as strong in itself as it was then.

I find that when I come back to America, which is a much younger and to that extent more vulnerable culture than the ones of Asia, I and most of my friends here are bombarded by the cultural influences of India and Thailand and Japan and France and Italy and Mexico and Guatemala. We thrive on it and remain as much ourselves as we ever were even while we're going to the Mexican restaurant in a Japanese car, on our way to the Ayurvedic clinic and the tai chi session.

It can be a sort of cultural imperialism. We want Tibet to remain as it was twenty years ago even if it's not as sanitary or clean while the local people want modern facilities or KFC. Who are we to say what the local people over there should have? We welcome foreign influences and like our Thai restaurants.

Exactly. We want our DVD players and our cars and flat-screen TVs. We want these other countries to remain quaintly picturesque. And I think they're more able to withstand those kinds of changes and influences because they've been around two or three thousand years rather than two or three hundred years, and because they have their roots much deeper in the soil.

Bali is a good example because I think the fascination with Bali is that it's always a little bit out of reach. I think what draws us travelers there again and again is this tantalizing sense there's something in the soil and in the air and culture that we can't touch, but that is the beating heart of Balinese society. Insofar as it remains outside our understanding, it also remains beyond our ability to corrupt it.

You've probably heard the joke: What did the first tourist say to the second tourist arriving in Bali? "You should have seen it when…" And that gets to projection, which is what you often deal with in your books, projections on cultures and countries as well as projections on individuals.

That's been my theme from the outset. And a bit of that arises out of my background, because one of the curious features of my upbringing is that it was cheaper for me to go to boarding school in England and return here to California three times a year than to go to the local private school in Santa Barbara. So from the time I was nine years old I was going to school by plane. I realized only a few years ago that it was a perfect training in seeing how cultures project their longings and fantasies and dreams upon one another.

In those days, every little English boy had one dream in life and that was to be a Californian. In a fifteenth-century English boarding school, what we longed for were broad horizons, the possibility of reinvention, the space, the freedom, the pleasures that California was a byword for. When I came back, I thought that what a lot of my California friends longed for was that sense of tradition and history and continuity, solid foundations and a past that Britain has in abundance.

It was almost as if I was going back and forth between two cultures that were dreaming about one another. Later, when I wrote about the influence of American culture around the world, I was able to write about it less critically than some people might, because I remember listening to the Grateful Dead in rainy England and watching *I Love Lucy*. I remember how my hometown of Oxford was transformed by McDonald's in the late '70s because it was the first restaurant that was clean and inexpensive and incredibly tasty, much better than the English equivalent.

We're always very attuned to the deficiencies of our culture and the wonders of other cultures, which is why we travel. And maybe I

>
>
> For if every true love affair can feel like a journey to a foreign country, where you can't quite speak the language, and you don't know where you're going, and you're pulled ever deeper into the inviting darkness, every trip to a foreign country can be a love affair, where you're left puzzling over who you are and whom you've fallen in love with…. All good trips are, like love, about being carried out of yourself and deposited in the midst of terror and wonder.
>
> —Pico Iyer, "Why We Travel"

have the advantage of not belonging to any culture, and so I hope to be open to the wonders of every culture, American included. Even though I've lived here on and off for forty years, a part of me is an outsider which is to say a part of me is still enchanted by America. Even though I know the reality of the place now, it's still exotic and romantic and glamorous to me because I'm still a little removed from it.

So the ideas that cultures project or cast upon other cultures have always been my theme. In the first chapter of my first book I described a large American dancing with a young Philippine woman in Manila and imagined how she might project some of her longings on him, and he on her, and neither would know how much they were interacting with the culture and how much they were interacting with the individual. I think that's one of the exciting confusions about traveling: we're taken in by a culture and we're often open to the people we meet. We don't know how much they are symbols to us and how much we're understanding them as real people. And, equally, we don't know whether we're symbols to them or whether they're responding to us because we're such intrinsically irresistible individuals (laughs), or because we're emissaries from this land of abundance and opportunity.

Your work made me rethink some of my perceptions. When I was in Thailand, I saw these svelte, delicate Thai girls—and they were girls; some were sixteen or younger—with these large, somewhat boorish, lager-bellied Germans. And I thought, These girls have to tolerate these gruff Germans. One thing that appeals to me about your work is that you try not to judge, but rather approach the world with beginner's mind.

That's a lovely phrase, thank you. Foreignness is an intoxicant. As when we're drunk, we don't know how much it's our true selves coming out and how much it's the drink speaking through us. And so I think those young Thai women walking through the street with the large German men wouldn't be able to say how much they're attracted by what the German men represent or how much by something else. The first thing I noticed when I traveled around Southeast Asia, when I talked, say, to the young women who worked in the bars in Thailand, was that they had nothing good to say about Thai men. And when I went to Bali, young Balinese girls had nothing good to say about Balinese men. And I don't think that means that the Thai and Balinese men are inherently worse than any others. I think it goes back to what I was saying a minute ago: when we see people from our own community we're particularly sensitive to all the things that are wrong with them. When we see people from another community we're alive to what's refreshing about them.

I travel in search of ambiguity. To me, the beauty of travel comes in dissolving one's judgments. When I sit inside my house in Santa Barbara I'll think about a couple in Thailand and decide that the German is an imperialist who's corrupting this sweet and relatively impoverished society. And the beauty of going to Thailand is quickly to have to throw out all those notions, and to see a reality that's much more human and complex and to some extent unfathomable.

In terms of what you say so nicely about beginner's mind: the one advantage I have is that when I began traveling, especially when I began writing about travel, I don't think I was seeing any place with a typical English mind. Although I was born and grew up in England, I'm nobody's idea of an Englishman. And I wasn't seeing things with a typical American mind, because although I've been resident here for forty years, you can hear by my voice that I'm not a typical American; and I wasn't seeing them with a typical Indian mind though my blood is 100 percent Indian, because I've never lived in India.

Living outside cultures and traditional definitions allowed me to approach places in a different and ideally a more open way. I grew up having to entertain simultaneously a lot of different systems of values, going back and forth between England and an Indian household in California, and so might be less likely to be entrapped in any one of them. And that's one way travel writing to me seems to have gained a whole new life. People often worry or wonder whether travel writing will lose its reason for being now that so much of the world is so accessible to so many people.

But my sense is that the nature of humanity is changing because of this mish-mash of cultures and the different kind of human beings who see the world with new eyes. Even when I was growing up—when I was born in 1957—a lot of the travel writing in English was the legacy of empire, and now, forty years on, it's very different. More women are traveling and the people who are traveling and writing about their travels come from much more mingled and multicultural backgrounds.

You look like you could be from any number of places. Does that help you?

Very much. It's a huge advantage and I really do have a completely chameleon complexion, which allows me to pass as a local in most places, to fade into the background, in a way that you and most people from America and Europe traditionally never could. Whether it's South America or the Middle East or Indonesia or Cuba, I can pass as a local and that's sometimes an advantage. But in Cuba I've been barred admission to hotels because people assume I'm Cuban. I've been thrown off beaches because Cubans aren't allowed to walk on some of their beaches, only tourists are. By and large it's allowed me to drift around like an invisible vessel, which is what I like to do. It's also allowed me to choose my nationality when people on a foreign street ask the archetypal question: Where do you come from?

In Cuba I might say I come from India and they're very excited because they don't see many people from India and they're often fascinated by yoga or Gandhi. And in the Philippines I might say I come from California and they're very excited because lots of them have relatives in California or long to be Californians. In Burma I might say I come from England and they're excited because they might want to discuss Trollope with somebody and haven't had the chance for many years.

I'm even blessed, through no feat of my own, with this useful name. Most people wouldn't recognize Iyer as an Indian name. Pico is actually an Italian name that sounds Spanish or Portuguese. So I grew up with these advantages for being a sort of global citizen.

Before we go on, I want to address the question about Burma—are there countries because of their government that good travelers just shouldn't visit? I went to Guatemala in the late '80s and people said I shouldn't be there because of the military government, but I remember buying things on the street from impoverished people who were so grateful I was there. I see the other point of view, but I also feel that if you go and engage as much as possible in person-to-person interactions, that you're really doing the local people a favor.

I've strongly felt that the more closed and the more oppressed a country, the greater is its people's hunger for contact with the world. And I think tourists can be the eyes and ears of people who are imprisoned in cultures that want to keep them completely isolated from the world. In Tibet, for example, tourists are the ones who can take the stories of Tibet out into the world, who can record the sufferings of the people there and who can be the only way that the Tibetan people, occupied by a culture 200 times larger than themselves can begin to have a voice in the world.

Burma's more troublesome because its most notable figure of conscience, Aung San Suu Kyi, has told people not to go. I've been to Burma only twice, but my feeling there was that tourists offer a sliver of imaginative freedom that is one of the most precious things that people in constrained countries can have. We can't hope to save their lives or even to make their lives a lot better. But what I find when I'm in Cuba or Burma or potentially in North Korea is that just for those people there to have the sense that they know someone from California, that somebody on the other side of the world is thinking about them, or corresponding with them, opens a small window in their lives that wasn't there before.

There's also a sense that people in closed countries long more than anything for information about the world. And their governments, by definition dictatorships, are trying to screen them from the world and keep them in a self-enclosed universe. We are the only people who can tell them what America's really like, for better or worse.

Famously in many cultures, Tibet and China included, the only way the citizens could follow what was going on among their own leaders was through the Voice of America, or nowadays maybe through CNN. But I think travelers are the individual Voice of America even if we just tell people we meet what our life is like in California, what we're thinking about, what music we're listening to, and what the discussion is in America about Burma and Tibet. And if we take that news to people in Burma and Tibet, I think that's significant assistance. The money that we spend is most likely going to go into the least deserving hands—often into the hands of the dictators who are keeping those people down. And the dictators will cruelly exploit the people in order to set up a tourist market. I'm not suggesting that we overlook those grim realities, but every place I've been, and especially the difficult places I've been, has reminded me of the power that even a single traveler can bring to somebody whose life is repressed.

It seems even more important now that our government here in the U.S. is rattling its sabers and taking a more militaristic approach to the world. Its citizens can show the American spirit of generosity and kindness.

People, as you say, are much wiser and more tolerant and open-minded than their governments. What I've found everywhere is this disjunction you're suggesting, which is that most people I meet are quite suspicious of and hostile to the American government; the same people are transfixed by American culture and long to make American friends and long to be Americans sometimes.

Burma is an interesting example because it has one of the cruelest, most remorseless governments on earth and has among the most good-natured and guileless, innocent people that I've met anywhere. And that's a good way for us to see past our simplified notions of Burma. Mostly what we hear about is the government and what we don't hear about is that human reality.

I went back and forth between Cuba and the United States a lot at the end of the '80s, when very few people were doing it, and I always felt that one good thing I could take to Cuba was a human, balanced sense of what America was like. And one good thing I could bring back from Cuba was a human, balanced sense of what Cuba was like, neither a paradise nor a hellhole but a confounding mixture of them both. And I remember soon thereafter I actually made a practice of going to all the countries that were listed on the U.S. Treasury Department's Trading with the Enemy Act, precisely because I felt they were places I could never learn about sitting in California, that all I would ever read or hear about them would either be propaganda against them or the response to it, which was wild propaganda in favor of them.

I felt it was my duty to educate myself about them, and since I'm lucky enough to have the time and resources to travel, I wanted to see what they were really like. We've heard a lot about the clash of civilizations, in recent years especially. I've always been interested in the other half of the equation: the romance of civilizations. We're unsettled by the foreign, but we're also fascinated by it and drawn towards it. We in California, say, often do have the time and money to go and see other parts of the world. People in other parts of the world seldom have the time and money to come and see us. So insofar as there's any potential for human interaction, and for beginning to get past these divisions of "us" and "them," the responsibility falls with us. The only way most Cubans are going to meet an American is by us going there.

I was there a couple of years ago and I found it refreshing to see that almost all Cubans could distinguish between Americans and the American government. They didn't hold our government's actions against us—they were so eager to befriend us and show us around their towns and sell cigars…

Havana days are the softest I know, the golden light of dusk spangling the cool buildings in the tree-lined streets; Havana nights are the most vibrant and electric, with dark-eyed, scarlet girls leaning against the fins of chrome-polished '57 Chryslers under the floodlit mango trees of Prohibition-era nightclubs.

—PICO IYER, *Falling Off the Map*

I just recently wrote this novel *Abandon* that plays on the fact that exactly at the time when America is at war with radical Islam, the single most popular poet in America is an Islamic mystic, Rumi. Many people in this country think of Islamic governments as our enemy. Yet when we meet somebody of Islamic origins, we're often as friendly to them as a Cuban is to an American.

My sense is that cultures and individuals are subtler than their governments and actually are the only way we can make bridges between them. Governments are rooted in their ideologies and survive by keeping up the sense of "us" versus "them." They have to have a keen sense of enmity; whereas many individuals don't have that. So that's one reason I've become a great advocate of travel, especially for Americans. I think it's dangerous in a global world to screen ourselves away from realities.

We talked a bit about Video Night in Kathmandu. *I'd like to talk about* The Lady and the Monk. *I think one of the most fascinating aspects of that book is your discussion of what you are projecting and how you are being seen by others. How did the relationship go after the end of the book?*

Even though I published that book twelve years ago, to this day, people are constantly coming up to me and asking that very question! I think the end of that book is very frustrating, because everything is so much up in the air. The story's been moving towards some resolution of this romance, of my projecting my hopes on this Japanese woman and her projecting her hopes on me, and then everything is unresolved at the end.

But the short answer is that, fifteen years on, I live with that woman full-time in Japan. For all intents and purposes, it's a completely happy ending. For literary reasons I wanted to end that book ambiguously because so much in life is unresolved. In real life it seems to have had a much clearer and better conclusion.

In writing nonfiction travel, as much as in writing fiction, one has to construct a persona, which is a variation on the truth, but never a full embodiment of the truth. In order to make a story work, you have to construct a facsimile of yourself. So the character that I represented as Pico Iyer in *The Lady and the Monk* is one tiny fragment of one aspect of myself—not necessarily a very appealing or interesting aspect, but to make the narrative work I had to create this character who exasperatingly finds an ideal woman, as it seems, and then flies away at the end of the book. In real life I was a little more canny than the character I created and knew it would be irresponsible and self-destructive to do that.

There was a small sequel to that particular story because the last chapter of *The Global Soul* is a return, twelve years on, to my life with that same person. She doesn't speak English much better than she did in 1987 and I certainly don't speak Japanese better than I did in 1987, but it's an informed chapter two to that story.

And it's fairly conscious in my mind that I published *Video Night in Kathmandu* in 1988, and I deliberately wrote a kind of sequel to it called *The Global Soul* twelve years later, twelve years being one full turn of the Chinese calendar, and wanting to visit exactly twelve years later some of the same issues and see how they had developed.

I wrote *The Lady and the Monk* and published that in 1991, and twelve years later exactly I brought out another romance that's got to do with the mutual fascination of cultures. In some ways I'm fairly conscious of trying to revisit my old themes and places sometimes, but assuming that I've moved on and they have, too. So for example, *Video Night in Kathmandu* was really about the external clash of East and

West; and then twelve years later I wanted to see how that clash had been internalized. When you see a young Thai girl with a German man, the next question is: What happens to their kids?

I appreciate in your work how you've moved from the kaleidoscopic Video Night in Kathmandu *to a very intimate and personal book. I'm sure there was a lot of pressure on you to write* Video Night in Timbuktu. *It seems like a lot of writers both within and outside of travel almost become brands now. If you read Peter Mayle you're going to get Provence. Was it challenging to move from one type of work to another as a writer who works in the publishing world which makes its demands?*

It was very challenging and for me, that's the excitement of the process. I'm a traveler at heart, which means not that I'm eager to cross borders or acquire new stamps in my passport but that I'm hungry for the next challenge. I always want to look around the corner and do something and go somewhere I haven't been before. And I think that applies in literary as much as geographic terms. So precisely because I'm a traveler, I'm driven by my sense of curiosity and adventure toward something I don't know about.

Having written *Video Night in Kathmandu,* the traveler in me says my next project should be as different as possible. I've worked in that form a little, I know that territory slightly, so I want to go somewhere I've never been on the page. Each time I've finished a book, my idea is that the next book should be as different as possible and should be as unknown as possible and often should be more difficult and larger than I am; that is to say, I am drawn to things I don't know how to do.

I suppose in strict publishing terms the natural impulse might have been to do a *Video Night in South America,* since I already knew that continent quite well. But I would feel that I wouldn't really be traveling if I had done that. I would be retracing my steps and I wouldn't be able to generate that sense of excitement that is the lifeblood of travel and of travel writing. I could generate that sense of excitement much more by writing a very intimate romantic story in Japan, which was *terra incognita* to me.

Thoreau, who's been one of my guiding spirits all along, says that to travel and to describe new lands is to think new thoughts and have new images. And he also says, "I measure travel inward," and I think that's always how I've been. So my notion of imprisonment would be to write the same book twice, and if I'm going to write about the same subject, I will force myself to address it in a way that I haven't begun to think about before.

I think a writer has to keep himself interested if he's going to keep the reader interested. And the writers I love are the ones whose books are constantly shifting, and perhaps running out of their control. My publishers might well have been happy if I'd written more *Video Night* books because that's the book of mine that has sold the most. And many of my readers would be happiest if I were to write a variation of that book again, because it's got much more light and charm and personality than some of my recent books.

I feel I could write that book many times over if I wanted to, but then I wouldn't really be living and I wouldn't be writing. The reason I got into writing is to find new ways to shake myself up. And so, as you can tell by the way I'm talking, the process of writing and the process of traveling are next to indistinguishable for me. The reason I travel is to get turned on my head and shown how I'm wrong and get spun around so quickly that I can't tell right from wrong.

What kind of research do you do before you go to a country?

I tend to read guidebooks a fair amount. These days I mostly read the Lonely Planet books and look at a couple of other guidebooks so I have a vague sense of itinerary in mind and I also have a vague sense of some of the themes and questions that are likely to come up or guide me on my travels. And although I don't read the newspaper, I find because I'm a voracious reader of books, I usually have some sense of what I'm getting into in a country.

For example, the place I most want to go to now is Mali—if I were to make that trip six months from now, I would try to find a couple of the narrative books that have been written about Mali. I would probably get one guidebook and consult it a fair amount before I left, and then I suppose that I would hope that everything I thought I knew would be tossed out. In other words, I would lay foundations but I would be happy, as with a mandala, if the foundations dissolved and I suddenly found myself in a place I hadn't expected to find.

We've spoken about Thoreau and Emerson being influences for you; in terms of more modern influences, who shapes your literary approach and who do you enjoy reading?

That list is too long! I think some of the people I most enjoy are not necessarily people who have had a big influence on me except invisibly. So, for example, Graham Greene has been my great talisman and inspiration for his mix of wisdom and compassion and for his ability to see the world in its shabbiness and sadness and yet always to try to work toward some hopeful or faith-filled sense of humanity. But many people reading my books wouldn't necessarily see his ghost there, though I feel it everywhere.

Just yesterday I was reading a new collection by Jan Morris and thinking that if somebody were to see her influence in some of my writing I wouldn't be surprised. Even though I've never consciously thought of her as an influence, I devoured her books when I was young and something of their rhythm and resonance, and especially her great mixture of kindness and shrewdness, may have influenced me.

Most writers about place don't like to be called travel writers. And one aspect or symptom of that is that I'm less and less interested in reading books about travel, but more and more interested in reading novelists like Graham Greene or D. H. Lawrence—or John le Carré— who catch place brilliantly even though place is not their main interest.

Or people who just explode the form. I think the most exciting discovery of the last few years for me has been the late German writer W. G. Sebald, who in some ways is writing travel. But when you pick up his books they're characterized often as fiction, history, and travel. Even the publishers won't say whether they're fiction or nonfiction. He's taking travel in such an unusual angle, it's almost as if he's revolutionizing the form.

I'm not the kind of person who's excited about reading generally about a trip crossing Tibet or Indonesia. But somebody who will write about even his hometown in some way that's revolutionary to me is the real traveler.

You've called yourself a global village on two legs—what most intrigues you now about the emerging global village and is that different than four years ago when you wrote The Global Soul?

What I've always been interested in is what's uncharted, the inner life of globalism. In writing *The Global Soul*, I was interested in how the global village was changing our dreams and our relationships and challenging our sense of self. There's a whole new race of people coming to birth who to me are the spiritual citizens of the twenty-first century, who don't fit into any of the old categories, who can't answer instantly what's their tribe or community or enemy, who have to create those answers from scratch and whose interactions with the world are going to be utterly different.

Those are people who are whole new cultures in themselves and whose take on places will be utterly different from people limited to one culture. So I think we're the first stage of seeing the first fruits of this sort of mongrel citizen. I've always been interested in them not just because I'm a mongrel citizen myself but because it's something new. I'm realizing as we're talking today that I suppose I'm just by nature drawn to what's undiscovered not so much in the sense of going to some part of the Amazon rain forest that no human has been to before, but seeing something taking place on the globe that many of us may be registering but nobody has actually sat down to think about yet.

You mean like a KFC in Beijing or baseball in Cuba?

Exactly. Or in this case, a new kind of person, perhaps, that's all around us but it's so quiet a development that many of us haven't stopped to think about it. I have a chapter in *Sun After Dark* about jet lag and it's a perfect example because it's a state of being that no human had visited until forty years ago. And now it's more and more a part of many people's lives. Yet it's not been documented the way drug states have been or mystical states have been. It's a fundamental new aspect of human life that many of us experience but few of us stop to think about. Another example would be that a few years ago I lived for two weeks around Los Angeles airport and I thought that it represented a whole new kind of city that will be the city of this coming century and one that many of us pass through many times a year. But nobody had inspected it as if it were a new culture. My instinct is trying to send me to these overlooked countries that are all around us.

A colleague of mine, a travel technology writer in his mid-fifties, lived for about two years without a home. He was going from hotel to hotel, occasionally staying with friends or family. His laptop was his office, a phenomenon that ten or twenty years ago was almost unheard of. We can work almost anywhere but he felt a sense of loss after a while—he longed for home and his own place. I wonder if you see some sort of loss in this faster and faster pace with fewer and fewer roots and less and less of a communal connection with our family and friends.

Very much. I think I wrote *The Global Soul* as a cautionary tale about the dangers of a world that was accelerating to the point where everything was a blur and people were perpetually jet lagged even if they had not left home. And the texture of life is coming to seem more and more like an MTV video and less and less like a spacious novel, more and more fragmented and dissonant and quickly exciting but not nourishing deep down.

So that's one reason I live in rural Japan without any means of transportation and without an ability to watch TV. I've never been on the World Wide Web. And when I noticed that I had 1.5 million miles on United Airlines alone—that funny system whereby you spend six days in hell and get the seventh day free—I consciously began spending a lot of time in a Benedictine hermitage. I'm lucky enough to have a lot of movement and novelty in my life, but I make sure that I also have a lot of stillness and changelessnes, too. And I do worry about the way the world is spinning out of control, almost like a car that's going 110 miles per hour around blind curves. That's why I've been a conscientious objector to a lot of the accelerating forces in the world.

In terms of your deeper question about home: I've written a lot about the new opportunities facing the people who live in the cracks between cultures, but the great danger for any of them is that they fall between the cracks. And I think a lot of the people who grew up with access to many cultures face this desolating question of "Where do I really belong?" or "What is my home? Will I end up stranded in the metaphorical equivalent of an airport all my life, in a passageway between places, utterly anonymous?"

So I think people who are lucky enough to grow up multicultural have advantages their grandparents couldn't dream of. But with those advantages come challenges: they have consciously to stop themselves and choose certain affiliations or else they'll just get lost.

Those choices can be a burden too. If you were growing up 100 years ago in a small village in Europe you knew who your people were —you didn't have to choose.

So I think one of the challenges we're facing now, for a few people at least, is having to invent their people and having to think about their people in new ways.

And their community, as well.

Exactly. Bereft of the traditional forms of community, having to form different types of community, and cyberspace is often one way that people do that. The traveling population forms its own community, a kind of fourth world, so that when you are on the road in Thailand you can go to Ko Samui or the Khao San Road in Bangkok, and you're in this whole floating universe of people like yourself from Australia and Germany and California and Japan, who are constantly in motion and who are without that settled sense of community.

But because travelers are prey to normal human urges, they have formed this community of like-minded souls who are perpetually moving, a little like the Deadheads, who form a floating community linked by choice and linked by common interest, rather than by circumstance. Which potentially sounds like a nice thing, because many of us feel that we didn't choose our families but we do choose our friends. So there's always the possibility that you can make an even better community with people who share your interests and affiliations than with people who merely share your blood.

It's nice to choose your own community, but it seems more…I was going to say shallow, but I'm not sure shallow is the right word because these communities can be deeply supportive. For all their constraints, the old communities provided a safety net that the modern communities may lack.

You're right to say "shallow" in that they don't have hundreds of years behind them and they don't have roots deep in the soil. The global village is built on much more shallow foundations than the traditional village. I think "global village" is a term we use to con ourselves in some ways because a village does have deep roots. In truth, I think we're in the equivalent of the global city and we use the word "village" to persuade ourselves we're all gathered round a campfire with a shared tradition, like the villages we imagine, but that's not the case.

My novel, *Abandon*, which is a romance between California and the Islamic world, was partly about that sense that traditionally when somebody faces a difficulty in her life, she will go to her mother or to her temple or to her community. But in a place like California, which is so young, people are often very separated from their immediate families. There isn't a strong sense of community or history to hold people up here, and instead of a temple there may be one hundred temples which comes to the same as zero. Part of the poignancy of California is that it's crying out for some of those things that a traditional society has too much of.

Has racism been an issue in your life?

No it hasn't. I was the only Indian, the only person of dark skin out of 1,200 boys in my boarding school. And yet I was the only one of the 1,200 boys who didn't realize I was Indian, because I was the only one who couldn't see myself. As far as I was concerned, I was born in Oxford and I grew up in all the same schools as my friends. I was just a typical kid growing up in England. So in the way I spoke and the way I thought and the experiences I had, I was indistinguishable from most of the kids around me.

I think in certain ways an Indian in California has the benefit of positive prejudice. People project all kinds of wisdoms upon me that aren't mine, just because they know I come from an old culture. Even though I've never lived in India, they assume I'll be a source of this Yogic wisdom, and I have to tell them that they know India more than I do. Japan is an interesting example in that context because the Japanese are not very excited to see people who look like me coming into their country. But because I'm an outsider and I always have been I don't mind that they exclude me as they exclude all foreigners from their society.

It's interesting you say that because in your first book it seems like you're very much an outsider taking quick peeks into various cultures, whereas in Kyoto perhaps you're not a part of the culture but it's a much more internal portrait. You're writing more from the inside whereas it seems as though you're writing more from the outside in Video Night in Kathmandu. *Should a travel writer be an insider or an outsider or does it depend on the project?*

There's no prescription for that. It really depends upon the person because some of the beautiful books of travel, like Heinrich Harrar's *Seven Years in Tibet* or Isak Dinesen's *Out of Africa,* are by people who settle deeply into a foreign place and write about it with the love of somebody for their home. And some of the great and exciting writing about foreign places has been written by people like Jan Morris or say P. J. O'Rourke who go quickly from place to place and always are an outsider there but bring such keen instincts and such a shrewd eye to everywhere that they see things that a resident never would. The challenge is for each person who is going to write about travel to figure out what is best suited to them.

And I actually discovered at an early stage that I was the kind of person who couldn't write well about being settled in a place for a long time. On the other hand I was at home being an outsider and moving quickly through places. I noticed that if I stayed two weeks in a place I felt I would have more to say about it and more interesting things to say about it than if I were there for two years. So I had to first come to that understanding and decide how best to work with it. There are other writers who have a slower, more spacious way of entering the culture—for them it would be folly to stay less than a couple of years.

And yet you seem to prefer to travel alone when you're working.

Very much. Because I feel that if I'm not alone I'm not really traveling at all. If I'm with somebody, I'm taking a piece of home with me. When you travel alone you quickly find that you make many more friends because people invite you into their lives much more quickly. If they see two people together, they assume it's a self-contained unit. And also I do travel to empty myself out and lose myself in a culture as much as possible and also to leave as much of myself at home as possible.

So I want to slough off all the ways I define myself in Santa Barbara and just be this anonymous invisible kind of vessel, and that's much harder to do if you're with somebody else. I sometimes think that my method of traveling and therefore travel writing is almost that of a Method actor, which is to say that my goal is to empty myself out, and for the duration of the trip try to fill myself up with another culture and with the perspectives of that culture.

Even when I write about the Philippines, the person that you meet on the page is very different from the person you meet on the page when I'm writing about Japan. For the three weeks that I'm in the Philippines I want to incarnate the particular qualities of the Philippines, a certain open-heartedness and exuberance and emotional directness. And when I write about Japan, I want to write in terms of reticence and veils, I hope to be a different person in each place that I visit, and that's only possible as long as I'm alone.

In silence, suddenly, it seems as if all the windows of the world are thrown open, and everything is as clear as on a morning after rain. Silence, ideally, hums. It charges the air. In Tibet, where the silence has a tragic cause, it is still quickened by the fluttering of prayer flags, the tolling of temple bells, the roar of wind across the plains, the memory of chant.

—PICO IYER, "Silence,"
Tropical Classical

It seems that when you're writing about a culture that's tranquil and peaceful it shows up in your prose and if it's a very chaotic experience, the actual structure of the sentences seems to reflect that.

I really try to do that, to empty myself out and then fill myself up with the coloration of the place. So that when I wrote about jet lag in *The Global Soul*…I get dizzy and seasick reading those passages myself. It's a swirl and I was trying to put the reader entirely in that sensation, turned around, seasick and uncomfortable. And I think a lot of the writing I've done recently has been about imparting that sense of dislocation and discomfort, which is not a very pleasant thing for a reader willingly to take on. But I feel that it's reflecting the reality—one reality—of the world as I see it.

I've written three romances—set in Japan, Cuba, and California—and when I brought out the Japanese romance many people asked me why is it so coy and so teasing and so reticent. And that's because those are the qualities that are distinctive to Japan for me. When I wrote a similar story in Cuba it was very oversexed and passionate, and people might have recoiled from that. That was my attempt to try to catch something of the distinctive texture of Cuba. In my recent book, *Abandon,* the two main characters are fairly neurotic and self-enclosed and really exasperating to be with, and very much walled in within their own concerns. It wasn't easy for me to keep them company for a couple of years. But my sense of California is of a place where God-made paradise is colliding against human-made drift and chaos.

When I saw you speak in San Francisco it was right at the beginning of the war in Iraq. It seems like a lot of people, because of fear, are more hesitant to travel abroad. What would you say to someone who says, "I don't know if I should travel around the world anymore because I'm just too scared."

I'd say this is the time you need to travel more than ever. To begin with, I always say to myself that one advantage of living in Southern California is that almost anywhere I visit is safer than Los Angeles. I remember when I was traveling in the '80s, Washington had a higher murder rate than Beirut, Kabul, or El Salvador.

In May 2001, in fact, I published a piece in *Condé Nast Traveler* advising people to go to Damascus and the Middle East, saying that home is no safer; you can be just as unsettled in New York and Los Angeles. And, sad to say, four months after that, people in New York did experience that destruction can come to your home.

Here I am sitting in Santa Barbara and I was in the middle of a fire that was much more dangerous than anything I experienced in Nicaragua or Syria or Ethiopia. I think the most dangerous thing in a world that is ever more connected is to close your eyes and to draw the curtains. In any neighborhood the person who doesn't even try to look at the neighbors is the one who is endangering himself and others. And I think the other danger is, you can get in a vicious cycle, scared of seeing the world. You don't go out, and if you don't go out, you get more scared of the world, and before you know it, you're a sort of cultural agoraphobe.

I traveled a lot in the week of September 11th and shortly thereafter, and during the bombing of Iraq I deliberately went to Dharamsala, to hear about peace, not war. I think it's presumption on our part to assume we know what's dangerous and what isn't, and my life has shown me that danger comes when least I expect it. And safety, too.

You wrote a story about a Cuban man who asked you to mail a letter to his brother in the United States thinking his brother was wealthy and powerful and could rescue him. And the brother in the United States was in jail and hoped his brother in Cuba could rescue him. It reminded me of a time when I was in Cuba and someone wanting to make conversation came up to me and said, "Hello, where are you?" Well, I was less than 100 miles from Florida but in a different world entirely. I really wasn't sure where I was. That seems to be indicative of the modern condition—can you comment on that?

Even as people talk a lot about the world getting smaller and even though we do have more access to other cultures than we used to have, in some ways I'm more conscious of the distances between places having increased. And sometimes the distances are intensified by the illusion of closeness. So my travels around the world don't make me think that Cuba or China or India are really any closer to us than they used to be, even though we're all sharing some of the same things.

We're all seeing the same movie but taking away a different picture. The example I've used is that of *The Sixth Sense*. I saw it in Japan, and there people were not frightened or unsettled by the ghosts, because they have plenty of ghosts in Japan. They were unsettled by the psychiatrist because there are almost no psychiatrists in Japan. I can imagine many cultures, say in the Middle East, where what was spookiest about *The Sixth Sense* was the notion of a single mother, because that's so outside the domain of what they're familiar with. I saw the same movie here in California, and people were most shocked by the fact that Bruce Willis could act. We're all seeing exactly the same movie, but we're taking different things away from it. That's a trivial example of what to me is going on in the world as a whole.

You've written about Bhutan where the king talks about Gross National Happiness. Would the world be a better place if more leaders had that idea instead of seeking to maximize Gross National Product?

I think he's very wise to concentrate on immaterial successes as well as material success. It's interesting that a lot of religious leaders often take that position. When the Dalai Lama has been in Los Angeles, people say, "Oh, the poverty in India must be terrible," and he says, "I see a lot of poverty here, spiritual poverty, loneliness." The people he meets in Bel Air or Hollywood may be very rich in material terms, but why are they going to psychiatrists and why are they getting divorced four times? And why are they crying out for any wisdom that he can bring?

I think the king of Bhutan is very wise in reminding us that we can't measure the things of the world just by what we can see and count. There is a whole other dimension, which is one of the things that travel teaches you. Bhutan is an interesting example because I think every parent finds that any prohibition is an invitation in disguise. When I was there a few years ago, they had no television and everyone still wore fourteenth-century costumes, and lived in traditional houses, yet I saw more video stores there than I see on Melrose Avenue in Los Angeles. They kept out TV but that only meant that people found another way to import images of the outside world. It's hard to keep the world out these days.

You've talked about what you've learned as a travel writer. Could you distill it into one or two central themes? How has travel shaped your philosophy of life or approach towards the world?

The world is much more diverse than we imagine; the world is much larger than our conceptions. Most of my conceptions before I go to a place are wrong and limited. I've been humbled by the kindness I've met almost everywhere I go. Often, the poorer the place, the kinder and the more generous are the people. Travel is, as much as anything, an exercise in trust—and a challenge of one's trust because we're naked and somewhat undefended when we're in a foreign place. And lots of people are coming up to us with all kinds of offers and we can't read their motives very often. Travel asks you how much are you going to surrender to the unknown. Even though I've probably sometimes failed that test, I'm still glad to confront it and have myself asked that question.

If you weren't a travel writer in this life, do you have a sense of what you might have done otherwise?

As Salman Rushdie has said: I would have loved to have been an actor, but I don't have it in me. *TIME* magazine rescued me from graduate school and I was stumbling through the back door towards becoming a professor of literature. But I wouldn't have been happy in that. All the time I was in graduate school—and I spent eight years studying nothing but literature—all of me was longing to be out in the world and at least attempting to make literature rather than picking it apart. But that might have been something I fell into.

How long were you at Harvard before you started working for TIME?

Four years; four years going nowhere except through Let's Go for those two summers.

It's funny how life twists and turns you in the direction that can be most fulfilling.

Yes, if you're open to it. I often think that Harvard experience really taught me a lesson. I had no good reason for entering graduate school. I knew that I didn't want to profess literature, but I was just there by force of inertia. And a part of me really wanted to write and I suppose wanted to travel too, but I couldn't find a way to do it. Finally, after four years, I plucked up the courage and decided, I've got to just commit myself to this. If I'm going to be a writer, I've got to just haul myself into the unknown, be unemployed and try to make it work.

I made that decision at the end of my fourth year of graduate school and out of the blue, two weeks later, somebody from *TIME* magazine arrived on the campus. He was traveling around various campuses in America looking for somebody to hire, and he met various people of whom I was one. Suddenly, out of nowhere, I got offered a job at *TIME* magazine even though my only qualification was reading *Beowulf* three times.

You must have impressed them with something.

Well, while I was in graduate school I used all my free time to write pieces for magazines—book reviews because that's what I was qualified to do—and I wrote those Let's Go things. So it meant that when opportunity arose, I had a lot of clips. I really worked overtime, and then when suddenly a man appeared on campus and said, "Why should I begin to hire you as a writer?" I was able to show him things I had written for small magazines here and there.

Beyond that, my sense is that there is a sort of poetic justice to it: when finally I decided to commit myself to it, instead of just wavering, then suddenly an opportunity came out of nowhere. And I think that if I hadn't had the resolve to take the plunge at last into the unknown I might never have been rescued in midair so miraculously. I think the whole process of traveling is about pitching yourself into a circumstance in which you don't know how things are going to work out. But that initial act of faith can bring about good results. There was a line I used a couple of times in the first chapter of my first book: "Faith is its own vindication." A lot of that runs behind my sense of travel, which is that you open yourself up to a country or to a person and you find in that opening up more riches than you ever imagined.

Europe Through an Open Door

Rick Steves
EDMONDS, WASHINGTON

RICK STEVES DREADED HIS FIRST TRIP TO EUROPE. HE HAD JUST completed his freshman year of high school and planned to spend the summer of 1969 hanging out with his buddies. But his father, a piano importer, insisted that Rick accompany him on a buying trip, and an unimagined new world opened up to the lanky kid from Edmonds, Washington.

Four year later, Steves returned to Europe without parental supervision, riding the rails on Eurail passes. Traveling on a shoestring with a friend, Steves survived for two months on a few dollars a day, pilfering apples from orchards, sleeping on trains, and sneaking into museums. Perhaps that's where he first got the phrase "Europe through the back door."

By the late 1970s, Steves was teaching courses to Europe-bound travelers and noticed that his handouts of tour itineraries kept disappearing. In 1980, he decided to put all his advice into a book, and self-published 2,500 copies of *Europe Through the Back Door*. Steves forgot to include an ISBN (International Standard Book Number, an identification code) making the book difficult for stores to order, but caught a break when the travel editor of the *Seattle Post-Intelligencer* serialized the book. Steves's independent, do-it-yourself tone was a hit with the newspaper's readers, but not with its advertisers, and Steves says it cost the editor his job.

During his early travel talks, Steves sold Cosmos tours, a mainstream "if this is Tuesday it must be Belgium" outfit. By getting twenty people to sign up for a Cosmos tour, Steves would earn a free trip and accompany the group. In his book, *Postcards from Europe*, Steves writes: "On my last Cosmos tour…we tumbled off the bus and met our harried guide. Monica, a German, picked up the microphone and said, 'I was to be finished for the season today. Finally going home. Yesterday I said goodbye to my last group. It was a difficult group. I am ready to go home. Then I receive a message that I must do you.'"

Steves knew there had to be a better way. When a friend asked him to guide her group, he rented a van and drove seven women through Europe. He knew he'd landed his dream job. In those days he often arranged lodgings as the sun set; today Steves's tours are planned months in advance. But tours are just one component of Steves's $20 million travel publishing empire—he's the author of twenty-seven guidebooks to Europe, including more than a dozen country guides and the handbook, *Europe Through the Back Door*. He's the producer and host of the PBS show *Rick Steves' Europe*, which has an audience of millions. He's become so influential that his back-door discoveries, like Italy's Cinque Terra, quickly become mainstream attractions. Steves almost single-handedly popularized Paris' Rue Cler, which *San Francisco Chronicle* travel editor John Flinn calls Rue Rick Steves.

Even with his renown, Steves still offers free travel classes, raises money for PBS during pledge drives, and donates time to causes ranging from his church to social justice groups. Casual viewers familiar with the folksy TV host may not know about Steves's political side. In an essay posted on his Web site, "Innocents Abroad: How Travel Made this Young Republican a Liberal," Steves tells how his global journeys led him to see the "vast gap" between rich and poor. "Lessons I've learned far from home combined with passion for America have heightened my drive to challenge my countrymen to higher ideals. Crass materialism and a global perspective don't mix."

Among the groups that Steves, a Christian who's active in the Lutheran Church, supports are Bread for the World, Greenpeace, and NORML, which advocates the decriminalization of marijuana. His trips to Holland, he says, have shown him there are more compassionate and sane policies for managing marijuana use and prostitution.

I met Steves on an overcast, mid-winter day in the coastal town of Edmonds, about a half-hour drive north of Seattle. The ground floor is a store selling tours, Eurail passes, guidebooks, and travel gear like lightweight carry-on bags.

From the window in Steves's corner office, one can see the junior high school he attended. On the wall is a map of Europe, a picture of Clinton and Gore, and an FSLN (Sandanista) placard. Steves whirled into the office like a tornado, his six-foot-two frame closing like scissors behind his desk. He answered my questions in staccato bursts, clearly enunciating each syllable.

As we spoke, I could see how all the elements of Steves's empire fit together. He's created valuable products, marketed them brilliantly, and persevered relentlessly, even when the odds were stacked against him. He even has a mission statement: maximum travel thrills for every mile, minute, and dollar of your vacation. All this brought to mind another visionary businessman in the Seattle area, this one based in Redmond. Could Steves be Bill Gates's good twin?

≈≈≈

Could you tell me about your first trip to Europe and your first impressions?

The most important thing I remember about my first trip to Europe is that I didn't want to go there and my parents dragged me—I was a fourteen-year-old kid. I thought, I work hard as a student, and my pay is my summer break, and they're taking it away from me. And then I got over there—my dad used to import pianos and we had relatives to visit in Norway and so on—so we got over there and I remember being fascinated. There's different candy, different pop, women with hairy armpits, and one-armed bandits in the hotel lobbies. I just thought, This is fascinating. It broadened my world.

Right off the bat, I was just fanatic about keeping notes and records. I kept a postcard journal—every day I would buy a postcard and track how much money I spent, how much money I had left, what we did, what the weather was like, what my impressions were. So just as a little kid, I was sort of a travel researcher ready to happen. On the next trip I saw other kids without their parents, with Eurail passes and rucksacks and the world by the tail, and it occurred to me that I didn't need my parents—Europe could be my playground. I've vowed to go every year since then and I have. Gradually my trips dissolved from being purely adventures to research trips to help other people have adventures.

Can you tell me about the first time you went to Europe without your parents?

That was my Europe-through-the-gutter trip in 1973. I went with Gene Openshaw, who is my co-author in some of my books, one of our tour guides, and my right-hand man here. We did the whole trip—it was on peanuts, something like two dollars a day. We were sneaking into youth hostels and stealing desserts from grocery stores. We were like two little ruffians in Europe. I remember when it was harvest time outside of Rothenberg and there were apples, free apples on the trees. It was a bonanza for us because we could get this fresh fruit. If something cost, we couldn't go in, we couldn't do it.

Most tour groups are territorial about their guide's services. Self-appointed vigilantes sheriff the back row making freeloaders feel cheap and unwanted.... Suddenly I'm being leaned on by a woman who whispers harshly, "Private tour, private tour." Leaning back I whisper, "Public attraction, public attraction."

—RICK STEVES, *Rick Steves' Postcards from Europe*

You mean like a museum?

Right, if we couldn't get in the front door, sometimes we would sneak in the back—we were just little street urchins slumming around Europe. We finished the trip trying to get out to the airport in Frankfurt on an expired Eurail pass. The conductors were coming down from either end of the train closing in on us and we wondered if we were going to get to the airport in time. We got there just in time, jumped out, and flew home with pennies in our pockets.

Every week we'd pile our money on the bed and see where we were at, and if we were a couple of dollars over our budget we'd have to tighten up the next week. In retrospect it was the most exciting and educational trip of my life, a great, great experience. Of course now I pay for things instead of scamming them, but I sure had a vivid experience back then. That kind of tuned me in to how nice it is to have a good roof over your head and reasonable food. I came back from that trip and was literally sick. I was anemic. I ended up taking classes in nutrition so I could treat myself better.

I think we've all had one of those trips and remember it more fondly than any other.

Yup, but that was when I was eighteen.

In your writing now you espouse a very open-minded type of travel, open to places, to people. What are the keys to traveling in a way that's broadening rather than stultifying?

Psychologically you really need to be there. Too many people go to Europe never leaving home, and it's like going to a high-definition travelogue. They're looking at it onstage; they're taking photographs of it; they're seeing people wearing traditional costumes; they're not really connecting with anybody. They've got a camera just bouncing on their belly that says, Yodel. And it's not good travel. You need to stow the camera and you need to be there.

You can go to church and take a flash photograph of Michelangelo's *Pieta* or you can go to mass at five o'clock any day of the week, two different ways to experience a church in Europe. Most people don't go to a church in Europe to worship—they go to a church to see art. They worship at home but they think they can't worship there because they're not at home. They put an artificial barrier between themselves and experience. You can go to the market and feel awkward because you don't speak the language, you don't understand the metric system, or you can go to a market and remind yourself you're not a tourist: you're one in a thousand-year-long line of hungry travelers. Hold your ground, you're part of the scene. That's a real important approach when you're a traveler.

For a lot of people travel is seeing if you can eat five meals a day and still snorkel when you get into port. In the old days people used to stand on the decks of cruise ships and throw coins into the water and photograph black kids jumping for them. That's one kind of travel that makes a gap between you and the rest of the world. And when I grew up, that's what I thought travel was. And then I thought, Boy, if you can travel in a way that connects you with the world, then travel becomes a real constructive way to spend your time and money.

In your book, Rick Steves' Postcards from Europe, *you say travel for you is a quest for roots. What do you mean by that?*

A lot of people are interested in their family roots—that means looking for their name on a tombstone or going to church and paging through yellowed pages of the names of parishioners from generations ago. They are putting together a family tree. I've seen tourists under Gore-Tex parkas in a driving rain, writing down the names on the tombstones. I could care less about seeing my ancestor on a tombstone. I want to understand my cultural roots, and they happen to be European. So when I go to Europe, I am trying to put together that puzzle and I love that. The more I know about that, the more fascinating the story is. I have an appetite for the history and art of Europe. I'm not a scholar, but I enjoy it to the point where I got a history degree. So now in my teaching, I have that same enthusiasm and that helps my writing. It helps my tour guiding.

In your guidebooks you emphasize that good travel is more than seeing a bunch of sites. It's interactions with people, it's meeting locals, it's striking up conversations in a café or train station.

And it's leaving home, it's leaving your norm. To me that's the essence of good travel, plus living out of suitcase. I live out of a carry-on-sized suitcase for a hundred days a year. I spend a quarter of my adult life in Europe living out of one suitcase and it's a beautiful thing. I don't need all that stuff. I come home and I've got milkmen to deal with, car insurance, all this stuff. In Europe, it's me, my suitcase, and Europe.

And there's a freedom in that minimalism.

It's a beautiful freedom, yeah, I feel so much healthier and so much younger. I feel like I'm just surfboarding on history. You can't do that when you're encumbered by material concerns.

And that comes through in your guides and on your TV show. It's almost as though one of the commandments of the Church of Rick Steves is "Thou Shalt Travel Light." It seems to be much more than the efficiency of it—it's a philosophy.

Well, it's a philosophy that has a bigger impact on Americans—the impact is correlated to how material your normal world is. I have a friend in Turkey who is a tour guide, and she just can't believe how many shoes Americans need. She just has one pair of shoes and she can outrun any of us.

I used to work up here (in the Northwest) for a bike tour company and for a week of biking people would bring coffee makers; they would bring hair dryers.

You can't preach this to people. It's sort of related to why I would not take a group to India. It's a personal thing. India is my favorite country, but I would never take a group to India because it's unpredictable. I wouldn't want to be in charge of making twenty people happy in India. I can be in charge of making twenty people happy in Denmark or Madrid or Ireland, because it's kind of predictable. But in India it's much more mystical and spiritual.

Is that why it's your favorite country?

Yeah, the good thing about travel is it moves around your furniture, and India moves it around more than any other country.

You write about European train stations and how magical they are, the sense of possibility. I remember walking into the train stations in Milan and Venice and thinking, I could go anywhere and I can be there in a few hours.

I love that, yeah. There's a lot that contributes to that: first of all, the train system is so great; secondly, there's so much diversity or variety per square mile; and also we know a lot about Europe. I'm excited about going to Prussia instead of Franconia—you could go all over China and a typical American wouldn't know if it's Mandarin or Cantonese or whatever. But in Europe, these are Walloons and these are Flemish—I'm coming into Wallonia. There's just an ambience in the train stations—it's like molecular motion, everyone is just moving.

There's a buzz.

You can just sit there and listen to it. In the old days I'd be on a platform in Munich and in ten minutes this train is going to Prague, and in fifteen minutes that train is going to Salzburg and I've yet to decide which train I'm going to be on. That kind of thing is pretty cool. That's freedom. Travel is freedom.

And I think that's part of the appeal of the Eurail pass. You're all paid for...

And if you're frugal like me, it's nice to take the pain of the cost out of it. You get hit once and then, hey, it's a buffet.

And sometimes trains are rolling hotels, too.

Exactly. I've been doing this for thirty years and it's very gratifying to see people one generation behind me having exactly the same magic that I had back then.

Great European train stations stir my wanderlust.... I stand under the station's towering steel and glass rooftop and study the big black schedule board crowned by the station clock. It lists two dozen departures. Every few minutes, the letters and numbers on each line spin and tumble as one by one cities and departure times work their way to the top and flutter away.

—RICK STEVES, *Rick Steves' Postcards from Europe*

Essentially travel has not changed—of course we have e-mail and cell phones and ATMs and euros and bullet trains and English Channel tunnels, but the magic of travel, being all alone on Dun Aenghus [an iron age fortress on the west coast of Ireland] or coming into a town in Poland and being completely disoriented and eating soup for fifty cents in the milk bar, the magic of travel is the same, charging across the Greek sea with the sun going down and dolphins playing in your wake, that doesn't change.

Whether you're a college kid in the 1970s with your girlfriend or a college kid in 2004 with your girlfriend, it's the same great hello-world experience. One of my favorite experiences is when things I wrote in my journal in the early 1970s—that are still in the book—inspire people now to have that same kind of magic.

Speaking of magic, what are some of the other places in Europe that you find most magical, churches, museums, nature?

Well, art. Art can be the closest thing to a time-tunnel experience Europe has to offer if you can understand the cultural and economic and historical context that it was created in. So to be standing in front of a painting by Fra Angelico, the greatest painter of the high Middle Ages, a man who was so spiritual that he couldn't paint a crucifix without crying, and to him painting was a form of prayer, to be standing there in a monastery where Savonarola worked, the guy who turned Florence into a theocracy, that's a heady experience.

To know enough about the art to be able to experience the art in the context in which it was created is a real challenge for an American, and it's very rewarding when you get it. Another thing is to just be engaged, clued in, that you're very fortunate to be able to be a traveler in 2004 and witness history in the making. A lot of Americans, a lot of tourists, are oblivious to history that's happening all around them.

An example is being in the Reichstag building in Berlin on opening week. It's a new glass dome that's open and free all the time so people can literally look over the shoulders of their legislators and know what's on their desk and keep an eye on them.

Which is such a symbolic thing given Germany's history—the people are watching.

It's incredible: no more fascism, no more communism, no more division, no more war. It's the beginning of a new century—they're free, hopeful, united, and looking into a great future. I was surrounded by these teary-eyed Germans—you know any time you're surrounded by teary-eyed Germans something exceptional is going on—and I realized they were closing an ugly chapter in the history of that great nation. It was a great new morning in Germany, and I don't think one in ten American tourists up there had a clue of the goose-bumpy experience that was for a German.

I was so thankful that I was engaged enough to know symbolically what was happening there—it was history and I was there. That makes travel much more gratifying and exciting. One thing I'm trying to do in my work is to help travelers not be dumbed down. I think so much in our society is dumbed down now and it's very, very important that Americans don't get dumbed down even if everybody wants them to be dumbed down. It's not just a shopping trip.

It's not a theme park.

Right—this is reality and these are real people having real struggles. And that's magic: we're talking about letting art take you back, about being aware of history right now. It's more important than ever that Americans are able to step away from their country to get a better understanding of what is our country's place on this planet. That's something I am more committed to than ever: helping Americans become better citizens of the planet. That's a good kind of globalism, I think. And travel is a powerful force for that.

One thing I admire about your work is that you don't hesitate to express your political viewpoints. Right now I think we're in an interesting time because of how the U.S. government is perceived overseas. I wonder if you think that's having an effect on how people from the U.S. are being treated in Europe?

There are two issues there: first of all, is it smart for me to let my political beliefs be known because I am a business, and I want people to buy my material so my business will work? I don't think it's smart from a business point of view to let people know where I stand because any entertainer is better off not being able to be put in a box that way. I realize Dennis Miller is a conservative or that he supports a lot of Republicans and it's strange for me to psychoanalyze my opinion of Dennis Miller's work now that I realize that he is quite a bit different than me in his politics. It shouldn't affect it, but it does.

So a lot of conservative people that love my work have sworn never again to use my books because they think I am some sort of an unpatriotic liberal. I feel I'm as patriotic as anybody. I'm so committed to my country and it's my drive for us to be smarter on the world scene. But other people hold it against me.

Now I'm sitting here in a building employing sixty people. I'm a businessman—I can't be a romantic or idealist. I gotta have my feet on the ground. I'm still right where I grew up—that's my junior high school, that big yellow-cream building right down there. Isn't that something. It's kind of fun to be thinking, this is where I belong and this is what I belong doing. So this is what I am, I'm an American and I teach Americans how to travel and this is where I live, this is what I do and I love it. I'm very thankful for it. That was a big tangent, excuse me, your question was?

Are Europeans distinguishing between Americans and the actions of the U.S. government?

First of all, everybody knows there are differences between peoples and their governments. Eighty percent of England was against unilateral American attack on Iraq and the British government supported our government. Eighty percent of Spaniards are that way, eighty percent of Turks are that way—people realize that. So thankfully nobody holds my government's actions against me. In the same way I am not going to hold a South African guilty for apartheid. Having said that, I don't know how long Europe is going to cut us that slack.

I noticed on my last trip that Canadians are making it really clear that they're Canadians. They polish their Canadian flags. I would never wear a Canadian flag—I am an American, take it or leave it. It's kind of like [the British comedy] *Fawlty Towers*; there's this funky little hotel in England. There is a joke when a German customer is coming to the hotel where they tell the staff, just don't talk about the war. And it's like that with Americans now, just don't talk about the war.

I went on a tour in southern France this summer in some little wine village and this dear woman had eight or ten people for a little wine tasting and half of them were Americans. She started her talk: "I just want to thank the Americans for delivering us from the Nazis—we'll always be indebted to you." There's this sort of nervousness on

Europe's part that we don't feel appreciated. The point I'm making is that Europeans are bending over backwards to accept Americans. They're not going to treat you badly.

In Europe a lot of people like to talk politics, but nobody's going to broach this issue with you because it might be impolite. So if you are a unilateralist and you think that America's right all the time, and you want to go to Europe and teach them to appreciate us, nobody's going to fight with you unless you start the conversation. So you gotta look for a fight to get a fight. If you're apolitical, Europe would just as soon be apolitical, and let's enjoy the cheese and the wine. If you're multilateral or a European-style liberal, and you let Europeans know, all of a sudden, wow, you've got yourself a party. Everyone's celebrating that you are a multilateralist. So my point is: if you're going to Europe, it doesn't matter what your politics are, it's not a bad thing unless you're looking for a fight.

One quick follow-up about your own personal opinions and having to run a business. You're probably the only person I know who's active in the Lutheran Church and also is a member of the advisory board of NORML (National Organization for the Reform of Marijuana Laws), and you're open about it.

Yeah, well, first of all I don't see any contradiction. Secondly, I'm in a position where I can get away with being outspoken. I don't want to do it in a divisive way. My goal is to be challenging and cause people to think carefully about things and have a broader perspective. It's a fundamental truth that if you travel a lot you have a broader perspective of things.

I just gave a talk in Bellingham to 500 people and it was a fundraiser for a local peace group sponsored by an independent bookstore. Everybody there was so hip and progressive, I just felt like, why even bother talking politics? It was oddly disappointing. And then I talk to conservative groups in the Midwest or Texas, and I find it very challenging and very stimulating and I find it more enjoyable for my audience, if I can present this as a Christian advocate for the decriminalization of marijuana who believes that we don't lead the world in self-evident, God-given truths, and that half the people on this planet are trying to live on two dollars a day and we're 4 percent of the planet with 50 percent of its wealth who's elected a government to try to get us richer at all costs, and there's blood on your banana.

If you can say that in a caring way, everybody thanks you for it. I've been talking to rich people in gated communities and golf clubs, and they had a jar in the back of the room called Pennies for Pathways and they would toss their coins to house homeless people. I just stood right up there and in a very loving way told them: "You're living here in this gated community and you're jetting all over the world and there are homeless people with children out there and they're getting pennies. It's very poignant for me and I would imagine it's poignant for you too, if you'd think about it."

People have good hearts and they want to be challenged. And that's really a beautiful part of my work, the opportunity to do that. I think if someone can effectively share their global perspective with them, they can be happier with their affluence.

Getting back to Europe, when I hear talk of increased European unity I think of an experience I had in Aerøskøbing in Denmark: I started talking with this old mariner who'd had a few pints and he said, "Denmark has a king; England has a queen, how can we be one?" In Europe there seems to be a lot of forces moving the continent toward a greater European community. I wonder what you think are the pros and cons of that.

A very basic part of how I'm so charmed by Europe is the diversity, all the cultural diversity. The diversity is not necessarily national—it's regional—and throughout our lifetimes we've been hearing regions bickering with nations. I think there are three different levels of loyalty: regional, national, and European. In the last twenty years, nations have been withering away as Europe emerges as the power. I think the consequence of that is suddenly people in Brittany no longer threaten Paris; people in Scotland no longer threaten London; people in Basque country and Catalonians no longer threaten Madrid because the nations aren't quite as important as they used to be.

Because of the superstructure of the European community?

Yeah, because the power is migrating towards Europe as a big free-trade zone. That's my hunch, and news events sort of bolster my belief, because now Catalonians are waving their flags and Madrid doesn't really care. In Brittany, for instance, when I first started traveling, if you named your child with a Celtic name, that child would lose its French citizenship. Celtic music was illegal—you couldn't play it because it was secessionist. Celtic music no longer threatens France. For the first time since 1711, the Scottish Parliament is meeting in Edinburgh. They got their parliament back because London's really not threatened by it anymore—it's not that big a deal.

As Europe unites, some people think it's all going to be Starbucks, but I think as Europe unites the regions are going to waive their flags with a little more vigor. You'll find these minor languages thriving, and the variety is going to stay healthy. As Europe gets more powerful, regions are doing better. So that's my positive spin on the unification of Europe. From a travel point of view, it's just great. You don't have the visas, you don't have coins to worry about. As Europe unites as an economic unit, it won't unite as a cultural unit. I think people like being Belgian; they like being Dutch, and they like the difference.

It seems sometimes that Europeans have a greater appreciation of life, of time to savor what's important. Is that a myth or something you feel is true?

I don't know—I think I probably have a romantic approach to Europe. I believe what you're saying is true, but I don't know if I'm romanticizing Europe or not.

They do have more vacation time.

They live longer, they consume less, they get more vacation time, they get more of a social safety net. They don't have the stress that comes with being a driven society that believes more in this Darwinian survival of the fittest economically. Time is money in America. We're taught to talk about it in terms like its money. We save it, we spend it, we invest it, we waste it.

There's this whole idea of the social contract: how does the society live together? We are the rugged individualists like Locke. In Europe they have the Rousseau model: everyone has to give up a little bit of their freedom so everybody can live together peacefully and civilly.

Part of that is because Europe has been around a lot longer than us, and Europe is much more densely populated.

And Europeans are into this. In Holland they say they cut the wheat that grows too tall. Why grow too tall? Anybody gets too much money, they lose it to taxation. There's that great equalizer. To me as an American capitalist, I'm glad I'm working here because I want to work hard and have power and affluence and make a difference. That's just what I get out of bed in the morning for.

From a quality-of-life point of view, Europeans would laugh at me. They would just say, "C'mon man, you've got those mountains over there, when is the last time you've walked in those mountains?" It's been years. So we can learn a lot from the Europeans—we really can. I don't think anybody's got a corner on truth. I don't like to be afraid of different answers—I like diversity. I'm real comfortable with the fact that I shouldn't condemn a billion Hindus for feeding their cows and starving their children. I don't understand the whole thing. I don't understand their concept of religion, of pain, of love, plus I don't know what it's like to live in a country with no trees where you have to have cow pies for fuel. There are a lot of reasons for things that we don't get, but we're quick to condemn it.

In Afghanistan I sat down in a restaurant and a professor joined me and said, "A third of the planet uses spoons and forks like you; a third of the planet uses chopsticks; and a third of the planet uses their fingers like I do, and we're all equal. Just because you use a spoon and a fork doesn't mean you are more civilized than me." That was the only point he wanted to make and then he left me. I'm not offended by it—I'm charmed by it.

>
>
> When you let your time become money you cheapen your life. One measure of a culture is its treatment of time. In the United States time is money: we save it, spend it, invest it, and waste it. Not so in traditional Italy. Here life is rich and savored slowly. In Italy—like in India—time is more like chewing gum. You munch on it and play with it … as if it will be there forever.
>
> —RICK STEVES, *Rick Steves' Postcards from Europe*

Today the guidebook business is very different than it was a generation ago. In the 1950s and '60s, each guidebook line had its personality, but you've remained a strong personality. Do you think that's part of the success of your guidebooks?

I don't know for sure, but good travel is fundamentally people to people. If I'm writing a guidebook, if I'm taking a tour, if I'm making a TV show, if it doesn't have people, it's not going to be good. I don't care who lived there, that building is just as dead as they are. I don't care to see Beethoven's birthplace—a bunch of buildings is nothing. You gotta connect with people, so when I'm putting a guidebook together, I connect people with people. When I'm making a TV show, I'm scared to death if my script doesn't have people in it. My guidebooks are unique in that they have you connecting with actual people—my readers know these people. They send them Christmas cards.

People know when they read my guidebook who is writing it. It's written by Rick Steves—he's a guy who lives in Edmonds and they can learn a lot about me if they want to. You gotta be careful that you don't get in the way of information. On the other hand, I remember quite vividly reading a book about Japan. I didn't know if the author was a man or a woman. I wanted to know something about that person, but it was as if an editor came through and scrubbed out any personality.

It's natural—you want to know who your guide is.

Exactly. My definition of "funky" has some consistency—if I say this is a funky place, people who have used my book in Norway will know what funky means when they go to Dublin. After a while they know that Rick is really into open-air folk museums so he overdoes it on these things.

So do you update all of your titles yourself?

I've got people helping me now—I can't go to every place. [Steves shows me his whirlwind itinerary for the coming summer.] We're very committed to getting back to these places in person—it's very labor-intensive, but I'm thankful the books are selling enough to make that viable.

A generation ago there were all these big shots: Birnbaum, Fodor, Fielding, Frommer, and now most people don't know who the technicians are behind the cover of Frommer's books and so on. And I think publishers like it that way because they can just pay for the piecework and not have to deal with royalties—they don't have to deal with the person. They can just discard him and hire somebody else.

You've done a brilliant job marketing yourself. On my way up here I saw a flier for a weekend of free workshops. So the workshops draw people who buy the guidebooks, viewers see the TV shows then buy your famous carry-on bag or sign up for a tour.

Nothing would succeed on its own. If I didn't do tours, my TV shows wouldn't be as good. If I didn't do TV shows the books wouldn't sell as well. If I didn't do the guidebooks I couldn't research the TV shows—everything helps everything else so everything can be a better value to the consumers and we can still be profitable, which is really quite amazing. My tour guides are the best paid in Europe—I'm the second biggest fundraiser for PBS. When public broadcasting makes money, they are part of the family. When my publisher makes money, it's part of the family.

Do you still give away your shows to PBS?

Yes, that's just a choice a TV producer has to make. I could charge for them and then stations would have to decide whether to pay for Rick's shows. My profit, honestly, is how many people I'm influencing, how many people are watching the show, how many people are using the book in Paris, how many people are enjoying the fjords because of our tour guides. We had 5,000 people take our tours, 500,000 people use the books, 5 million people watch the TV show. That's really profitable to me because all these people are being affected. And with that seemingly altruistic approach to business, we are viable and profitable in a difficult economic environment because we're committed to the travel experience.

I used to charge ten bucks for people to take my travel class back in the '70s at the University of Washington. Then I realized traveling couples were having to decide that one or the other would take the class so they didn't have to both pay for it. I honestly thought, this is terrible, this is a travel partnership and only one person is going to take the class because you don't want to pay the extra ten bucks. Then I thought about it and said, Heck, lets do the classes for free and people can buy my guidebooks, so that worked out better. The classes have been free ever since.

With all the guidebooks and TV shows, you're very well known now. Can you do the work incognito?

It's a problem in some cases because I come into town and there's a buzz: Rick's coming down the Rhine River. All the B&B people are out scrubbing their doorsteps, saying, "Oh yes, Rick, I've been scrubbing all day, just like every day." One year I wrote about a little B&B and said, it's not very clean but it's friendly. I try to call a spade a spade. It was painful for this woman to hear that her place was not very clean. So the next year I'm coming down the Rhine and the word gets out. I come up to her place and she's wearing her apron and she's on her knees scrubbing. And she says, Rick, "I've been scrubbing all day— that's all I do is scrub and scrub. You can eat off these floors." I had to just laugh because I knew it was set up.

Nowadays if I come to a restaurant and they know who I am, I don't rely only on my experience—I talk to people who are eating there. That's one of the great things about having a book that's established. I can go into a restaurant or a pub or whatever, talk to four different groups who are enjoying their food and I sit down with each of them. I'll even sample off their plate—it's kind of fun. And they want to talk to me and I just ask: "How is your meal? Is the service O.K.?"

And they say, "We've eaten here three nights in a row—it's just awesome." Who am I to say it's not great? This couple here they've been in Sorrento for three nights and they love it and they're thankful I put it in the book. Good enough for me. Next. I'm realistic about it— I can't eat everything on every menu. I can't sleep in every hotel myself, but I can talk to people who do. I can get a sense of the place because I'm pretty efficient—I go through Europe like a tornado.

And you do a nice job on the Web—I imagine you get a lot of reader feedback.

I love the reader feedback—it's very, very helpful—it's crucial for us.

If by some miracle you had two free weeks, if you could go anywhere, would it be India? Just to go, not to write about it, just to enjoy it. Or would you stay here in Edmonds and hang out with your family?

That's a good question. Well, if I had two wide-open weeks, I'm such a workaholic, I would go to Europe and do things that are nagging me. I would do the Peloponnesian Peninsula and get up to date on Greece. Or I'd check out St. Petersburg and the Baltic capitals. I love sharing what I love. I've only had two jobs—I used to be a piano teacher and now I'm a travel teacher. I love music and I love travel. When you start making your hobby your work, you risk ruining your hobby. But I've always been thankful that when I teach what I really like, it doesn't take back how much I love it. I just love my work, so if I had the time I would just work more, which sounds kind of pathetic. But I get a certain vicarious joy from helping other people experience something really cool.

A couple of Sundays ago I was in Paris in St. Sulpice Cathedral. After the first mass you wait at the back of the nave and the little door opens up and people in the know can scamper up the spiral staircase and go into the organ loft and sit with one of the greatest pipe organists in Europe and see him working. There were a dozen people with my book scampering up that spiral staircase. It's pretty cool to be on the appreciation end of all those people's experience—they're all thankful to me for opening that door to them.

Right now there are probably twenty people at Walter's Hotel in a little village in the Swiss Alps on his doorstep having a nice coffee schnapps, watching the moon rise over the Jungfrau. That's pretty cool—I get selfish joy thinking of all the people who are enjoying the travel thrills I've enjoyed.

Now if I couldn't do that, I'd probably stay home and play backgammon with my children and go biking with my wife and sit in a hot tub, and go skiing. That's what I'd do, go skiing. If I was to travel, I'd go to India. I love India but I haven't been there for years because I don't teach India.

In your book, Rick Steves' Postcards from Europe, *I've seen images of your postcards. You probably could be in the* Guinness Book of World Records *for cramming the most information in tiny writing on the back of a card. Do you still send postcards, or is it all e-mail and cell phones these days?*

That's a good question: I do not send postcards. That's funny, yeah I used to do that. I am so intense when I'm in Europe and I'm so efficient and I'm so energized, it's exhilarating. I just don't go into a post office and buy a stamp and send something. I use e-mail.

Do you sleep?

I sleep, yeah. I'm very careful to get my sleep so I get eight hours a night, but I don't waste a minute when I'm in Europe because I've always got twice as much that needs to be done for the time I've got.

It seems that you plan very efficiently.

I won't even tell you how fast I update these books because it would discredit the books (laughs). I know what my readers need. We used to say on the back of our books, "Don't be fooled by overweight guidebooks."

Is there any unrevealed place that you love in Europe that you just thought, this is too precious or too delicate, I can't talk about it or it'll be overrun?

Arthur Frommer, I went to a talk by him, and I think Arthur Frommer is great, he's my inspiration—he opened the door to independent travel for people back when it really was radical. So I went to a talk by Arthur Frommer and he said he's got his favorite little pension in Rome that he keeps to himself because it's too precious. My gut reaction was, Arthur how can you do that, because I just work so hard to find these gems and if the very best gem I kept for myself, it would just make no sense at all. I'm there two nights a year, and there are 363 other nights—why can't people enjoy that?

And also it's real important for the economies of all these little places to get this business, and I love to support small businesses that are idealistic, that are keeping the character of their societies going. This mom-and-pop kind of thing is more than just cute—it's part of the fabric of a healthy society. So to answer your question, I'm so passionate about the experience my readers are going to have, I could never in good conscience keep a secret from them because I wanted it just for me.

Now there is the case of a place that's too fragile to send everybody to, and I'm aware of that. I take the temperature of places every year and see how much they can handle. Gimmelwald and Salema and Cinque Terre, these places are being overrun with my readers—now is that a bad thing? I go there and I talk to the locals and they're very thankful—they're naming streets after me. They're opening up new little businesses—they're not out in the field so much. They're doing Internet cafés and little restaurants and bed and breakfasts and they're having the economic boost that my readers bring, and my readers are all just having a blast.

It's not quite as romantic as it used to be, but there's a laundromat and there's a comfortable little hotel, and there are English menus, and there are boat rides you can take, and on and on. So it's an evolutionary thing. Yeah, I'm changing the character and the economics of that area but the locals are happy, the tourists are happy, I'm happy. A few people think that I should just tell them alone about it. There's something a little hypocritical about a reader who says, "How can you send everybody here?"

What you do feel is your greatest accomplishment or contribution as a travel guide?

There's a curiosity and a wide-eyed enthusiasm that my readers have that I try to stoke through my enthusiasm. It's not normal to be poetic for a lot of Americans and that's really a shame. Something I try to do in my books is let people know it's O.K. to be a poet and to be aware that Victor Hugo sat right there and he wrote about the ivy dragging its fingers down the ruins of that chapel and he looked down at the river and saw the boats coming as they had since Roman times. He was aware that this was the palace of the Holy Roman emperor. Today it's the Sleeping Beauty town that everybody left and it's sort of in a mothball situation now, reawakened only in the age of modern tourism. This kind of romantic approach is a beautiful thing, and a lot of people miss that in their travels. So that's my challenge as a writer, to give people the opportunity to be a poet in their travels.

A World of
Wonders

Simon Winchester
GREAT BARRINGTON, MASSACHUSETTS

S IMON WINCHESTER CREDITS STORMY WEATHER FOR HIS
greatest literary success. On Monday, September 7th, 1998,
dark clouds blanketed the New York metropolitan area, washing out the plans of many prospective beachgoers and others who
hoped to spend the Labor Day holiday out of doors. Instead they
stayed home in the company of *The New York Times*. On that day the
paper of record printed a lengthy story about Simon Winchester's new
book, *The Professor and the Madman*. The next week it was on *The
New York Times'* bestseller list.

After decades spent roaming the globe as a war correspondent,
political reporter, and as Asia-Pacific editor for *Condé Nast Traveler*, it
may seem ironic that Winchester's greatest success has come from a
book about the creation of the *Oxford English Dictionary*. But it
shouldn't be that surprising: Winchester's scholarly curiosity—he
studied geology at Oxford—and love of language have served him well
in his travel books, such as *The River at the Center of the World*, about
a trip up China's Yangtze River.

Among his recent books are *Krakatoa: The Day the World Exploded*, a groundbreaking account of the 1883 eruption that was heard thousands of miles away and caused 100-foot waves to wash over distant islands; *The Map that Changed the World*, the story of William Smith and the birth of modern geology; and *The Meaning of Everything: The Story of the Oxford English Dictionary*. At press time, he was working on a book about the 1906 San Francisco earthquake in advance of the temblor's 100th anniversary.

Winchester is known as one of the great raconteurs of our time. As the following interview shows, a question about his literary influences can lead to an account of how *Lord of the Flies* got published. If you ever have a chance to hear Winchester speak, seize it.

On a crisp, early-autumn day, after the first New England leaves had begun turning shades of yellow and orange, I visited Winchester at his recently purchased farmhouse outside of Great Barrington. When my wife and I arrived, this imposing writer greeted us with a plate of lemon tea cake and offered us lapsang soochong tea. The late afternoon sun slanted through the trees, casting golden light on a pair of tawny, chocolate-maned, Norwegian fjord horses, as they stood shoulder to shoulder behind a wood-plank fence.

Winchester's office, perhaps a hundred yards from the main house, was full of books, including an ornately decorated edition of the *Oxford English Dictionary* propped up on an antique schoolteacher's lectern. I didn't want to leave a ring on his wooden table, so Winchester suggested I put my steaming mug on an envelope—the envelope turned out to be embossed with the Queen of England's logo. When I asked, Winchester mentioned that it carried a letter of royal recognition for his parents' sixtieth anniversary. "It had to be delivered by a postman in a jacket and tie," he mused.

After the interview concluded, I sampled one of Winchester's tea cakes—he'd called a friend in England for the recipe—and found they were light and tasty. As we walked back toward his home, Winchester brushed a crumb from my goatee, called to his companion to feed the horses, and asked if we would be so kind as to stop at the Old Inn on the Green on our drive out to cancel his dinner reservation.

≈≈≈

What inspired you to become a travel writer?

First, I'd say I'm not a travel writer and I don't want to be thought of as one really. I went through a period when I worked for *Condé Nast Traveler* when I was one, but without meaning to sound pretentious, I think I'd rather be known as a journalist or a writer who travels. I remember Jonathan Raban talking about being a travel writer—there's this perception that your job as a travel writer is to help plan people's holidays—and I think I'd rather slit my wrists than do that. I like traveling and writing when I travel, but not always about foreign places. The last two books [*The Professor and the Madman* and *The Map that Changed the World*] have not been about faraway places.

What started me off being a writer was reading this book called *Coronation Everest* by James Morris [who later became Jan Morris].

[Simon shows me a picture of James on the book jacket.]

This is the book that changed my life—that was the seminal event for me. What propelled me into specific travel writing was a rather bizarre business. I was working for the *Sunday Times* (of London) in Hong Kong being a reporter and traveling around the region, and Rupert Murdoch had just taken over the paper.

When was this?

In 1987 or 1988, something like that. I was in Perth in western Australia and the foreign editor rang me one day and said, "Go to Manila—there's been a coup." And I said, "I know about this coup and it's the fifth coup this year and believe you me, Philippine coups are very rarely major events. If I fly from Perth to Manila, which will take me a long while, the coup will be over and you won't be interested—it'll be a waste of energy, time, and money. Meanwhile the story I'm doing here is a good story."

And he said, "No, the editor is insisting you go." So I rang *The Guardian* and I said I'm sick and tired of working at the *Sunday Times*, and I'd like to go back to *The Guardian* where I used to be. *The Guardian* salary was not good—one thing about Murdoch is that he pays very well—but I thought it was the noble thing to do. So I sent a fax to *The Guardian* accepting and thought, Well I've really cooked my goose because I've halved my salary just like that, just because I didn't want to go to Manila.

About 2:30 in the morning the phone rang, and it was Harry Evans calling from New York. He said, "Hello Simon, we've not talked for several years and I've just been given a new magazine to edit which hasn't started publication yet but will soon. We're going to call it *Condé Nast Traveler* and would you like to be our Asia editor? You can remain in Hong Kong and carry on working for a British paper. And the figure I have in mind is…" It was almost exactly the shortfall that I'd just two hours earlier accepted. It's a classic example of one door closing and another door opening.

Aside from Jan Morris, have you had other mentors who have influenced your development as a writer?

Very much so. I had this wonderful editor called Harry Whewell—he had the wonderful habit of putting up a list of difficult words on the bulletin board of the newsroom every Monday and urging us to try to get these words legitimately into copy. Any reporter that did would win a pint of beer. He did these sort of lexical games and I was in Belfast and he put up the word "poetaster" which means a composer of doggeral, bad poetry. I was writing a piece at the time—and I think he knew I was writing a piece at the time—on graffiti. Protestants and Catholics would insult one another and they were in the habit of writing bad poetry so I managed to get in a line which said: "The standard of the poetry on the gable ends of houses in Falls Road [the Catholic part of Belfast] was such that even the meanest poetaster of Ireland would not wish to put his name to it."

And Whewell rang me and said "O.K., that's going into the paper tonight—you've won your pint of beer." He was enormously influential in urging me to sort of look for the weird, strange idea, the quirky, off-center piece, and write it beautifully. He had very high standards about good writing. So he was a huge influence.

When I started writing books, after I left Belfast in 1972, my first editor—who wrote to me out of the blue and said would you consider writing a book—was a man called Charles Monteith; he's now dead—Harry is still alive. Among other things he worked for the firm Faber and Faber. He was Philip Larkin's editor. Larkin is my favorite modern poet. Monteith became quite famous in the 1950s. In those days, Faber and Faber had a woman called Edna who was an outside

editor, and any manuscript that was sent in uninvited would be given
to her. She would give it a cursory review before passing it on to a real
editor to decide whether it was worth looking at.

Charles told the story of coming into his office at a quarter to five
on a Friday night in the summer—it must have been about 1952—
with a view to going down to his cottage in Gloucester for the weekend and seeing a manuscript which had clearly done the rounds. It had
got coffee stains on it and was dogeared and dusty and had circles
where glasses of wine had been put on it. And it had a note from Edna
which said, "Some rubbish about schoolboys stranded on a desert
island. I suggest you ignore it." And for some reason he put it in his
briefcase and took it down on the train to Gloucester that night and
on Monday morning he rang William Golding and said, "I'd be
delighted to publish *Lord of the Flies*." So Charles was a huge influence.

*You wonder what wasn't published, what didn't get past the Ednas of the
world. To touch on another topic: With your geologist's training you often
write about the forces that shape the Earth. What forces in your life have
shaped you—what's made the deepest impression upon you?*

I was first and foremost a reporter, so I was covering wars and nasty
situations like Ireland and India. So I saw a lot, mankind behaving at
his very best and his very worst. I really enjoyed chronicling that, but
also chronicling the little things that happened in the interstices of the
great things. I think that was something, and this is going to sound
very self-serving, but if anything did mark me out as a reporter in
those days in Ireland, India, and America during Watergate, it was that
I didn't just concentrate on the big stories. I was looking all the time
for light relief. And I think that still marks what I do now. Even in this
book on Krakatoa, there are heaps and heaps of footnotes and little
things that just seem to bring the reader back down to Earth. So it
wasn't a conscious technique—it was something I enjoyed doing.

*Well it's very human—that's what I notice in a lot of your work, and I
think it's something that readers grab onto.*

Jan (Morris) was this huge influence. If you look at any of her books
they're littered with these kinds of footnotes. I think my favorite book

of hers is a book simply entitled *Oxford,* about a city that I know very well. But she would tell me so much that I didn't know—it was just a joy. I was just being bombarded with strange and unanticipated delights. I think in a way readers like that. They're getting the main story, but they're getting all the additional odds and ends which maybe give it a human dimension or just make it more fun to read, and certainly more fun to write.

A question about journalism: Traditionally journalists are outsiders—do you think that the best travel writing comes from being an outsider or an insider?

To me, the best travel writer, and almost one of the best writers in the world, is V. S. Naipaul. I just think he's so wonderful and fully deserving of the Nobel Prize (for literature, which he won in 2001). He's been personally an outsider all his life, in the Indian community in Trinidad, and then no community in England. In the same sense, here am I, an English-man here in Great Barrington. I think somehow keeping yourself off-balance all the time is a good idea because you're constantly being amazed or surprised. I think if you try too hard to assimilate yourself, in an attempt to get under the skin of a country you're reporting about, then you lose that capacity to be surprised.

>
>
> For all of my life, enthusiasm and fascination have dominated, and the wonders of the world have entirely enraptured me. The man who first suggested that I write—he is now a woman, but that's quite another story—insisted repeatedly that the world was so brim-full of delights that it would and should be impossible for any aspirant belletrist to ignore them all.
>
> —SIMON WINCHESTER, *The Best Travelers' Tales 2004*

Jan Morris is insistent that you always try to retain a sense of wonder about wherever you are, and she's managed in a way because she's relentlessly Welsh. She's an outsider—well, certainly in England. You have a sense of detachment or otherness that keeps you on your toes. Jonathan Raban lives in Seattle. Geoffrey Moorhouse, he's a north country Englishman and lives in north country England. He goes a great deal to India, and makes no attempt at all to assimilate himself. So, I think you do need to be an outsider.

Certainly it's my experience that what comes with it is a sense of unsettlement. You're at home everywhere and you're at home nowhere. That may be good for your writing; it's not necessarily good for you as a human being.

For instance, here. This is the first place I've ever really settled down, and I really love it. I'm just looking out at a field that I've created out of the forest. I've just sowed winter rye, which is coming up thanks to the weekend rain, and I get an enormous pleasure out of that. I feel, though it sounds too corny a metaphor, that I'm putting down roots for the first time, and I wonder what effect that's going to have on my writing. I'm not feeling quite as off-balance and able to be surprised, and yet I am still an outsider here. I've been here a year, not very long at all—maybe after five years I'll just be restless and I'll go somewhere else, but I sort of think not.

I still travel a lot. I was in London last week and Hong Kong the week before and I'm going to Indonesia. The places I love most of all—I'm a cold-weather person so I'm a high-latitude person—anything over 60° north and 50° south really engages me. Above 60° north the people continue to astonish me, particularly the Inuit of Canada. I haven't yet seen this film that everyone's raving about called *The Fast Runner*, a film from northern Baffin Island—apparently it's just magical.

Really, the first traveling I ever did was to east Greenland. When I was a geologist at Oxford, the Oxford University Exploration Club allowed students to organize expeditions. We went off to east Greenland and ran into all sorts of trouble. I had to shoot a polar bear because we ran out of food. We had a very, very adventurous time.

And that really whetted my appetite for the Arctic and anything to do with people who lived under conditions of enormous difficulty and struggle, yet managed to achieve a remarkable life. I am constantly amazed by people who live under conditions of extraordinary cold. I'm not amazed by people who live in hot countries. But people who live in very, very cold countries where death is just around the corner all the time, and yet live happy fulfilling lives, they're wonderful people. So I go there as often as I can.

I read of piece of yours in Condé Nast Traveler *a couple of years ago—*

That would have been Ellesmere Island—I was thinking about doing that book about Greeley—I loved that trip.

So that's where you were when you got the call from The New York Times *saying they'd like to interview you about* The Professor and the Madman?

Well it was interrupted because of that—but I was there maybe forty-five or fifty days. The season is very short up there and we were very, very lucky to get out. We almost had to overwinter there—it would have been from August until May.

Should good travel writing encourage readers to follow in the author's footsteps?

That goes back to the original question: I don't like to plan people's holidays. With travel magazines like *Condé Nast Traveler* you are going to an exotic and perhaps little-known location and turning around to the reader and beckoning, saying come on, it's fun; it's interesting.

But I think in books you're not trying to do the same thing. In *Traveler* you're trying to engage the reader—you're trying to tell him or her about places that it might be possible to visit. It's not just vicarious pleasure you're giving him or her. But I think that's magazine writing. When you write a book about someplace extraordinary like Calcutta, you're simply saying this is an amazing place; in fact, perhaps don't visit because it's disease-ridden and complicated, full of thieves and vagabonds.

With a magazine it's rather different, and they tend to select where they send you according to whether it's possible to go there. And that was one of the reasons I'm no longer writing for magazines, because increasingly I wanted to write about places that I didn't care whether people visited or not. In fact, some I'd rather they didn't.

It came up because I was going on a trip where I was on a ship journey that went to the Antarctic, Easter Island, Pitcairn Island, and Bora Bora. I said, "Where do you want a piece from?" And the editor said, "Bora Bora." I said, "Well of those four places, Bora Bora is by far and away the most boring." There's nothing to say about Bora Bora—it's just palm trees and dusky maidens and blue seas. It's beautiful but…

Have you ever been to a place where you went with the intention of writing about it and then thought, It's too pristine, I don't want hordes of tourists coming?

Several times, but only in recent years—earlier on I wouldn't have cared about that, but now I care about it very much. I wrote a piece for *Salon* about an inn in southern Patagonia, and I just didn't want anyone ever to go to it because it was so wonderful. The thought of lots of ghastly readers descending upon it in coachloads...so I wrote about it in code and put clues as to where it was, and I said anyone who's smart enough to get these clues deserves to go there. And the rest of you can stay away because it's too lovely.

The Antarctic is a case in point: I go there quite often and the last time I went there I was appalled. There was a man from a golf club in Monterey who stepped out onto the Antarctic Peninsula, put a flag up, and had a photograph taken of himself driving a golf ball into the sea, just so he could go back and tell his mates that he had hit a golf ball in Antarctica. I wanted to say, just step back and think for a moment about where you are: the majesty and pristine nature. That kind of travel, which is thought to be amusing by a lot of travel magazines, doesn't interest me in the least.

Overall do you believe that the type of travel most often practiced today is beneficial to humankind?

That's a very interesting question and deserves a long answer. The cliché is world travel leads to great understanding between peoples, to peace and harmony and everything else. But of course that's not what often happens at all—it often increases prejudice at least among some people. People travel in the wrong way if they go to somewhere like Calcutta and they find the Bengalis dirty and argumentative. Or it makes them create in these countries little islands of comfort and Western civilization so a traveler can go there and feel perfectly at home, and so the whole world becomes the same in a way. And I think that's ghastly. I want places to be hugely different. I want cultures to be as varied as possible.

That begs the question: Do I want poverty to remain? No, but I don't want the reverse to happen. I want the dignity of relative lack of money. I do not want India to be in the thrall of poverty for the rest of its days, but on the other hand the people there in certain cities and certain communities that I have come to know and love wouldn't know what to do if they were suddenly showered with heaps of money. It would ruin them.

To somehow try and preserve them in their relative lack of money—is that a condescending attitude? I'm not sure—it's something I wrestle with all the time, but I don't want there to be so much travel that the whole world is rendered essentially the same, so that you can find yourself in the Sheraton in Bombay or the Sheraton in Mauritius or the Sheraton in South Africa where life is almost exactly the same. There's no sense of wonder and astonishment, which there was fifty years ago.

I'm afraid in a way a magazine like *Traveler* fosters the sanitizing of the outside world so that you get sort of Potemkin villages created everywhere. *The Atlantic Monthly* wants me to write a piece, which I think is going to be quite difficult to write, on the really remote villages in places like Papua New Guinea that are selected by cruise liners to take their passengers to. What they do, apparently, is send their researchers to a place like Papua New Guinea and find a village that is picturesque and import into this village a sufficient number of naked people, and a sufficient number of basketmakers, and a sufficient number of people pounding maize, so that when the tourists come in, they get one-stop shopping. So the world is Disneyland—it's a very depressing thought.

I'm constantly reminded of the quote by Pascal which paraphrases that all of mankind's ills stem from his pathological inability to remain quietly in the peace of his own living room. When you think about that it's sort of true, that once you leave your living room, you go out and start wars with other people, you invade, you become a missionary. He thought about this through his life and concluded in the end that if you don't travel, if you do remain in your living room, then you become dull and you die. So you've got to accept that when you do leave your living room and go do things, you should do them in a sensitive sort of way, respecting and not trying to change the people that you're going to visit. And this keeps you alive and engaged as a human being and allows the other people to remain separate and different. You don't try and put a Sheraton down or Wal-Mart the world.

Do you think one should avoid countries for political reasons?

I think one should go. I go to Burma a lot, because you do make contact with Burmese, and in North Korea, you do make contact with North Koreans. Sure your minders will be listening to everything you say. Sure, if you're not careful and you do talk to the Burmese or the North Koreans or whoever, they do stand in jeopardy of getting in trouble. But I think they appreciate it so much, contact with you, and you come away—if you're a sensitive person—enormously sympathetic to their plight.

The other argument is about Cuba. I think it's just an outrage [that the U.S. government prohibits most travel there]. Cuba is the one really nice place in the Caribbean because it's so not American. There's no McDonald's —it's how the Caribbean used to be.

I recently went on a bicycle tour of the countryside there.

I bet you loved every minute of it. It's a magical country, wonderful people.

Yes, and almost everyone there was intelligent enough to distinguish between the American people and the U.S. government.

Now there are said by biologists to be only 100 *baiji* left in the entire river, maybe 150. Did the fisherman feel responsible? I asked. He nodded, and he did indeed look contrite…. "Yangtze fishermen have good hearts, you know. We love this river. We love the fish. We love the dolphin and we revere her. But back then— back then it was very different. It was very difficult. Mao did some terrible things. We had to eat. We thought we had no choice. It was the dolphins, or it was our children. Which would you choose?"

—SIMON WINCHESTER, *The River at the Center of the World*

Exactly, and there's one case where you should defy your government. But I think when you're urged by peace activists and Suu Kyi's friends not to come to Burma because the government will get the money, I think you've got to accept that simply by being there, if you're going to go, you have to make an effort to make contact with the locals. It's enormously important to them to know there are sympathetic people on the outside and that you can get their message out and back to America or Britain. Some money is bound to trickle down.

Do you have any advice for aspiring travel writers, any suggestions or tips?

I must say I'm not the classic travel writer, but I was a foreign correspondent for a very long time so I've always written about abroad and still do. I would say the best way to report from abroad is to be abroad and start writing. Find yourself a country, obscure enough so there will not be legions of American or British reporters, a country that has got an interesting domestic situation, with perhaps a little bit of war, a little bit of insurrection, something that's newsworthy. Go there. Set yourself up and find out the names of a number of newspapers that do not have representation in this town. Find seven or eight of them in non-competing markets and then write to them and say, "I am in Colombo, or Phnom Penh, or Jakarta, and if anything happens, ring me up. And if anything happens that I think might be of interest to you, I'm going to tell you about it." You can sell the same piece to all of your potential clients.

So that's a piece of practical advice: Go abroad. Don't just stay here and hope to be sent abroad. Secondly, be doggedly persistent. Never stop writing or telephoning or e-mailing editors and sending ideas in, because in the end you'll wear down the most jaded news editor. Thirdly, and it may sound cliché, never lose the sense of wonder. Be constantly thrilled to be seeing all the things you're seeing, because if you can convey this sense of enthrallment to your reader, you'll win the reader's attention.

What's a typical day like for you—do you keep to a schedule when you're writing?

I absolutely do. I'll outline it for you but may think it sounds horribly...well, I get up every morning at 6 and I come here at 6:10. If I'm writing a book, whatever I wrote the night before I will read until 8 o'clock and tinker with it until I'm relatively satisfied. At 8 o'clock, on the dot, I will print it up so I then have my twenty pages of printed material. Then I go running or exercise or something and have breakfast until maybe 9:30, and then I come back here and write for the rest of the day until about 5. And then at 5, I finish the writing and go into the house and watch the BBC news. At 6:30 or 6:45 I come back here and begin the reading for what I'm going to write the following day, and then at about 9 o'clock, I stop.

And then the following day I come back at 6, I look at what I wrote, tinker with it till 8, print it up, and so another twenty pages becomes forty. So it goes on day after day after day.

Do you work on the weekends?

Yes, when I'm doing a book. I just find I like the concentration, I become so totally immersed. This is going to sound…well, it's not awful because it's exactly how Trollope [the nineteenth-century British novelist], who is my idol in terms of writing…he had a metronome and every fifteen minutes he'd produce a thousand words. He was amazing, astonishing, totally focused.

I have a counter. [Winchester shows me a spreadsheet on his computer.] For the last book, I had an early target of 100,000 words, due on the 30th of June, present date 20th of May, the number of days remaining until 30th of June was forty. These are the chapters and the number of words, total there of 116,932 words.

That's a very workmanlike approach.

Very workmanlike! But it works for me. I'm sure you'll find other writers work in a completely different way. So there it is.

After seeing you at a recent book event, it's clear you're one of the world's finest storytellers. In travel writing, how much leeway is acceptable? Should travel writers stick to just the facts or are they entitled to some artistic license?

I have a debate with Geoffrey Moorhouse about this, because Geoffrey believes you should stick absolutely to the facts. Jan Morris, on the other hand, believes that providing what you write in your heart of hearts fairly evokes the place you have just been, then you do have some leeway. There are no hard and fast rules.

I think composite characters are a bad thing. You should stick to the names of the people you talk to unless for some reason you want to disguise their identities. I have, on one or two occasions, been tripped up badly, once very badly indeed. There's no harm in confessing it because this is something I feel quite badly about. I couldn't get to a particular village in the far east of Russia once so I telephoned them and wrote as if I had been there. A fact-checker found out, and I felt so appalled with myself. So that's as bad as I've ever done, and I wouldn't do it again. I, in a way, pushed the limit, so I know where the lines are drawn.

Having said that, there is some leeway. I don't think total, rather pedantic and fussy, just-the-facts-mam lends itself to good or better travel writing. But it's a very dangerous area to get into. I think the masters like Jan Morris and Jonathan Raban who do airbrush things to an extent, do it very delicately and very carefully, always holding to a principle that what they produce is fair.

Strange
Travel
Suggestions

Jeff Greenwald
OAKLAND, CALIFORNIA

A S HIS FORTIETH BIRTHDAY APPROACHED, JEFF GREENWALD realized that he'd already seen more of the planet than Magellan and Marco Polo combined, but travel was losing some of its allure. He had begun to tire of jetting halfway around the globe in less time than it took early explorers to cover forty miles. So he set a unique challenge for himself: to travel around the world without leaving the ground.

While visiting Nepal in his late twenties, Greenwald was drawn to Buddhism and incorporated some Buddhist practices into his life. His global odyssey would be more than a travel adventure, it would describe a *kora*, a Buddhist devotional circle, around the object he considered most sacred: the planet Earth.

As he traveled around the world in 1994, Greenwald carried a laptop computer and filed trip dispatches for a nascent online magazine called *Global Network Navigator*. He was the first person to publish trip accounts for a widely-read Internet publication while circling the globe, and he shares the electricity of the trip in his 1995 book, *The Size of the World*.

In a 1996 interview for a magazine called *Internet Underground*, Greenwald told me: "I had this sense of being almost on fire, that the excitement and heat of my journey was something I could broadcast in no time at all. It was a very giddy feeling." Yet he noted the irony of transmitting his impressions at light-speed while taking nine months to travel around the planet. "The point of my trip was to forsake technology, so my presence on the Web became an ironic counterpoint. While my brain was telecommuting at the speed of light, my body was compelled to travel at a snail's pace, face down in the sand."

Like several other authors profiled in these pages, Greenwald's writing ranges far beyond travel. Since his teen years he's had a ferocious love of science fiction, and his science writing has appeared in *Wired* magazine. He counts Arthur C. Clarke among his closest friends, and his book, *Future Perfect: How Star Trek Conquered Planet Earth*, illuminates the cult of Trekkies.

Yet Greenwald is best known for his travel writing. His early visits to Nepal led to the 1985 publication of *Mr. Raja's Neighborhood* and, five years later, of *Shopping for Buddhas*, a hilarious and at times haunting tale of seeking the perfect statue of Buddha. In his modest apartment in Oakland, California, Greenwald showed me the small Buddha statue that would become the object of his desire in *Shopping for Buddhas*.

On the wall was a bronze and wooden plaque earned by his father, Robert Greenwald, a sales manager for General Electric, for flying 100,000 miles on United Air Lines. Awarded in 1965, it reads: "In Appreciation of Your Valuable Contribution to Air Transport Progress." The plaque contains a globe with four circles around it, representing a distance of 100,000 miles. "That's what they gave you in the days before frequent-flier miles," he quipped.

Greenwald, who spent much of his twenties pursuing the visual arts and sculpture, has some of his own art decorating his walls. One piece, showing a watch, symbolizes time slipping away. "I felt like I was wasting time not being in Asia," he said.

In 2002, he self-published *Scratching the Surface*, a collection of his best travel writing, stories that appeared in *Adventure, Islands, Geo,*

Salon, and top newspaper travel sections, as well as in Travelers' Tales anthologies. In 2003, Greenwald premiered a solo theatrical performance called *Strange Travel Suggestions,* in which he told his exotic and compelling tales to audiences in San Francisco.

≈≈≈

How did you get started as a travel writer, and was it intentional or did you just start traveling and then decide to write about your trips?

It's hard to say when I became a travel writer. A lot of writers, myself included, begin writing very young. My earliest memory is of writing something that I had to read in public, when I was eight years old. At that point, travel was more or less out of the question—although I did consider running away from home quite a few times!

From a very young age I've loved science fiction, and I feel that sci-fi has a very strong component of travel in it. I never could hope to travel to the places that I read about in science fiction books, of course, yet back when I was a kid—in the early days of the Apollo program— it didn't seem impossible that, by the time I grew up, one would be able to go to the moon or even visit Mars.

Two movies that I saw when I was a teenager influenced me a great deal: I think I was about fourteen when *2001: A Space Odyssey* came out. Something about those infinite vistas, and the astronauts alone in space, gave me a deep longing to travel, even if it was going to be confined to the planet Earth.

The other movie that had a huge impact was *Lawrence of Arabia.* It was the most beautiful landscape I had ever seen. And the sensibilities of T. E. Lawrence, as portrayed by Peter O'Toole, as a person traveling by his wits through a land that was so exotic and strange, really inspired me. It made me feel as though I could only have true control of my life and of my destiny if I traveled; that I could be fully alive in a way that would be impossible if I were to stay at home.

It was when I was in my late teens, or early twenties, that the idea of travel writing reared its head. What happened was that in 1979 I went on an extended trip that took me through Europe, Egypt, India, Southeast Asia, and that introduced me for the first time to the country that would become my second home: Nepal.

When I got back from that trip I was in love with Asia and obsessed with the idea of putting writing together with the traveling I'd done. I lived in Santa Barbara at the time, and sold my first few stories to *Westways* magazine. Once I'd published a few pieces in *Westways*, I had a few ideas that I pitched to *Santa Barbara* magazine, which I'd heard paid a little better.

The first one they bought was about the Amtrak *Coast Starlight*, which ran down the West Coast from Santa Barbara to Union Station in Los Angeles. It was a short trip, but I managed to cobble together a mildly unusual story about my experiences. The editor enjoyed it, and gave me other assignments. Soon after, the publisher of *Santa Barbara* magazine began a new magazine, which he called *Islands*. When I went abroad again in 1983-84 on a journalism fellowship through the Rotary Foundation, *Islands* gave me assignments in Sri Lanka and Indonesia. They were a very literary, writer-friendly magazine, and encouraged me to stretch my skills.

Before my 1983-84 trip to Asia, I stopped in New York. Being a very brash young man in my late twenties, I felt like the world was in the palm of my hand. I just stormed into the offices of *Geo* magazine in New York. I met one of the editors there, Richard Conniff, and said, "Hey you don't know me but I think you want to. I'm heading off to Asia and I want to do something for you." He looked at me up and down and said, "You can't just barge into an editor's office like this." I said, "Oh, well, I'm really sorry. Please forgive me, but here I am. Is there anything we can do together?"

He said, "Well, I'm certainly not going to forget who you are…so if you come across something interesting, drop me a line." After a couple of months in Asia I got an idea to do a story about the cave temples of Ellora, in Maharashtra, India. I pitched that to Conniff, and he assigned the story. It appeared as the cover story of the October 1984 issue—and then the magazine went out of business.

Coincidence?

I certainly hope so.

It seems like a lot of great assignments come from such serendipitous encounters.

When you teach at travel writers' conferences and do classes and seminars, a lot of people tend to ask you what your trajectory was, as if it were something someone else could imitate and somehow duplicate. I've found that every writer's career takes a completely different track. It's almost impossible to advise anyone else how to begin a career in writing, or what assignments or contacts they're going to make that are going to shape their career and move it forward.

I would look at almost every assignment I've done as having a component of serendipity to it. If I hadn't taken a Club Med junket to Tahiti to write about their new cruise ship for the *San Francisco Examiner*, I wouldn't have met my friend Mary Roach—and if I hadn't met Mary Roach, I never would have written for *The New York Times Magazine*, because it was she who put me in touch with the editor there. Everything is so interconnected—wherever you shake the tree, a fruit is going to fall from someplace.

The most serendipitous thing that ever happened to me happened in 1979—when, on a whim, I wandered into the Athens Museum and struck up a conversation with a beautiful woman who was walking through the galleries alone. I was not the sort of person who approached women easily, and it turned out this woman was going off to a place I'd never heard of to do a residency in Ayurvedic medicine. Over the next two weeks she and I traveled together. I fell in love, and swore I'd do anything I could to meet her there. Because of that chance encounter in an Athens museum, I was introduced to Nepal—which became perhaps the single most influential place in the world as regards my development as a human being, a spiritual person, and a writer.

And that's certainly not a blueprint for anybody except yourself.

Of course. Who else could possibly duplicate that string of romance, coincidence, and happenstance?

One thing I've noticed in my travels is that not only can't you go home again, you can't go back to the same place where you had that magical experience. For me, Guatemala in 1989 was utterly magical, the people I met, the old friends I ran into by chance. When I went back in 1994, the serendipity wasn't there.

Well, I've had the opposite experience with Nepal. Every visit has had a completely different component of magic and coincidence and has reminded me anew of why I fell in love with Nepal in the first place—and why I have to keep going back. There's a deep connection that never seems to run dry. As polluted as Kathmandu is, as noisy and politically screwed up as it is, it still has the capacity to surprise me and astonish me in ways that I didn't know were possible.

So it's become a second home for you?

I'm not there for three or four months a year as I once was. I'm sometimes there for only three or four weeks a year, so to call it my second home is a bit of an exaggeration. But when I think about my spiritual life, I consider Nepal my primary home, because it's where my heart goes to be restored. It's where my spirit's batteries are recharged after being drained by the West.

When you first started traveling were you consciously seeking anything, or perhaps running away from something, or did you just have a curiosity about the world?

I think I was running away from my family life in New York, which was extremely oppressive to me. Again, identifying with T. E. Lawrence, the idea of being alone in strange and exotic lands where I had to fend for myself was enormously appealing. Of course, I was completely unable to do this. The first time I left home alone in 1971 on one of those cheap $99 SAS fares, I panicked the minute I landed in Copenhagen, and raced home in disgrace after just a few weeks.

It would be eight years before I traveled abroad again. That time I was away for eleven months and had a completely different sense of self-confidence, and an insatiable curiosity about the world. By that point I'd moved from New York to California, and had established myself independently. It was no longer about standing on my own two feet—it was about seeing the world and learning what the world had to offer me.

But I still did not see myself, primarily, as a writer. Between 1975 and 1983 I identified myself mainly as a visual artist. I was a sculptor and graphic artist, and I tried very hard to make a go of that. Writing was on the back burner for me. When I traveled to Europe and Asia in 1979, in fact, I had my sculpting tools with me. My original idea had been to live in Greece for twelve weeks and sculpt marble on Paros, but the trip took me to Egypt and Nepal and put me right back into a writing mode very quickly.

What led you to choose the types of places you went and what publications you wrote for—how actively did you shape your career?

To be frank, I don't really think I shaped my career as well or as wisely as some other writers that I know. I never went to New York and lived there and made the necessary contacts that would have put me at a higher level in the literary community. I was always the sort of person who liked to be moved around by the world, and when I found places that I resonated with I would just stay there, and write about them. I spent an awful lot of time in Nepal when I might have been in New York doing freelance pieces for magazines and trying to put my name on the map. I was more interested in writing as an artistic form of expression rather than as a career path. My first book, *Mr. Raja's Neighborhood: Letters from Nepal* is a year's cycle of letters written to my visual artist friends in California.

In March of 1994, I would turn forty. As a birthday present to myself—and as the ultimate challenge of my career—I wanted to rediscover that the Earth is round. I wanted to embrace its mass, feel its gravity, ambulate its circumference. I wanted to travel forward, without a return ticket, and let the topology of the planet's sphere carry me back to the place I had started from. There was only one way to do this. I would have to travel around the world—from Oakland, California to Oakland, California—without ever leaving the ground.

—Jeff Greenwald,
The Size of the World

Let's talk for a moment about The Size of the World *and the idea of transmitting travel essays to readers almost instantly. What a departure from getting an assignment and several months later your story appears in a magazine. In 1994, you'd write something and several hours later it would appear on GNN. How was that for you as a writer?*

It was astonishing—it was like I was no longer *writing for* the world, but *talking to* the world. There's such an incredible sense of freedom and artistic spontaneity that comes when you know that your writing is going to appear within a day or two. It's nothing like news writing, where news editors go over your piece and they cut it and trim it. A lot of the writing I did for GNN was published word-for-word precisely as I'd written it—and I knew it would be. So it was like tightrope walking. When I sat down at the computer to write something, I was always aware that my thought processes would be transferred to thousands of readers all over the world. It was exhilarating.

I felt very wired. It was a huge relief to be able to write on a laptop, something that was small, light, and portable. In the past, even while I was traveling through Asia in the early '80s, I'd always carried a typewriter with me. This is because my penmanship is so bad. I write with my left hand, which I have to twist up like a pretzel in order to form a string of letters, and after ten minutes I get a cramp. So all through 1983-84, I had a seventeen-pound Smith Corona Mark IV in my backpack. And not just a Smith Corona, but typing paper and carbon paper and typing ribbons and white-out, and all the things I needed to type letters to friends and notes to myself.

And I traveled all over Asia with this huge typewriter taking up half my backpack. I feel kind of sorry for whoever was staying in the rooms next to me, because I would just be up clacking and banging away on that typewriter all night long. It was almost like a Buddhist chant or meditation in the background. When you're typing, you're inspired and you're just pounding on the keys: this rhythm and clackety-clacking train sound that never ceases. I didn't hear it while I was writing, but it must have driven everyone around me stark raving mad.

I just can't imagine carrying around twenty pounds of writing equipment.

It was completely insane. When I think about it now I realize the answer to the question, How did I do that? along with the answer to so many other questions I ask myself now, is simply: I was much younger.

How do you prepare for an assignment? For a typical travel story, what do you do a few weeks ahead, a few days ahead?

I used to go to the library and read whatever was most current: books, magazine articles, most months or years old. Now I go on the Internet and try to find out all the latest—not only the geographical situation and historical background, but what the current political situation is in every country I'm visiting. I'm always very interested in the political problems and the environmental issues, because it's on those sorts of rough edges that you find the most interesting people.

What I'll do these days, which I find tremendously valuable, is try to make direct contact with specific people in a country before I go. In a recent assignment to write about Palau for *Islands* magazine, I knew that I'd be doing a lot of scuba diving and that I'd be looking into coral reef issues—so I first made contact with Francis Matsutaro, who is the director of the Coral Reef Ecology Center in Palau. He and I had a correspondence going for weeks before I arrived in Palau, and we hit the ground running. By the time I got there, we were ready to buy each other beers—we were nearly friends.

That's one of the most extraordinary benefits of the Internet, and one that has made my so job so much more rich and profound: the relationships get kick-started. When you land in a country, you don't have to tell everybody who you are; the red tape is behind you, and you can get into relatively intimate exchanges with people very quickly.

Before an assignment, do you have a sense of the structure a story is going to take, or do you let the story unfold and then use what you find?

I almost never have an idea going in of the structure a story is going to take. That always happens to me there. I never know who I'm going to meet, who's going to be the central character in a story. Often the person who I think will be the central character will not be. I don't know what's going to move me—I don't know what the metaphors are going to be. I have to be on the ground to really understand that.

The best example of this is my assignment to the Solomon Islands, again for *Islands*, in the late 1980s. The Solomon Islands had very little tourist or travel infrastructure when I landed there in 1986, and I was completely at sea. I had no idea who to turn to for information, or where to go. Speaking with a local tribal man in a small restaurant, I learned about the tradition of the *wontok*. This is pidgin for the words "one talk." In the Solomon Islands, the only people you can rely on for anything are your own clanspeople, the people who literally speak your language.

Once I discovered this I sought out my own *wontoks*: the Peace Corps volunteers who had been assigned to the Solomons. They immediately took me in and began introducing me to aspects of the island that I never would have found through any other means. That was something that I never could have predicted, and that I couldn't know until I hit the ground.

It's that way everywhere. In Phuket, I didn't know that Thai boxing would be the metaphor for my story until I'd been to a Thai boxing match and saw how these peaceful Buddhist Thais were transformed in the boxing ring. It showed me, very viscerally, how much fight they have in them. This is something that's come out historically, but that the average tourist doesn't see.

How has being a travel writer shaped your view of the world?

It has made me aware that the things one reads in the newspaper and the things one sees on television are very superficial indications of what's really going on—like Indonesian shadow puppets that give an outline of the world and its people but don't give any sense of depth. You hear the news from Iran, and you hear that some students are rioting, and it's all very two-dimensional and chaotic. But having

---

It was a shock to walk down the streets of Tehran…and feel no sense of menace at all. Everyone I met was helpful and hospitable, and quite eager to talk about Iran/American relations —within limits. Even my taxi driver, who spoke perhaps ten words of English, pumped my hand when he heard where I was from. "Oh, America! Very good! J.F.K., very good!" "What about Bill Clinton?" I ventured. "Very good, very good!" "George Bush?" "Very good!" "Ronald Reagan?" "Sorry…" he shrugged. "No English."

—JEFF GREENWALD,
Scratching the Surface

been to Iran, you know what these people are like—what color their eyes are, how they huddle in cafés over coffee in the evening, and how it pains them to hide their affiliations from some of their closest friends.

Or you hear about the Maoist activity in Nepal, and that a bomb went off in a marketplace somewhere in Kathmandu. A person who's never traveled to a place like that may imagine the whole city erupting in flames. But you know what it really means—you can picture the place in your mind. You know that it must have been a wild scene of devastation in a small area, with radishes scattered and bicycle rick-shaws shattered, but that two blocks away there could have been peo-ple simply going about their business, with no idea the blast even occurred. You realize that the picture is a lot bigger than one is led to believe by the Western media, and you feel a sense of gratitude for being able to see the world on its own terms.

I don't know how my life would have unfolded if I wasn't a travel writer. I don't know if I'd be a more conservative person, if I'd be a more ignorant person, I don't even know if I'd still be alive. It seems quite impossible that my karma could have led me to any other life other than the one I'm leading.

But you have suggested that travel has opened your heart and opened your mind...

I like to think that I'm an open-minded person with an open heart. In the abstract, I think about the people on this planet and I recognize that they have a lot more in common than they have dividing them. Simple things like a kind act, a smile, or a hand on the shoulder, will break down barriers more quickly than any battering ram.

When I'm in places like China or India or Vietnam, where it can be difficult to travel, I find myself doing what any normal human being might do: I lose my patience; I get irritated; I get depressed; I get lonely. All the things that happen to me here, happen to me there. I believe that most of the world's conflicts are less a function of the way people are, and more about the way governments and power-mongers are. It's my conviction that the vast majority of people on this planet would like to be left alone to live and work in peace, to raise their fam-ilies, and to exist in a generous and rational way.

There are exceptions, of course, but I think when you see major exceptions, like religious fundamentalism, it's because people are being used; their poverty or grief or desperation are being exploited. I'm very forgiving of the human race. I think that people complain about how primitive humans are, but consider that concepts such as children's rights or animal rights, completely unknown in the developing world twenty-five years ago, are now major issues worldwide. This is after only 10,000 years of human social science and government in the world. As I'm fond of saying: wolves have been around for 50 million years, and they can't even make a good cup of coffee.

But they have pretty sophisticated social organizations and don't tend to kill thousands of their own kind in battles or disputes.

Exactly; they appear to be in stasis, whereas we continue to evolve socially. We not only have the capacity to destroy the planet, we also have the capacity to preserve the planet as a paradise, and to achieve creative feats in every realm: astonishing works of art; the first moon ships; new kinds of flowers; ships that can sail miles beneath the surface of the sea. I don't think these are bad things—these are fantastically creative things. As they say in the old comic books, "If only we could use our brilliance for good instead of for evil." There's a lot of good done by human beings. I really think it's just a minority of the species that's driving the rest of us to extinction.

What changes have you seen through the world in the twenty-five years or so since you began working as a travel writer.

Well, environmental awareness has not kept pace with environmental pollution. As the world gets more accessible, it also gets more accessible to mining companies and lumber companies and exploitive corporations that use up every resource they can get their hands on to make a short-term profit. We've seen a lot of horrible things happen in the past twenty-five years in the rate of species extinction, the destruction of the coral reefs, the decimation of our rainforests. The environment of the planet is being severely degraded; there's no question about that.

It's the classic race: What's going to happen first? Is the planet going to enter an irrecoverable period of environmental and social destruction, or are the forces of wisdom and conservation going to prevail? It's a question that might actually be answered during our lifetimes. Right now, during the first term of the George W. Bush administration, the outlook seems grim—arrogance, selfishness, and wastefulness have become global contagions, led by the U.S. and China. But I think that most of us have a sense of how quickly things can be turned around by changing just a few of the people in power.

And even if we can't change our leaders—we seem to have freedom of choice, but so little to choose from—we are gaining the tools to change things globally on a populist level. The Information Age has reached nearly every corner of the world: There seems to be a deep, deep compulsion among humans everywhere to communicate with each other, and to experiment with manifestations of other cultures—whether it's Americans looking at an incredible show of Mongolian art, or kids in Calcutta watching *Star Trek*. This is a kind of ultimate democracy, as well as an ultimate window to peaceful co-existence, because a fascination and delight in the world is a long step toward caring for the world.

The one thing that human beings do better than anything else is communicate. A lot of the communication is nasty, but a lot of it is very useful and valuable. That's why, among all the people I admire in the world, the top person on my list is Arthur C. Clarke. Nearly everybody knows that he wrote, with Stanley Kubrick, *2001: A Space Odyssey*. But he also came up with the concept of the communication satellite, which is one of the most useful tools that's been invented in the past hundred years.

You've met him, right?

Clarke has been a friend of mine since I was fifteen, when I wrote him an almost pathologically gushing fan letter after seeing *2001* and reading all of his books. He answered the letter and invited me to come meet him at the Chelsea Hotel in New York. We soon became friends, and our friendship has endured. During the past thirty-five years, I've visited him three times in Sri Lanka. One of those visits is recorded in *Mr. Raja's Neighborhood,* and another in my book about *Star Trek, Future Perfect. Wired* magazine and Salon.com have published several of my interviews with him.

Do you have any advice for aspiring travel writers?

I would suggest they take the craft of writing as seriously as they would take learning how to play the oboe. It involves a lot of practice, an unflagging commitment, and a surprising amount of failure in order to become any good. I also think it's very important to read what you love to read—and to write about what you love to write.

The well-worn adage to "write what you know" remains true, at least in the sense of knowing what interests you. When neophytes travel, they have this idea that they must write something very broad, describing every aspect of a place like Paris or Bangkok or Canyonlands. Far more interesting would be a piece about the men or women who collect the bits of tile used to cover certain Thai temples, or the story of how Brancusi's beautiful sculpting studio ended up outside the Pompidou Center. If you're a firefighter, write a story about the firefighters of Paris, and how quirky and unusual it is to fight fires in Paris. When was the first major fire in Paris? People should write about what fascinates them, rather than try to do a general story that covers all the bases.

At a writers conference a couple of years ago, Tim Cahill suggested following a potato from a French field to the truck to the market to the restaurant to the plate.

That's exactly what John McPhee did in his book about oranges, and what Michael Pollan did with apples, potatoes, tulips, and cannabis in *The Botany of Desire*. People love it when they can read about something that they're familiar with and see how it's put together. That's why Simon Winchester's *The Professor and the Madman* was such a success. It dealt with words: a subject that is universally fascinating to people who love to read.

And that's a nice story, too, because an agent's first take might be, "Are you kidding me, a book about the Oxford English Dictionary?" *But it really struck a chord. It was a bestseller, and you never really know where that's going to come from.*

I think a lot of people pick up *Shopping for Buddhas* not necessarily because they're fascinated with Nepal and its mythology, but because they have shopped for Buddhas. They have been in countries where they have wanted to buy themselves a Buddha statue, and so they gravitate towards the account of an experience that they are familiar with.

The title of that book is great because of the unlikely juxtaposition of shopping and Buddha. You think of the Buddha as tranquility and peace, and when you're shopping for one…

…You're materialistic and critical. Using that process as a metaphor for the Western mind might be one of the better ideas I've had. But as you know—again, we talk about serendipity—*Shopping for Buddhas* did not begin as a book, but as a staged monologue. Thanks to a coincidental encounter, it was turned into a book. Another example of how strange things happen to strange people.

Do you consider travel writing a noble calling?

Absolutely. And I think travel is a noble endeavor. I strongly believe that launching yourself into the world, putting yourself face to face with other people, on their turf, where you have to account for yourself on unfamiliar terms, is a noble way to live and to move ahead as a human being. As for travel writing per se, there are many different approaches. There's the kind of travel writing where you go out and try to conquer a mountain, to prove to yourself and the world that you can do it. That's certainly fascinating, but it can be exploitive as well.

There are many travel writers, especially recently, who travel to bring a greater sense of political and environmental awareness to their readers. I'm tremendously in favor of that approach. One of truly great writers in this genre is Joe Kane, who wrote *Running the Amazon* and *Savages*. He's a deeply political and extremely articulate champion of the South American Indians. And then there are the fabulously funny writers like Mark Twain, Dave Barry, Tim Cahill. It's wonderful to read funny travel writing, to read adventure writing, to read a book like Jon Krakauer's *Into Thin Air,* which is so metaphorical for the relentless sense of desire that drives so many Western travelers.

It can be a noble vocation; but almost any vocation can be noble. As the Buddha said, it's all about intention. If you go into accounting or car repair hoping to help people and make their lives a little easier, and if you enjoy what you're doing, you're on the same path as a Tibetan monk. That's what the Buddha taught. Liberation comes not just from studying and meditating over sacred texts, but from doing whatever it is you do in a conscious and compassionate way. If you travel and write about your experiences with an open eye and an open heart, you can teach people valuable lessons about the way their fellow human beings face desire and suffering and happiness on this planet.

Ultimately, all that people care about is other people. That's why a magazine like *People* is so successful, and why *TIME* and *Newsweek* are now devoting so much space to gossipy articles. People are keenly interested in how other people live, suffer, and strive for happiness.

And that also informs the best travel writing—it's not just a description of the land and the place, but...

...it's character-driven. You meet a couple of good, or at least interesting, people. The reason *The Size of the World* is my favorite of my books is that, for a nine-month period, the universe conspired to throw me together with some of the most interesting human beings on the planet: people like Paul Bowles and scores of others. There are smart, creative, articulate people everywhere you go. What they're doing is completely unusual and wild—they're trading USDA butter for computers on the Silk Road in Kazakhstan, publishing the first free speech magazine in Hong Kong.

You recently began performing a one-man show in San Francisco called Strange Travel Suggestions, *based on your travels. I assume the title is from Vonnegut's line, "Strange travel suggestions are dancing lessons from God." What inspired you to do this show? It must be a very frightening thing to do a live solo performance.*

It is frightening because when you write you try to craft your material, but when you're on stage telling stories, it's very much what comes to your mind. You can pass through a whole section of a story and realize you forgot one of the juiciest observations, but you can't go back and add it. The idea of the show is to somehow find a way to bring the experience of travel, the spontaneity and the surprise of it, onto the stage. To do that, I built a big wheel of fortune with thirty symbols on it, each one standing for a different idea or notion about travel: The Ugly American, Meals of Misfortune, Creature Karma, Doors Strangely Open. People from the audience come up and spin the wheel, and whatever it lands on, I improvise a story from my travels based on that theme. And it's really wonderful, because evening to evening, I don't really know what kind of stories I'm going to tell or what kind of journey I'm going to go on with the audience, so it really does capture for me the sensation and the feeling and the emotion of traveling, with all its surprises and an awful lot of its anxiety.

You recently created a non-profit called Ethical Traveler (www.ethicaltraveler.com). Would you tell me a bit about it?

Tourism is a huge industry, and travelers have, whether they recognize it or not, a tremendous amount of power and economic clout. Where travelers choose to go—and where they choose *not* to go—can have a big impact on cities and even on countries, and serve as a lever for profound change. We're trying to create a worldwide community of politically aware travelers who support human rights and environmental protection. We also believe that travel is a tremendously effective form of diplomacy, and that all travelers are de facto ambassadors.

Can you offer some specifics about what Ethical Traveler is doing?

We contributed to the effort to stop Nepal from deporting Tibetan refugees back to China during the summer of 2003. We are conducting letter-writing campaigns to help control the poaching of deep-sea fish and lobsters around the Galapagos and Cocos Islands; and to ask the Chinese to withdraw their plan to build a road around Mount Kailash, in Tibet, and nominate the area as a UNESCO World Heritage Site instead.

If you hadn't been a travel writer, what do you imagine you'd be doing right now?

I'd be an astronaut. My lifelong dream—from the time I was thirteen until the day I drop dead—was and will always be to visit outer space. There's nothing I ever wanted to do more, and there's no disappointment I feel more keenly than the premature end of the civilian space program, which got its death blow with the explosion of the *Challenger* and the death of civilians in space.

Otherwise—given that I was probably too tall to be an astronaut anyway—I might have gone into astrophysics or astronomy. It's an exaggeration to say I'm an amateur astronomer, but cosmology and the universe are supremely fascinating to me, and I try to keep abreast of the latest developments. I just really enjoy hanging out with the people who are making discoveries in those sciences.

That all ties in very neatly, of course, with my love of science fiction. I'm as fascinated by what might be Out There as I am by what's down here. The only places I can really explore are down here on this planet. And I do my best, be it on land or in the ocean. But some day, *inshallah*, I would love to be coaxed aboard a spaceship by some relatively friendly aliens and given a little tour of the neighborhood. I'll hold out as long as I can, watching the skies and waiting for that to happen.

One last question: Why do you make Oakland your home base?

I happen to think Oakland is one of the most ethnically diverse and integrated cities in the world. You go downtown to Le Cheval, a popular Vietnamese restaurant, and on almost any day of the week you can count six, seven, eight racial groups in every kind of configuration you can imagine. You've got blacks lunching with whites, Lao sitting with blacks, Latina nurses sharing plates of spring rolls with Khmer doctors. Oakland is wonderfully international, and it's a place with a very vibrant jazz and art scene.

Personally, I wish it was still considered the "ugly duckling" sister of San Francisco, but it's gotten a lot more trendy since Jerry Brown took office as mayor. Oakland has always been underappreciated, if not shunned, by outsiders. And though I prefer it that way, for selfish reasons, I think it's deeply worthy of the appreciation of anyone who enjoys human civilization at its most vibrant and expressive.

Any rebuttal to the alleged Gertrude Stein quote about Oakland, "There's no there, there."

Well, there's here, now.

Through Love and War

Eric Newby
GUILDFORD, ENGLAND

ERIC NEWBY'S LIFE STORY READS LIKE A HOLLYWOOD SCRIPT. After a comfortable, middle-class English upbringing, Newby left home at eighteen to join the crew of one of the world's last commercial sailing ships, the *Moshulu*, which hauled grain from Austrailia to Ireland. A few months later, World War II broke out. After serving in India, Newby volunteered for the Special Boat Section, which sent squads of soldiers ashore to blow up enemy aircraft. On an August 1942 mission off the coast of Italy, Newby was unable to return to his submarine after attempting to attack a German airfield and was captured.

He spent thirteen months in P.O.W. camps before escaping in September 1943, immediately after the Italian armistice. A sympathetic Italian commandant, who was later beaten to death by the Germans, let the prisoners escape. Newby, who had recently broken his ankle, left atop a mule. A Slovenian couple with anti-Fascist sympathies sheltered Newby, who became smitten with their daughter Wanda as she taught him Italian. When it became unsafe for Newby to stay with Wanda's family, he sought shelter in the maternity ward of a nearby hospital. But as the Germans closed in, Wanda's father risked his life to drive Newby through Parma to a mountain hideout in the Po Valley. Ultimately Newby was recaptured and returned to prison camps but survived the war.

When hostilities ceased, Newby returned to court Wanda (pronounced "Vanda") and thank her family for saving his life. They were soon married and settled in England, where Newby worked in the family clothing business. After a decade in the rag trade, Newby and a British foreign service officer traveled to Afghanistan, which resulted in Newby's still-popular 1958 book, *A Short Walk in the Hindu Kush*. They ventured into territory almost never visited by white men and came close to summiting Mir Samir, a near-20,000-foot peak, with almost no training in mountaineering. It's a classic piece of old-school British exploration, and established Newby's trademark self-deprecating wry humor.

Unlike many travel writers who prefer to wander alone, Newby has traveled with his wife whenever possible. Wanda accompanied her husband on the first part of his trip to Afghanistan, until it was no longer feasible to have an unveiled woman about. Wanda floated with Newby in *Slowly Down the Ganges*, hauling gear during portages and moving boulders to clear a channel in the riverbed when they ran aground. While in their sixties, the Newbys bicycled around Ireland in December, a sodden, and at times, exasperating trip chronicled in *Round Ireland in Low Gear*. Eric said he quite enjoyed the trip. Wanda hasn't been on a bicycle since.

In 1964, Newby became the travel editor of *The Observer,* accepting the job only after the newspaper agreed to let Wanda join him on trips as his traveling secretary. After a decade in that post, Newby moved on. "I thought I could make more money on my own," he told me. "And I did." An accomplished photographer, Newby captured his journeys on film. Sadly, his Hindu Kush pictures were lost when a pack horse crossed a deeper-than-expected river. But his *Moshulu* images were published in 1999, sixty years after the ship made its last grain haul, in a book called *Learning the Ropes: An Apprentice on the Last of the Windjammers.*

Love and War in the Apennines appeared in 1971, a riveting account of Newby's imprisonment and a tribute to the courageous Italians who helped him survive. After our interview, Newby remarked on Wanda's courage during the war and she said dismissively, "When you're young you have courage to do anything." In 2001, Hallmark made a movie called *In Love and War,* based on Eric and Wanda's story.

Wanda, who speaks with a strong Slovenian accent and calls her husband "Newby," remains his steadfast companion more than sixty years after they met. I traveled by train to their home in Guildford, about forty minutes southwest of London. Their modest Surrey home overlooks St. Martha's Cathedral in the North Downs where Chaucer's pilgrims trekked in medieval times. A bust of Newby stands in the entryway. On the mantle were artifacts from the Newbys' travels, including a Mayan ceramic head acquired in Mexico.

Newby, who was eighty-four when we met, occasionally had difficulty recalling distant events, but Wanda sat by his side and prompted him. Throughout the interview Newby's pale blue eyes sparkled, reflecting, I imagined, the sheen of a Nuristani glacier or the shimmer of the flowing Ganges. At times his face would open into a wide, wistful smile, as he remembered a stirring moment from years gone by. As our interview ended, he said, with characteristic humility: "Sometimes I look up what I consider to be funny bits and read them to myself, and think, Could I have written that? I can't believe it's so good."

~≈~

You were born in 1919, just after the Great War, right?

I was born by Hammersmith Bridge in London on the River Thames on the night of December the 6th, 1919. It was a wild and stormy night. The surgeon who delivered me—the delivery was at home—was not very pleased when my father telephoned him at three o'clock in the morning saying that my mother was in labor.

I went to St. Paul's, which is a very famous boys school. I stayed at St. Paul's until 1936 and then I failed algebra. My father took me away from school, much to my horror, and put me into a business, which I wrote about in the first chapter of *The Last Grain Race.* That put me in an advertising agency, which had very, very beautiful typists, they were actually delicious. I stayed there for two years learning the business, and I got more and more disenchanted with London.

One day I went home from Piccadilly Circus where our agency was, and still is, and I went down in the Underground. It was absolutely crowded during the rush hour—there was only standing room. I suddenly felt a hand groping in my pocket and pulling out my handkerchief and blowing his or her nose on it. I never found out who it was, but I was so disgusted by this that when I got to my destination, which was Hammersmith Bridge where we had the flat, I told my father that I would like him to give up the idea of me going in for advertising and that I'd like to become a sailor.

I asked him if he would apprentice me to one of the last of the big sailing ships going around Cape Horn, which he did. This was in the autumn of 1938. I got my orders to go to Belfast and join a ship there, the four-masted barque, *Moshulu*, the biggest sailing ship in the world at that time. After that come events that were quite hair-raising for me and quite amusing for other people. As soon as I got on the deck, one of the mates came up to me and said, "Go up the rigging." The top of the rigging was the height of Nelson's Column, in fact it was ten feet higher [198 feet]. It's all in *The Last Grain Race*.

So you had just gotten onto the ship, before you even could change out of your nice clothes, and they're saying climb up the rigging!

He wouldn't let me take my shoes off, which was extremely dangerous because I had very slippery shoes. The only support you had up aloft was a wire hawser under the yards. The yards were crossed, and I was terrified of course, but they did the right thing. Everybody was made to do this because if you didn't, you would put it off forever. The captain would get fed up with you and you would be a waste of time and money.

So we sailed to Australia from Belfast in eighty-two days. We loaded a cargo of grain there, 63,000 sacks of grain, which we lowered into the ship's hold. It took us a month to load this cargo. We sailed for Europe from Australia, and we were thirty days to Cape Horn and fifty-five days to the equator, and eventually arrived in southern Ireland in ninety-one days, the fastest passage of the year. There were twelve other ships, and ours was the fastest. It was the last grain race ever done—the ship is now anchored in Philadelphia. It's been turned into a restaurant—they've cut windows in the side of the ship.

It was the last grain race because World War II broke out a few months later. Would you discuss your experiences during the war?

During the war, I went to India for five or six months, which was fascinating. That provoked me to go and make this journey down the Ganges later on. We both felt that it [the Ganges trip] was one of the most marvelous experiences that we could possibly have had.

When the war began I joined in something called the Special Boat Section, which was formed to land troops on the enemy shore and blow up their aircraft and then, if possible, return to your submarine. The first place I ever landed in was Sicily—I was landing with half a dozen men to attack a German airfield. This was in 1942. We failed to get back to the submarine because we got cut off. We managed to swim out to sea to avoid being captured by the Germans, but we didn't escape. We were eventually picked up by Sicilian fishermen after having been six hours in the water. That was in 1942 when I was captured.

And then in 1943, after the Italian Armistice, we all broke out of the prison camp we were in, several hundreds of us, and there I saw Wanda, looking very beautiful. When the Germans came to take us to Germany, we broke out of the camp, and I had to be on a horse because I had broken my ankle. I couldn't walk. It was at this time that Wanda met me and hid me—this is all described in *Love and War in the Apennines.*

Tell me about the first time that you met.

The main road ran in front of the prison camp, which was a large Italian *palazzo*-type building. You weren't allowed to look at the road, and if you did they'd fire shots at you. I don't know whether they intended to kill you or just frighten you, but they did certainly frighten me. I could see girls on bicycles—they were all pretending that they were going to visit the cemetery, but what they really wanted to do was see the Allied boys in the camp.

I saw Wanda, and she looked pretty attractive to me. She waved to me and I waved back. The sentries did what they were told to do and fired but missed. Then it became apparent that the Germans were not going to be able to be driven back out of Italy as we had hoped. But we were let out of the camp by the Italians.

Wanda: After he escaped he went to a farm and stayed there for two or three days. After that it became dangerous. He needed help because he couldn't walk, so he was moved to the hospital. It was all terribly strange. We were terribly fascinated to see some English people. We'd never seen them—it was another country and far away. The only thing we knew about the English was they had very good raincoats. I said, "Well look, you can't stay here. I'll help you." My father was a great friend of the town's doctor…

Eric: And they were both violently antifascist, dangerously so for their own safety.

Wanda: So they decided to put him near the maternity ward. I used to teach him Italian there, and he wasn't concentrating very much.

Eric: I'm still not concentrating, but I did succeed in that.

Wanda: Yes, you learned quite a lot. And then the Germans got to know where he was, and I said, "You must escape." And he escaped from the hospital at night through a window. My father and the doctor waited for him and they took him to the mountains.

Eric: We had a hair-raising ride down the Via Amelia, that long road that goes from Bologna to Rimini. We were driving the doctor's car which had a red cross on it. If the Germans had found him carrying a prisoner of war, he'd have been shot instantly. Anyway, we drove all the way down this Via Amelia, and on the way passed the 16th Panzer Division on the march. It was the first time I saw our enemies close to. We got to the main town, Parma, where we would have to turn off to go to the mountains.

As we entered the main square, which was full of Germans, our car broke down. It worked on methane gas and got a leak in the gas pipe. So we were putting our heads inside the radiator, which was the most sensible thing to do because there were all these German military police responsible for discipline. All they were interested in was getting this square cleared for the 16th Panzer Division. So we drove unscathed through the mountains which was really fortunate. In fact, we're probably lucky that the Panzer division had been there. I must say it's a very strange feeling sitting in a queue of German lorries when we'd been taught that if you got as near as that to a German you'd be dead.

Wanda: But the Germans got to know about my father and the doctor, and they put them in prison in Parma, a civilian prison. The thing was that there were a lot of partisans around, and when a German soldier was killed, they took at random, say, five prisoners and shot them. That was the great danger. Twice I went to see if my father was among them but he wasn't. The reason he was saved was that the interpreter of the prison was a Slovene—and we are Slovene—and I started talking to him. I asked him where he came from and he told me: a village near Ljubljana. And that was my village. It's all described in a film called *In Love and War*.

He said he would help me on one condition, that I come and tell him every week about the partisans in the village. And I said yes. Of course I would never have told him anything—I just gave him very silly messages. I think he got fed up—he told me not to come anymore. But the doctor wasn't released and he had to fake appendicitis. He was operated on and never really recovered. He was a marvelous man. That's war.

What did you do after the war?

I got myself working in the family fashion business. That made it difficult to contemplate any travel. We started traveling to see Wanda's family in Slovenia, but we didn't do any serious traveling at all until the 1950s. *The Last Grain Race* was really successful, and my publisher asked me what I would like to do more than anything else. I said I would like to go on a journey through wild country in central Asia. And he said, "Well, you shall."

Here on the Arayu, one of the lonely places of the earth with all the winds of Asia droning over it, where the mountains seemed like the bones of the world breaking through, I had the sensation of emerging from a country that would continue to exist more or less unchanged whatever disasters overtook the rest of mankind.

—ERIC NEWBY, *A Short Walk in the Hindu Kush*

Before we discuss the Hindu Kush, I'd like to ask, when you embarked on that sailing ship, did you think that someday you might write a book about it?

I had kept very detailed accounts every day about what happened on the ship. It was the only way—you can't remember things and say, I'm going to write them down later. You must write them instantly. I've always found that. I knew that if you go to sea, you had to keep a log book. It may sound monotonous, but it made it possible for me to write what was really quite a good book about the sea.

"What I don't see," I whispered to Hugh, "is what happens if the leader falls on the first pitch. According to this, he's done for."

"The leader just musn't fall off."

"Remind me to let you be leader."

—ERIC NEWBY, *A Short Walk in the Hindu Kush*

Wanda: When the coronation came in England in 1953, we went to a party—a publisher we knew invited us. Eric hadn't written anything, and this publisher said, "Have you got any pictures?" Eric said, "Yes, I've got a lot of pictures." So the publisher said, "Why don't you do a book on the pictures with captions?" And he started writing, writing, writing, and it became more than captions. That's how they published the book.

So how did the Hindu Kush trip get started?

At this time I was working in a couture house in London. I sent a telegram to my friend Hugh Carless who was in the British Foreign Office, saying: "Can you come, Nuristan?" This was a part of Afghanistan which nobody ever visited. And he sent a telegram back saying, of course. When he came to England, we only had five days before we were leaving, and we both found that neither of us had ever done any mountaineering at all, which was rather terrifying. We telephoned a pub in Wales near Mount Snowdon and went there and found people who were prepared to teach us to climb.

In five days?

Yah, it was pretty amazing. Although I shouldn't say it myself, the whole thing was quite funny—it's one of the funnier books. Just before we left, one of the waitresses in the hotel gave us a little book showing how to cut steps in ice. And that's all the instruction we had—we actually found ourselves stuck on this rather large glacier with one ice ax between us, reading this little book for instruction about how to proceed. It was a very dangerous situation because this mountain was having the picturesque habit of appearing to fall to pieces. Great rockfalls were taking place all the time.

At any rate, we failed to get to the top. We could easily have said we got to the top because there were no porters or anything like that. In the end, tormented by what we should say, I sent a telegram to the editor of *The Times* in London saying Newby and Carless have failed to climb the 20,000-foot peak in the Afghan Hindu Kush. Nobody could accuse us of not telling the truth.

Many of the writers I've interviewed prefer to travel alone, but you often travel together—how is that for you as a writer to travel with your wife?

I was travel editor of *The Observer*, and it meant being abroad a lot. I was very emboldened when I said to them, I'd like the job but I would like to have my wife to act as my secretary and fellow traveler, and I promise you she'll be made to work. And she was, actually. I couldn't have done the Ganges trip by myself.

Tell me a little bit about the Ganges trip and what you recall about it.

We had an interview with Mr. Nehru (India's first prime minister who served from 1947 until his death in 1964) and he gave us a wonderful letter which we embalsamated in plastic. The only occasion we used this thing was when we were far south on the Ganges. It was just before Christmas—we had no idea what we were going to do for Christmas; we knew everything closed up as it does in Britain. We went to the Kanpur Club which had been a stronghold of sahibs. We asked the secretary if we could be put up for the Christmas holiday. I gave him Nehru's letter and he looked at it, and he said, Mr. Nehru is not a member of the Kanpur Club.

The most impressive thing of going down the Ganges was the visit to the great fair at Allahabad, which was at that time barely known in the West. There were reputed to be something like 5 million pilgrims there on a sandbank. This, from time to time over the years, caused terrible losses of life amongst the pilgrims because stampedes take place and a lot of people get crushed to death.

It was terribly cold at night. We slept in the open on sand islands in the middle of the Ganges, which in some places was five or six miles wide.

Wanda: We got a fright one night. Mr. Nehru had said beware of robbers so we always slept in the middle of the river on some sands. One night we saw some men and thought they came to rob us. But in fact they were only curious because they had never seen a white man.

The difficulty of the Ganges was the first forty or fifty miles because every so often we heard *shhhh*; that means there was a rapid. We had to take everything out of the boat and carry it, and the sand was red-hot in the middle of the day. That was very tricky. I dropped the stove in the river and we couldn't cook, so we had to rely on cow dung.

>
>
> I love rivers. I like the way in which they grow deeper and wider and dirtier but always, however dirty they become, managing to retain some of the beauty with which they were born.
>
> —ERIC NEWBY,
> *Slowly Down the Ganges*

Eric: And there were lots of corpses that were semi-burned. The poor can't afford anything but a partial cremation because the cost of wood is so fantastic. The shortage of wood must be worse now than it was when we were there [1963-64]. From the start, we went twenty yards and the boat stuck. We were stuck at the beginning of the 1,200-mile journey, before the first rapids even.

Wanda: But it was a good journey.

You've both traveled quite a bit by bicycle.

Yes, we went round Ireland.

But you went in December—why?

Well, we had other things to do in the summer, our garden…

Why do you enjoy traveling by bicycle?

I explain about that at the beginning of *Round Ireland in Low Gear*: Because it's quiet and unless you load yourself with too much gear, there is very little that can go wrong.

Wanda: I've never bicycled since. When you bicycle and it rains, all the water goes into your shoes, and you have wet feet all day. It's very uncomfortable. But I loved the Irish. Then the beer was very cheap and they used to drink a lot of Guinness in the evening. And they used to talk, now they don't talk so much. We met some very nice old men who would talk about their lives.

Eric, what have your greatest gratifications been as a world traveler?

I've always been fascinated to know what's over the next hill or around the next corner. As one music-hall man wrote, "With a ladder and some glasses, you could see the Hackney Marshes, if it wasn't for the houses in between." That more or less sums up my attitude.

Is there still one trip you'd like to make or one place you'd like to visit that you haven't seen yet?

I'd like to go back to Turkey. I've been many, many times to Turkey. I'd like to go to southeastern Asia minor, Syria. And I'd like to go back to Mexico.

Who are the writers you admire?

I must say that Patrick Leigh Fermor would be quite high on any list, starting with *The Traveller's Tree*, a wonderful book about the Caribbean, absolutely splendid. Everything he does, he has a sort of magic touch with. And I think Evelyn Waugh is very observant, very funny. I've read his books more than once.

He wrote the foreword to your Hindu Kush book, yet you wrote that you never met him.

I gave him a princely gift of three magnums of burgundy, thanking him for the foreword. And he said rather waspishly, because he was a rather ill-tempered man, he said, "When you say that Wilfred Thesiger was wearing the same sort of tweed coat that Eton boys wear, how do you know? You were never at Eton." I wrote back to him and said, "In point of fact, I met Wilfred Thesiger in Piccadilly the other day, and incidentally he was wearing a bowler hat, and he said the Eton jacket is my old change coat from Billings & Edmonds."

He invited us to join him on his birthday (and share the wine we gave him). But I wouldn't go because he was very forgetful and he might easily have said to me, I don't know who you are. He might have said, there's a common little man at the door, who could he be?

I remember you wrote that you saw him in a restaurant but chose not to say hello.

Wanda: We were having tea at the Ritz [in London] with our children, and the children said to Eric, why don't you go to him? But he wouldn't. And then you saw him in the street, and you both turned...

Eric: He was going to our wine merchant and we passed one another and both after a few yards turned round and looked at one another, and then went on (laughs). That was rather silly. I was rather timid.

After fifty years of traveling and writing, what are you most proud of, what do you feel have been your greatest accomplishments?

One of the books I really did like is *Something Wholesale: My Life in the Rag Trade*. That's a truly amusing book actually. Reading that now, I wonder how I stood it all those years, going up the backstairs of London stores with armfuls of suits and dresses to sell. I went on doing that for years and years until I finally broke away when I went to the Hindu Kush. Even then I had to go back and work as a fashion buyer. I've really worked hard in my life because it's tough being a writer and also a fashion buyer as well. They don't normally come together.

With your pioneering adventures, do you feel that you have inspired other people to travel?

I think that is one of the principal things I will have accomplished. Whether I did it consciously or not, I don't know. But I do think that

I have inspired oceans of young people to travel. I can tell that because of the mail one gets, the letters one gets, the reviews one gets even...

Do you think the world is a better place because of the opportunities for travel we have today?

I think that people have been lucky to be able to indulge in it. The future looks particularly black for travelers.

Wanda: Before he went anywhere, he read a hell of a lot about the place he was going, so he knew what he wanted to see and what interested him. One of our most exciting travels was to Libya when it was completely forbidden—you just couldn't go, and he wanted to go to Libya. He asked the embassy and they said, "No, no you can't." So I said, "Why don't you write to Khaddafy?" After that, a huge letter arrived saying, "Please be our guest." He showed it to the embassy, and they couldn't believe it.

Eric: We went there and failed to meet him because somebody had attempted to assassinate him that week. And then the policewoman was killed in St. James Square [in 1984 by Libyan terrorists], and after that nobody could condone travel to Libya, so I never went back. But we did see some remarkable things in Libya.

I can't leave without asking you: do you still have the Rolex that got thrown into the vat of hot stew towards the end of your Hindu Kush trip?

Yes, I have. [Newby shows it to me—it's on his wrist.] This is the only thing of my past that I've got now.

Southern Exposure

Sara Wheeler
LONDON, ENGLAND

A CLASSICIST WHO HAS STUDIED ANCIENT GREEK CIVILIZATION, Sara Wheeler burst onto the literary scene in 1994 with her richly imagined narrative about Chile, *Travels in a Thin Country*. The book chronicles a country in transition as it emerges from the brutal sixteen-year dictatorship of Augusto Pinochet. A finalist for a Thomas Cook travel book award, *Travels in a Thin Country* showcases Wheeler's ability to mesh sharp insights with sympathetic portraits of a people torn asunder by their country's political turmoil.

Next Wheeler turned her attention to Antarctica, an Eden-like tabula rasa she considers the Earth's ultimate travel destination. Freed from the distractions of her everyday London life, she found beauty and contentment in Antarctica's vast open spaces. In her elegiac *Terra Incognita*, she spends seven months with polar scientists, exploring not just the physical geography of the land, but the emotional topography of an extended stay near the South Pole.

Wheeler's time in Antarctica stoked her interest in early twentieth-century polar explorer Apsley Cherry-Garrard, who accompanied Captain Robert Scott on the expedition on which Scott perished. Cherry's book, *The Worst Journey in the World,* widely considered one of the greatest adventure stories ever written, made Wheeler curious to "see the man behind the mask." Her biography *Cherry,* the first authorized account of his life, examines, among much else, the remorse Cherry felt after Scott died just twelve miles from where Cherry was camped.

Now married and the mother of two young sons, Wheeler lives in London's upscale Hampstead neighborhood, near Hampstead Heath. I met her on a chilly December day, entering a chaotic household as Wheeler was trying to manage her squealing toddler, Reginald. Her older son, Wilfred, then age six, is named after Wheeler's grandfather, but she said she likes the association with the writer Wilfred Thesiger, who died shortly before I met Wheeler. After the interview, Wheeler showed me a picture of her with the elderly Thesiger, whom she greatly admired.

Reginald, who was fifteen months old, often joined our interview by shouting gleefully into the microphone, tossing the recorder around, and once pulling a lamp onto himself. Still youthful looking at forty-two, Wheeler wore a black, long-sleeve t-shirt reading "Live from Antarctica." She moves with cat-like agility and speaks so quickly that it's hard to take in everything she's saying. Thankfully, the mini-disc survived young Reggie's gymnastics, and I was able to review her words at my own pace.

≈≈≈

Could you tell me how you started writing and whether you were a writer first or a traveler first.

Definitely a writer first—traveling came naturally to me as a vehicle for writing. I was always a very keen traveler. What I mean by vehicle is, I could weave my ideas and my preoccupations and my concerns within the form of the travel narrative. I'm not really very interested in places—I'm interested in ideas and what it is to be human. I was looking for a form in which I could smuggle all that stuff in. I've always thought that if I was a better writer I would have been a novelist because I think that the travel form gives one a much firmer structure and much more to hold onto, as opposed to a novelist who has to get everything out of his or her imagination.

So it was a natural form for me because of the kind of writer I am and the kind of person I am. And I got started like most people do, by sending things off unsolicited to newspapers and magazines, getting lots of rejection letters.

Yes, I know the feeling. So when you first started traveling, beyond the writing, what were you seeking? Was it adventure, meeting different kinds of people?

Well, since I became a writer, I only travel for one purpose, which is to get material, whether concrete material, i.e., observations about what things look like and so on; or ideas, conceptual material. I'm always saying to my husband that I want to go on holiday without a notebook and I make plans to do that, but it never happens.

My editor at the San Francisco Chronicle *says he takes one trip a year without his notebook just for the sheer joy of travel.*

He's right. And I always used to say that when I don't get a hit from the smell of aviation fuel, that's when it's got to stop.

You're best known for your books on Chile and Antarctica—but where did you first travel when you were starting out?

The first piece I ever had published was about Prague. I'd sent it to *The Times* of London and I just opened a copy of the paper a week or two later and it was there. They hadn't written to me or anything—nothing had been negotiated—they weren't intending not to pay me, and I duly received a check in the normal way. But they just thought, this is all right and they put it in. I had no idea. So that was very amusing, but it wasn't that easy after that.

My first book, which is no longer in print, was a book about a journey around a Greek island; it was called *An Island Apart*. I feel, as many people feel about their first books, that it should have been consigned to a drawer and discreetly tucked away. Now that those two books [*Notes from a Thin Country* and *Terra Incognita*] have been very successful, people often say to me, why don't we reprint your first one, but I couldn't face it.

I'd like to talk a bit about polar exploration. It's hard for us to understand today the magnitude of Scott's journey there almost one hundred years ago, and what a big impact that had on English society at the time, just how large it loomed in the public consciousness of the early 1900s. Could you give a sense of how important it was?

Well, there are two things: one is the importance of polar exploration in general at that time. So not just Scott's second expedition, but Shackleton and all the other polar explorers. And that's quite straight-forward: it's the only area of the globe that was left to be explored. So the South Pole was the last field in which nations could prove them-selves. For Britons, who lived through the nineteenth century when they did rule everywhere and get places first, it was the last bastion. And the South Pole in particular was the Holy Grail. It's like how the moon was, and then everyone lost interest in the moon after we got there.

The second thing, specifically about Captain Scott and his second journey, has to do with timing. Scott represented a whole set of ideals. He died in 1912, and by the first war, no one could believe in the glory of death after seeing the horrors of the Western front. So Scott repre-sented the last flowering of the imperial ideal. And that's why still now he is a hugely important figure in terms of Britain's history of itself. And that's why biographies of Scott, even though there have been thousands of them, get massive amounts of coverage. He's a national figure because of the time in which he lived.

In the same way, until Caroline Alexander's book brought Shackleton back into fashion seven or eight years ago, nobody had even heard of him. Whereas Scott is one of the most famous Englishmen who's ever lived. And that's all to do with timing, I think.

What intrigues me about the poles is that the coordinates by which we locate ourselves collapse. Time collapses: in the summer it's all daylight, in the winter it's all darkness. The lines of longitude converge. When you're at the South Pole, everywhere you turn is north. So how does that affect the psyche when you're down there?

Two things: one is physiological when you lose your diurnal clues. There's no time zone. When you set up an Antarctica science camp, the leader says, "O.K., what time zone shall we have? What time will it be now?" You have a time so you can synchronize your watches.

But I think the most significant thing from a writer's point of view is how it affects you when you are totally loose, not just from your own cultural moorings but from any cultural moorings. And to me, that was always the most potent thing about the Antarctic because it is the ultimate tabula rasa, and I think the most gripping destination for any travel writer. That's why I had to go on and do other kinds of writing after that, because there could be no territory that was as gripping as that. I think that for a writer, the more casting off you can do, the more you can concentrate on important issues.

When someone asked Jonathan Raban why he was making his way down the Mississippi, he said he was having a love affair with it. Antarctica was my love affair, and in the south I learned another way of looking at the world.

—SARA WHEELER, *Terra Incognita*

What did that mean for you personally, was there a certain freedom in being in a place that was so open?

Yes, it was immensely liberating. I think everyone who goes to the Antarctic says that it's very liberating to be there, and a great privilege, because it's like stepping outside of the world.

But it almost seems that for you and for some of the early explorers, that you stepped into your world and not out of it. In Terra Incognita, *you say you felt like you were coming home.*

Yeah, I still feel like that.

So what was it about Antarctica that felt like home to you?

Well, I suppose it's almost the reverse—the civilized world doesn't feel very homely, and so it's the absence of the things I find alienating.

It seems like a lot of the explorers who went there early on talk about how alive they felt, how they just miss it so deeply after they return. What do you think accounts for that?

A lot of the things that we all have to go through in our daily life, then and now, are very stultifying, just the daily grind whether it's traffic jams, paying the electricity bill, writing boring features for money. But none of that's there in the Antarctic—there's no telephones to ring. And even the drudgery of life in the Antarctic, chopping ice and so on, it's a new kind of drudgery, therefore it's interesting. And not many people around to annoy you, just being surrounded all the time by beauty. And the sense of great proximity to the elements as well, that elemental proximity to nature, and nature in it's most austere and most brutal. I think that's all very uplifting to the human spirit.

Is it also how close you are to the edge of survival, that you have to be vigilant about taking care of yourself or else you might perish?

The need for vigilance puts every day into sharp relief. Being in the big outdoors in any country in the world is uplifting and liberating— that's an almost universal human experience. So you just get that in the Antarctic, but times a thousand.

One thing you say in Terra Incognita *is that humans are not only battling exterior elements, they're battling their internal demons, man against himself, as it's been put. Can you say a bit about that?*

The battle with the inner self is something that preoccupies me greatly as a writer. There's no difference in the Antarctic; it's something that goes on all the time. To a certain extent, the external battle for survival against the elements is a good symbol of that. And also the fact that one didn't have things like the gas bills to worry about meant that that internal battle was perhaps nearer the surface, which is a good thing, in that one can engage with it perhaps in a more meaningful sense.

This is a place, Antarctica, that really had no human history until about a century ago. How do you feel human history is unfolding there and do you feel it's to the detriment of this pristine place?

Not at all. Everyone's always trying to get me to say that I don't think tourists should go to the Antarctic, but I feel that the human footprint now and the damage caused by tourism or indeed by science or explorers is so minuscule compared to the damage being done elsewhere. Still there's been less pollution caused by people in the Antarctic than there is on one single day in New York City.

I'm not an environmentalist, but I care about the environment like most ordinary people. And if you make a list of the major causes for concern of environmental destruction of the world, things we should really be doing something about, I think Antarctica would be about a millionth, a thousandth, or a hundredth. Animals dying out, environments just about to die out, the horror of radiation fuel...so of course it's vitally important to protect this one place that we haven't mucked up yet, but I think we are sort of doing that. Anyway, what are you going to do, start saying we mustn't let tourist ships go there? That's just not realistic—you can't stop people going places. And I'm not going to say, I've been there but it's not O.K. for anyone else to go.

Let's talk a bit about Apsley Cherry-Garrard. What intrigued you early on when you first started to learn about him?

Well, it was his book that spoke to me (*The Worst Journey in the World*). It was the one book which seemed to be about the here and the now and about me, rather than about crampons and testosterone, which were things I felt the world has probably already had enough of. It was striking that he didn't have his biography. I felt he'd written a masterpiece, not just a polar masterpiece but a masterpiece. And that's a view that's widely shared by any critics who have read the book. So I wanted to see the man behind the mask.

And what did you see? What did you learn about the man?

Well I sort of feel that if I could tell you that in two sentences, I might as well not have bothered to write 130,000 words (laughs). I mean, a lot.

Let me ask you this: Cherry seemed to blame himself for Scott's death— he may have been only ten or twelve miles away and later felt that had he continued on instead of waiting for Scott, he might have rescued him. How do you think that feeling of responsibility colored his life?

Cherry is a man who would have been diagnosed today with clinical depression. He had a few spectacular nervous breakdowns, and he had a lot of difficulties with his psychological and emotional well-being. The fact that he, as you say, in his worst moments felt that he could perhaps have saved Scott, which actually he couldn't really have, I think made his dark periods darker. It's always difficult to say what causes depression, whether it's external events or internal neuro-transmitter imbalances. It's probably a combination of the two in most cases.

So how far his experiences in the south contributed to his depression was a question I spent a long time thinking about, and I think that probably Cherry would have been terribly unwell had he not gone to the Antarctic, but I think that it made his problems worse.

Do you find that people, especially the early explorers, who have been in such a remote place had felt such a high about being there that when they leave it, that the lows are lower?

Cherry leafed through the flimsy notebooks, recalling the rippled glaciers that tumbled down Mount Erebus, their gleaming cliffs casting long blue shadows; the crunching patter of dogs on the march; the pale, shadowless light of the ice shelf and a smudgy sun wreathed in mist. "Those first days of sledging were wonderful!" he had written. In the quiet of his library he heard again the hiss of the Primus after a long, hard day on the trail, and smelt the homely infusion of tobacco as the night sun sieved through the green cambric of the tent. He tasted the tea flavoured with burnt blubber, and felt the rush of relief as tiny points of light from the kippered hut glimmered faintly in the unforgiving darkness of an Antarctic winter. "Can we ever forget those days?" he wrote.

—SARA WHEELER, *Cherry*

I would say, not necessarily, because most people, unlike Cherry, have got something to get their teeth into when they get back. For example, scientists, most of Scott's officers, were people on a par with Cherry, and went back to have extremely distinguished scientific careers. Life takes over. But that was one of his problems—he didn't have to work and he was able to dwell on things.

Moving on, it seems your trip to Chile was inspired by a strange travel suggestion from a man you met who said, "Why don't you visit my country?"

I made that up.

You did, really? Well, it gave the book a nice start.

That was the idea.

So where's the line in travel literature between reporting what you see and creating a character, as you did in the Chile book?

Well it's not a line. I think that most writers who do the kind of thing I do, which is not being a reporter, it's the opposite of what reporters do in a way; we're trying to convey a poetic truth, and the tools that you use in order to achieve that poetic truth or to try to...I don't see it as a line.

I write a lot of things which constitute geographical facts and history. Obviously one would be extremely foolish not to treat that as a reporter would. But if I meet a guy in January or in June...I think I'm allowed to shape all that material in the service of my narrative. And I think any travel writers who don't admit that are not really aware of the processes. Colin Thubron would absolutely say, "It all happened just like that." And I'd say, "Well look, to start with, what about all the conversations you didn't put in, because that's manipulation of data. You are choosing one sentence and leaving out nine others." We all manipulate material—it's a very controversial issue, and readers always want their money back when they learn this.

But did the person actually exist or did you create him from scratch?

I created him.

So who were his family that you meet down in Chile?

I made them up as well.

Really, wow, O.K.

But I was there in that place and I saw people like that. The notion of exiles, political exiles, political refugees, was a very important one to me, a very important part of my portrait of Chile. I could show that pain of separation caused by a tyrannical regime, aided and abetted by Kissinger and the CIA. There was a point to it. And, of course, I have met loads of Chilean refugees—I know lots of people exactly like him (the character who suggests she visit Chile), and so it was appropriate to my portrait to have a refugee in there at the beginning.

I could have started off the book with a paragraph of reportage saying that there are lots of refugees in London and I've met several of them, but it wouldn't have been the same kind of book. People would not have been quite as interested in it—it probably wouldn't be in its fourteenth printing—I mean, you're trying to make something readable. My readers tend not to be political scientists.

So do you see him as a composite of the different people you met?

Yes. The Antarctic book was a bit different because they were all known to me and a lot of them appear by name.

Chile is such a country of variety, of deserts, the frigid south, the coast, the Andes Mountains. What parts really appeal to you and what made the biggest impression on you during your travels there?

I'd have to say southern Patagonia just because it's such a beguiling landscape, but I like the desert, too. Extreme environments always appeal to me, but I would say Patagonia and the glaciated south—it's such a spectacular landscape.

Have you been back to Chile since you wrote the book?

No, I haven't. I was going to go back to do a tenth anniversary edition; I was going to leave the text the same but just do an essay at the beginning, telling about Chile now, bringing the Pinochet story up to date. But I realized that to do that, I would have to reread it, and it was just something I couldn't quite face.

Why is that?

Well, I don't know if it's any good, and it's a young woman's book as well. I'm forty-two now. I was thirty-two when it came out; I must have been about twenty-nine or thirty when I went.

I guess that's the hope as a writer: that when you're five or ten years away from a book that you've improved to the point where you feel like you can do a lot better. It's a good book though. One thing I like about your work is you seem to be having a good time. You have a quote in there from Peter Fleming, "We wanted to travel because we believed we should enjoy it." That's reflected on the pages of your books.

Sure, yeah, I think very much it's about having a good time. I think there's a long history of travel books about people having a miserable time—what's the point? It's not a particularly easy way of making a living.

That's an interesting question because I'm very keen on all that Hemingway stuff about pain being the best thing for a writer. But in terms of travel stories, I don't know if you approached Paul Theroux, because that's why people went off him so spectacularly, because he's so fucking miserable all the time. I'm very keen on him, but people didn't like that middle lot of books when he just didn't like anywhere.

So two things, one is, it is about having a good time. I mean Jan [Morris], you can't imagine her not having a good time anywhere really. She tries to make out that she's not having a great time in Trieste, but I don't think it's very believable.

Several of the people I've interviewed say they don't view themselves as travel writers.

That's because they think it's demeaning.

Do you?

Not remotely! Absolutely not. I think that's rubbish, all of that. I'm very keen on it. I edited a book called *Amazonian: The Penguin Book of Women's New Travel Writing*. And in the introduction, we wrote about Bruce Chatwin who won a travel-book award and gave the check back because he thought it was demeaning. As if it's a lesser form; I don't think that's right. The only reason I'm slightly equivocal is I've moved away to a more hybridized form of nonfiction. But that's not because I don't want to be a travel writer, sort of (laughs).

So what are you working on now?

I'm writing about Africa which I don't know anything about at all—it's a dark continent to me. I quite like what I did in my last book: having a figure in a landscape, so writing about place but having a person in the middle of it. I wanted to do another figure in a landscape, and I wanted the same period, 1890s to 1920s. I'd written two books about the polar regions, and if I'd done one more that would have been it—I would have been typecast. I could have gone on churning out books about little wooden ships forever and they would have paid me, but what's the challenge in that.

So I wanted to get far from the polar regions which is how I ended up on the equator. I'm writing about a bloke called Denys Finch Hatton, who was played by Robert Redford in *Out of Africa*. I'm writing about east Africa—I've just come back from Denmark, the Karen Blixen (whose pen name was Isak Dinesen) archives.

I've just written a short story that might interest you, the first thing I've ever written that's made up.

Well, completely made up.

(Laughter.) Except of course it isn't—how could it be? It's people I met and know just transmogrified into a fictional form. Everyone says, "It's all made up, isn't it?" And I say, "Yes, but it isn't." In the same way when people think nonfiction is all true, but it isn't.

It's not a sharp line between fiction and nonfiction...

No, it absolutely isn't, and anybody who says that it is, I would really question whether they are really examining themes and material.

So you're suggesting it's about the pursuit of truth, not the pursuit of facts.

Yeah, the poetic truth.

If someone, say, twenty years younger than you, who had just graduated college came up to you and said, "I want to be a travel writer," what would you tell her?

All I could say is: don't give up, just keep going. Read as much as you can all the time. Decide what you believe in. Never trust a man who drives a Porsche (laughs).

Any reason for that?

Just empirical data. You know, it's difficult because everybody does want to be a writer and a travel writer. There are no mysteries; just work very hard. People do ask me that question all the time and I'm often shocked as to how little people read. You've got to read all the time—that's partly why I still do masses and masses of book reviewing. Look at what other people do; examine why it works or doesn't work, and it informs your own writing.

Who are your favorite authors of travel narrative?

I like very much a lot of the writers of the '30s, of course Robert Byron—all English travel writers worship Robert Byron; Norman Lewis of course; we all like the same people really. I'm looking for a pattern in the carpet—I'm looking for it to be about something, which a lot of the modern books are not. They're just about people hanging around, doing some spurious journey through China looking for something that I don't care about. It's got to be about something real—it's no good to go off in search of this or in search of that unless you really make us believe in it. I look for the same thing in all books—at the end of the day, I think the quality of the writing is the only thing that really matters.

What have you learned about yourself through travel, or how do you think your life would have been different if you hadn't traveled?

Well, I think it would be facetious to say it has given me a greater perspective, because the implication is that people who don't go anywhere have a narrow perspective, and that's simply not the case. And we've all met people who are immensely widely traveled who are incredibly narrow minded.

I taught a travel writing course and a student asked, "How can you realize your true nature?" And they all thought that was a good thing, and I suppose it is a good thing, but I feel that I probably know too much about my true nature and that my whole life is a struggle to keep it down, keep it suppressed (laughs).

That reminds me of the movie, This is Spinal Tap, *where the members of this rock band are at Elvis's grave. One of the guys says, well, it gives you perspective, and the other guy says, yeah, too much fucking perspective. Anyway, if you weren't a writer, what do you think you would be doing with your life?*

Well, it's inconceivable to me that I wouldn't be a writer—that would be like not existing. I think anybody who is really a writer in their heart knows they couldn't possibly be anything else. Because it's so difficult that unless you felt like that, you wouldn't do it. If I thought I could be happy being an accountant, I'd much rather be one.

You know it was Graham Greene who said, "For writers and priests there is no such thing as success." And I think that's right, it's never good enough. I get paid well now, so I don't have to work as hard as I used do, but for twenty years it was pretty bloody relentless. I don't regret that, I have a great life, but it is hard work. Ask Jan: she works hard and she's in her late seventies and extremely distinguished.

One last question: Is there any place you haven't been that if you had one trip left to make, you'd say that would be the place?

There's lots of places I haven't been and lots of places I want to go, but to single out one: I'm very intrigued by all those "-stans" in the middle of Asia: Kyrgyzstan, Uzbekistan, Turkmenistan. There are still some toponyms that make the heart beat faster, Samarkand, Kyrgyzstan; they just evoke the whiff of the souk because they're unknown, but I don't go to those places because I can't speak the language.

Phew. Sorry about that, that must have been difficult for you. In twenty years time someone will ask you what was the most difficult interview you've ever done, and you'll say, "There was this woman in London…"

Giving It All Away

Brad Newsham
OAKLAND, CALIFORNIA

"SOMEDAY, WHEN I AM RICH, I AM GOING TO INVITE SOMEONE from my travels to visit me in America."

Brad Newsham was a twenty-two-year-old backpacker sitting alone on a rock outcropping in Afghanistan's Hindu Kush when he made that vow. Watching a caravan of camels march solemnly across the distant sand, Newsham decided he wanted to share the joy of travel with someone who otherwise might not be able to savor it. Though he never became wealthy, at least by First-World standards, two decades after making that promise Newsham embarked on a round-the-world trip to invite someone home.

Traveling to give something back transformed the journey, Newsham said. He soon realized that every encounter could change someone's life, which lent the trip a certain magic. At the end, Newsham placed in a hat the names of four people he'd met and pulled out the card reading "Tony." A rice farmer on the Philippine island of Luzon, Tony had left home only once, to visit Manila.

It took Newsham eight years of driving cabs on the streets of San Francisco to raise the money to bring Tony to America. The sale of his second book, *Take Me With You*, Newsham's account of his round-the-world trip, put him over the top. He was finally able to send Tony a plane ticket. During Tony's wild month in the States, he and Newsham enjoyed a private plane ride over the Golden Gate, a taxi-cab road trip across the country, and an ambassadorial reception at the Philippine Embassy in Washington.

Like many Americans in the early '70s, Newsham discovered the joys of backpacking to remote places. But he never considered writing about his travels until a friend handed him a copy of Paul Theroux's *The Great Railway Bazaar*. That planted a seed which germinated with the 1989 publication of *All the Right Places*, an engaging account of Newsham's travels in Japan, China, and Russia, after his first marriage disintegrated.

The son of a CIA cartographer, Newsham grew up in suburban Washington D.C. After "majoring in basketball" at a Midwestern college, he moved to San Francisco, where each day he felt like he was stepping onto a movie set. Though his writing has received critical acclaim, Newsham has never earned enough with his words to pay his bills, a source of frustration. He has remarried and lives with his wife and daughter in the Oakland hills. In 2002, Newsham founded Backpack Nation, a nonprofit effort to send "ambassadors" from wealthy countries to the remote corners of the world with thousands of dollars to give to worthy groups, villages, or individuals.

I met Brad on a sun-splashed August morning. He was warm, sincerely friendly, and displayed a keen interest in my life. I could immediately see why his travels were so full of rich encounters. Brad suggested we drive up to nearby Mountain View Cemetery, which has a breathtaking view of the Oakland hills, the San Francisco Bay, and the Golden Gate. We set up our chairs near the mausoleum of a wealthy San Francisco family and marveled at the landscape below us. A stiff breeze, so brisk it seemed to have circled the world, ruffled the pages of my notebook.

≈≈≈

What have you been up to lately? Are you still driving a cab?

About sixteen months ago I had two rides back-to-back that scared the daylights out of me. On the first ride, I knew that the two guys in my cab were either going to rob me or run on me. Fortunately, they ran on me without paying when I let them out at a housing project. The next guy I picked up didn't respond to my question about where he was going. So I turned around and he was fumbling under his baggy shirt for something. I heard a voice in my head saying, Sarah needs a father, Sarah needs a father. I pulled in front of a hotel and told him I'd become ill and had to go use the bathroom, and that he'd have to find another cab. He was O.K. with that.

I sat there afterwards just shaking. That's one thing that I, and certainly my wife, won't miss about cab driving. Prior to that I've had a gun held to my head, been punched in the face, and been robbed three times. So there is some excitement involved with driving a cab that I probably don't need in my life right now. My wife got a nice promotion about two years ago and has been fully supportive of me not driving. I've been hanging out with my daughter quite a bit—it's been much better for our family to have me home on weekends instead of driving a taxi cab. I also started Backpack Nation. That's been my creative focus for the past year or so.

How did becoming a father change your life?

I was forty-five when Sarah came into our lives and I had never given much thought to parenthood. It's been a shock and a real adjustment, completely different than the life I had before and completely different than the life I imagined I would be having right now at fifty-one. It's had its stresses, and it's had more joys than I could possibly have imagined. Somebody told me before I became a parent that you can imagine all the bad things about parenthood. I could imagine them and they're all true, the lack of time and the lack of freedom. But you can't imagine the good things until you experience them. I've had so many moments of unjustifiable joy just hanging out with my daughter, more moments of joy in the last six and a half years than in the rest of my life combined.

Were you concerned that the life of the happy wanderer might end when your wife became pregnant?

It was a surprise, and I was terrified. Any parent will understand: I am absolutely in love with this little girl, and at the same time I really miss my freedom. I've been trying to surrender into this life and it's been a real struggle. In that ten-year period when I wrote both my books, that was my number-one focus. I was able to clear the decks of pretty much every other concern and write—that's what it took for me to get two books written.

My preferred writing hours have always been between about nine at night and three in the morning. I used to drive my cab between five at night and three in the morning so for years I'd been a night person. Now I get up at seven in the morning. Yesterday a friend sent me an e-mail with a quote: "You have to give up the life you had planned so that you can have the life that's waiting for you."

When did you start thinking about becoming a writer and what sparked your interest in travel?

I fell in love with stories and writing on my mother's knee—she'd read me these great stories. I always thought, Wow, to be a writer you had to be born with some magical power. I couldn't tell a story—I still have trouble doing that. The Irish call writers failed talkers; I feel that applies in my case.

When I was a kid we used to take trips in the family station wagon all over the country; I loved that. There was a five- or six-hour drive we'd make from Washington D.C. to the hills of western Pennsylvania where my grandmother lived. Every now and then you'd see a guy with a mule tilling a field. I just loved looking at these little towns with kids my age and wondering, What would it be like growing up in their town—who would I be if I lived there? My father was with the CIA—he traveled all over the world—and he would send each of us four siblings our own personal postcards. I felt very special to get my own postcard from Dad from Bangkok or Buenos Aires, and it got me thinking about travel.

I never thought I was a good writer, but I dabbled at it; I worked for the high school and college newspapers. After college I did a lot of hitchhiking around the United States and then went off to Europe and just fell in love with travel. In about 1976, a friend and I were hitchhiking around the country and we went to an Air Force base in Florida to see a friend of ours who had become a pilot. My hitchhiking buddy and I were just back from Afghanistan, and we had hair down to the middle of our backs. We didn't look like our Air Force friend—he had a buzz cut. He heard our story and said, just a minute. He came back with Paul Theroux's *The Great Railway Bazaar* in hardback, handed it to me and said, "You guys are going to like this book."

I had no clue that this genre of literature existed, that people could take trips like I had just done and write about it. I never saw my writing as something to share, but here was a guy, Paul Theroux, who had gotten on a train in London, exactly the sort of stuff that I dreamt about; he'd done it. And he'd written a great book about it.

You're approach to travel is very progressive and open—that seems a far cry from the CIA.

Well, that generation fought World War II and I tip my hat to them. My father was a cartographer with the OSS, the forerunner of the CIA. He was in Ceylon and stayed on with the CIA. I once asked him when I was thirty-five, "Why'd you go to work for the CIA?" And he said, "I got out of college and that's who was hiring."

Having seen Afghanistan a generation ago, how do you feel about what's going on there today?

I like to think that people who have the chance to travel and get a sense of other cultures, as I have, come back with some brilliant wisdom. But all I feel personally is sadness and confusion. I'm a bit aghast that these things can happen. My sense is that 99 percent of the people in this world just want to be left alone. They want to live their lives; they want to feed their children; they want to have peace. The trouble gets caused by just a few people, it seems.

I just finished Jason Elliot's *An Unexpected Light*. It put me right back in Afghanistan. I could see that the culture that's been developing there for thousands of years is still basically the same, and they've just been washed over by different troubles. There were a million and a half Afghanis killed. I don't know what to say.

Your first book, All the Right Places, *starts with your wife at the time asking for a divorce. You say, "Let's hit the road." Do you feel that travel can help solve your problems?*

My premise for that book was: travel heals, I hope. My conclusion was: time heals, and travel is about the best way to spend time. That first chapter of *All the Right Places* is ten lines long—originally it was 160 pages. Boy, those 160 pages were some of the best, most brilliant, most polished, most worked over pages I've ever written. And when I realized they didn't belong in the book, it was kind of crushing. One day I said, Oh, that's too long by 159 pages; once I got the rest of the book, I could see that. But I had to write those 160 pages to get to that insight. So it was time well spent, I like to think.

I came to that insight while participating in a writing group. People said they really got engaged with the book when suddenly I had left the country. I thought, I can't just waste these 160 pages, and then I thought, Who says I can't?

At the end of writing that book I had an interesting moment walking down Haight Street with my ex-wife, Beverly. I told her I had just finished a chapter that I really liked. I saw that I had three or four more months of work ahead of me. As I was walking, I realized, that book's finished. It was like a lightning bolt. I ended it on the train coming out of Moscow, instead of recounting coming back through Europe and driving across the United States. It was over—that was great—and it was perfect because I was so far in debt that I had to go back to work. I started driving a cab pretty much the next day.

Earlier, when my wife told me she did want a divorce, I was working at Wells Fargo Bank. I was putting together a newspaper for our division, and the people who ran the division offered me a promotion with a 20 percent increase in salary—I would have been writing speeches and doing communications. It was like somebody showed me the corporate ladder: here it is, if you want to climb it. I never had an inclination in that direction, but suddenly realized, Oh, this is how it works. I said, Whoa, no, I don't want to do that.

What I did want to do was be a travel writer. I wanted to be Paul Theroux. So I thought, My wife wants a divorce; I don't owe anybody anything; I'm thirty-three—I have a chance to act on this impulse that I may never get again, so I went for it. I had a few thousand dollars left at the end of the trip; I got a room in the Haight and spent nine months writing that book. In the middle of that I ran out of money. I went down to Yellow Cab and realized they would hire me. I said, "If you will hire me, I'll come back when I'm done with this book." I racked up $6,000 on my credit cards while I finished the book, then paid back that $6,000 in three months. Cab driving has been absolutely great—I loved the activity, I loved the people, coming home with cash, staying up till almost dawn every day—it was good.

Driving a cab seems like traveling in a way, a new adventure every day.

Oh, absolutely. And in San Francisco you've got this world-class scenery and people from all over the world. At some point in every shift, you're going to see the Golden Gate Bridge and the bay and the Pacific, things people travel thousands of miles to see. That was my workplace—it was beautiful. I loved driving a cab in San Francisco. I miss it.

When seeing a new place, I often think: I am going to come back here later—when I am rich, or when I have more time, or when I have a purpose, or when I am with someone I love—and do this right. But it is self-deception. More often than not, my feet lead me somewhere new rather than somewhere I've already been. And as I sat at that window watching the train bore through the heart of China, I had a different, more probable thought, and I wrote it down: *I better remember what this place looks like. I will never be back.*

—BRAD NEWSHAM,
All the Right Places

You aren't by chance The Night Cabbie (a columnist for the San Francisco Chronicle*), are you?*

Ha, that's great! I would be able to retire forever if I had a dollar for every time I've been asked that question. I'm not The Night Cabbie. I don't know exactly who he is, though we've corresponded by e-mail.

This gets to how hard it is to make a living writing—I had written my first book, and I thought, I've got all these cab stories. I could sit here and tell cab stories all day. So I wrote three columns and sent them to the editor of the Datebook section of the *San Francisco Chronicle*. She wrote back and said, "I love them—I'll buy all three and run them soon." So I watched the paper every day for a couple weeks, and they didn't run. That woman had left to run a magazine, and the guy who took over the page said he'd run one as a favor, but that no one is interested in cab stories and to please quit bugging him. Not much I could do about that.

Six months or so later *The Examiner* [San Francisco's other major newspaper at the time] started "The Night Cabbie." It's not me, but I'm jealous of his platform.

One thing I really like about your first book—and this is true of a lot of my favorite travel literature—is that it's about more than the places. It's about the people at the destination, as well as the author. As soon as you started talking about your divorce on the first page, I was hooked.

You have to hook the reader—it has to be compelling. I grew up attending Christian Science testimony meetings. Some people would stand up and give a testimony that was so boring and unengaging. And there were other people who would stand up and from the moment they opened their mouths, you couldn't stop listening to what they had to say until the moment they sat down. That's what everyone wants. When you read a book or a newspaper column, you want to be hooked from the start and pulled right through to the end. I strive for that. Sometimes you succeed; sometimes you don't. I thought the beginning of *All the Right Places* was effective; it would have engaged me. With both of my books I succeeded in writing the book that I envisioned, and I'm happy with the way those turned out.

At the end of our lives, all we will have left behind is our stories. They will be told or not told, and the better story you have, the better chance it has of being told once you're gone. What's going to engage someone is not the description of a place so much; they will remember the stories of people. We can all relate to human dramas and dilemmas. When I read a travel book, or anything, I want to know about the people involved. It's nice to have a sense of the writer. I want to know enough about the writer so that I think that person is interesting.

When I read I'm thinking, Would we like each other? Would it be fun to travel with that person? So I as a writer try to give the reader something to engage with, not just political discourse or scenery, but the sense that they're moving through this place with me. People like that—they say they felt like they were there with me. I like to hear that because that's what I'm trying to achieve.

Running through both of your books is the thread of idealism, an attitude that if we could all travel and get to know each other, the world's problems could be solved. Do you feel that was unduly idealistic or do you think that travel is the engine that really could bring peace to the planet?

The latter. I feel travel really is the engine that could bring peace to the planet, and I don't feel it's idealistic at all. I've gotten thousands of e-mails from people all over the world that this idea—Backpack Nation—really resonates with them. I think it's a suppressed urge in a lot of people. If we really had our druthers about what we'd like to do for the next six months—take away all our financial or familial obligations—we'd go traveling much more than we do. I haven't been out of the country for eight years and I'm dying to get out of the country.

According to an article in *The New Yorker*, in the typical human sex act, the act that brought each of us to this planet, there are between 60 million and 900 million individual sperm involved. So each of us on a cellular level, I think, has a memory, a clear sense that we have already beaten about the biggest odds that we're ever going to face, before we even got here. This life is like the bonus round. This is the prize—we're here. We should enjoy this baby! Why would we talk ourselves out of being idealistic and settle for something practical and pragmatic?

When the twin towers came down and I saw those people in the Middle East cheering, I had this thought that they could never have cheered the death and destruction if they had known the people involved. And conversely if we, the haves of the world, knew the reality of life for the have-nots, we would live our lives differently.

I tried to put myself out 100 or 200 years from now and look back at this very interesting time in history, and try to see what happened that brought the world out of that chaos and led it into the harmony and order that is surely coming. I thought that if 100 travelers a day from the have countries went to the have-nots places, and each of them gave $10,000 to a compelling situation that they encountered, and there are millions of compelling situations out there, that would change the conversation that we have in the world, which is an ancient and outdated conversation. To make this conversation real, we have to take some action, and I thought this was an action worth taking.

To people who have said that it's too idealistic and not pragmatic: we are spending $400 billion a year on our defense and our security, and we have never felt so insecure and undefendable, we have never felt so vulnerable. That says everything to me that there is to say. For much less than $1 billion a year, you could send 100 travelers a day, each funded with $20,000 ($10,000 to pay for their trip and $10,000 to give away), around the world, and that would change things. I don't think that spending a billion dollars a week in Iraq is going to change anything. I think it's a horrible, unimaginative way to waste America's fortune and the world's fortune. So the more I hang out with this idea, the more convinced I am of its worthiness.

And I'm not the only one that's doing something like this. I think we're in the midst of an underreported phenomenon, this idea of people all over the world reaching out, person to person, country to country, culture to culture. But if you pick up today's paper, you won't read about that. Since I've been involved with Backpack Nation, I hear so many people talking about things they've done, like what I did with Tony. Many people have done that, I've dramatized it. Many people have started organizations that are helping out villages and individuals in developing countries.

Do you worry about the unintended consequences of sending somebody with $10,000 to a remote village or bringing somebody back to America?

Inviting Tony to America, I wondered, Would this ruin his life? Would this upset the balance of his community? And I don't know, but if we are a human family, and I do think that we are, we are the rich relatives. And if rich relatives don't want anything to do with the rest of the family, we resent those people. As much as there is a danger in upsetting the balance with $10,000, I think there is a danger in *not* doing something like this. Planes flying into the Twin Towers in New York, that's what we'll get if we keep ignoring this separation.

Fifty years ago, there was no real mechanism for an ordinary person from the have cultures to have any sort of interaction with people from the have-not cultures. But now, because of the Internet, each of us has global reach. I've got global reach—I've proved that in my own life. And I'm not at all extraordinary or unusual. We all have global reach, and if we want to exercise it, we can.

I'd like to move on to Take Me With You. *What was it like to travel on a trip that wasn't just for you but for somebody else as well?*

That changed everything. I have never had a 100-day period that was so magical. For 100 days, I had nothing but conversations which could have been life-changing. This person I'm talking to, we could be on the other side of the world soon having a mind-blowing experience. Often when you travel the focus is inward—this shifted the focus outward. It was so powerful, the experience and its aftermath, with Tony coming here and the media attention. Suddenly there we were on Voice of America, the BBC, national TV. It was a thrill.

Once I was in India with my first wife, and we were having a wonderful time, but I felt kind of hollow. We'd been there for three months and we were on the beach at Goa. I got up one night at two o'clock and I was walking on the beach, trying to figure out why I wasn't enjoying this experience quite so much. I started thinking of all the stories of all the people I had met, and they were thrilling, good stories, but it was sort of all about me. And I could only stand so much of me.

During my "normal life" I've kept protective walls around myself—to keep out that vast faceless sea of people who want to do me harm. But shifting my stance—from *What do they want from me?* to *What miracle might our meeting produce?*—made me feel light, pleasantly tickled. Sometimes, writing notes about someone I'd met, I would get almost giddy imagining him opening the letter with my invitation and the plane ticket.

—Brad Newsham,
Take Me With You

When I shifted, with *Take Me With You*, it wasn't so much about me, it was more about the people I was meeting. It was great—I was giving something away—there's some hidden power in that. I stuck my finger in the socket and plugged into some universal law of taking the attention off yourself and giving to others.

The original inspiration I had for *Take Me With You* happened in the mountains of Afghanistan—that moment has reverberated in my life ever since. I was out in the middle of nowhere and felt I was touched in a way, like my previous life was erased. I knew that my future was going to be different than anything I had imagined, and it has been. The last thirty years have sort of fallen out of that moment, when I saw those caravans and thought, My goodness, I could have been born anywhere on this planet and could have had any life. I should somehow share this.

What was it like to come to America with Tony?

It was one miracle after another. Six months before he got here I was on NPR, and after that appearance on *All Things Considered* people called from all over the country with offers of things for us to do. One of them came from a San Francisco cab company owner who loaned us a new taxi cab that he'd just bought. He said, "While Tony is here you can drive it anywhere you want." I said, "New York, Washington, D.C.?" He said, "Anywhere you want." And off we went.

That was one of the most generous things that happened. Another was: a pilot called after that show and offered us a ride in a private plane. I didn't know if Tony would want that. The first airplane ride of his life had been four days earlier on a jetliner. I didn't know what he would make of a private plane, so I asked him, and he said "Yeah, sure." We got in a plane in Novato (twenty-five miles north of San Francisco) and flew over Mt. Tam and down the coast.

I had no idea this was going to happen: the pilot flew through the Golden Gate Bridge in this little four-seater; he flew lower then the tower tops. Looking down I could see people's heads turning up to look at our airplane. I could see faces of individual drivers at the wheel—unbelievable. We flew over this neighborhood to look for our house, and over the cemetery. We flew out to Lake Tahoe and landed. Tony moved from the back seat of the plane to next to the pilot, and I moved to the back.

As we're flying back to the Bay Area, the pilot asked Tony, "Would you like to fly?" Tony later told me that he'd been observing the pilot, and within two minutes of that offer Tony had taken the controls. In a private plane, there are auxiliary controls, so the pilot can take over if necessary. Tony was doing the foot pedals—the pilot coached him down from 5,000 feet to 800 feet. From the backseat, I'd say, "Scott, whose flying?" Scott would lift his folded hands up from his lap and his feet off the floor. For fifteen or twenty minutes, Tony flew the plane at 200 miles an hour over the Central Valley. I thought, If this is day four and we have a month together, I have no idea what's coming.

You know, Tony's eye was put out by a mugger who attacked him six months before I met him. And when he got here, his prosthetic eye looked pretty bad. Twelve years had gone by and the false eye had yellowed and didn't fit anymore. A doctor here made him a new prosthetic eye that he couldn't tell from his real eye. A dentist gave him three root canals.

The Philippine ambassador read a front-page article in the *Christian Science Monitor* about our taxi trip across the country, and called me on my cell phone. "When you get to Washington," he said, "you're coming to the embassy for a special reception in your honor." That was the one thing that Tony and I argued about as we drove across the country—he didn't want to go. He said, "You've seen my life—it's so simple—what am I going to say to those diplomats?" I told him he really didn't have a choice. I said, "If you go back and tell your wife that the ambassador invited you to the embassy and you said no, she's going to divorce you. Where are you going to live?" So we went to the Philippine embassy, and we had a wonderful time. He enjoyed it quite a bit, I think.

Do you stay in touch with Tony?

While he was here, we talked about what his future might be when he went back. One of the ideas we kicked around was—since he lives in this incredibly stunning setting—he could be a lodge-keeper. He and his wife could build a guest house. So I raised seven to ten thousand dollars and sent it to him, and he's built a guest house. But just about the time that he finished the guest house tourism took a huge dive.

I think his income is less now than it was then. I'm concerned—some friends and I have been sending him a little bit of money each month just to make sure that his family is taken care of. The other idea he had while he was here was perhaps buying land so that he could grow more rice. I'm as broke as can be right now, but I'm trying get six thousand dollars to buy him one hectare of land. He says that if he had that, his family would be self-sufficient.

I feel a responsibility. I've poked around in his life. Although there's this imbalance in our economic status, I think of him as an absolute equal. We've developed a real friendship—we've got a bond for life. We've had heart-to-heart talks, the sort that I rarely have with anybody. I got so much out of this. I hope that he got as much out of it. I'm pretty convinced that when we're old men, we'll look back and this will be one of the best things that ever happened in our lives.

What's next in terms of your literary career? Are you thinking about that right now or are you too busy being a parent?

I think about it every minute. I do feel like I have five or six more books in me. Whether I'll get any of them out or not, I don't know. I've written these two books that I'm proud of, but there's no money in it. My wife supports the family. For people looking at becoming travel writers, I try to warn them off. I say, take a hard look at the reality: It's really hard to make a living as a travel writer. If you have to do it, you might as well do it, but if you don't, you're probably better off doing something else. I've gotten a lot of personal satisfaction out of this, but I couldn't afford to have a daughter if my wife didn't have a real job.

I love that my book has done well in Britain. Here in America they've both pretty much fizzled. It's actually harder to get a second book published if your first book has not been a blockbuster. Thank god for the British; *Take Me With You* has sold almost 30,000 copies over there and on the strength of that, they've republished *All the Right Places* with an initial print run of 16,500 copies. But here I can't interest anyone in my next project.

I would have thought twenty years ago that I would be satisfied with getting two books published. There is satisfaction in it, but there's as much heartbreak as anything else. I know a lot of writers who would be jealous of this level of success, but there's nothing to be jealous about in my mind.

I think there is still a lot to be proud of. My friend Allen Noren wrote a book called Storm *(also published by Travelers' Tales). He didn't have great sales, but even before it was published he told me, I wanted to write this book—whether 5 people read it or 5,000 or 5 million, I'm going to be proud of it.*

That's great, but I hurt for Allen because I read that book, and it took my breath away, the way he put words together. Before your book is published, when you've got the contract, anything is possible. It could be those 5 million people. The author lives in the possibility for a while and almost never does that possibility turn into a reality. If you've lived in that possibility, the ride is downward for a good while. Hopefully you've enjoyed the ride up because you're going to get a down ride out of it, too. I've been on it twice now, and I'm ready to go again (laughs).

In your books you ask people, what's the best thing that's ever happened to you? So I'd like to ask you that.

It's gotta be my daughter, the experience of being a parent, seeing the continuity of life. It's been a thrill getting my books published, but there's no question which is more important in my life—it's my daughter. Next on the list would be my experience with Tony.

Is there anything you'd like to add about what you've learned by traveling around the world?

The thing that's had the most impact is how fortunate the accident of birth can be, and in my case has been. Had I been born in middle-of-the-road circumstances in the other half of the world, I would have a tiny fraction of the opportunities. Three billion people live on less than two dollars a day. Now that I've been to those places and seen how they live, I have an appreciation for this incredible richness. I'm a guy with no money and I'm infinitely rich in experience and opportunity.

Do you feel that you were born in just the right place at just the right time?

I'm constantly dissatisfied with my life. I always want a little something just out of reach. I would like to be able to make a living from my writing. I'd like a book contract. I'd like a magazine to send me to the Philippines to write about my experiences with Tony. Fifteen years ago I just wished somebody would buy *All the Right Places*. Ten years ago I just wanted somebody to publish *Take Me With You*. And now I wish somebody would drop a million dollars on Backpack Nation so I could achieve my vision for it. But I do try to remind myself—look at us sitting here on top of the Bay Area—I gotta be happy with this.

If you had just one more trip to make, where would you go?

Can I have two? If it's only one, I would retrace *Take Me With You.* I would take a copy of my book and some money to give to all the people that I wrote about who perhaps don't even know that they're in this book. And I'd thank them.

Why have you settled in Oakland?

I haven't met anyone who has moved across the country to settle in Oakland. They all think of San Francisco, and I was just like everyone else. On visits to San Francisco, I would always find myself feeling euphoric, the air, the views, this world-class scenery, and the sense of possibility in the air. I wondered what it would be like if I moved to San Francisco—would I always feel euphoric? So I moved and lived there for twelve or thirteen years, and I always felt like I was the star of a movie. You walk out and there's Arnold Schwarzenegger and Danny DeVito walking down the street. We moved to Oakland because we could afford to buy a house here.

Since we are conducting this interview in a cemetery, I'd like to close by asking you where would you like to end your life?

Can I have two? (Laughs.) There are two very different places—one is Secret Beach in Kauai where my wife and I spent a couple of weeks camping. It's only there six months of the year because in wintertime the waves bang up against the bottom of the cliff. But in the summertime the ocean recedes and there's 100 yards of white sand. At the bottom of the cliff at shower-nozzle height and shower-nozzle speed comes this pure drinking water. So you don't need clothes there, you've got drinking water, you walk about a mile away there is a little grocery store. Dolphins swim into the bay every now and then. That would a place to lay my head.

The other would be the burning ghats at Varanasi. When I was there I felt as close as I've ever felt to the door to the other side. It's a place that's dedicated to ushering people out of this world. It's pretty darn basic, bodies being burned on the banks of the Ganges.

Along the Border

Tom Miller
TUCSON, ARIZONA

BEST KNOWN FOR HIS SEMINAL WORK ABOUT CUBA, *TRADING with the Enemy*, Tom Miller writes about life on the border. His latest book, *Writing on the Edge: A Borderlands Reader*, is a collection of essays, poems, fiction, and song lyrics related to the U.S.-Mexico frontier. Miller is also well known for his engaging book, *The Panama Hat Trail*, which documents a journey deep into Ecuadorian jungles, seeking the source of these fashionable accessories.

After driving through the Sonora Desert during the night to avoid the searing late-May heat—my old pickup lacks air conditioning—I caught up with Miller at a Tucson café near his home. We chatted over coffee and pastries before retiring to his peach-colored, adobe house, fronted by prickly pear cactus, a home that complements the desert landscape.

Inside, Miller showed me archives of his published work, a copy of the *La Bamba* compilation album for which he wrote the liner notes, and field passes to the 1999 baseball game in Havana that matched the Baltimore Orioles against the Cuban national team. During the game

Miller worked for ESPN, though not on camera, helping broadcaster Jon Miller (no relation) provide commentary.

By chance, our interview occurred on the eve of Miller's tenth anniversary. He's married to a Cuban woman, Regla, a practitioner of the Afro-Cuban religion, Santería. Miller joked that he could have won a few bets with his friends who doubted his marriage would last a decade. Regla made some fresh mango juice, providing us with a refreshing break during the interview. Tom and Regla's plans for the evening entailed a voyage in the Goodyear blimp, a trip Miller won by entering a drawing when he bought a set of tires.

After the interview, Tom and I enjoyed a late lunch at Café Poca Cosa, its brick interior illuminated by color-splashed tablecloths and paintings. Located in a nondescript Tucson hotel, this Mexican restaurant puts inventive twists on traditional favorites, such as chicken *molé*. After lunch I bade Tom farewell and ventured south to meet a friend in the border town of Nogales, Arizona.

Being so close to the border, I felt compelled to cross it, so the next morning I visited Nogales, Mexico, stunned, as always, by how much can change when one crosses a line in the sand. The storefronts were ramshackle, the roads dusty and crowded, but most people were warm and friendly. I got a $5 haircut, in hopes of cooling off a bit, and then waited in a line of cars for an hour to cross back into the U.S. and start the long journey home. When I called it a day at 7 P.M. in Yuma, just a couple of miles shy of the California border, a flashing thermometer read 108 degrees—in the shade.

~·~·~

I know you grew up near Washington, D.C.—maybe you could start by telling me what led you west and towards Latin American culture.

First things first, I went to a Quaker high school outside of Washington D.C. For reasons I can't tell you to this day, I went to a small Presbyterian rural Ohio college, the College of Worcester. I was not rural or Presbyterian—I just had nothing in common with it— and left after two years.

I went back to Washington and worked as a journalist in the underground press. Part of my beat was Capitol Hill and Congress as it applied to students, for something called College Press Service. I saw guys who were five, ten, or twenty years older than me, stoop-shouldered carrying these briefcases around the halls of Congress, and I just recoiled at the notion that could be me five, ten, or twenty years from now. I knew nothing about the western United States; we're talking '68 or so, and there was an enormous amount of stuff about the antiwar movement.

A friend said, "Hey, you might try Tucson." I spent the summer of '69 hitchhiking around Mexico; it was a great introduction to Latin America. I made a point of coming up through Nogales and surfacing near Tucson.

There was a very active antiwar community here, a very active underground culture or alternative culture. For the first six months here, I'd look out of the window of the small place that I rented and there was this saguaro cactus and I thought, I'm living in a B-movie set. It took a long time to acclimate to the fact that this was not a movie set but where I live. It's that window in one's youth when you don't have emotional or economic or family or employment or academic ties to batten you down. I jumped through that window of opportunity and this is where I landed.

It seems that a lot of your writing involves not just the Southwest but particularly the border areas. You call the border "a third country" and say that border towns have a symbiotic relationship born of necessity. What do you find unique or fascinating about the border?

You see that cap I was wearing this morning, that was from a border horse race where they tear down the fence one day a year. This is just west of Douglas, Arizona. There's a horse race with the Mexican horse on the Mexican side of the border and the U.S. horse on the U.S. side. About 10,000 people attend this event, probably two-thirds of them on the Mexico side. There are six matches during the course of the day, and there is no fence between the horses, although one rides on one side and one rides on the other. There's something so anarchistic about it; and that's one of the things that appeals to me about the border: you can practically jump rope back and forth.

This border is close to 2,000 miles long and has its own identity, which changes over the years for reasons of migrations and drugs and the whole homeland security nonsense. But the integrity of border culture stays pretty much the same, how people live there and how people comport their lives. Almost everybody I know who lives in a Mexican border town has a P.O. box on the U.S. side.

What makes the border unique is the mix of language, the mix of music, the mix of law enforcement, the mix of literature—you could even say clothing. Almost every aspect of someone's life is affected directly or indirectly by the fact that they live within five miles of another country. The farther you get from the border, the more diluted that becomes.

There's a lovely photograph by Alex Webb showing a family hanging its laundry out to dry on the fence. People use the fence in just about any way they can—they make the border work for them as opposed to it constraining them.

You write about a volleyball game where the fence serves as the volleyball net.

Yeah, the whole notion of using the border instead of the border using you: in that case the fence was the net. At the end of the game, the players, government officials from both sides, tried to shake hands. But they couldn't because of the fence. The wonderful thing is that it just lends itself to great metaphors; the downside is that the metaphors are so poignant that there's a lot of bad poetry written about the border.

By the way, Tex-Mex food is a combination of the worst Texas food and the worst of Mexican food all on one plate. I just wanted to go on record with that.

What changes have you seen with all the intensive security, NAFTA, all the things that have come down the last twenty years or so?

More people are crossing in both directions—more people are aware of it. The amount of legitimate commercial trade has increased enormously—the amount of crime has increased enormously. But border culture itself is pretty much the same; a family may live on the U.S. side as opposed to the Mexican side.

This typewriter repairman has lived in Sonora since the mid-1950s and he's lived in the same house the whole time. He said, yeah, the neighborhood has changed and he has a closed-circuit camera on the entrance to his house that he can see from his living room. I assumed that he just had it in case there was any crime in the streets. He said no, no, no, it's just that the older I get the less I want to go all the way to the front door, so if somebody is out there, I'll know who it is before I get there, and I can see if it's a customer or not. I don't know if that's the real answer but that's the answer he gave me.

You have a lot of great stories about the Southwest, but what are the most memorable ones? Is it the saguaro cactus that got shot—what really strikes a chord with you?

There are probably two or three and each one tells a much broader story. You can condense the saguaro cactus story into one sentence: Drunken fool goes to desert, kills cactus, cactus kills him.

Would you elaborate a bit in case people haven't read the book?

Hard to believe that there are people who still haven't read the book. (Laughs.)

The saguaro cactus story is: There was a cactus, one of millions in the desert north of Phoenix. One day an ex-con, his buddy, a case of beer, and a dog go out into the desert target practicing, just shooting at cactus. This is on a weekday afternoon in February, no one else was out there and they loved to shoot at cactus until the cactus fell over.

These are majestic plants that are fifty, seventy-five, or more than a hundred years old. He was shooting more and more cactus and finally he gets to this one particular cactus and starts shooting at it and it doesn't fall. And he kind of moves around at a different angle and he keeps shooting and it stands. Finally, really frustrated that this cactus was not responding to his gunfire, he picks a real sturdy saguaro rib off the ground, and starts poking at one of the cactus's arms from below. This cactus was at least ten feet tall and had two very big, strong arms. While he poked at it, the cactus's arm came crashing down on top of the guy and killed him instantly.

How much do you think that arm weighed?

Probably 500 pounds, you know they're filled with water. It doesn't look like it, but these things are very heavy. That's what cactus do for a living, they fill themselves up with water whenever they can find it, and that's what keeps them alive during the summertime which is ten months of the year.

Now one of the many functions of the cactus arm is to give ballast to the trunk itself. With its arm dislodged, the trunk starts wobbling. The trunk could have fallen anywhere, but it fell right on top of its arm, right on top of David Michael Grundman and killed him yet again. You're laughing, and everybody laughs, but we have two deaths here. By killing the cactus, he essentially killed himself. This is nature's revenge. You don't need a metaphor here boys and girls—it happened. The story tells itself.

It's a story about nature, a story about mankind…it's funny, when it happened it was a little *ha-ha-ha* story on Associated Press. I clipped it out and put it on my bulletin board where it stayed for about twenty years. I said, "You know, one of these days I'm going to go look into that." It touched on so many elements of the Southwest: violence, beauty, nature, sudden change, urban growth.

The other story is the *Salt of the Earth* story. This was a militant labor union, a Communist union actually, of miners, almost all Mexican Americans during the 1940s. Near Silver City, New Mexico, they went out on strike against one of the major mining companies. It was a three-year strike and the demands were not just the conventional ones having to do with working conditions and salary, but the wives of the miners put in their own demands for company housing, running water, sanitation.

By law, because of the Taft-Hartley Act, the strikers could not continue picketing, but the miners' wives and the women in this town took up the picket line for the remaining part of the strike, about a year longer. And they were just tough as nails, very militant, they refused to let scabs in, and finally, after another year, the company and the union settled. The company gave in on most of the demands.

What happened during the middle of all this was some blacklisted Hollywood lefties learned about the strike and they were looking for a story line. They saw this strike and the struggle of these miners as a terrific story for a movie. So they made an agreement with the local union to make a theatrical picture based upon the strike. This movie was filmed in Silver City and its environs and a lot of the min-ers and miners' families played miners and miners' families in the movie.

As it was being filmed, some members of Congress started denouncing these Hollywood lefties for spreading Communist propa-ganda throughout New Mexico. All of a sudden all the yahoos in this immediate area of southwestern New Mexico started physically attack-ing the movie site until they had to stop shooting. The guy who was in fact the president of the local union played the president of the local union and the woman who played his wife was a very well-known Mexican actress, Rosaura Revueltas, and she was deported from the United States.

The rest of the filming and production was done underground with help from unknown or little-known people at the time, like Will Geer, who played the sheriff. The movie was finally finished and set for distribution. Howard Hughes, who was then very active in the film industry, told movie theaters, "If you carry this movie you'll never get another movie from my company again."

So the distribution of *Salt of the Earth* was effectively sabotaged. It had maybe three or four showings in New York, L.A., San Francisco, and Silver City at a drive-in. Basically it wasn't seen by the American public until the mid- or late sixties. Copies of it surfaced when it began to take on a certain legitimacy in college classes on labor history or Chicano history or women's struggles. It touched on a lot of different elements all based in the Southwest. Then it became available on video and PBS ran it and now you can get it at Blockbuster.

There are other nice Southwest stories such as the one about Rosa's Cantina, the bar from the Marty Robbins song, but to draw on all the elements at once, those two stories stand out.

It seems you pick a very narrow topic and follow that thread. The Panama Hat Trail *is a perfect example. You grab people with "Did you know that Panama hats aren't from Panama?"*

Just two weeks ago I went to a book sale and I found a book about *cuy*—that's guinea pig—it's a delicacy in the Andes. I have a chapter in my book about going to a restaurant that specialized in *cuy* in the city of Cuenca, Ecuador. This guy's academic obsession led to this book. I was fascinated by it—it probably had a readership of fifty, maybe a hundred; there just aren't a lot of *cuy* aficionados. But there are Ecuadorian restaurants in New York City where you can go get *cuy*. And there are people who raise *cuy* in the United States for consumption and restaurants.

What you're asking about is finding something very narrow and exploiting it as best you can. There is a lot of self-indulgent travel that passes itself off as travel writing. People say, "I travel, therefore I write."

Just because someone has been there doesn't mean it's interesting to anyone else. Usually when writing something there will be a subtext to it, and that's always the travel writing that I admire most in others: the reader draws a much larger conclusion than the book does. That's a successful book.

You mention *The Panama Hat Trail*. It got a lot of wonderful reviews and I'm quite pleased with that, but there was one review where the guy got it. It was in the *Chicago Reader* and the guy said, "What motivated Miller on this trip was anger, anger at the system that encourages exploitation where somebody earns fifty cents for weaving a hat that is eventually sold for $35." Exploitation is a word I did not use once in the book—I made a point of that. I quoted someone saying that, but I never used it myself. I wanted to lay it out, but I wanted someone else to say it, not me.

Hunched over, weather-beaten, and ageless, the Andean Indians seemed to be forever walking with heavy loads strapped to their backs.... From the waist up they stoop over at a three-quarter angle to the ground, always looking as if they are headed into a stiff wind. Even when they are walking downhill they tread as if pulling themselves uphill. At times it seems as if the Indians carry the Andes themselves on their backs.

—Tom Miller,
The Panama Hat Trail

It wasn't an angry book—your approach seems very measured. You don't seem to inject a lot of judgment into your work.

No, I like to think readers will make a judgment based on what I present.

I remember in Bruce Chatwin's The Songlines, *one of the aboriginal artists who was paid a couple of hundred dollars for his painting sees it in a gallery for $6,000 and he becomes enraged, shouting and stamping his feet. The gallery owner explains they have to pay rent and they have to pay people to work at the gallery and so on. But the artist says, you can't tell me that costs thousands of dollars and my art is only worth a couple of hundred. It's an interesting scene; Chatwin doesn't inject a lot of commentary; you just kind of get it. You can see where the shop owner is coming from, and the artist's outrage is completely understandable.*

The books that I admire most and the goals that I set for myself all involve that subtext where the reader walks away with a broader conclusion than the book itself states.

Which is a nice segue to Cuba.

You could say Cuba is the great story, I wouldn't say of our time but of recent years. It involves a lot of mythology: "Remember the *Maine*," Teddy Roosevelt, Fidel Castro, guerrilla warfare in the mountains, a revolutionary with a beard, the Bay of Pigs. There are all these things which have an element of truth and an element of mythology to them, and it's a story that's still unresolved. It's one of the last unresolved stories of the Americas.

Most other countries, either economically or politically or musically are well-defined and are unlikely to change. It's curious, but Cuba has a stable government. It hasn't changed a whole lot during the last forty-four years. Though they don't say so publicly, that's one reason the State Department likes Cuba the way it is; they don't have to change their policy every year. They just don't have new leaders there. Fidel, for all his bombast, is an extremely consistent guy. He hasn't said anything new in forty-four years.

And he's been in power since, when, the Eisenhower administration?

Right, January 1, 1959. And he's unlikely to willingly give up power until he dies. When I travel in another country, the last thing I want to see is another American. I come from a country full of Americans; I know where to find Americans if I want Americans. Cubans on the other hand, will go out of their way to find other Cubans. My wife and

I were with some friends in Juarez at a Caribbean nightclub and there was a Cuban band playing. My wife didn't actually know the musicians but they greeted each other like old friends. I would never do that with anybody in another country. Cubans can sniff each other out a mile away in any country—it's just incredible.

So there is that identity that they have; it's a very proud one, and it's also one of superiority. It's a very self-assured cultural identity and that plays into the larger story of Cuba, how Cubans overseas see themselves and see the island. Despite the reputation, there's a very wide range of opinions in Miami about what's going on in Cuba now and what should happen there in the future. It's not just one attitude. A lot of it depends on when you came over to this country, if you're part of the first wave or the Mariel wave, or if you came over more recently.

I've met any number of Cubans in this country who say, the day after Fidel dies I'll go back. And others go back three times a year. So what really appeals to me about Cuba as an ongoing story is that dynamic of how people there adapt to their situation and how Cubans outside of Cuba adapt.

I have found Cuba to be both a heartbreaking place and an inspiring place. I wonder if you see a similar dynamic. What strikes you as heartbreaking or inspiring, or both?

There are different levels of heartbreak. One is Cubans who used to live there go back for the first time in fifteen or twenty or forty years. I just met somebody who went back for the first time in forty-four years. And she was so glad—it had been bothering her for forty-four years that she couldn't see her homeland, but at the same time she was heartbroken. She said, "Look at those buildings—nobody has taken care of them." The city of Havana and most of the small towns simply don't look or feel as they did when these people left.

The longer they wait to go back, the more idealized it becomes in their mind. So for them going back is heartbreaking, to see what's happened to so much they left, and at the same time, they feel that *cubanía* that allows them to identify with the island even if they don't live there.

What's happening in Cuba is that the street is leading the government. If something is successful on the street, then the government will seize it and take it over. There were these *paladares*, these home restaurants. They weren't legal; they weren't illegal—they just existed. It was all word-of-mouth. They became so successful and so well known that the government stepped in and said, O.K., from now on we're going to license these places and impose a tax on your business. So from that point on you had to be licensed or you could suffer a gigantic fine and get closed down.

Same with these *casas particulares*, these private homes that take in travelers. It was enormously popular until the government stepped in and said, we're going to license these things. The first time I went to a *paladar* was before they'd been legalized. The maitre d' was an off-duty Havana policeman in uniform, and it was in somebody's living room and kitchen—that's the way they still are. And it was two dollars for dinner—I was magnanimous and paid $8 for a nice big dinner for everybody.

On Christmas Day in 1997, a well-known photographer who lives in Cuba, Ernesto Bazan, was getting married to a woman from Camaguay, a town in central Cuba. It was a nice big party at a rented house in Havana and sitting in the corner was this guy who we were told was a local baseball player. It was Orlando Hernández, El Duque, and at the time I kind of knew who he was because I heard he'd been banned from baseball in Cuba (for allegedly speaking with a U.S. baseball agent).

My wife is a Cuban baseball fan and she started dancing with him. Regla tossed me her camera, so I have a picture of Orlando Hernandez and his wife and my wife all sitting together. Well, that very day he took off. He went to a tiny town on the north coast and from there took off into the water and ended up in Yankee Stadium. So I saw him on his last day in Cuba and by happy coincidence I was in New York the following June on his first day in Yankee Stadium. So I had to go to that game to complete the cycle.

That brings up another issue of travel writing: The most compelling stories are human stories—wouldn't you agree?

Yeah, that may be why I'm bored silly when I go birdwatching.

When I was in your office and saw the complete works of José Marti, I recalled that in Trading with the Enemy *you describe visiting Plaza de*

Armas (where used booksellers vend their wares). You came back a year and a half later and a bookseller remembered what you were looking for and said he had the set of Marti's works.

Exactly. And that's how I got *Our Man in Havana* in Spanish. The real dealers there just put the touristy books on their stands at Plaza de Armas, but they have resources not only in their own homes but they know people around town who have extensive libraries and are willing to sell their books.

Though you don't usually comment on politics in your books, I'm wondering if you have any thoughts about the U.S. embargo of Cuba.

There is the U.S. law called the Trading with the Enemy Act which discourages commercial and personal contact between the two countries. With the recent roundup of Cuban dissidents, both sides are being as unfriendly as they can be.

In Trading with the Enemy, *revised in the mid-1990s, you have a line saying, "Visit now because it will never again be the same." People have been saying that for about a dozen years and Castro is still in power.*

I spent the next morning writing out my request to interview Castro. Looking back, I might just as well have sat on the Malecón wall spitting in the ocean…. I wrote that I wanted to chat with him about the places and personalities I had encountered during my stay, about baseball, about Cubans in exile, Caribbean music, Afro-Cuban culture, the Guantánamo navy base, literature from and about Cuba, and the aspirations of Cuban youth…. I didn't put it in my request, but I also was burning to know why Cuba, of all countries, had adopted the designated hitter, a decision I considered a metaphor for compromise and national disintegration.

—Tom Miller,
Trading with the Enemy

Visit Cuba now applies as long as he's in power. And I don't wish his death—on the other hand I sure hope I'm there when it happens. One reason there's so much interest in Cuba is the enormous success of the

Buena Vista Social Club CD and documentary. The documentary I don't think gives a very accurate portrayal of life in Cuba. I liked it; it was a nice soft look at a hard country. The documentary and the CD touched so little on the politics or economics that it had a much broader appeal. Cuba is also a border. The border is forty-four years long.

You're suggesting a visit to Cuba is almost like time travel.

Yeah, there is a linguistic border as well; there are cultural borders; you're in a different realm. In *Trading with the Enemy* is a profile of this woman who recently died, Nitza Villapol, the television cook. The shorthand is to say that she was the Julia Child of Cuba. She was on television from the early fifties till the mid-nineties, every week with cooking advice. She was extremely well known and well regarded because she actually talked about what was in people's kitchens and in the *bodegas*. She was real good at knowing what was available and what wasn't. When things were at their absolute worst in the early nineties she would show how to make grapefruit rind steak and things like that, which were almost embarrassing. But it was practical advice for people.

That sounds like the Cuban version of mock apple pie, only we had apples here. I don't know why anyone would want to make mock apple pie.

Ritz crackers. In any event, it turns out Nitza Villapol had a much more interesting history than most Cubans knew about. She was a very bitter woman who really had no use for most Cubans. She thought they were either sex-obsessed or had no interest in a balanced diet. She was born in New York City—she was a U.S. citizen—her parents were both Cuban. Her life paralleled the revolution and her middle-class existence, with all of her friends leaving in the late fifties and early sixties and her staying behind.

The way you describe her, she sounds almost disdainful of her audience, sort of like the Martha Stewart of Cuba. Anyway, one thing that strikes me about Cuba is that because of shortages and because of the embargo, much has been preserved. The façade of the Malacon is still there, it isn't riddled with KFC, Starbucks, and McDonald's. Much of the agriculture is organic because they can't afford pesticides.

The U.S. embargo is responsible for the flowering of Cuban culture in the last ten years or so, because the steamroller of globalized culture which emanates from the United States and rolls over just about every country it can, is not rolling over Cuba. There is no musical group from the Dominican Republic with the popularity of the Buena Vista ensemble, even though there's terrific Dominican music. To my way of thinking, the embargo has been good for Cuban culture.

I did an interview with Omara Portuondo, the singer from the *Buena Vista Social Club,* and I proposed that the flowering of Cuban culture owes itself to the U.S. embargo. I just wanted to see how she'd react to it. She was actually very thoughtful—she said, in a way that's true. Because of the revolution, cultural centers were put up in every small town throughout Cuba. Whereas arts education used to be concentrated strictly in Havana and was very commercial, after the revolution it lost its commercial identity and gained a much broader geographic identity. She was saying it wasn't the embargo but the revolution that was responsible for this flowering. She turned my question inside out.

That brings up a question you get asked in Cuba a lot, which is, "What do think of Castro?" or "What do you think of the revolution?" And it can be a tricky question to answer because you don't know where the questioner is coming from. I would often say, "It seems like the revolution has done some good things in education and health care, but the people here need a lot more."

Yeah, I would do the same thing—I had a fence-straddling answer. "It's a lovely country with severe problems." Who could disagree with that?

Let's talk a little bit about baseball in Cuba, because it's the same yet very different. What are the differences that you see, beside the salaries?

In the game itself there's probably more running; it's more scrappy than major-league baseball. There are fewer home runs and more base hits. Pitching a complete game is pretty normal—of course their arms are worn out by the time they're in their early thirties.

The game you're describing sounds a lot like American baseball in the 1950s and 1960s.

Yes, that's their model, but usually there are no trades. Each province has its own team.

Doesn't Havana have a couple of extra teams?

The province of Havana has one team; the city of Havana has two teams. One is the Industriales, which El Duque Hernandez pitched for. They're the Yankees of Cuba—they always win—and they are hated by everyone except the Habaneros. The other team is the Metropolitanos, which are just perennial losers.

Like the Mets.

Exactly. You go to see the Industriales and the place is packed and people are cheering madly. The next day the Metropolitanos are playing and you can be one of a thousand people at the stadium. The difference in loyalty to those teams is striking.

I spent part of a baseball game inside the scoreboard in Piñar del Rio. There are two guys back there who watch the game with binoculars, listen to it on the radio, and when it goes from Ball 2 to Ball 3, they'll quickly take out the slat that says 2 and put in the slat that says 3. Actually, they have more of a rotating turnstyle and turn it from 2 to 3.

These guys are great—they're the heroes of Piñar del Rio. They've been doing it for the last thirty years. I asked what they thought about electronic scoreboards and they said, "Well, we hope they never come."

Sure, it's their job.

Exactly. They were able to carry on a conversation with us and at the same time watch the game through these peepholes. There are no exploding scoreboards in Cuba. There's no Astroturf there. There's advertising, but it's all for the government or the Communist Party or Fidel. Or there will be some slogan like "Play Sports for Longer Life." But it's not "Drink Coca-Cola."

Now if you talk to the players, though most of them don't say it out loud, the goal of any baseball player is to play with the best, and the best are in this country [the U.S.]. Politics really slammed down right in the middle of them. Frankly, I'm surprised there haven't been more defections.

During a 2001 trip in Cuba, the bicycle touring group I was traveling with stayed in the same hotel as the team from Villa Clara. I met the manager, a guy named Victor Mesa, who's very animated and engaging, sort of like the Dusty Baker of Cuba. He signed a baseball for me, which one of the players had sold me for five dollars.

They also sell their jerseys and their caps. When they go overseas they'll take boxes of cigars with them and sell them and that's how they'll make money overseas.

It's hard to blame them because they don't make much more than their expenses and a little salary right?

The salary has gone up somewhat, and more and more of them are getting perks for outstanding play so they can live in better houses in their hometown. A typical Cuban baseball player earns about $40 a month, plus some stipends for housing and, perhaps, a car. An average U.S. player earns about $3 million a year.

Let's talk a bit about the business of travel writing…

It's a get-rich-quick scheme (laughs). There are times when I have this false sense of financial stability; there are times when I'm at the opposite end. I've been going through these highs and lows so long that I'm assuming it will continue like this. The instability of freelancing is still there, but it's built into my life.

I'm amused and delighted that *The Panama Hat Trail* is having a new life. Two years ago at the *L.A. Times* book festival, there was a panel that Pico Iyer and I were on and someone asked me: "*The Panama Hat Trail* came out in 1986—don't you feel obligated to update it?" I said, "No, it's what that place was like at that time." If I did a good job, someone who visits there now can see echoes of that. It's not a guidebook. These books are meant to show what this place was like at this time as seen by this one person.

Back to the question of making a living, have you been able to support yourself with writing?

For a few semesters I was teaching workshops at the University of Arizona, from one day to two weeks. These are things that are derivative of the writing. As far as income goes, I have probably earned more on things that have come about as a result of my book on Cuba than from the actual books themselves. The book has a certain notoriety and people have asked me to give a talk, or lead a group, or something like that.

You worked on a compilation of different "La Bamba" versions—how did that come about?

That started in 1957 or 1958 when the song "La Bamba" came out. I remember going out at age ten and buying it for a dollar, a 45-rpm pressing on the Delphi label. I still have it. Over the years I just thought of it as the Latino "Louie Louie." I never played guitar or was in a band—I just like the song. After moving to the southwest in 1969, I would hear different versions of it and I started to hear the slow versions—very Mexican versions—not rock-and-roll. I learned that it was a folk song that started in the state of Veracruz. At one point I convinced an editor at *The New York Times Magazine* to let me write a piece on "La Bamba."

The song did begin in Veracruz—the roots of the song go back to the slave trade with Africa. In southern Veracruz the culture is called Jarocho, and "La Bamba" is one of the initial Jarocho songs. Jarocho is a combination of Spanish influence, African influence, and native influence. The African influence came from slaves who were brought from Africa by the Spaniards to present-day Veracruz. Some of them came from a province called M'bamba in the Congo.

I saw that Rhino records had released *The Best of Louie Louie*, ten different versions of "Louis Louie." Absolutely cold, I wrote a letter to the president of Rhino records. I didn't know the guy—I just said, "Hi, I've written a few books; I admire what you guys are doing; I got an idea: let's do the best of 'La Bamba.'" A few days later I got a call back—he said, "Good idea. Let's do it."

I have a collection of seventy-five or eighty different versions of the song—I even went to the filming of the movie *La Bamba*. The essay on the back of the record, the liner notes, is essentially *The New York Times* piece rewritten to be in a liner notes fashion. It turns out the most popular cut on the "Louie Louie" album was by the Rice University marching band, the Marching Owls. Rhino got in touch with Rice and asked if they could do "La Bamba." So they did. I was happy with the way it came out, including the Mormon Tabernacle choir singing "La Bamba."

What advice would you give me if I were fresh out of college and said I wanted to be a travel writer?

I would recommend writing, not travel writing. My feeling is don't call yourself a travel writer—let somebody else do it. Travel writing is as much a marketing niche as it is a literary form, sometimes more so. There's a lot of schlock calling itself travel writing. Anybody with a laptop computer and frequent-flier miles can say, "Hey, I'm a travel writer." So I wouldn't say be a travel writer—be a writer.

The book *On the Border* came out and people said, hey, that's very good travel writing. I never thought of it as travel literature or anything of that nature, maybe current events or long-form journalism or some form of literature, but never travel writing.

One of the basic things when I do writing workshops is say, after your first draft go through your manuscript and circle every first-person reference and see how many of them you can knock out. When you get down to the absolute minimum, you've improved your manuscript a great deal. What I ask anybody is "What makes your travel so different from anyone else's?" People don't want to read for the tenth time about Antigua unless there's something startlingly new.

As a writer who travels, what have been the highs and lows, the greatest joys and pleasures, as well as the sacrifices you've had to make for this lifestyle?

The sacrifices came more recently. One is a conscious decision on my part to settle down. I've done as much writing but less traveling during the past ten years since getting married—actually the amount of travel maybe is the same, but it's been much more back and forth to Cuba; I spend much less time in Mexico.

The satisfaction comes when everything falls into place, when all the research and writing comes together and I know that I'm done. I don't want to turn it into a sports analogy about the long-distance runner—too many writers do that.

Are there any general lessons you've learned from extensive travel?

Always unpack from your last trip before you pack for your next.

If you had one last trip to make, where would you go, would it be your upcoming trip to Africa?

It may well be Africa because it's never been on my dance card. I hope this isn't my last trip.

If you hadn't been a writer, what do you think you'd be doing with your life right now?

I was asked by someone else, "Without literature, how would your life be?" He was expecting some grandiose, possibly pretentious answer. I said, "Less stressful and more stable."

The Snow
Leopard

Peter Matthiessen

T HE AUTHOR OF *THE SNOW LEOPARD*, A MEDITATIVE AND
elegiac account of a trek deep into the Himalaya, Peter
Matthiessen has written more than two dozen books, rang-
ing from the spare fiction of *Far Tortuga* to the evocative prose of such
recent work as *The Birds of Heaven*, a global odyssey in celebration of
cranes. A passionate advocate for threatened species and threatened
cultures, Matthiessen is a champion of environmental protection and
social justice. His travels with Cesar Chavez, whom he admires greatly, resulted in *Sal Si Puedes*, and his book, *In the Spirit of Crazy Horse,*
is a blistering indictment of the U.S. government's decades-long
imprisonment of Leonard Peltier.

Though Matthiessen has been widely acclaimed for his nonfiction,
which he likens to cabinetmaking, he's often said he prefers the creative freedom of sculpting fiction. His first story, published more than
half a century ago in *The Atlantic Monthly*, won the Atlantic Prize, and
he had a long association with *The New Yorker*, writing "fact pieces"

because that's what paid the bills. His 1965 novel, *At Play in the Fields of the Lord*, was nominated for a National Book Award, and was made into a critically acclaimed film in 1991.

Born May 22, 1927, Matthiessen began by writing "bad short stories" in high school. Just three years after graduating from Yale University, he co-founded *The Paris Review*. After a few years Matthiessen returned to the U.S., settling in eastern Long Island, where he captained a commercial fishing boat to augment his income from writing.

Matthiessen didn't feel well suited for marriage "but I didn't want to lose this beautiful girl," he said in a 1999 lecture entitled, *Zen and the Writing Life*. He had two children with his first wife before they split up. "Greed, anger, and folly have been the earmarks of my life," said Matthiessen, a committed Zen practitioner and teacher. His second marriage ended with the death of his wife in the 1970s, after she'd brought two more children into his life. He married a third time and lives with his present wife in the Long Island house he's owned since the early 1960s. Though committed to the well-being of his family, Matthiessen remains a writer first. His books are extraordinarily well researched, and he's a meticulous notetaker in the field, which reveals itself in his prose.

On an earlier visit I'd made to New York, Matthiessen said he "just didn't have the heart" to be interviewed that week but suggested I try again if I returned. Just as he never saw the snow leopard on his Himalayan trek, I thought I might never have the opportunity to interview Matthiessen. But just a couple of weeks before this book's deadline, I stopped in New York after a trip to Great Britain, and this time he consented. I drove across Long Island through a swirling snowstorm that intensified as I neared the Hamptons. Just before reaching his home, I crossed a bridge over a salt pond where white swans poked their heads into the frigid water searching for food. A brilliantly colored pheasant shot across the snow and plunged into the hedges as I turned into Matthiessen's driveway.

I found Matthiessen working in his study, about a sixty-yard walk from his home, dressed in a blue crewneck sweater and jeans. His austere, crevice-lined face suggested the imposing dignity of a Himalayan massif. A tall, agile man, somewhat similar in appearance and bearing to Everest climber Sir Edmund Hillary, Matthiessen was poring over his Everglades trilogy, reducing and rewriting the three books that began with *Killing Mister Watson* to fit into one volume. Photos, papers, and mementos of his travels covered the walls and a table.

After the hour-long interview, Matthiessen bounded out into the snow without a jacket and showed me a massive whale skull he'd found. Inside his home were artifacts from a 1961 New Guinea expedition, the same journey from which Michael Rockefeller disappeared forever. Down a winding, tree-shaded path stood a rustic and simple *zendo* (meditation hall) where Matthiessen teaches Zen to a small group of students.

Though reluctant to have his picture taken, Matthiessen posed briefly outside his study. His piercing blue eyes and silver hair were framed by the yellow flowers of the tree behind him. Clusters of snowflakes settled on his sweater like confetti. In that moment, as I prepared to say farewell, I realized anew what a gift my time with Matthiessen had been.

~~~

Would you say a few words about your early life and growing up?

Briefly, I was born in New York City on the day that Lindbergh crossed the Atlantic, so I've seen quite a lot of change. My earliest nonfiction book, *Wildlife in America*, was about wildlife and the environment, and I've always been concerned with it. A parallel concern was traditional people who are also threatened, their languages and their culture, and they too show up in *Wildlife in America*. One cannot really separate those concerns, the environment and biodiversity and social justice. They're all tied in very closely together.

Where did that concern initially come from?

I think it came from growing up in Connecticut and being wildly interested in birds from a very early age. My brother and I, we began with snakes—we had a copperhead den on our place in Connecticut. We were outside all the time. It was before TV had really gotten going. My dad was a hunter and a fisherman and taught us about that, and my mother had a bird feeder so the interest in nature was really built-in and then it broadened out.

When I was in prep school my social ideas began to change. My family had money, and they were good people; they were very fair-minded. They were always Republicans, but they voted Democratic after Eisenhower and still thought of themselves as Republicans; they just detested the Republican candidates.

When I was in boarding school, I served as a counselor in a charity boys camp. These were kids from a very tough area of New Haven, Connecticut, and they were only a year younger than I was—I was thirteen—so it was a little nerve-wracking at first, and a social shock. I saw these kids come into that camp, and I think for the first time in their lives they saw enough food. There were lots of hot dogs and lots of corn on the cob and ice cream, and they went absolutely hog wild. They just stuffed themselves, and as a result they were sick all night long—it was a hell of a beginning. But I thought, My God, what is it like when you have some uncle or big brother leaning over your shoulder to take your food away?

That opened my eyes. By the time I was in my twenties, I was going far left very rapidly, which made things a little awkward with my parents, though they behaved very well about it. I was very hostile to the Vietnam War, and I marched in Washington. In the sixties, I began taking a more active role in social justice issues while never losing interest in the environment. On the contrary, that was growing.

At this time I was writing travel pieces for *The New Yorker*. I was getting paid to go to the places I'd always wanted to go. In consequence, I learned a lot more about situations elsewhere and also peoples elsewhere, not just the wildlife. I loved Africa—my present wife was born in Africa and I have been to Africa many times, so all these interests have intertwined.

Even in my fiction, I've always felt that the landscape was a character that you had to reckon with, right away. You had to know how the characters related to the landscape and how it impinged on them. For many years, I kind of despised my nonfiction because I was much more interested in fiction, but then a friend of mine, Sheridan Lord, who was a wonderful landscape painter—he was my lifelong friend; he and I and George Plimpton started off in school together at the age of about eight, and he died of cancer a few years ago, alas—but he was the one who said: "In your fiction and nonfiction, your main theme is much the same: a kind of elegy for what's being lost."

At present, I'm working on this trilogy of novels—the Everglades trilogy that began with *Killing Mister Watson*—and reducing it. Originally it was a single novel which became so long, I had to split it into three, which made it even longer. That was a structural error, and I want to restore it to one book. It's a dangerous, scary project because I may be doing more damage than good, but I don't think so. It will be a lot shorter—short enough to be published in one volume.

Those books began with environmental work in Florida. I spent a lot of time down in the 'Glades, Kissimmee Prairie, and the Keys, and I also worked with the Indian people down there, too. I don't like the coast much, but I love backcountry Florida—it's still wild, with obstreperous people. But in this book, too, one sees the destruction of the birds and water systems of the Everglades, which is being perpetuated by Governor Jeb Bush; it's still a very threatened ecosystem. There is only one Everglades—there's nothing like it on earth, as a habitat, as an environment, nothing. In its strange, lonely way, it's a very beautiful place indeed, with wonderful birds and four species of poisonous snakes. I like working there and I go back as much as I can.

Beyond the bright-headed Tibetan geese, not eighty yards away in the open marsh, stand two white cranes with startling red faces and red bills, fresh as roses in the light of the new sun. Like most cranes, *G. leucogeranus* prefers open areas with unobstructed views, and since it is wary, I am scared I might flare the first snow wreaths I have ever seen, or cause them to move farther from the bank. I sink to my knees behind a bush, watching in relief as they resume feeding: they probe wet gleaming bills through the bronze duckweed or immerse red faces to the eyes to grasp sedge tubers and tug them from the mud.

—Peter Matthiessen,
The Birds of Heaven

Last night I was reading your book, Tigers in the Snow, *and I wonder what it's like to get so deeply involved in a project, like the Siberian Tiger Project, and then to see these beautiful animals struck down. Is that sometimes so overwhelming emotionally that it makes it hard to continue with this work?*

No, it spurs me on! Of course it's very saddening to have those great animals destroyed, and a lot of them were. As it happened, the three that I was most closely associated with in Siberia were all poached and destroyed. Depressing, yes, but I think overall the Siberian tiger is holding its own. Since that time I've been to India again. The first time I went I didn't see a tiger—that was after a big poaching epidemic all through central India—there was hardly a tiger to be found. But recently, I co-led a wildlife safari, and we went to four parks and saw tigers in every one of them—an amazing shift in only a few years.

Encouraging, and yet at the same time you're aware that tiger habitats in India are contracting and shrinking every year as human populations impinge on them. These Indian tigers are just being snuffed out here, snuffed out there, because their habitat is being taken away. So it's not a very hopeful situation.

Even though there are many more tigers in India than in Siberia, possibly six or eight times as many, the Siberians have a better chance, simply because they have a larger contiguous territory.

You're more hopeful about Siberian tigers, even with all the commercial pressure?

There's a lot of corporate pressure for forestry and mining exploration, but corridors have been established between wilderness reserves. A great cat, if there's any opening at all, will find it. They're terrific that way. They will spread to other populations so they don't get too ingrown. And the areas themselves are much larger and much less populated. One early morning, we drove on a logging road for four hours and never saw another vehicle. On the other hand, everybody there has a rifle and will shoot every tiger and elk seen on or near the road.

Because they're worth so much?

Yes. And the elk is a subsistence item of the human diet. Unfortunately it's also important in the tiger's diet, so there's a conflict.

In Tigers in the Snow *you include a quotation from the poet Elizabeth Bishop about the "sweet sensation of joy" one feels when seeing a wild animal. Do you think that sensation can be conveyed widely enough in time to preserve some of the great predators like the tigers?*

I was very touched a few years ago to see a poll in which Americans were asked if they would like to preserve the Arctic National Wildlife Refuge, the one that Presidents Bush one and two and the big fossil fuelers have been gunning for. In the Arctic refuge, there are no roads, no airstrips, no facilities; the only way you can get there is to trek or fly over one hundred miles of very rough mountains. So you've got to fly in, which is expensive, find a place to land, bring your own food, bring your own river craft. Few people will ever see it.

And yet the great majority wanted to protect it from Big Oil. This is the last stronghold of Arctic life, Ice-Age Arctic life even, and maybe their kids might see it or their grandchildren. It's only this appalling new breed of fossil-fuelers, for which the Bush politicians are the point men—these people are leading the charge. The Enron A-team is in the White House, incredibly greedy and shortsighted—these people are looting our country. It seems extraordinary that the American people won't see we've invited the thieves into the store.

I heard a report the other day on NPR about hunters and fishermen, typically staunch Republican voters, who are outraged about what this administration is doing. They spoke specifically about the Tongass National Forest up in Alaska, and one hunter said he'd vote for anybody except Bush.

But how many voters are getting the message? You see these polls and you wonder. These people are lying and lying and lying and lying, the environment, the economy, Medicare, Iraq. They'll do anything to get their errand boy back in office. George W. Bush is the errand boy for these interests and doesn't seem the least bit curious about anything else. There's a Bush hagiography which had one negative adjective in the whole book, and perhaps the writer failed to realized how damning it was. "Incurious"—imagine the head of the free world being incurious. Our president wants to grow up to be a redneck. A redneck is not somebody who is ignorant, but somebody who is ignorant and proud of it. How tragic to have such a person as the head of the free world.

One of the things I appreciate about your work is the poetry of it. You really have an appreciation of language. I wonder, are there poets or other writers who have influenced your work or who inspire you?

There are many writers who inspire me, prose writers and poets, too. Conrad and Dostoyevsky are the two I usually name because they were so powerful for me when I was a young. But I can't identify a direct influence on the prose itself, despite echoes of Melville and Faulkner.

Are you conscious about lending your writing a certain poetry?

Lyricism, yes. That quality makes the writing so much stronger, striking people in the heart as well as in the head—that is critical.

Are there writers you read as you were growing up whose work made you say, "Yes, that's it, that's how I feel." Loren Eiseley spoke to me in that way.

This clear and silent light of the Himalaya is intensified by the lack of smoke and noise. The myriad high peaks, piercing the atmosphere, let pass a light of heaven—the light on stones that makes them ring, the sun roaring and the silverness that flows in lichens and the wings of crows, the silverness in the round tinkle of a pony's bell, and in the scent of snows.

—PETER MATTHIESSEN,
The Snow Leopard

Eiseley was certainly one of those; he's wonderful. One of his books has that wonderful story of the frozen catfish in the Missouri River. He took it home in a chunk of ice. By God, it thawed and this catfish came thumping out. That enormous insistence on life, that is the last hope of endangered animals such as the tiger.

You captained a fishing boat in the 1950s. Was that because you wanted to or was it financial necessity?

It was two different things. I was writing and getting good reviews, but I wasn't selling enough. I had a new family and two little kids, so I needed to make more money. On top of that I compounded my problem. In the harbor at Rockport, Massachusetts, I saw this tuna harpoon boat, with the most beautiful lines I'd ever seen. The owner was selling her dirt cheap and I thought, I've got to have that boat. I was like Toad in *The Wind in the Willows*—my eyes were spinning. But to pay for that boat, I had to run her as a charter boat, and I had to go and get my captain's license. Those years are in a book called *Men's Lives*.

And then you went on and did quite a bit of work with The New Yorker.

I wrote a book in 1959 called *The Cloud Forest* about travels in South America. That's how I began with *The New Yorker*, and out of that South American material came a novel, *At Play in the Fields of the Lord*. *The New Yorker* bought a number of my books, at least seven. I depended on them for a long, long time. They paid very well, and they did not interfere with your prose. So I was devoted to Mr. Shawn [the editor] even though I hardly knew him.

What was it like to work with William Shawn?

Like me, most people hardly knew him. I worked with him for nearly thirty years, and I learned great respect for him. He had enormous integrity and was dead honest, never a smart-ass or anything like that, and very generous. You never asked for better payment because you were always pleasantly surprised by how much they gave you.

One time I heard about a sailing boat that was going down to Nicaragua to fish green sea turtles. I thought, My God, I've got to get on that boat. So I got Mr. Shawn to underwrite me, and I had to make three trips to Grand Cayman in three different years before I sailed. I'm very conservative about expense money, but even with all my precautions it was coming to quite a lot. We sailed from Grand Cayman and went to the Miskito Cays and down the coast of Nicaragua—an extraordinary experience. I was fascinated by how these men worked—no modern equipment. The spareness of their life, and their beautiful old English speech—they were a real racial and ethnic pot-pourri. I loved their stories, and I loved observing their Caymanian seamanship, which was famous.

I came back and I said, "Mr. Shawn, I can write you a fact piece, but I should tell you that I'm going to hold back the best stuff for a novel." I said the fact piece will be fine if you still want it; otherwise, I'll do my best to repay you the expense money. Most editors in those days would have climbed all over me. I didn't say it was open to negotiation—I said, I'm going to use the best stuff in my novel. And Mr. Shawn without hesitation said, "Mr. Matthiessen, you do what's best for your work." It was heartfelt and spontaneous, and I loved him for it.

Would you discuss how your practice of Zen has shaped your life and your writing?

I first understood that it had shaped my life somewhat when my kids said they thought my Zen practice had softened me—that was probably in the late '70s.

I could be harsh and I had a hot temper. Anger has been my life-long *koan*. But really, Zen has mellowed me out. I'm still a pretty wound-up guy. I think people look at me and say, "That's a Zen teacher?" But if it hadn't been for Zen, it would be worse. The practice has clarified my life, and I am devoted to my students.

I'm beginning to realize I can't do everything. Besides Zen teaching, I'm working very hard with this huge novel, I have a lively family, and I'm involved in environmental advocacy and also with American Indian matters. Something has to go. I was getting desperate, but now something has opened up, and I think I am gradually backing away from my Zen work. I think our Zen group is strong enough now to be self-sustaining. We have seven or eight strong senior students, terrific people, several of them potential teachers. I'm very happy about that.

I'm curious about when you went to the Himalaya in the early '70s. It was so touching reading about your being away and telling your son you would try to be home for Thanksgiving. I know you didn't make it back in time. How did it turn out, trying to balance your passion for travel and writing with your concern for your family?

I think my family understood, just as my Zen students have to. I'm not a full-time Zen teacher—I'm a writer. I came into Zen as a writer. But that everyone understands doesn't mean that it's been easy for them or for me. Nor does it mean that I handled it well. I've always been a responsible parent, but I was gone a lot of the time, and when I'm home, I'm an obsessive writer. I write seven days a week.

When his mother died, I took my youngest son, Alex, down to the beach here and told him about his mother, who had died the night before. He said, "You know Dad, she can't be dead; you're wrong." And I said, "Well, why can't she Alex?" And he said, "Well, Dad, if she were dead, I'd be crying." He hung on to that idea for a long time. It was very moving. Then when I was in Nepal, he wrote me a wonderful letter which he signed, "Your sun, Alex"—he drew the sun and its rays of light.

He is now the Hudson Riverkeeper, and the Hudson is kind of the flagship organization for all the Riverkeeper and Baykeeper waterway NGOs around the country. As a result he's on TV and in the papers all the time. I'm very proud of him—he's done a great job. So he came out O.K.

Staying with The Snow Leopard *for a minute, the trip is clearly a pilgrimage. Generally, what's necessary to make a pilgrimage—what does a pilgrimage entail? I remember the advice you received from Eido Roshi: "Expect nothing."*

A true pilgrimage has mystery. It can be an inner mystery—you can be searching the interior; you can be searching for the Lord who is seen within, as we say in Zen. Or it may be a mystery of circumstance, for example, the snow leopard, which is this elusive, extraordinarily beautiful beast in the Himalaya. My wife had just died, and I was making a Zen pilgrimage for her as well as for myself. It was just to clarify the mystery of life—that's what the driving force was. It turned out to be an extraordinary trip.

We walked 250 miles over the Himalaya up to the Tibetan plateau. It was like walking into the Middle Ages—just amazing. My partner, George Schaller, was a perfect companion, so able and thorough and resolute and responsible, and a good man as well. I remember saying to him early on, because I was just so stunned by what we were seeing and how everything was unfolding like a parable, I said, "If I can't get a good book out of this, I ought to be taken out and shot." (Laughs.)

I'm curious how meaningful the awards have been for you. For many authors, the National Book Award, which you won for The Snow Leopard, *is the crowning glory of a career. As somebody who has practiced Zen meditation for decades, I wonder how you view those accolades?*

When I'm in my Zen mode, they seem illusory. But of course it's wonderful to have your work recognized. We work with the ego in Zen training. I have a big fat ego; I'm thin-skinned, and in my past life I've been quite arrogant, so both are there. So it really depends where I'm sitting at the time.

What have you hoped to accomplish with your work, and do you think you have succeeded?

I never had an idea of what I might accomplish. I began when I was about fifteen by writing bad short stories. You just need to do it. Later on you get more ambitious; then you start thinking in terms of reviews and agents and money, and that kind of infects the process. I think people who want to write should write regardless of all that. They should write as a way of clarifying the way they see life.

And reading certainly is a great gift to us all. The amount of wonderful writing is such a blessing. It's like air and sun. Writing is a way of getting in touch with the reality of existence. You punch through to see something more clearly. As you said earlier, good writers articulate things for you. I used to be so amused by library books when I was a kid. It seemed to be a habit of old ladies to take library books and make little notations in the margin when they saw something articulated that they knew to be true. They all wrote the same thing: "How true, how true!"

Why have you settled here in Sagaponack?

Things in place. This county is my home country. Although I was born in Manhattan, I went within a day or so to a place called Fisher's Island over towards Rhode Island and Connecticut but still within Suffolk County. I still go occasionally—my brother still has a cottage there.

When I first came here, I lived in a little village called The Springs, beyond East Hampton. In my fishing days I lived in Amagansett, perhaps ten miles east of the village where I live now.

And then I came by this place—I was extraordinarily lucky because I met the owner, a gifted Russian photographer, at a party. I loved this property because I was a hunter then—I didn't tell him this part—but my hunting pals and I used to come in here and poach. There were so many pheasants in here—it was like a tea party. I just thought this wooded area so close to the ocean is exactly what I would like. I don't want to be right smack on the ocean for environmental reasons as well as aesthetic ones.

I said to him casually, "If you should ever decide to sell part of your acreage, please let me know." After a drinking bout, he was found under the hedge right here nearly dead. He told a friend, get a hold of that guy Matthiessen. So I acquired this place, six acres and three buildings, and came to Sagaponack. That would've been about 1960, so I've been here for almost a half century.

If you hadn't been a writer, what do you think your occupation would have been?

There are so many other professions I would like to have tried. My brother is a marine biologist; I don't think I would work in his field, but certainly I would be a field biologist. I would want to work with wildlife and wild places. George Schaller, my partner on *The Snow Leopard* trip, not only does wonderful work in the field, but he also has been instrumental in establishing wildlife parks all around the world. That to me is terrific and exciting work, and I've done a little bit of that myself, and promoted that. That would be a wonderful combination of fieldwork and social benefit.

Someone has said that the purpose of life is to help other people get through it. That's also in the spirit of Zen practice. I work on my kids—I would hate for them to go through life and not feel they'd made a contribution to human welfare or perhaps the environment. And, of course, I want that for myself, as well.

Isn't there a Buddhist saying, "Everything you do may be insignificant, but it's very important that you do it."

It's not that it's insignificant; you may feel it's insignificant, but it's the doing that's important. We speak of fulfilling your life, fulfilling your true nature, what you were meant to do. Some of my students are very insightful, they're very clear about the teachings; others are wonderful entrepreneurs, and they're all making very important contributions.

But we all have the idea we want to be something else. We're living in the future or we're living in the past, and we suffer. The nature of that suffering is the feeling that something is missing in our life, and we don't even know what it is—we're just yearning for something that's missing. We're never quite present and content with what is. That includes me after thirty-some years of Zen. I'm a senior teacher now, and I still see myself responding to those very human impulses.

In The Snow Leopard *you write about the end of that magnificent trip. You're descending and somebody pokes his head into your tent and you tell him to get out. He's ragged and mangy and you're angry at his neediness. Yet it's not just his neediness, but your own neediness.*

My neediness, yeah. It's not that you don't enjoy things, it's perfectly O.K. to enjoy a beautiful bowl or any other possession really. It's when your life depends on it, when you cling to it, when you gotta have more and more and more, and the more you get the more you want.

It's funny how things have come full circle. Do you remember in *The Snow Leopard* there was a man called Tukten Sherpa? He's the one I come out with, and he disappears at the very end. I knew very little about Tukten, and out of the blue has come this extraordinary photograph of him taken about three years before I knew him. It's right here somewhere. [Matthiessen looks for but can't find the photo.] Tukten is very mysterious; he looks actually like this Buddha.

What has his life been like since you traveled with him in 1973?

Unfortunately his life didn't last very long—he died of, I think, TB and drink. Turns out he was a Tibetan, I didn't know that. He was a Gurkha soldier for a long time. He even was in Singapore for a while; he was a well-traveled fellow. He spoke Malay—I didn't know any of that.

Jan Morris has written that the Welsh have a word, hiraeth, *which is that ineffable longing.*

I wrote about that in *The Snow Leopard* and in some of my Zen writings. As close as I can come to it, I think that nebulous yearning that you can't define has something to do with purity, with the lost paradise. For me I know it does, I can't answer for others. I'm not thinking of a literal lost paradise where there's a people who are untouched, or a landscape that is untouched; I'm thinking more of the purity of childhood. I think we come into the world in this extraordinary pure condition, and all the trouble that mankind brings on itself is all incipient.

The wildwood brings on mild nostalgia, not for home or place, but for lost innocence—the paradise lost that, as Proust said, is the only paradise. Childhood is full of mystery and promise, and perhaps the life fear comes when all the mysteries are laid open, when what we thought we wanted is attained.

—PETER MATTHIESSEN,
The Snow Leopard

But for a time we are this extraordinary blank slate. I describe it as a child in the sandbox in the summertime, watching the birds go by and the leaves dancing and the sun coming through the leaves. He has no ego at all—he's completely part of that. You see a little kid playing in the sandbox, his eyes are absolutely wide, he's not separate from that at all. He's absolutely what you try to become through all these spiritual disciplines. You're trying to return into the one.

There's a wonderful Zen metaphor, that we are like a bottle of seawater floating in the ocean. We are encased in a bottle of our own construction, and we are separate from the whole, from the one. If that bottle were to melt or dissolve, we would then rejoin the whole, which is our natural condition. We aren't separate from other beings.

The End of the World

Jan Morris
Llanystumdwy, Wales

"A<small>RE YOU SURE YOU KNOW WHAT YOU'RE UNDERTAKING? IT'S</small> hell getting here, the weather will be awful, you'll almost certainly need to spend a night somewhere, nearly everything is closed for the season, and I don't consider myself a travel writer anyway. However, if you're fool enough to insist, you'll be very welcome and we'll put the kettle on." So wrote Jan Morris by email when I proposed a winter visit to her home. Earlier, she'd said I could interview her when she came to San Francisco, but of all writers it seemed that Jan Morris should be interviewed in her place.

Born in 1926, Morris revels in her Welsh heritage (her father was Welsh, her mother English) and her home, called Trefan Morys, is a multifaceted reflection of who she is, as revealed in her book, *A Writer's House in Wales*. I wanted to see Trefan Morys's ancient stone walls, its bookshelves sagging under the weight of thousands of volumes (dozens of which she wrote), and its hybrid weathervane with E and W for east and west; G and D for *gogledd* and *de*, Welsh for north and south. I hoped to sign her guestbook, hear the gentle music of the River Dwyfor rolling by, and introduce myself to Ibsen, her Norwegian forest cat. I looked forward to meeting Morris's life partner, Elizabeth, with whom she's shared more than half a century. And I sought to pay tribute to one of the great writers of our time.

Morris began life as James Humphry Morris, but from childhood felt that she was a girl. In her book, *Conundrum*, she offers an intimate, matter-of-fact account of her desire to shed her male identity and become her true self. Though doctors had warned that a sex change could have unforeseen effects upon Morris's personality and literary talent, she never doubted she was pursuing the right course. In 1972, after years of hormone therapy, Morris had sex-change surgery in Casablanca. Elizabeth, Morris's former wife and the mother of their four children, has supported Jan through all her transitions, and the couple live together in Trefan Morys to this day.

As a reporter for *The Times* (of London), Morris, who earlier had served as an intelligence officer in the British army, accompanied the 1953 Everest expedition that reached the mountain's summit for the first time. Thanks to Morris's swift descent, the news hit the London papers on the Coronation Day of Queen Elizabeth II, lending exultant celebration to the ceremony. "I felt like I'd been crowned myself," Morris said upon hearing that the news had reached London in time.

A few months later, Morris was in the U.S. on a fellowship, which she recounts in her first book, *Coast to Coast*, a collection of essays written for *The Times*, and reprinted by Travelers' Tales in 2002. Yet Morris wasn't following journalistic convention. Rather than write descriptive pieces, she painted impressionistic portraits resulting from a place's affect on her. Her essays don't discuss solely what a place looks or sounds like, but rather present "a wanderer's response," as she has said. Her most beloved books about places have probably been *Venice* and *Oxford*, but she says her recent volume, the insightful and melancholy *Trieste and the Meaning of Nowhere*, is her favorite and most self-revelatory book.

Morris's most acclaimed literary endeavor is the ambitious *Pax Britannica* trilogy, a character-driven, anecdote-filled, historical analysis of the rise and fall of the British Empire. Though a Welsh republican and an admirer of small independent nations worldwide, Morris harbors a fondness for the pageantry and grandeur, even the arrogance, of the now-passed British Empire.

I first met Jan in 1992 at a travel writers conference, held at a bookstore near San Francisco. She gave a delightful keynote address that began with a lighthearted story about pilfering the hotel's washcloth and using it as a handkerchief, and then thrilled the audience with her tales of intrigue and discovery. At the conference's final lunch, Jan sat with the bookstore's owner and the travel editor of the *San Francisco Examiner*. One chair remained vacant at their table. As I diffidently approached, they all welcomed me, a great thrill, and I listened as they discussed Apsley Cherry-Garrard's *The Worst Journey in the World*. The second time I sat down to lunch with Jan, twelve years later in Wales, I told her how appreciative I was to be included then. "Well, we didn't really mean it," Jan said with her classic wry humor. "We probably said, 'Oh, no, here comes another one.'"

Despite Jan's cautionary note about getting to her home, the journey to Wales went smoothly. During the six-hour train ride from London, I marveled at the mortarless stone walls of Wales and watched just-born lambs scamper across spring-green hills. Upon arrival in the old slate port of Porthmadog, in the long shadow of Y Wyddfa (Mount Snowdon), a couple of kindly women helped me find my way. "Take a right at Woolies," they said, and when I reached the Woolworth store I did just that and found the tidy B&B where I had a reservation.

As I read Morris's *A Writer's House in Wales* in my room, someone knocked on my door. It was the ever-hospitable Jan—her phone was out so she came by to say she'd pick me up tomorrow, show me nearby Portmeirion (a fanciful Italianate village designed by an architect friend of hers), and then we'd go to her home for the interview.

Morris's home is down a narrow country lane fronted by a sign reading "This is a Welsh speaking district." The River Dwyfor sings sweetly nearby; a proud stuffed red kite, magnificent in its tawny plumage, casts a watchful gaze over the living area; and the eighteenth-century stone walls promise protection from the capricious outside world. During the interview, conducted in the presence of the forty-some volumes Morris has authored, Ibsen made himself comfortable on top of my Cordura briefcase. When we finished talking, Jan, an avowed cat-lover, said, "I hope Ibsen's not still on your bag," and before I could finish saying he'd moved, she continued, "because if he was I wouldn't let you move it!"

Afterward, Jan gave me a quick tour of the sturdy house with its models of old slate ships, drawings of Venice, and two bronze busts, one of herself and one of Admiral Jacky Fisher, about whom she wrote a biography and with whom she plans to have an affair in the afterlife. In her library she showed me a rare edition of E. M. Forster's *Alexandria*, number 129 of only 250 printed, and an ancient volume of Alexander Kinglake's *Eothen*, "my favorite travel book."

Elizabeth, who is as warm and kind as Jan says in her books, joined us for lunch at a Portmeirion restaurant. Elizabeth slipped off to pay the check before it arrived at the table, thwarting my plan to pick up the tab. When I thanked Elizabeth, Jan chimed in: "I must say, it is a joint account." Before dropping me back in Porthmadog, Jan and Elizabeth took me to Borth-y-Gest, a broad crescent beach where the slate-hauling ships were built. Across the bay a white house gleamed in the late-afternoon sun. "That's where Bertrand Russell lived," Jan said.

As I bade them farewell, Elizabeth helped me with my jacket and I remarked on her kindness. "Fifty years of that," Jan said, "what could be better?" I offered some parting words of thanks. "Shall I give Ibsen your love?" Jan scolded in a tone of whimsical reproach. As they zipped away, Jan's hand popped out of her Honda's sunroof with a final wave, a gesture embodying all the warm hospitality of Jan, Elizabeth, and, I could easily imagine, just about everyone in Wales.

≈≈≈

You started as a journalist—would you talk about how journalism shaped your later work and your life as a writer?

I cheated really, because it was journalism but I only worked for two newspapers, one was *The Times*, the other was then the *Manchester Guardian*, now *The Guardian*. Both these papers were very civilized broadsheets, and they soon realized that I wasn't much good at plain reportage and I was much better at writing sort of essays. So I did that. I was a foreign correspondent for both of them, but I used to send dispatches back more or less in essay form. Although in some ways I regret having started in newspapers, in other ways I think that was quite good for me.

I thought, in those days, that going into newspapers was the entry into literature, largely on American examples, like Hemingway and Steinbeck. I was wrong. I think if I hadn't gone into newspapers, I'd have probably gone into the writing of fiction, which would have changed the whole course of my life really. But as it was, because of these two liberally-minded newspapers, I was able to interpret journalism as a form of literature, a lesser form, but still a form of literature.

One of the big scoops you had was from Mount Everest. You accompanied John Hunt's expedition, with Edmund Hillary. Could you say what that was like at the time? I think it's hard to understand today how important that was.

When you say one of the scoops, it was the only scoop I ever had (laughs). It had a totally different meaning for everybody. You must remember that 1953 was the time when the British Empire was dispersing—it was the end of the empire. It wasn't altogether finished, but the imperial sensations and the excitement of ruling the world had left the British. So there was a sort of flatness in the air, and the nation was pretty depressed in many ways, economically it wasn't prospering. The grand pride of the war had faded rather. So when a British expedition climbed the highest mountain in the world after so many years of trying—it was a great boost to the national ego. It was different from going to the moon because America didn't need such a boost—the British did. So that meant a lot.

And it was the end of a whole era of terrestrial exploration. Finally, just sort of allegorically, it so happened that it coincided with the coronation of the present Queen of England. The British especially, and to some extent the world, thought this was the kind of totem of a new start for the flagging old British Empire. They thought of it as a new Elizabethan age that had sort of a glamour for everybody, not just for the British. It had sort of a Shakespearian feel. And this news arrived in London on the very evening before the coronation of the queen, which was an immense pageant in those days with gilded carriages and cavalry. It was exciting and glamorous and romantic and the whole world felt it, too. So that's why it meant more than it would mean now.

Would you say a bit about your part in it? Almost as heroic as the ascent, in a small way, was your descent to get the news to London in time.

It may seem heroic because I wrote the book about it. It wasn't heroic, but it was sort of romantic because I was up at Camp IV in the Western Cwm when Hillary and Tenzing came down, and we had no way of knowing whether they'd got to the top or not. I met them in the Cwm and got the story. And then it occurred to me that if I could get down the mountain that night, I could get the news back to London just in time to hit the coronation, which would add a gloss to it all, wouldn't it?

So one of the climbers, Mike Westmacott, volunteered to come with me. We staggered out into the night; it was getting dark. And it was a long way down—it was fairly heroic, it was! And so I stumbled and staggered down, falling over the whole time, and once saying, "Oh let's give up," until he pulled me on. And so eventually, long after dark, we did get down to base camp. There, I wrote a dispatch.

The problem was getting the news back to London. Most of the time I had sent it by runner to the nearest telegraph station. But I did know that there was an Indian Army radio post quite near us. I had persuaded them that if there was one really vital message from the mountain, that they would send it for me to Kathmandu and then it would get on to London.

I knew I didn't dare tell them what the message meant because they would certainly have spread it around the world, and I would have lost my scoop as you kindly call it. And so I'd arranged a code beforehand for this very contingency, which merely said who had got to the summit, and whether everybody was O.K., and so on. So I wrote this short dispatch and sent it by one of my Sherpa runners down to this radio post that was about thirty or forty miles away, to ask them to send it, which they did without knowing what it meant—it seemed to mean the opposite. And that did get back to London.

The Times, being in those days a civilized newspaper, could have sat on it until the latest edition so that no other newspaper would have got it. But in their gentlemanly way they put it in the first edition so that every other paper was able to pick it up for their second editions. It's rather funny, *The Times* was entirely anonymous then so I didn't even get a byline (laughs). Nor was it on the front page because *The Times* in those days didn't print news on the front page—it was all small ads. They just put a little tiny headline in the top right corner saying, "Everest Climbed." Those were the days.

But when it did get into the papers it truly was a cause for great rejoicing, not only in England but around the world. It gave great pleasure to people, I'm sure.

I can only imagine the kind of pageantry and exhilaration of all of that coming together. That must be gratifying.

Fun, more than gratifying—I enjoyed it very much.

Aside from the members of the expedition, you were the only one who knew Everest's summit had been reached. Was that as cool as it seems, to be one of the few people on the planet who knew?

It was a good feeling, I enjoyed it very much indeed. Especially being up there in that rarefied atmosphere which heightened that feeling: Wow, I'm the only one! And tomorrow, I'll give it to the world. I was young you know.

Let's move on to America in the mid-'50s. You traveled around quite extensively with your family.

Actually, I began traveling around the U.S. with an Everest lecture tour; four climbers came over and since I was in America already, they invited me. They thought by then—I'd been there about a month—they thought I must be an enormous expert on everything American. So they invited me to take part, which took me all over America, and then my family came over and joined me. I had a fellowship to spend the whole year traveling, and made my first book.

Of course that was Coast to Coast. *Would you talk a little bit about the mentality in America at that time? You've said it was "the apex of American happiness."*

Part of it was contrasts. I'd come from Europe, which at that time was still pretty depressed after the war. The whole continent was pretty shabby and drab and sort of demoralized, and tired really, very tired after all those exertions. Rationing, I think, was still going, the lights kept going out, all of it. So to come to America, which had prospered greatly from the war and was in the height of victorious celebrations still—they felt, with some reason, that they'd won the war—we thought so, too. It felt young and happy and vibrant: people were very pleased with themselves in a generous sort of way. I loved it—it was a marvelous time to come to America. People who remember it share this feeling with me, that it was a wonderful moment in American history, with reason. They'd done well, and they bore themselves with a becoming mixture of self-congratulation and modesty. I thought it was wonderful.

The purpose of the fellowship was to bring young European people over to America and indoctrinate them with pro-Americanness. And for me it certainly worked, didn't it? You couldn't have chosen a better moment. I would have been tempted at the end of the year to stay on in America, but it so happens that a predecessor on the same fellowship had done just that—he'd never gone home—he stayed in America and lived there ever after. And so they put in a rule that you had to go back to Europe after you finished your fellowship. The guy who had done this was Alistair Cooke, but he fulfilled their purposes, too, didn't he, because he became the spokesman for America in Europe, certainly in Britain, and to some degree the other way around.

Twenty years later, I thought that when Alistair Cooke retired, I am the best person to succeed him. And I think it was true, I was really. I thought I'd hang around for a bit and see if it happens. But I've been hanging around ever since—he retired last week! I've just written a piece about the funny thing of waiting for a job until you're so old yourself you can't do it, and he's still at it. [Alistair Cooke died in New York on March 30, 2004, three weeks after this interview was conducted.]

When you were touring with your latest book, The World, *you made a comment about the American Empire, and you said, "Don't worry—yours will subside too." Do you feel that the American Empire is subsiding now?*

Yes, visibly. Morally, certainly. I suppose economically and politically, probably not. But the rot is setting in. And a good thing, too. Hubris has most clearly set in and hubris is the precursor of the end. I think it's gone too far, but then I think the whole democratic capitalist system has gone too far. There's too much of everything.

Too much capitalism or too much democracy?

Both. It isn't working very well, is it? I know Churchill always said that democracy was an awful system, but that there wasn't anything as good. And there is that, but at the moment if you look at the democracies, by and large they don't seem to be pursuing the aim of human happiness very successfully. And so one has to wonder if it is necessarily the right system. In America, particularly, it's assumed that it is the right system, that it's the end of all, is it not?

I think it's assumed that it's the only system a civilized society should have.

That's right, and I think that's debatable. I was reminded this morning by a magazine in New York that I had said some time ago that I thought it was time the world ended and made a fresh start. And I do rather feel that as a matter of fact. I think the world's tired of itself and sick of itself and things aren't working. Maybe it's a moment like the end of the dinosaurs. I think it ought to be—I'd be very happy if some immense convulsion came and put an end to it all. But that's easy to say when you're my age, I know.

What about your kids and grandkids? What about your hopes for them?

Tough luck. They wouldn't know—the dinosaurs didn't know after all, did they? Sometimes I seriously wonder whether people bringing babies into the world now can truly be happy about doing so. Are they going to live in a happy world? Is life going to be agreeable for them? I expect people have said this down the generations, don't you?

That's exactly what my father said to me when I told him I didn't think we were going to have children. He said look at history—he was born in 1929 and he talked about the Depression and went on to talk about what life must have been like during the plagues or during the great wars. I think every era feels its problems are the worst.

But nevertheless we have to express what we feel.

Let's talk about Wales. This is clearly your home and it's clearly your element.

The reason I stay here is that I like it. I've never envied expatriates. I believe in communities. I no longer believe in the nation-state, but I do believe in the nation-community. And Wales is sort of family-sized as nations go. I know an awful lot of people in Wales, and my son knows more than I do. There's nowhere we go where we can't meet friends and feel at home. That's one reason I like it.

Another reason is I admire it very much. I think it's wonderful that this little country sitting here beside what was the greatest nation on earth and is now a surrogate for the present greatest nation on earth, so an Anglo-American civilization is pressing on us all the time, and has been pressing on Wales for several centuries, and yet the little country seems to have survived and kept its soul and spirit. I've always liked rear-guard actions. This is one of the longest rear-guard actions in history, and it's still being fought with some success. I find that romantic and attractive and aesthetically pleasant to take part in.

And I like the nature of the Welsh civilization, which is basically very kind—it's not very ambitious or thrusting. It's based upon things like poetry and music, which are still very deeply rooted in this culture. And I love the look of the country—it's extremely beautiful and changes so much. It's so small and has so many different visual pleasures. I like to live in surroundings that excite me, and these do.

Finally, I like to live in Wales partly because we're so near other places, not only one of the world's great cities, London, down the road, but also the whole of Europe. I jump in my car and I'm in Paris or Brussels or anywhere else you'd like to mention. I'm going next week to Burgundy. I just jump in the car, go through the tunnel, and I'm in Burgundy—isn't that wonderful?

So you like to drive mostly, as opposed to flying or taking the train—you just take the car?

I do when I can, but from time to time I like the train journey because you can work at the same time.

Does having such a strong foundation here in Wales make it easier to go all over the world?

Yes, I used to say I have one foot in Llanystumdwy and one in Manhattan. I do like to have a firm base here. I'm homesick all the time when traveling, but as long as I know this is here, it cheers me up. That's why I've never envied expatriates—they're always so pleased with themselves, but I'm always sorry for them. I think, Good god, you poor things.

Do you feel they're lost in a way?

I do, but they don't, so that's all right. I'm made to be rooted.

In A Writer's House in Wales, *you write, "I live, though, in a Wales of my own, a Wales in the mind, grand with high memories, poignant with melancholy. It is in that Wales, that imperishable Wales, that my house prospers." So your house is very much of its setting and you're very much of your setting.*

Yes, but it's partly, as I said, the imagination. We create our own worlds as we go along. And I invented this one a long time ago, and I'm sticking to it (laughs).

What are your hopes and concerns for the future of Wales and Welsh culture?

My chief hope for Wales is that it can become a truly independent, bilingual, equal member of a confederal Europe; my chief fear, that before that can come about, its identity and its culture will be swamped by the inexorable influx of English settlers, who bring with them all their own habits and customs, and may well extinguish Welshness and the Welsh language by sheer force of numbers.

Your writing is so personal—you've even said it's "egobiography." Have you always approached cities as a mirror in which you see yourself?

Well that's grown on me, and not always in a very attractive way. I got more and more thinking about myself—I got a bit tired of myself—and I began to realize that all these books I've written have been largely about myself, but less so in the early years because the world was fresher to me then. It was more interesting and so I could stand back and look at it more, but now as the years have gone by, it's more and more my own feelings when I'm in the city and less and less about the city itself. And it's gone too far in the end, I think.

So in my last book [*Trieste and the Meaning of Nowhere*], I frankly recognized that the city I was writing about was how I thought of myself. I saw myself in the city, and as a city really, and the city as me. Then I thought, Well this really has gone a bit far—you're going a bit nuts here about this—you better give up. So I didn't write any more books.

You still have a lot left in you. You seem healthy, vital, sharp. Why would you want to say that was your last book? Who knows how you're going to feel in a year?

I don't want to publish any more books. I might write more books. But I don't want to publish any more books, partly because I think the Trieste book was my best book. I don't think I can do better than that, and I don't want to start doing worse. That's partly it, and partly because I carry this identification with place a bit too far. When you begin to see a city as you, I think it's come far enough. I could only do it with Trieste.

The last time I saw you speak at a bookshop, you talked about leaving a manuscript under the stairs to be discovered later.

Absolutely, that's it, and flogged to Random House for a billion dollars!

Let's talk about the spirit of place, because when you started writing you did something different from most people who wrote about place. It wasn't, here's what you'll find in New York and this is what Venice looks like, it was more impressionistic. Would you talk a little bit about how you convey the spirit of a place?

I very rarely tried to describe a place. I was only talking about its effect upon me. So what you call the spirit of the place is the spirit of the confrontation between two forces, the city itself and the writer. I didn't do that consciously, but I do realize that's what it is. And that's why it doesn't feel like, and isn't in my opinion, travel writing.

But as to the spirit of the place, I have several rules: one is to grin like a dog and run about the city. Another thing is from E. M. Forster, who wrote an alleged guidebook to Alexandria. He said the way to look at Alexandria is to wander aimlessly around and to have all your antennae out in all directions so that nothing, absolutely nothing, is uninteresting. I've written that I don't mind going to the dentist in a foreign city because it's bound to be interesting. It might not cure the toothache, but it gives you something for the essay you're writing. So that is my technique for getting the spirit of the city, just to be absolutely open to it in every way. And it is fun because if you're in the mood, absolutely nothing is boring, nothing at all. Think of the most boring thing you can—what's the most boring thing?

Going to the motor vehicles bureau.

That would do—I'd like it very much. I'm sure I'd get material out of it.

You alluded to your smile test—what have you found by grinning at people in different cities?

Oh, that's a very useful device indeed, though unnerving for the recipient. But it's true that if you smile deliberately at people, their responses are very revealing because they show every degree of confidence, or shyness, or self-doubt, inhibition, all things which can be extrapolated not only into a civic meaning but even into a national meaning if you're rash enough to do it.

I began it in Vancouver which was a lovely city really, but very unassertive and very unconfident—it was then anyway. One particular response I'm always sympathetic to is this: sometimes when you see a person smiling at you, you're pleased, but you're not necessarily certain it's intended for you. It might be for somebody behind your back. And that shows a nice tendency, because you don't want to be so presumptuous to think they are smiling at you when they might not be. The Vancouver people seemed to carry that particular attitude to extremes. They never thought you were smiling at them and so they didn't know quite what to do, what their response ought to be. That's very revealing about Canada, not only about Vancouver.

You cite Lawrence Durrell's quotation, "I imagine, therefore I possess." Is that an attitude you've adopted toward cities as well: you've created these evocative descriptions of cities so they become yours?

Yes, they do, not only cities really, but the relationship between imagination and truth is something that has always interested me. I said somewhere that even imaginary love could be true, and some critics said this is a lot of balls. But I stand by it. I think if you imagine something very strongly, that is a reality isn't it?

Don Quixote, my master, he lived his life for that, didn't he? He imagined things which he knew weren't true on the normal level of truth, but they became true for him as he believed the whole chivalric thing. He knew it was nonsense, but nevertheless it had become true for him, and he lived by it, too, even though it was an entirely fictional way of life. And I agree with him. If you've thought about a city so long and you've made another entity of it by making a book of it, then in a way it is yours.

Let's talk about Oxford and Venice. They seem to be cities that have really touched you.

That's true, in a different way from Trieste. Oxford I have known all my life—as a child I went to what we call a prep school in Oxford when I was very small. I went back as an undergraduate, and now I'm a fellow of my old college there. So it's meant something to me all through my life. It's always seemed to be an epitome of England, an England that was lost before I was born, but which in Oxford has sort of survived, still lamely struggling on. It's based upon an old idea of England, which is sort of ornery but bloody-minded, romantic, elitist, all those things which I rather like (laughs), but which have gone out of fashion a bit. Rear-guard actions again, I like the way Oxford has managed to make those things survive in itself. So that's what Oxford has always meant to me, and I still love going there.

Venice is a different kettle of fish altogether because my response to Venice has been the same from the very first moment I set eyes on it. I think it's just marvelous. For my money it's the greatest of human artifacts. I think of it as one artifact, the best thing mankind has made. The worst thing mankind has made is Auschwitz, but the most beautiful place that's ever been on earth is Venice, and luckily so far it remains that way. When I first saw it, I was perfectly dazzled by it and I've never lost that. The scales have never dropped from my eyes. Every time I go, I get the same feeling exactly.

I think the happiest book I wrote is the book about Venice—that's the one that breathes a spirit of happiness for me, and it seems to have breathed happiness to people ever since. I'm still hearing from people who read *Venice* and take it with them to Venice on successive visits. But when I get one of these letters I think, gosh, that must be a good book, and then I take it out of there and have a look. But I don't think it seems all that good. As a matter of fact, the only thing I like about it is the feeling of happiness.

Oxford made me…. For near the heart of the Oxford ethos lies the grand and comforting truth that there is no norm. We are all different; none of us is *entirely* wrong; to understand is to forgive.

—JAN MORRIS, *Conundrum*

On the one hand you express deep admiration for places like Wales and their rear-guard actions, but you also maintain a fondness for empire, for pageantry, and maybe for England as it was a century ago when it was at the height of its powers.

Well it's true. I don't mind being self-contradictory, not a bit. The chief intellectual focus of my life has been the British Empire. I never believed in the principle of empire, ever. But I was aesthetically seduced by it—I like the swagger of it; I like style of it.

The confidence?

The confidence, even the arrogance. Fortunately I wasn't subject to it—I was writing after the event, but I saw the end of it, of course. In a way I took part in the end of it.

Are you referring to being in Hong Kong in 1997 when the British left?

No, no, long before that. I'm thinking of the army. I covered the retreat of the empire for years and years. I was attracted artistically by the decline, too, the creeping melancholy that came in, and the poignancy. And not least the contrast between the great, pompous, splashy days of Victorian supremacy and the Diamond Jubilee and all that stuff. And then the wars came, and gradually the whole thing went sour and got sadder and sadder. The British themselves lost their taste for empire, and the subject peoples realized what it was.

I liked watching that and trying to describe it, and trying, I hope, to feel what both sides felt about it. I hope I wasn't a sucker for empire. And my empire was the empire that ended with the death of Churchill. I wrote *fini* for it then.

The subject is a marvelous subject, especially as it's ended. I prefer writing about things that end, and that's why Venice has particularly appealed to me because it doesn't end. It's the one city that really stays more or less the same. All other cities that I've written about: Hong Kong, even Oxford, Manhattan—the one book about Manhattan that I still like is *Manhattan '45*, where I chose a particular year in the past so it wasn't going to be overtaken.

I imagine this comes up in almost every interview: you started life as a male and exulted in one of the greatest masculine journeys of all time, the ascent of Everest. Now you've spent the second half of your life as a woman. Could we talk about this in terms of your writing and in terms of how or if it's affected your view of the world?

I don't know. I have no idea—other people say it has affected the prose, but I don't notice it myself. When I did this book [*The World*, a collection of previously published articles spanning Morris's career], I honestly can't see much difference between the prose at the beginning and at the end. As you get older your experience widens in every way, and it's hard to know how much of that is simply age and how much is the difference between genders. Of course I changed, but I would have changed anyway.

I was struck by two things when I read Coast to Coast, *first that it was so clearly you. You could have given me that book without a cover and I would have said: No question, this is Jan Morris. The second thing was that there's a certain ease to it. It almost seems like you came into this world as a writer, and you've said that it's not hard for you to write. You hear many writers say that they struggle and sweat blood, but you're one of the few I've met who says, I just do it—it comes naturally.*

We had a relative called E. V. Lucas who was sort of a belletrist of the 1920s. My grandfather rather despised him and used to say, Ah well, E.

V. Lucas, he'd be a good writer if he'd only suffered a bit. His life had been so easy. And I have to say sometimes when I pick up one of his books, they do remind me of me. There's a feeling that he never had to try terribly hard; it came naturally to him. I've always enjoyed writing, but I suspect I'd be a much better writer if I'd had to struggle a bit more.

Haven't you had struggles in your life?

Not artistically, no.

But aren't human struggles a crucible for your development as a person which helps you become a better writer?

I don't know. I've always felt them to be separate, oddly enough, in the same way that I've felt that my judgment has been separate from my description. For example, what I felt about the rightness or wrongness of the empire was separate from how I felt it aesthetically was. And maybe they [the *Pax Britannica* books] would be better, too, if I had managed to combine the two more. But there we are—you take me or leave me.

People have said to me, we've so much enjoyed these empire books, but we don't quite understand how, if you disapprove of the idea of empire, which as a Welsh nationalist I must, how you managed to make the whole thing so happy. And that's the reason, that the two sides of me are separate.

That gets back to journalism. Is your ability in Pax Britannica *to look objectively at empire, separate from your Welsh identity, is that something you learned as a journalist, to keep your personal viewpoints out of the scholarly work, or does it just come naturally?*

It just came naturally. I've never been very analytical, especially about writing. I just wrote—that's what my life has been really. That should be my epitaph: She just wrote.

Is that what you would choose?

I've only thought of it now.

It's getting shorter—I recall an epitaph in A Writer's House in Wales *that was three lines.*

Now it's three words, yes (laughs).

You've written that since your childhood you've felt different or separate or outside.

That gets you back to *Conundrum*, and that hasn't been a bad thing on the whole. This is so maddening, isn't it, that everything comes back and seems quite happy to me. It would be much more interesting if I said, "Oh, I've suffered so much from being an outsider." But I never did. I'm quite proud of being different. It may be sometimes a bit lonely I suppose. All this I've expressed best in the Trieste book, which is a much more autobiographical book than any of the other things I've written, even the most overtly autobiographical.

In Conundrum, *you say on your fortieth birthday, "What a wonderful life I've had." I thought: What an optimistic viewpoint, because* you had written about feeling lonely, struggling, not content with your gender. Yet you still felt you'd had a wonderful life.

For thirty years our gravestone, awaiting the day, has stood amidst the almost impenetrable muddle of boxes, papers, duplicate copies and long-discarded children's toys that is under the library stairs.... *Here are two friends, Jan & Elizabeth Morris, At the end of one life.* And if our ashes blow in the wayward wind beside the river, I am sure our spirits will often wander up to Trefan Morys itself, wishing whoever lives here after us, through every generation, happiness if they honor the house and its Welshness, ignominy if they don't.

—Jan Morris,
A Writer's House in Wales

Yes, it's true because there have been anxieties and worries, but nevertheless, on balance I'd rather have had this life than any other.

So how does the second half of your life compare to the first?

I hesitate to say because it gets better and better. It comes out smug though doesn't it?

No, it sounds genuine.

I'm grateful for it. Of course it's very largely due to her [Jan's partner Elizabeth]. That has been a constant in my life and has saved me from a lot of the worries that would have been much more crippling if I hadn't had such a friend as this all these years. We've lived together for well over half a century, and we know each other well.

And she supported you all the way through.

She did—that's the constant, but there's the constant of Wales, too, so I've been very, very lucky. But the more I say this the more conceited and self-satisfied it sounds. I've tried to be more unsatisfied, but I can't make it (laughs). Of course, most of my worries have been about my children. I think that's true of everybody, that people worry much more about their children than they do about themselves. I suffer for them much more than I ever suffer for myself.

Even as a young writer you seemed very confident. You always had faith that you could do what you want.

It's something to do with upbringing, I imagine, but of course the basis of it was the writing. I'm no good at anything else, I'm pretty hopeless at most things, but I always knew that I could write. And I suppose that if you have one thing that you're absolutely confident about, you don't worry too much about the others. You always say, "Well I can't do that, but I can write."

Is there something special about writing? So many people aspire to be writers, and if you have that skill you can understand yourself and understand the world because you can put it into words.

Yes, you know the feeling yourself, don't you? Of course you do, because the whole world is sort of embodied in it. I'm working on Shakespeare now and I constantly marvel at the feeling you get from reading him. It's all there—it's all his. If he cares to tap on one emotion or one geographical aspect, he can do it easy as pie. He just clicks his fingers and out it comes. Wonderful. Shakespeare above all gives one that feeling. And you feel that he just sat down and wrote it, when in fact he probably slaved away over the sentences.

A quick question about process: How much research do you do before going to a city?

Mind you, this is mostly in the past because nowadays there are few cities I go to that I don't know already. But when I was going to cities that were foreign to me, I most distinctly didn't read anything of a literary nature about them. I didn't want to catch other people's attitudes or responses. But I read history before I went, as much as I could, and then when I was there I used guidebooks. When I came home, if I was writing a book especially, I would try and read all around it as well and see what other people thought. But the main thing was to make sure that all the ideas and responses were genuinely my own.

Do you have any advice for aspiring writers, young writers who want to learn from somebody like you?

The only advice I would give is: enjoy it. It's a marvelous thing to write at all, isn't it?

Yes, it's a privilege.

It's a terrific thing and it doesn't matter if you don't get published. I've given up wanting to be published. I think the joy of it is in the writing itself. In the feeling that you can bottle this stuff up and think about it and then put it out there, and it exists in front of you on the page. That's the great thing I think, to have written at all. Even writing a letter is an achievement, isn't it? The pleasure of it lies in the aspiration, for my money.

That recalls a comment you made recently: you said you were beyond ambition but not beyond aspiration.

And I agree with it (laughs). But not beyond smugness—that's my weakness really.

Well, I'm not sure that you're smug, but if you are, I feel like you've earned it.

I'm smug inside. These are my books here [the shelves facing us have numerous editions and translations of Morris's forty-some books].

Sometimes I sit here and I think, Wow!, what a wonderful thing to have done. And then I think, You're only thinking about yourself and how marvelous you are.

I think that's O.K. if it's not bragging, to be proud of what you've accomplished. What's wrong with that?

It's bragging to yourself, and perhaps that's even worse than bragging to others. I've never thought of that before, but it might be.

But if you can observe it...

If you can laugh at it, laughter helps doesn't it?

At that travel writers conference when I first met you, I overheard a travel editor saying that people who have achieved tremendous success often profess false modesty, but Jan's not falsely modest. She's not boastful or unduly proud, but she recognizes what she has accomplished.

Oh, that was nice, I hope it's true.

I think it was spot on, as they say here.

Is "spot on" an Anglicism? I thought it was an Australianism.

Well, Australia's just an English penal colony, right?

Absolutely, you're getting the hang of it, aren't you now—you're catching the imperial mood!

In the Trieste book you write about a Fourth World of people, many of whom are travelers, whose only real ambition is kindness. I really like that, because even as a teenager I felt so at home when I traveled and felt such a kinship with the community of people I met on the road and in hostels. You articulated it for me: this is the Fourth World, and these are my people. Would you say a bit about the citizens of that Fourth World?

Well, we all know them. And everybody thinks they're a member of that Fourth World. We know each other, too, do we not? Despite what I say about it's time that the world came to an end, there seems to be just as many citizens of that pseudo nation now as there ever were, perhaps more. That's the sad thing really, there's so much decency; there are so many nice people in the world.

Take America, the best example of it all, really. It's swarming with citizens of the Fourth World, and yet when it's converted into a nation-state, look how it behaves. None of them want to behave like that, but they're sort of sucked into it. But if you get them individually, everybody finds that Americans are extremely decent people. We all know that. I know people here who have never been to America, and they've been brought up on the image of America that it itself projects, unfortunately. They think it's going to be awful, and they go there and find it's enchanting. People are very kind, and ordinary, and nice.

The difference between that false public world and the private world is a very substantial one, and a rather tragic one. So we have to search out our fellow citizens, whatever awful nation-state they happen to live in and realize that we stand above nation-states.

There are people everywhere who form a Fourth World, or a diaspora of their own…. They share with each other, across all the nations, common values of humour and understanding. When you are among them you know you will not be mocked or resented, because they will not care about your race, your faith, your sex, or your nationality, and they suffer fools if not gladly, at least sympathetically. They laugh easily. They are easily grateful. They are never mean…. They are exiles in their own communities, because they are always in a minority, but they form a mighty nation, if they only knew it.

—JAN MORRIS, *Trieste and the Meaning of Nowhere*

Do you see this Fourth World as the hope of the world?

It always was, I suppose. It's *a hope* of the world, short of the dinosaur solution.

You wrote one book about a totally imaginary place, Last Letters from Hav. *Do you see that as a novel, or as an imaginary travelogue, or does the label even matter?*

I thought it was a novel, but it came after a period of uncharacteristic modesty because I began to realize that I had written lots of books about cities and that I rarely got the hang of any of them. I didn't really get to the depths—I don't know who could have, but I didn't. So I thought I'd write a book in which somebody, me really, goes to a city and gets more and more confused by what's going on until in the end the reader is confused. It ends with an unexplained mystery and so you're left in the air, as I began to think I was being left in the air by all these cities I was writing about. So it was a sort of self-allegory, also it was fun to do. There's a lot of Trieste in it.

Have you ever received correspondence asking where it was?

Lots of people wrote to say, "Where is it?" The extreme example was the Royal Geographic Society map room wrote and asked me where it was.

Would you say you've had to make any sacrifices to pursue this life, being away so much, traveling so much?

The only one is the homesick business—that has been a slight problem with me. On the other hand, I'm footloose. If I'm here too long I want to go away. Otherwise the only sacrifice that I made…I suppose if I had stayed in journalism I could be a great deal richer than I am, but I don't count that as a sacrifice.

You use the Welsh term hiraeth *(yearning) in your writing. What are you yearning for? I believe you say you're not a religious person, but I wonder, are you yearning for a connection with the divine?*

I don't know what religious means. Sometimes I say I'm a pagan or an agnostic or a pantheistic pagan. But I suppose everybody must be religious in some way; even atheism is a sort of religion isn't it? I certainly like things that do have an end. The empire had an end; I like things to be neatly packaged. My life has been a consciously rounded life which I hope to end aesthetically in some way.

The yearning, the *hiraeth*, is by definition a longing for something you don't know what it is, just a bit like *deja vu*. You always feel there's something more over there. Maybe it is a yearning for the divine. Fortunately, I always feel I'm going to find it. But these are mystic feelings rather than religious feelings. And they're almost indefinable feelings, which is why I fall back upon that particular word, *hiraeth*, which has no English equivalent.

But religious yes. I'm religious, but that doesn't mean I go to church. But I think about it, only a fool wouldn't think about it. It has nothing to do with the afterlife—I don't know what the afterlife will be if there is an afterlife. That's the one mystery that we can't solve.

You were just talking about endings a moment ago and you've witnessed the ending of James Morris in a way. Does that give you any perspective?

No, because it's a blur. People always think I went to bed one night as a male and woke up the next morning as a female. It was nothing as simplistic as that. It's partly the body, partly the spirit, the gradual movement from one to the other. So, no, I don't think that's a good analogy you've produced.

O.K., we'll scratch that one then. Is there anything you'd like to share about what you've learned about human nature or about the world by such extensive travel throughout more than fifty years?

The only lesson I've learned from a lifetime of wandering is that on the whole people are decent. That's the conclusion I've reached. If they aren't, it's usually because something has happened to make them not decent. So I don't believe in the original sin; I believe in original virtue, as a matter of fact. That's a rather profound conclusion, isn't it?

Afterword

When I began working on this book, I felt a little like Tom Sawyer rounding up his friends to paint his fence. Though I didn't charge anyone a dime to be part of *A Sense of Place*, I felt like I was profiting from these authors' words, without offering much in return except some small gifts. Yet as I progressed with the interviews, several authors told me how pleased they were to be included in this book, and that they appreciated the recognition of their contributions as writers.

Early on, I thought *A Sense of Place* would be about travel writing. My goal was to seek advice from the masters about how aspiring and working writers could develop their skills. But it quickly became much more: a set of linked biographies, a collection of thoughts on human nature, a multi-faceted view of the world at the dawn of the twenty-first century.

The travels for this book became a pilgrimage, and a way to honor the writers who have expanded my horizons, stoked my hunger for exploration, and enhanced my appreciation of this wonderfully diverse world. When I realized I was on a pilgrimage, I did my best to remain open to receive whatever gifts might come my way. Looking back, I feel that I've been showered with offerings, and in creating this book I've sought to share these gifts with the global community of travelers, writers, and readers, especially, as Jan Morris so eloquently puts it in her Trieste book, the Fourth World.

I also had a heck of a lot of fun. So many wonderful moments come to mind: Morris showing me her guest book and the intricate drawings she added under the names of the visitors to her Welsh home; walking through the snow on the Dartmouth campus and joking around with Bill Bryson; enjoying pasta and bay laurel liqueur at midday in Cortona with Frances and Ed Mayes; bouncing over a rutted dirt road behind the wheel of Tim Cahill's pickup truck and learning the proper way to wave at oncoming drivers, (just lift one finger slightly off the top of the wheel, anything more enthusiastic and they'll know you're a tourist).

Not coincidentally, many of these memorable moments occurred when the tape stopped rolling. During the first few interviews I constantly checked my recorder. But I soon realized what I was missing—a wistful look in Eric Newby's eyes, the rueful smile of Jonathan Raban as he puffed thoughtfully on his cigar, the emotional depth of a life fully lived revealed in Isabel Allende's compassionate expressions—and I began to give my attention to these details.

My meetings with these authors gave me an even greater appreciation for books. Though I grew up in a tradition that reveres texts, and I can recall my grandfather kissing a prayer book that accidentally fell to the synagogue floor, my travels have deepened my respect for the written word. When I heard Redmond O'Hanlon recall his traveling companion, Manou (described so eloquently in *Congo Journey*), who just wanted a book, any book, I realized anew how fortunate I am to be able to walk into my favorite bookstore and have thousands of volumes to choose from.

These conversations reminded me of the traveler's responsibility. It's virtually impossible for most people in the developing world to leave their countries, for financial or political reasons, so it's incumbent upon us, the "rich relatives of the human family" as Brad Newsham says, to travel abroad and give something back. Pico Iyer reminded me how much it means to someone in Burma or Cuba to simply meet a traveler from the United States or Europe, and how important that connection can be for local and visitor alike.

As the journey continued, I began to see more links among the writers I chose to include in this book. (A word on my selections: it's a highly personal list. I chose writers whose work has had a profound impact on me, and whom I simply love to read.) Simon Winchester, the first author I interviewed, cited Jan Morris as a mentor. Paul Theroux compared his writing style to that of Raban and O'Hanlon and the late Bruce Chatwin. At the end of Raban's *Passage to Juneau* he writes a letter to his friend Paul, which on second reading I recognized as Theroux.

As I re-read Bryson's *A Walk in the Woods*, I came across a line where Bryson writes that Indians would "porcupine" a grizzly bear with arrows. A few years ago my editor at the *San Francisco Chronicle*,

John Flinn, cited this as an example of a colorful verb, and Flinn used it in a story about donating a kidney to his wife, saying physicians were "porcupining" their arms with needles. I vaguely recalled seeing "porcupine" somewhere else, but it wasn't until I went back to O'Hanlon's *Into the Heart of Borneo* that I found O'Hanlon fearing his traveling companion James might get "porcupined about the rear with poison darts." So, to bring it all back home, I used "porcupine" as a verb in the introduction to my conversation with O'Hanlon.

As I traveled from place to place, I wondered: How much do these great travelers and writers care about where they live? As frequent travelers, is their home important, or is travel their priority? I found that all the writers profiled in these pages care very much about where they live, and that each is shaped in some way by the places, exterior as well as interior, they've chosen to call home. Tim Cahill said it best when he cited a weightlifting expression: "You can't shoot a cannon from a canoe."

I especially appreciate how several writers have named their houses. The O'Hanlons reside in Pelican House, Jan Morris lives in Trefan Morys, and Frances Mayes's Tuscan home is aptly called Bramasole, yearning for the sun. Such personalization gives these houses a presence and enhances their personality, an acknowledgment that a home is a being in its own right.

Appreciating the sense of place these authors feel has led me to think that someday soon, I'd like my wife and me to have a place of our own. Maybe we'll even give it a name. Yet I can also hear the roar of the road. There's a fascinating world out there that we've barely begun to explore. Our desire to put down roots has grown stronger, but I think that can wait just a bit longer. It's time to dust off our backpacks and go.

—Michael Shapiro

Appreciations

This section is typically called Acknowledgments which connotes recognition. But I want to do more than recognize all the people who have helped *A Sense of Place* come to fruition, I want to express my gratitude; thus, Appreciations seems a more apt title.

First and foremost, I'd like to thank all the writers who participated in this project. Every single author I asked consented to an interview. It is their words that make this book so compelling. And many of them went above and beyond: Frances and Ed Mayes surprised me by meeting me at the train station near Cortona and took me to lunch. Jan Morris showed me around Portmeirion and Borth-y-Gest in Wales and she, too, invited me to lunch. And Tim Cahill told me to save my motel money and spend the night on his couch. These are just a few examples of the kindness and generosity of the writers profiled in this book.

I'd also like to express my gratitude to the people who helped along the way. My friends Gary and Emma Schwartz gave me a base in London and their eighteen-month-old son Joshua was kind enough to share his room. Jeff Booth and his wife Francesca put me up for a night in Italy, and my ninety-seven-year-old grandfather Stanley Kreutzer on Long Island was always happy to share his apartment and loan me his car.

The talented team at Travelers' Tales deserves the utmost appreciation. Executive Editor Larry Habegger and Publisher James O'Reilly helped give this book shape and hone the list of authors. Our ongoing dialogue during the project kept refining and improving the material. To Susan Brady, Director of Production, I extend my utmost gratitude for keeping us all on track; and to Krista Holmstrom, Senior Publicist, thanks in advance for all your promotional efforts.

Warm thanks to John Flinn, Executive Editor of the *San Francisco Chronicle* travel section, who helped me reach Bill Bryson and Redmond O'Hanlon. And a special appreciation to Elaine and Bill

Petrocelli, owners of Book Passage, the San Francisco Bay Area bookstore that holds an annual travel writers' conference where I've taught for five years and where I've met many of the authors interviewed in this book.

Finally, to my extended family, some related by blood and all connected by love, who kept me going during a very difficult year. To my parents, Phyllis and Larry, and my brother Andy, who always encouraged me to keep moving forward. And to my wife Willow, my foundation through the vicissitudes of life. Thank you.

Acknowledgments

Selection from "North Pole the Easy Way" by Tim Cahill excerpted from *Pass the Butterworms: Remote Journeys Oddly Rendered* by Tim Cahill. Copyright © 1997 by Tim Cahill. Reprinted by permission of Vintage Departures, an imprint of Random House, Inc.

Selection from "Exotic Places Made Me Do It" by Tim Cahill excerpted from the March 2002 issue of *Outside*. Copyright © 2002 by Tim Cahill. Reprinted by permission of the author.

Selection from "The Entranced Duck" by Tim Cahill excerpted from *Hold the Enlightenment* by Tim Cahill. Copyright © 2002 by Tim Cahill. Reprinted by permission of Villard Books, a division of Random House.

Selections from *Under the Tuscan Sun: At Home in Italy* by Frances Mayes copyright © 1996 by Frances Mayes. Reprinted by permission of Broadway Books, a division of Bantam Doubleday Dell Publishing Group, Inc.

Selection from *Bella Tuscany: The Sweet Life* in Italy by Frances Mayes copyright © 1999 by Frances Mayes. Reprinted by permission of of Broadway Books, a division of Bantam Doubleday Dell Publishing Group, Inc.

Selection from *Hunting Mr. Heartbreak: A Discovery of America* by Jonathan Raban copyright © 1991 by Jonathan Raban. Reprinted by permission of HarperCollins Publishers.

Selection from *Passage to Juneau: A Sea and Its Meanings* by Jonathan Raban copyright © 1999 by Jonathan Raban. Reprinted by permission of Pantheon Books, a division of Rand House, Inc.

Selection from *In Trouble Again: A Journey Between the Orinoco and the Amazon* by Redmond O'Hanlon copyright © 1990 by Redmond O'Hanlon. Reprinted by permission of Vintage Departures, a division of Random House, Inc.

Selection from *No Mercy: A Journey to the Heart of the Congo* by Redmond O'Hanlon copyright © 1996, 1997 by Redmond O'Hanlon. Reprinted by permission of Vintage Departures, a division of Random House, Inc.

Selection from Editor's Letter from *Arthur Frommer's Budget Travel* reprinted by permission of Arthur Frommer.

Selection from *The Global Soul: Jet Lag, Shopping Malls, and the Search for Home* by Pico Iyer copyright © 2000 by Pico Iyer. Reprinted by permisison of Alfred A. Knopf, a division of Random House, Inc.

Selection from "Why We Travel" by Pico Iyer copyright © by Pico Iyer. Reprinted by permission of Pico Iyer.

Selection from *Falling Off the Map: Some Lonely Places of the World* by Pico Iyer copyright ©1993 by Pico Iyer. Reprinted by permission of Vintage Departures, a division of Random House, Inc.

Selection from *Tropical Classical: Essays from Several Directions* by Pico Iyer copyright © 1997 by Pico Iyer. Reprinted by permission of Alfred A Knopf, a division of Random House, Inc.

Selections from *Rick Steves' Postcards from Europe: 25 Years of Travel Tales from America's Favorite Guidebook Writer* by Rick Steves copyright © 1999 by Rick Steves. Reprinted by permission of John Muir Publications.

Selection from the Introduction by Simon Winchester to *The Best Travelers' Tales 2004* edited by James O'Reilly, Larry Habegger, and Sean O'Reilly copyright © 2004 by Simon Winchester. Reprinted by permission of Simon Winchester and Travelers' Tales Inc.

Selection from *The River at the Center of the World: A Journey Up the Yangtze, and Back in Chinese Time* by Simon Winchester copyright © 1996 by Simon Winchester. Reprinted by permission of Henry Holt and Company.

Selection from *The Size of the World* by Jeff Greenwald copyright © 1995 by Jeff Greenwald. Reprinted by permission of The Globe Pequot Press.

Selection from *Scratching the Surface: Impressions of Planet Earth from Hollywood to Shiraz* by Jeff Greenwald copyright © 2002 by Jeff Greenwald. Reprinted by permission of Naga Books.

Selections from *A Short Walk on the Hindu Kush* by Eric Newby copyright © 1958, 1986 by Eric Newby. Reprinted by permission of Viking Penguin, a division of Penguin Books USA, Inc.

Photograph Credits

Photograph of Tim Cahill used courtesy of Michael Shapiro.
Photograph of Frances Mayes used courtesy of Michael Shapiro.
Photograph of Jonathan Raban used courtesy of Michael Shapiro.
Photograph of Redmond O'Hanlon used courtesy of Michael Shapiro.
Photograph of Isabel Allende used courtesy of Michael Shapiro.
Photograph of Bill Bryson used courtesy of Michael Shapiro.
Photograph of Paul Theroux used courtesy of Greg Martin.
Photograph of Arthur Frommer used courtesy of Michael Shapiro.
Photograph of Pico Iyer used courtesy of Derek Shapton.
Photograph of Rick Steves used courtesy of Michael Shapiro.
Photograph of Simon Winchester used courtesy of Marion Ettlinger.
Photograph of Jeff Greenwald used courtesy of Michael Shapiro.
Photograph of Eric Newby used courtesy of Michael Shapiro.
Photograph of Sara Wheeler used courtesy of Michael Shapiro.
Photograph of Brad Newsham used courtesy of Michael Shapiro.
Photograph of Tom Miller used courtesy of Michael Shapiro.
Photograph of Peter Matthiessen used courtesy of Michael Shapiro.
Photograph of Jan Morris used courtesy of Nigel Hughes.
Photograph of Michael Shapiro by John Burgess.

About the Author

Michael Shapiro is a writer who has bicycled through Cuba for the *Washington Post*, celebrated Holy Week in Guatemala for the *Dallas Morning News*, and floated down the Mekong River on a Laotian cargo barge for an online magazine. He is the author of three books about using the Internet for travel, including *Internet Travel Planner*, and maintains NetTravel.com, a list of top travel sites alongside some of his travel stories.

For four years Shapiro wrote a column for the *San Francisco Chronicle* travel section. His work also appears in the *Los Angeles Times*, *Sunset*, and in Travelers' Tales anthologies. For an investigation into frequent-flier programs, Shapiro won a 1998 Lowell Thomas award from the Society of American Travel Writers. In 1994, he joined O'Reilly & Associates to help develop Global Newtork Navigator, the first online directory of sites on the World Wide Web.

Shapiro's first travel story was about a bicycle journey he took across the U.S. the summer after he graduated from U.C. Berkeley. He's worked as a river-raft guide and is a volunteer sea kayak guide for ETC, a group that takes disabled people on outdoor adventures. Shapiro has also interviewed Barry Bonds, discussed the blues with B.B. King, and been blessed by the Dalai Lama. A native of New York, he lives in Sonoma County, California, with his wife and cat. He can be reached by email at senseofplace@nettravel.com.